RELIGION
and
SCIENCE
in
Early
Canada

FRYE LIBRARY OF CANADIAN PHILOSOPHY

General Editor: Douglas Rabb
Lakehead University

The Library will include volumes on:

William Lyall

William Albert Crawford-Frost

Charles De Koninck

George Paxton Young

Jacob Gould Schurman

George John Blewett

Herbert Leslie Stewart

John Clark Murray

John Watson

RELIGION
and
SCIENCE
in
Early
CANADA

Edited by J.D. Rabb

Ronald P. Frye & Company

ISBN: 0 919741 76 2

Published by:
Ronald P. Frye & Company
273 King Street East
Kingston, Ontario CANADA K7L 3B1

Printed and Bound in Canada

CONTENTS

Introduction

This work is intended, in part, as a general introduction to the **Frye Library of Canadian Philosophy**. The purpose of the **Frye Library** is to provide ready access to primary source material, in the first instance, written by early Canadian philosophers. Each volume will consist of archival material never before published, annotated reprints of principal works or new collections, along with extensive commentary. Each volume is intended to extend and deepen the pioneering work of the two classic histories of Canadian philosophy A.B. McKillop's *A Disciplined Intelligence: Critical Inquiry and Canadian Thought in the Victorian Era* (McGill-Queen's U.P., 1979) and *The Faces of Reason: an essay on philosophy and culture in English Canada 1850-1950* by Leslie Armour and Elizabeth Trott (Wilfrid Laurier U.P., 1981). As excellent and useful as these two histories of Canadian philosophy are, they are still secondary sources. Those few Canadian universities so alive to our culture inheritance as to offer courses in Canadian philosophy are thus forced to deal with the material indirectly. This is somewhat paradoxical because it is a long-standing tradition in Canada to study philosophy from the original works of the philosophers themselves. Thus if one wishes to study the philosophy of Plato or of Kant one reads Plato or Kant, in translation of course — another of our long standing traditions inherited from Scotland. The most famous of the early Canadian philosophers, John Watson of Queen's University, as early as 1908 gave rational expression to both of these Canadian traditions in the preface of his book, *The Philosophy of Kant Explained*:

> This book is the result of a not unsuccessful experiment in the art of teaching continued over many years, the main object of which was to provide a method by which the tendancy of the student to lean upon the authority of his   teacher should be counteracted. Nothing can well be more fatal to any real progress in philosophy than the habit of listening to lectures without a corresponding reaction of one's own mind. Various plans have been suggested for the avoidance of this fatal defect. The plan that I was led to adopt with more advanced students a good many years

ago was to introduce them to the direct study of the Critical Philosophy through the medium of the translated passages, published under the title of "The Philosophy of Kant in Extracts from his own Writings," which I made expressly for that purpose. In this way I was able to count upon the co-operation of the class, while the method seemed to me to have the additional advantage of recognising that the mind can only be aroused to powerful reaction when the matter upon which it is exercised is of the first rank.[1]

Watson goes on to state that his own explanations of Kant "are not intended as a substitute for Kant's own words, but as a commentary upon them."[2] In a similar way the two histories of Canadian philosophy mentioned above are not intended as substitutes for the primary sources, but as commentaries upon them. McKillop's work is clearly intellectual history. Armour and Trott describe *The Faces of Reason* in part at least as "a reference work which may be consulted by readers interested in particular figures, ideas, movements and periods."[3] It is important to note that their work is also "a continuous story which makes a point about the development of philosophical reason in the Canadian context."[4] However, the primary source materials upon which this story is based are not easily available. Most of the books are long out of print. Though many may be found in university libraries scattered across Canada, some are not available even at The National Library in Ottawa. The Canadian Institute for Historical Micro-reproductions (CIHM) is attempting to develop a microfiche collection of all early monographs, pamphlets etc published in Canada, or outside Canada written by Canadians. But this is a very long term project and it is far from complete. Its usefulness is also somewhat limited, as anyone who has spent even a few hours in front of a microfiche reader well knows.

Questions concerning why the works of early Canadian philosophers are not readily available, even in Canadian university libraries, and why until very recently, philosophers in Canada expressed little or no interest in their early Canadian counterparts have been addressed by Armour and Trott in *The Faces of Reason*.[5] Their book, published in 1981, is something of a watershed. It has been a prime factor in making the case for Canadian philosophy.[6] The reluctance of some Canadian universities to offer courses in Canadian philosophy is now due more to the lack of easily available primary source material than to any scepticism about the merit (or existence) of the subject matter. **The Frye Library of Canadian Philosophy** is intended as atleast a first step in an attempt to rectify this situation.

As a general introduction to the **Frye Library of Canadian Philosophy** this volume presents the work of a number of early Canadian thinkers centred around a common theme, the impact of science on the religious beliefs of the day. Each subsequent volume in the series will be devoted exclusively to the thought of one philosopher. Volume Two, for example, is entitled, *Crawford-Frost's Philosophy of Integration: The Christian Cosmology of an Expatriate Canadian*. and contains two of the major works of this former student of

George Paxton Young along with some miscellaneous papers and critical introduction. Subsequent volumes will include *Charles de Koninck: an Anthology of his works in English*, edited with a critical introduction by Leslie Armour and a biographical introduction by Thomas de Koninck. At least one major work of most of the philosophers discussed here will be included in the Library. It is hoped that a parallel library devoted to the work of French Canadian philosophers will follow.

As will the critical introduction to each of the subsequent volumes, the introductory essays in this volume locate the selected work in relation to the philosopher's thought as a whole, and present a preliminary analysis of that thought. The philosophers represented here have been selected from among the many thinkers who have contributed to the development of philosophy in early Canada. They form a representative group. Further, each has something of interest to say about the relation between religion and science. Only philosophers whose work is not easily available elsewhere have been included. Hence thinkers such as, for example, Richard Maurice Bucke, whose book *Cosmic Consciousness* is still in print, have been excluded.[7] The order of presentation is roughly chronological, with some important exceptions. A place of honour in the opening sections is accorded to the two most famous early Canadian philosophers, John Watson of Queen's University and John Clark Murray of McGill. A large part of *The Faces of Reason* is devoted to an analysis of Watson's thought, Chapter Seven: Reason as Social Understanding, and Chapter Eight: Reason as Constitutive of Knowledge and Reality. Although Armour and Trott devote only one chapter to the analysis of Murray's thought, they open that chapter with the statement: "If one had to choose only one Canadian philosopher to be rescued from oblivion, one could make an excellent case for John Clark Murray."[8] They have since published Murray's *The Industrial Kingdom of God*, based on a manuscript in the McGill archives.[9] Still most of the work he published in his lifetime remains out of print. Not only have Watson and Murray been granted a place of honour in the opening sections of volume one of the **Frye Library of Canadian Philosophy**, but since Leslie Armour has written the introduction to the section on Watson, and Elizabeth Trott the one on Murray, they too share the place of honour. This is most appropriate as it is really their book, *The Faces of Reason*, which has made the case for Canadian philosophy.

The concept which provides the unifying theme for volume one of the **Frye Library**, the relation between religion and science, has received recent treatment in Carl Berger's *Science, God and Nature in Victorian Canada*. Berger argues that:

> The idea of evolution through natural selection -inevitably brought into question the notion of the Bible as an inspired text in which God had spoken to man of his history, his duties, and his destiny . . . For a benevolent, supervising deity it substituted a blind relentless, physical process; for adaptations deliberately designed, random adjustments; for

harmony, abiding violence and conflict;. . . for nature arranged for man's benefit, a natural law operating without apparent regard for human values.[10]

As can be seen from the essays republished in this volume of the **Frye Library** the response of religiously minded Canadian thinkers to the idea of evolution was not so much to do battle with it as to accommodate their religious beliefs to it. Most of the philosophers represented here are, in some sense, idealist. As McKillop has argued, "The idealism that so dominated the intellectual life of the pre-war years in Canada was very largely an attempt to maintain the universal moral authority of traditional Christianity in the face of the massive challenge posed by empirical sciences to the pre-Darwinian monistic world view."[11] According to Armour and Trott one of the distinctive features of Canadian idealism, as opposed to British or German idealism, is the way it attempts to accommodate, to take seriously, the opposing view. The term 'philosophical federalism' is used to describe this feature of Canadian philosophy. They explain the concept as follows:

The single point which we would make if we could make only one point in this book would be this: Dominantly in Canadian philosophy reason is used as a devise to explore alternatives, to suggest ways of combining apparently contradictory ideas, to discover new ways of passing from one idea to another. Only rarely is it used as an intellectual substitute for force — as a device to defeat one's opponent . . . There is, in short, a kind of philosophical federalism at work. . .[12]

This philosophical federalism manifested itself in Canadian idealism as an acceptance of realist claims. The notion of "the other," of the "not-self," must be taken seriously. As Margaret Atwood has pointed out, the "Nature" encountered by the early settlers in Canada did not live up to their expectations of a Wordsworthian romanticised English Lake District in which "Nature was a kind Mother or Nurse who would guide man if he would only listen to her."[13] As Atwood puts it "If Wordsworth was right, Canada ought to have been the Great Good Place. At first, complaining about the bogs and mosquitos must have been like criticising the authority of the Bible."[14] She goes on to note that.

Nature seen as dead, or alive but indifferent, or alive and actively hostile towards man is a common image in Canadian literature. The result of a dead or indifferent Nature is an isolated or "alienated" man, the result of an actively hostile Nature is usually a dead man, and certainly a threatened one.[15]

If this is the view of nature shared by the early Canadian idealists, then they would not be likely to regard the concept of nature imposed by the idea of evolution as all that incompatible. As is suggested in the introductory essay in Section Ten, "Darwin Among the Canadian Poets," there is in fact a close parallel in the views of nature found in the imaginative and philosophical literature of Canada. The eleven sections of this book can be read in any order. However, Leslie Armour's somewhat longer introduction to Section One does provide useful background that is helpful in understanding all the philosophers presented in this volume.

J.D. Rabb

Notes

[1] John Watson, *The Philosophy of Kant Explained*, (Glasgow, 1908), Garland reprint (New York, 1976),p. v.

[2] Ibid, Watson, p. vi.

[3] Leslie Armour and Elizabeth Trott, *The Faces of Reason: an essay on philosophy and culture in English Canada* 1850-1950, (Wilfrid Laurier U.P.., 1981), p. xxv.

[4] *Ibid.*

[5] See also their article "The Faces of Reason and its Critics," *DIALOGUE*, Vol XXV, No 1, pp. 105-118, especially pp. 116-117.

[6] Also important is the pioneering work of John Irving.See, for e.g. his article on "Philosophical Literature To 1910," in the *Literary History of Canada*, ed. Carl F. Klink (Toronto 1977), Vol 1, pp 447-460. Of Special note is Jack Stevenson's admirable defence of the study of the history of philosophy in Canada against five possible objections, and actual oppositions, to it. See "Canadian Philosophy from a Cosmopolitan Point of View.," *DIALOGUE*, Vol XXV, No 1, 1986, pp 17-30. This particular issue of *DIALOGUE*,Vol XXV,No 1, is devoted to philosophy in Canada. It is the twenty-fifth anniversary issue of the journal of The Canadian Philosophical Association.

[7] R.M. Bucke, *Cosmic Consciousness, (Philadelphia, 1901), reprint paperback edition, New York: E.P. Dutton, 1969.*

[8] *The Faces of Reason*, p. 105.

[9] John Clark Murray, *The Industrial Kingdom of God*, ed. Leslie Armour and Elizabeth Trott, (University of Ottawa Press, 1981)

[10] Carl Berger, *Science, God and Nature in Victorian Canada*, (Toronto, University of Toronto Press 1983, p. 53.

[11] A.B. McKillop, *A Disciplined Intelligence: Critical Inquiry and Canadian Thought in the Victorian Era.* (McGill-Queen's U.P., 1979), p. 228.

[12] *The Faces of Reason*, p. 4.

[13] Margaret Atwood, *Survival: A Thematic Guide to Canadian Literature*, (Toronto, Anansi, 1972), p. 50.

[14] *Ibid*, p. 50.

[15] *Ibid*, p. 54.

Section One

JOHN WATSON
(1847-1939)

1

An Introduction to John Watson

Leslie Armour

Watson the Man

Inaugural lectures, given when a new incumbent takes over a university chair, mark the beginning of a new career. One might expect them to reveal the professor's plan for a life devoted to teaching, research and writing. They rarely do. But John Watson's is an exception: there in Convocation Hall at Queen's University, on the 18th of October, 1872, he laid down a plan for the reconciliation of science, religion and philosophy. In the 67 years remaining to him he carried it out.

We can imagine him there, twenty-five years old, upright, a little on the solemn side (there are no jokes in the printed version, at any rate), speaking with the slight burr with which an educated Scotsman lets it be known that he is not an Englishman. Perhaps he was uncertain about how it would all turn out. He had already remarked that Queen's University conformed precisely to Aristotle's definition of a building: "four walls and a roof." But he came with the fulsome praise of Edward Caird, the leading Scottish philosopher of the hour, who was later to say "Watson is perhaps the man of the 'driest light' that I know. I do not know any man who sees his way more clearly..."[1] Watson stayed in Canada for the rest of a long life. (He died in 1939.) By the time of the First World War, he was recognised not only as the moving force of Canadian idealism, but as one of the most competent metaphysicians of the century. He had given the renowned Gifford lectures in Scotland in 1910-11. (The Gifford Lectures were the occasion on which many eminent philosophers including William James, Josiah Royce, and Alfred North Whitehead chose to unveil their major work.) And he was generally reckoned, among idealists in North America, as second only to Josiah Royce. When the young idealists in California challenged the communitarianism of Royce, their erstwhile hero, in 1896, Watson was summoned after Royce to take up the defense. His *Christianity and Idealism* was the result.[2] It was one of three major works on the philosophy of religion and one of nine substantial philosophical works he was to produce.

An ardent billiards player and amateur playwright and painter, he was a commanding figure on the Queen's campus for more than half a century. His work in religion was, according to H.H. Walsh, one of the major forces which brought about the United Church of Canada, though he never seems to have joined it;[3] his *State in Peace and War*[4] was a Bible of political reform; and his students played prominent roles in the public service and in churches across the country.

Watson's inaugural lecture is directed to the conflict of science and philosophy — but it becomes obvious, long before the end, that what he is concerned with above all is the defense of rational religion. His main targets are Thomas Henry Huxley and Herbert Spencer. Huxley, the great popularizer of Darwin and bane of bishops, was painted by Watson (not wholly unfairly) as an out-and-out materialist who believed that science must replace both philosophy and religion. Herbert Spencer, the man who coined the phrase "survival of the fittest," believed that religion should be confined to the realm of the "unknowable" and that the centre of science was a theory of evolution which would eventually embrace all events from the origins of the stars to the rise and success of the capitalist system.

The Philosophical Background

To see what Watson and his antagonists were about, we must look at their background. Religion had scarcely recovered from its struggle with the two opposing forces of the eighteenth century — the lassitude engendered among many believers by rationalism and the over-exertion engendered in others by Methodist enthusiasm — when it collided head on with the history and biology of the nineteenth century.

In Germany, David Strauss' *Leben Jesu* (1835), though not the first assault on the authenticity of the orthodox accounts of the historical Jesus, became a symbolic turning point. After Strauss, historical criticisms — including the so-called "higher criticism" of the Bible —set in with a flood. The very existence of Jesus was called into question. The historical status of the four gospels was challenged on every count. Even those who clung to a belief in Biblical veracity began to be influenced by scholars of Aramaic and Hebrew and to believe that the texts did not always really say what the English translators said, and even to accept that it was sometimes hard to find any clear meaning for them.

In France and England, the study of biology was in ferment in the eighteenth century and became revolutionized in the nineteenth: first Buffon, then Lamarck and finally Darwin and Wallace. The quarrel with religion was not over the idea of evolution itself. Evolutionary theories went back to the Greeks. But, in the eighteenth century, Buffon had gradually come to accept the idea that the *facts* demanded some kind of evolutionary theory and, by the end of that century, after the philosophical writings of Hegel, evolution became a philosophical commonplace. The real blow to religion was Darwin's theory that evolution actually took place by chance — that new species occurred through random mutations which (very occasionally) turned up specimens better adapted to their environments than their rivals. Religion could survive an evolutionary theory based on natural law, for one could easily believe that the Deity chose to plan the world that way. But a *chance* universe seemed clearly to be a universe outside the control of the Deity.

The combination of historical criticism and the new biology caused a great flurry. Historians and biologists were attacked by angry clerics. (The direct attack on historians centred on those who applied historical techniques to the Bible itself, but it applied to those, as well, whose findings about secular matters in ancient civilizations conflicted with "the Bible's view.") Some theologians beat strategic retreats, others gave up science. New sects and subsects emerged to fight one battle or another. The effects on the day-to-day practice of religion varied a great deal; but Christian thinkers were in considerable disarray.

The Church of England, for instance, was a state church with powerful ties to governing classes and important functions ranging from the crowning of monarchs to participation in parliament through the House of Lords, tended to look for the sources of its validity neither in the literal reading of the Bible nor in philosophical theories but in its own institutional history and the collective experiences of the nation. Its most dramatic response — crystallized in the "Oxford Movement" —took the form of an insistence on the continuity of the church as an institution going back to the New Testament events. John Henry Newman (who greatly interested Watson and exercised, as we shall see, a considerable influence upon him) proposed a theory of "development"[5] which suggested that the church gradually, through its collective experience, came to understand the full range of meanings of the traditional texts. It was thus open to change. What mattered was what the institution itself made of its collective experience — not what the Bible literally said or what outside sources of knowledge such as science insisted upon. Science, after all, was just part — even if an important part — of the collective experience.

This argument allowed for a good deal of flexibility. Beliefs might change, scientists could be (and should be) listened to without necessarily having the last word. But the argument almost inevitably led Newman out of the Church of England (generally known in Canada as the Anglican Church and in the United States as the Episcopal Church) and into the Roman Catholic Church. For an argument which depended on continuity and collective experience seemed naturally to lead beyond the spatial and temporal limits of a single state church (unless, of course, one could argue, as some did, that the Church of England represented the "real church" from which others had strayed.) Some of Newman's friends followed him; most did not. The result, in general, was a further source of confusion and dispute. But Newman's theory survived and played a part in the philosophy of religion developed by Watson. (It had some influence on Edward and John Caird, too, but they converted it into a rather simple evolutionary theory while Watson used it more nearly as Newman intended.)

In England, most of those who belonged neither to the state church nor to the Roman Catholic Church (Dissenters or Non-Conformists as they were called) tried to consolidate their position around a dependence on the Scriptrue The German "higher criticism" of the Bible left them in large part untouched because its pedantic scholarship had little appeal to the people they served. Constricted by laws governing Oxford and Cambridge, they had turned inward, created Dissenting academies, and toughened their stand around the Bible and Bunyan. New and revived institutions (beginning with the University of London, a mediaeval institution which had largely fallen into disuse but began to take on new life in the 1820's) were intended to broaden the outlook of those to whom the old universities had been closed, but the Dissenters often regarded them as godless or, if not, as further appendages of the Church of England. (Jeremy Bentham was the guiding spirit of University College, London, dubbed by the Archbishop of Canterbury the "Godless University of Gower Street." The Archbishop promptly founded King's College.)

In Scotland, however, the situation was quite different. The Presbyterian Church of Scotland drew heavily on the argumentative aspects of Calvinism. Calvin had sought to demonstrate his central doctrines rationally as well as to found them in Scripture, and Calvinist churches had derived much of their strength from their ability to conduct public controversies.

This tradition fed upon (and in turn fed) the Scottish tradition of public education. The Scottish universities, though not quite as old as Oxford and Cambridge, went back some hundreds of years and had always been open to rich and poor alike. The stories of poor farm boys arriving on foot in Edinburgh from the Highlands with a sack of oatmeal to see them over the winter were not necessarily apocryphal.

Thus there was in Scotland a large educated population able to understand the point of German biblical criticism and able to understand the impact of science on religion. And there was little chance there of emulating the Oxford Movement. Watson, as I said, put Newman to use, but that was in *Canada* and that, as we shall also see, made a difference. In Scotland, however, one could hardly join with the Church of England in taking refuge in institutional continuity. For the Scots Presbyterians were familiar not with continuity but with a tendency to splinter. The practice of "disrupting" as it was called led finally to the Great Disruption of 1843.[6] Both disrupters and their opponents *argued*, and so debate was the order of the day.

The great figures in Scotland from whom Watson adapted his position were the Caird Brothers. They are so closely tied to the roots of Watson's thought (though Watson's finished philosophy was very much his own) that we must spend some time explaining their positions. John Caird — first a clergyman, then a professor and finally Principal of the University of Glasgow and thereafter always referred to as "Principal Caird" — developed a new historical theology, with strong roots in Hegel, which redirected the main lines of intellectual traffic in Scottish religion. In retrospect his achievement seems astonishing. Scottish theology always had its own subtleties, but, in the popular mind, the heart of the traditional Scots Calvinism was most often the doctrine of predestination: immediate eternal bliss after death for the chosen few, eternal hellfire for the many whom God had damned from (and *for*) eternity. God knew from the first moment of time who these sinners were. Sin was clearly defined in Scripture and the sinner's apparent fall from grace was simply evidence that, in all likelihood, he had been damned from the beginning of time. Success, including the worldly success of shipyard owners and the proprietors of coal mines, was a sign that God smiled on enterprise and that the capitalist was very likely saved. When John Caird's *Introduction to the Philosophy of Religion* appeared in 1880 under the staid imprint of James MacLehose, printer and publisher to the University of Glasgow, many people expected an explosion. For he insisted that religion was based on reason, that religion had to become scientific, and that there was a development in religion — not the development in already given ideas which Newman had insisted upon, but the appearance of genuinely new and distinct ideas. Caird insisted on a humane understanding of human failings, based partly on the inability of men to know everything in the past — or even in the present — but, above all, on a human failure to understand, except through a long historical process, the nature of the human condition. The idea of God, like other ideas, was in a process of evolution.

This, from a Scots clergyman who was Principal of the University of Glasgow, seemed to a few people quite shocking. There was grumbling and a little agitation. But no explosion. Eventually, a small band of dissidents brought a lawsuit urging that the Church of Scotland had abandoned Christianity and darkly suggesting that it had adopted the philosophy of Hegel. They ultimately lost on appeal. No one disputed that Hegel had entered into Scottish theology, though apparently, that was not enough to persuade the judges that Christianity had been abandoned. But, for the most part, it was as if those who understood — and they were many, for Caird had been preaching to packed churches — had simply been waiting for a thesis which could provide the tramlines along which they might travel to a modern understanding.

John Caird was the great reformer in Scotland, but it was his younger brother, Edward, who gained most repute as a philosopher and social thinker. Edward became a fellow of Merton College, Oxford, in 1864. His account of the "evolution" of religion provided a much more radical thesis than that of Newman's *Development*, published fifteen years before Caird became an Oxford Don. For, by extending the doctrine of religious development to all religions — and not merely to Christianity — and by allowing for the introduction of genuinely new ideas in religion, the younger Caird freed Newman's doctrine from its close association with Roman Catholicism. Two years later Edward returned to Glasgow to become Professor of Moral Philosophy at the University of Glasgow — where he influenced John Watson — but in 1893, at the age of 58, he became Master of Balliol College, Oxford, thus cementing his connection with English philosophy and ensuring the spread of his ideas to a wider public.

Edward Caird was a man ahead of his time in many ways. He was a pacifist in the Boer War and was in trouble for using Balliol College as a centre of pacifist work. He campaigned tirelessly for the rights of women students to receive the same degrees as men. He attacked racism at a time when racism was thought merely normal, and shocked all of Oxford by mounting a strong (and, in the end, nearly successful) campaign against the plan to give an honorary degree to Cecil Rhodes, the man who had endowed **the Rhodes scholarships, on the ground that Rhodes' activities in Africa** (where he founded Rhodesia) were "despicable." But he also deepened his elder brother's philosophy. If one simply considers religion as such, it is concerned only with the "elevation of the soul to God." It is a process which needs no explanation or justification. Either it happens or it does not. Nevertheless, a *theory* (or philosophy) of religion is necessary because there comes a time, inevitably, when questions are raised from the outside, when existing practices and techniques seem to fail, and when we want to know whether or not we can order our conduct so as to make the "soul's elevation" more or less likely. Theology deals with the internal structure of theories of religion, philosophy of religion with their justification.

The idea of God, however, is clearly the idea of something which transcends the experience —and the logic — of the subject-object relation. To be with God is to be with what is no longer relative, incomplete, puzzling. It is to have complete knowledge. All knowledge, therefore, in so far as it leads to an understanding of the unity of experience and the completion of the activity of experiencing, leads on to God. But, at any moment, we can only grasp this completion obscurely.

Religions go through various phases which are related to the knowledge, the experience and the culture of their time.

Hence one should not look back to the *beginnings* of religions for the truth, but rather watch the process through which ideas are clarified and purified of their accidental elements. The tendency, Caird thought, in all religion, is to move toward a notion of God which is rather like the Hegelian Absolute, a concept which many people continue to find obscure, but which is intended to embody a total rationality and ultimately to overcome all disunity, even that caused by the distinction between subject and object.

We cannot explicate this idea fully, but we can see the direction of the development of thought. Modern Christianity, in the younger Caird's view, is less devoted to magic, less prey to cultural oddities, less prone to utter dogmatism than it once was. Even the Church of Scotland was abandoning its traditional notions of predestination and election. We are more ready now to realize that we can only do our best to conceive the ultimate.

How, then, do religion and science clash? Religion is, after all, practical as well as theoretical. Souls have always found their way to God through all the difficulties. Science, however, very often seems to clash with received opinion about how this ascent to God is to be achieved and about how God is made manifest in the world. In reality science's effect on religion can only be to remove impediments to clear thought. Newman (and Matthew Arnold, the poet-philosopher), of course, would have added that science may also take away the ground in which religious emotion takes root and that, without religious emotion, salvation is surely improbable. Thus Arnold clung to the arts as a way of keeping a rich soil in which the emotions might grow, and Newman clung to the Church. In the sterner Scottish tradition — a tradition which stands on the side of Aquinas, the champion of the intellect, in the mediaeval debate with the Scotists over the will and the intellect — Edward Caird was prepared to meet God coolly on his own terms.

Watson's Philosophy

Watson would have acknowledged the Cairds as the chief influence on his philosophy, especially his philosophy of religion. But he was not simply one of their followers.

Somewhat more conservative in politics than Edward Caird, he was more flexible in religion, both more inclined to insist on the relevance of Christianity's past, and to give serious credit to Catholic philosophers from Aquinas to Newman. He was certainly more radical than either Caird in his concept of God. *Christianity and Idealism, The Philosophical Basis of Religion,* and *The Interpretation of Religious Experience* all go well beyond Caird's position.[7]

Edward Caird seized upon the then popular idea of "evolution" and applied it to religion. His "evolutionism" was sometimes rather mechanical. He believed that religion naturally went through a series of phases, prodded on by human nature and the nature of the universe at large, which constituted progress.[8] The implication seemed to be that primitive religious notions had been superseded and primitive religious practices overturned. Watson is by no means sure of this. Like Newman, he thought that there was a development in religion: we can understand things which the first Christians could not. In particular we can see the universe in scientific terms as a rational whole, and are less likely to be distracted by idle superstition. But for Watson the first Christians did have their privileges. As Watson says, Christianity promises deliverance from evil.[9] For this nothing will suffice but the understanding of the human being as a whole. Both human moral codes and those often propounded by the church have tended to emphasize a kind of morality which can be developed independently of other values, even those of art and science. While — as Watson insists — metaphysical understanding helps in this too, "the conception... elaborated by the Church in the person of Christ"[10] is the only conception which seems to be free of the limitations which characterize man-made moral codes, for it presents God as expressed through the whole human being. The first Christians were in a position to grasp this embodiment immediately — through the life and person of the Founder (as Watson likes to call Jesus). I think Watson believed that the legitimate claim of fundamentalists was the insistence that this original experience is not to be forgotten, but rather to be protected and re-enacted as best we can. Hence there is a place for Scripture as well as for the rituals of the church.

There is not straightforward progress but rather, as Newman thought, development. Unlike the British idealists, indeed, Watson frequently mentioned Newman favourably, as did George Blewett, the Toronto philosopher who was Watson's chief rival for the title of leader of the Canadian idealists.[11]

In Watson's philosophy weight is given, in fact, to nearly all the main lines of nineteenth-century religious thought. No coherent movement is simply dismissed. Circumstances in Canada — the tendency for church union to become a serious issue, especially in the west where the small towns that grew up along the railway could not support indefinitely many different denominations, the need to reckon with a very large and influential Catholic minority, the absence of any single dominant church, all encouraged this kind of scholarly "accommodationism." One might think of this aspect of Watson's philosophy as rather conservative, inclined to preserve as much as possible of human religious experience, just as in his political theory Watson wanted to preserve a political tradition which had given Canada a stability and a relative freedom from violence which distinguished it from the United States which, even then, had a good deal of civil violence and had recently undergone a civil war.

But his central concept of God is radical. The Cairds' view of God is both traditional and puzzling. We have already met some of the views of Edward Caird, and the statement at the end of John Caird's *Introduction to the Philosophy of Religion*, for instance, while it invokes all the traditional pieties, does not seem to be of much help in the problem of adjusting questions about God to the modern outlook on the world:

> Christianity contains in common with the Monotheistic religions the idea of a god elevated in His absolute being above the world, unaffected by its limits, incapable of being implicated in its imperfections, it yet enables us to think of god, not merely as an omnipotent power and will above us, but also as infinite love within us. [12]

One is moved to ask what this statement means and whether or not it contains contradictions.

Watson is clear that we can no longer accept the notion of a God literally above and beyond the world who functions chiefly to explain things or events which science fails to explain. Unexplained phenomena may lie at the beginning of the world (before the "big bang" as we might now say) or they may be the fashionable miracles of the hour. But they are likely either to be explained in the future by science or else to turn out to be such that no proposed explanation really adds anything to the description of them. (We can answer Leibniz's question "why is there something rather than nothing? by saying "there is something because God decided that there should be something," but obviously this evades the question. For the question then is: Why is there God rather than nothing?)

The need for a concept of God does not arise from the unexplained (or inexplicable) features of the world, but rather, Watson thought, from the features of self-consciousness itself. Consciousness can embrace everything that is possible within its own store of knowledge. It has no limits as consciousness. Its limits are always those of the body through which it is expressed. (Indeed, if we want to explain why someone's awareness is diminished or unstable, or his capacity for knowing less than normal, we do not usually nowadays first seek the explanation *within* consciousness. The natural place to seek is in his brain, or his glandular system, or some other feature of his anatomy.) Watson, though an "idealist," agreed with this contemporary propensity, though he would have said that bodies, after all, are only the means through which consciousness instantiates itself. If consciousness is really unlimited *in itself* then it, after all, has the properties usually assigned to God: It is infinite and unflawed. It is only in contact with the flawed world that it becomes limited.

And this, indeed, *is* Watson's conclusion. Each of us is *identical* with God in His *essence* as a conscious being. But consciousness must be expressed through the world. By itself, it is empty as well as incomplete and unstructured.[13]

It is this *expression of consciousness in the world* which constitutes God. All the expressions of God in the world constitute a natural community, the same in essence but different in expression. Christianity insists upon the doctrine of the incarnation. It also insists, as Watson several times reminds his readers, on the doctrine of the Trinity. According to orthodoxy, there are three expressions of the same essence and all are perfectly equal.

But so it is with each of us in principle, except of course that, though our essence as conscious beings is perfect enough, our expressions fall short. We must live and learn in the world. Watson could well have drawn on the New Testament which says, after all, "be perfect even as your father in heaven is perfect."[14] The purpose of life is the perfection of these expressions. Christianity maintains that perfection can be achieved and even offers an example.

Nothing in this view conflicts with science, nothing imposes on human beings an external constraint on behaviour, nothing suggests a world in which everyone is to become alike.

Thus Christianity has, in Watson's view, been relieved of the burdens which had tended to make it unacceptable. But none of its most central traditional tenets has been denied. The Divinity of Jesus, the doctrine of the Trinity, the centrality of the New Testament all remain and yet belief has been revolutionized.

The Message of the Inaugural Lecture

We can now return to the inaugural lecture. Its essential message is that:

1. truth is one — religion, and philosophy are all parts of the same whole;
2. science, religion and philosophy all stem from the same basic source —reflection on the difference between what is and what seems to be;
3. knowledge is an activity involving creativity and not merely passive receptivity; and finally,
4. the highest truth in morals as well as in science and religion derives from carrying out the Socratic injunction: know thyself.

Let us look at each of these notions in turn.

1. *The Unity of Knowledge*: it has become a commonplace in our time to believe that knowledge is fragmentary. The biologist does not know and does not need to know what the physicist knows because the understanding of the one does not depend in any way upon the other. More dramatically, many people (including some philosophers) believe or appear to believe that science and religion are logically independent of one another in the sense that it does not matter if the one denies what the other asserts. (For instance a physicist may believe in the bodily assumption of the Virgin Mary — a doctrine which appears to assert that the living person, normally embodied, of the mother of Jesus was taken from a point on the surface of the earth through space to heaven without any of the separations and transformations which usually accompany death. But, he will probably not believe that a sufficiently powerful telescope could detect her still moving through outer space some 2000 light years from us even though it is evident that no body can travel faster than light and even though heaven has not been discovered within a radius of 2000 light years from the earth.)

Watson insists, however, that truth must be a unity for, if it is not, we have no *logical* way of dealing with *any* claim to knowledge. His argument indeed is precisely that if contradictions are to be allowed, then propositions can be equally proved and disproved and the human intellect must be fatally flawed. In that case. *no* knowledge would be possible at all for no amount of human evidence would be adequate to demonstrate any proposition whatsoever.

2. *The Source of Science, Philosophy and Religion*: Watson in effect argues that science, philosophy, and religion have their origin in thinking, thinking which arises when the superficial view of the world conveyed to us in our unreflective moments and our ordinary language proves not to be enough. To begin with, science calls attention to regularities which are hidden from the eye which is not informed by the mind.

We might think that every apple falls for a different reason, that the tide rises and apples fall for reasons unconnected with each other, or that the orbit of the moon and the passage of the tides are independent of one another.

Newton taught us that they all form examples of one and the same principle — that bodies attract one another directly as their masses and inversely as the square of the distances between them.

Serious religion — as opposed to mere superstition or magic or the thoughtless performance of prescribed rites — arises when we begin to see that not only is there a regularity of forces but that the whole adds up to something meaningful which is related to whatever it is that gives rise to our own natures. It is this link, in Watson's view, which finally reveals the God of Christianity mentioned (as fits His status) only towards the end of the lecture.

In other writings, Watson explores this notion in further dimensions: Art and morality also arise from the distinction between what is and what appears to be.[15] Art is not mere representation of nature but rather something which reveals part of the real not otherwise apparent to us. We think that Shakespeare probes into human nature, that Milton exposes some nerve of the real, that Picasso sees with the mind as well as the eye and so sees more than the unaided eye might see. Morality tells us what is *really required* of us as opposed to what mere social custom and belief and ordinary desire tell us to do. Morality may justify rebellion — but only, as sensible men would say, in a *real* cause. Philosophy, of course, seeks to codify the differences between what seems to be and what really is.

3. *Knowledge is an Activity* We can see from the above that knowledge requires the activity of distinguishing between what seems to be and what is. If so, then the project of sitting still (as the more extreme empiricists suggested) and letting nature write its own message on the mind —the project of attending to the *effects* of sense data on the human awareness — is self-defeating. It can only produce accounts of what seems to be.

Knowledge is produced, not given. If it is not to be freed from attention to immediate experience, it is, equally, not to be freed from reason either. Objectivity for Watson has two dimensions: completeness and rationality. To be objective, one must leave nothing out. But to understand what one has included, one must develop a rational structure. For meaning derives from order (try jumbling the words in this sentence and see what happens to the meaning) and order is limited, in the end, on Watson's view by the principles of logic. That is to say that disorder destroys meaning and violation of logical rules destroys meaning also. The best anyone can do by way of finding truth is to meet the criteria of completeness and rationality. To put the matter the other way around, if someone suspects error, one's choices are either to maintain that something has been left out, or that the facts have been wrongly ordered. What other kinds of error are there? Since Watson believed that the arguments led inevitably to claims about the existence of God and only one God, given his nature, could exist, he did not believe that there could be two or more complete and rational orders. Of course, since each of us is identical in essence with God and each of us has an order determined by our own perspective, there may be very many sub-orders, but each of these is seen to be limited by its perspective.

4. *Know Thyself*: The need to distinguish between what seems to be and what is comes partly from the fact that we can reason and thus see that what seems to be *need not be* what is. It also stems from the fact that we are conscious and so can give meanings to events — events can come to count for (or against) something. The unity of knowledge derives from considerations of logic and also from the fact that consciousness cannot operate except as a unity. You cannot think of your scientific and your religious beliefs without thinking of them together — without, that is, thinking of some relation between them.

Consciousness, thus, in Watson's view, constantly drives us on in the search for the final unity. It is this which leads to the search for universal laws and it is this which, in religion, leads us to think of the world from the point of view of the totality —that is from the point of view of a conscious being for whom it all *is* a unity. This in turn leads us to the notion that, in essence, we are identical with God and different only because of the way in which consciousness is expressed in the world. Finally, this identity forces us to think of all conscious beings as forming a community within which in the end none can profit at the expense of others. And this is the essence of morality.

Some Difficulties in the Inaugural Lecture

It is important to see how Watson tries to associate himself with the main line of a perennial philosophy which begins with the Greeks and extends by logical addition to the present, and to dissociate himself from the skeptical lines in the history of philosophy. Socrates' dictum "know thyself" is still Watson's watchword and guide. Aristotle is carefully included in Watson's side as one who thought that there was soul in everything (i.e., that the world was a unity held together by spirit), though this is surely pulling Aristotle closer to Hegel than most contemporary commentators would wish.

Herbert Spencer (1820-1903), along with T.H.Huxley (1825-1895), looms in the front ranks of the enemy, though the inventor of "social Darwinism" was then generally ignored in the universities and he has been largely forgotten now. Spencer, for most of his working life the editor of *The Economist*, had originally been trained (though briefly) as a civil engineer, and he had a great success as a popularizer of science. His following in Canada (again outside the universities) was substantial, for, after all, a good part of the educated population was engaged in necessary technological tasks and shared much of Spencer's outlook. Watson does not attack the theory of evolution, but he is clearly annoyed at Spencer's simplifications and particularly at the notion that all reality exists on a single level, so that no deeper notion of reality emerges with the understanding of mind than with the understanding of matter. According to Watson, matter is just a brute given for which no further explanation would be forthcoming if mind and God did not exist and work on different levels. Thomas Henry Huxley was a British biologist. He collected marine life on the celebrated voyage of H.M.S.Rattlesnake and became the principal popularizer and defender of Charles Darwin. Unlike Spencer, however, he believed that philosophy was doomed by the advance of science. Watson, of course, bristled at every separation of science and philosophy.

For the same reason Watson attacks Alexander Bain (1808-1903), a pioneer Scottish psychologist who claimed that we form our ideas of space from our muscular sensations. Watson wants to insist that it is only through reason that such notions can be formed; for sensations (of whatever kind) have no generality and pass so fleetingly that nothing can ever be deduced from them although they can be understood when organized by more general concepts. Mill is included in the same assault. We think of John Stuart Mill (1806-73) chiefly as the moral philosopher who believed that it was everyone's duty to maximize his own pleasure (he defined happiness in terms of pleasure) and that of others, and who introduced the doctrine of kinds of pleasure in opposition to the quantitative theory of Jeremy Bentham; but when Watson was writing, Mill was highly thought of as a metaphysician and critic of Sir William Hamilton's theory of knowledge. Mill believed that space, once again, can be inferred from the simultaneity of sensations, but Watson wonders (as would any modern relativity theorist) how this simultaneity can be discovered except by using reason to create a concept of time.

Watson's attack on "passivity" as the basis of knowledge centres on Locke. Watson's view of Locke is one current at the time but will seem odd to contemporary scholars. Locke did attack "innate" ideas — the doctrine that we are born with some ideas already in our minds —(as would Watson himself) and did write of the human mind as an "empty cabinet" (the famous expression *tabula rasa*, the blank slate, seems only to occur in a Latin text on natural law which Locke did not publish and in a summary of his essay done by him for the French translator). But Locke was also the champion of the unity of knowledge and, ultimately, of the notion of *activity*. It is true that he believed that the basis of knowledge of the external world was to be found in the passive receipt of sense data — and Watson may well be right in doubting if this scheme actually works — but it is also true Locke thought much else went into knowledge of the world as a whole: *intuition* of one's own existence, *demonstration* of the existence of God, and *reasoned arguments* to show the unity of knowledge. (Locke, indeed, thought that if God did not exist, knowledge of *any* kind would be impossible — which shows that he did not think sense data alone constituted Knowledge.)[16]

Some have doubted, indeed, that Locke was an "empiricist," but, even if he was, he was not so extreme as some who came after him. In attacking the Englishman Locke as the instigator of what Watson thinks of as an intellectual disaster, Watson shifts some of the blame away from the Scotsman Hume and other less cautious Scots who wrote about Hume. Hume could be portrayed as the inheritor of difficult problems. Watson could give a philosopher the benefit of the doubt if he thought he was on the right track in any case: Berkeley is not pursued here, for instance. His attitude to Hume is more complex. he says Hume was an out-and-out skeptic. Contemporary Hume scholars tend more and more to see him as the defender of "natural beliefs." Like any other High Tory, he simply did not believe that there was ever enough evidence to overturn these natural beliefs. But Watson also describes Hume's view of knowledge as "bitter sarcasm." This hardly sounds like a compliment. But it is possible that it is meant more kindly than one might think. Scots intellectuals of the time not infrequently prided themselves on their sarcasm and sometimes, as well on being dour between their great occasions of celebration. Hume, it is said, was misled by Locke. The gravest sin — the belief that knowledge depended on passivity, a view that undercuts the heart of the Scots work ethic — is ascribed to Locke.

Kant figures as an author whose terminology is "barbaric" (Hegel is not mentioned in this regard!) and the Moralists (with a capital M) who appear toward the end of the lecture are surely Kantians who suppose that there is absolute freedom to act rightly or wrongly, and who want to separate moral judgment from motives involving one's personal situation. Watson, however, was to go on to become a noted Kant scholar. (Indeed, his writings on Kant[17] have recently been reprinted and are still consulted.)

Finally Watson is following a common view of the time in dividing philosophy into Logic, Metaphysics and Ethics. The Scottish universities generally had a separate chair in Logic and courses in England as well as Scotland were often organized under these headings. The theory of knowledge tended to be divided between Logic and Metaphysics. Many books of the period follow these distinctions. Thus, for instance, Bernard Bosanquet's magnum opus is entitled *Logic or the Morphology of Knowledge*.[18] Natural theology and the philosophy of religion generally went with Metaphysics while social and political philosophy and other "value theory" topics frequently went with Ethics.

Notes

1. Cited in Robert Charles Wallace, ed., *Some Great Men of Queen's*, Toronto: Ryerson Press, 1941, p.24.
2. John Watson, *Christianity and Idealism*, New York: Macmillan, 1897.
3. H.H.Walsh, *The Christian Church in Canada* Toronto: Ryerson, 1956.
4. John Watson, *The State in Peace and War*, Glasgow:James MacLehose, 1919.
5. John Henry Newman, *An Essay on the Development of Christian Doctrine*, London: Longman's Green, eighth edition, 1891. (This is the last edition published in Newman's lifetime, but it is not significantly different from the third edition of 1878 which is most frequently quoted. There are, however, substantial changes between the first edition of 1845, written just before Newman's conversion to Catholicism, and the 1878 edition and there are minor differences between the editions of 1845 and 1846.)
6. The "Great Disruption" began over the issue of the right of the Established Presbyterian Church to "intrude" clergymen, i.e. to appoint them independently of the congregation, but the dispute between the newly created Free Church of Scotland and the Established Church of Scotland came to include many issues. The "Disruption" spread quickly to Canada and its leader,

Dr.Thomas Chalmers, has left his name on a good many United Churches in Canada. See Thomas Brown, ed., *Annals of the Great Disruption*, Edinburgh: MacNiven and Wallace,1893.

7. *Christianity and Idealism*, New York, Macmillan, 1897; *The Philosophical Basis of Religion*, James MacLehose, 1907; *The Interpretation of Religious Experience*, Glasgow, James MacLehose, 1912.

8. Caird, Edward, *The Evolution of Religion*, 2 vols., Glasgow: J.MacLehose, 1893; London: Macmillan, 1894.

9. *The Interpretation of Religious Experience*, ch.12.

10. *Op. cit.*, p.288.

11. See John Watson, *The Philosophical Basis of Religion*, Glasgow: James MacLehose, 1907, pp.9-24 and 362-381; and George Blewett, *The Study of Nature and the Vision of God*, Toronto: William Briggs, 1907, especially pp.17-23 and 333-348. Compare Bernard Bosanquet, *Logic or the Morphology of Knowledge*, Oxford: The Clarendon Press, 1911, vol.I, Chapter IX.

12. John Caird, *An Introduction to the Philosophy of Religion*, Glasgow: J.MacLehose, 1880; London:Macmillan, 1881, p.357.

13. *Interpretation of Religious Experience*, ch.12.

14. *Matthew* 5:48.

15. See e.g., *An Outline of Philosophy*, Glasgow: James MacLehose., 1908, chapters IX, X, and XI.

16. John Locke, *An Essay Concerning Human Understanding*, ed.Peter H.Nidditch, Oxford: The Clarendon Press, 1975; second edition, with corrections, 1979 (first published 1689), Book IV, ch.10, section 10, p.625.

17. See especially *The Philosophy of Kant Explained*, originally published by James MacLehose: Glasgow, 1908.

18. *Logic or the Morphology of Knowledge*, Oxford: The Clarendon Press, second edition (revised) 1911.

The Relation of
Philosophy to Science

John Watson

The object of an introductory lecture is to indicate, in a general way, the sphere and limits of the Science which has afterwards to be treated in a detailed and systematic manner. We cannot at present be expected to give more than a vague idea of the topics afterwards to be discussed at length, and may, therefore, seem occasionally to be deficient in that definiteness and accuracy of thought, which are all-important in a teacher of Philosophy. With a view of obviating, as far as possible, the difficulties that unavoidably lie in our way, we propose to discuss, as fully as time will allow, the relation of Philosophy to the Special Sciences; a course which will, by the force of contrast, throw into bolder relief the nature of those problems with which we shall be afterwards occupied.

Truth, from its very nature, is a complete unity, and if it could be proved that the results of one department of human enquiry directly contradict those of another, the whole edifice of knowledge must fall to the ground. For such a disharmony would imply that there is something in the nature of intelligence itself which precludes it from ever attaining to truth. If equal evidence can be brought to shew that what may be proved in one way may be equally disproved in another, we should be forced to take refuge in the unwelcome conclusion that we are the sport of a desire for knowledge that can only lead to irremediable disappointment.

It is, therefore, matter of some surprise that most — we might almost say *all* — of those scientific men who have spoken of the relation of Philosophy to Science, maintain that there is an absolute opposition between these two spheres of knowledge. One of the most eminent living Biologists of England deliberately asserts, and enforces with all the ability for which he is distinguished, the startling proposition that Philosophy no less certainly leads to Idealism than Science to Materialism. "Follow out the teaching of the one," says Mr.Huxley, "to its legitimate conclusions, and you are forced to admit that matter is a mode of mind; accept the results of the other, and you

* First published by *Queen's University*, William Bailie, printer, Kingston 1872

cannot deny the inference that mind is a mode of matter." That Science inevitably leads to absolute Materialism, or the position that man is simply the product of the forces of nature, Mr.Huxley endeavours to prove upon scientific principles. In all organisms, whether vegetable or animal, there is one common basis of life out of which they spring and which is identical in all, whether it is regarded from the point of view of form, of function or of substantial composition. This physical basis of life, or protoplasm, as it has been called, is found upon analysis to be composed of water, carbonic acid and ammonia. The composition of these in certain proportions gives rise to life, and hence life is due solely to chemical elements. Moreover, as thought or consciousness is dependent upon life, and life upon material elements, it, too, is ultimately resolvable into forces of nature. The conclusion, therefore, to which our author comes is that the most rigid scientific demonstration leads us to believe that man is of the same nature with the ground on which he treads. Let us hear Mr.Huxley's own words: "It may seem a small thing to admit that the dull vital actions of a fungus or a foraminifer are the properties of their protoplasm, and are the direct results of the nature of the matter of which they are composed. But if, as I have endeavoured to prove to you, their protoplasm is essentially identical with, and most readily converted into, that of any animal, I can discover no logical halting-place between the admission that such is the case, and the further concession that all vital action may, with equal propriety, be said to be the result of the molecular forces of the protoplasm which displays it. And if so, it must be true, in the same sense and to the same extent, that the thoughts to which I am now giving utterance, and your thoughts regarding, them are the expression of molecular changes in the matter of life which is the source of our other vital phenomena."

This is the scientific or materialistic side of the theory: philosophy conducts us by a different path to exactly the opposite conclusion. Having led us into "the slough of Materialism," as he aptly calls it, Mr.Huxley would extricate us from it by showing that an inspection of consciousness leads us with equal certainty to the Idealistic position that matter is dependent on mind. The external world, he says, is only known to us as states of our consciousness, and all knowledge is made up of such states. Some of these we attribute to self and some to not-self, but in either case we never get beyond our own consciousness. By Philosophy we are thus taught a different lesson from that inculcated by Science. Between the two there is an irreconcilable contradiction, and we can only say, that as we neither know what matter nor what mind is *in itself*, but only as it presents itself *to us*, there is probably some method of reconciling their antagonistic deliverances, if the limitations of human thought did not prevent us from ever discovering it.

It does not belong to our province to enter into the scientific question raised by Mr.Huxley — whether, namely, life is the mere product of chemical composition; and we shall content ourselves with remarking that, whether true or false, the theory has not yet been proven. Approaching the problem from a purely philosophical point of view, we shall endeavour to show, that even if it were established, as a matter of *fact*, that life is evolved from matter, the inference that thought is resolvable into material forces is utterly untenable.

There is nothing new in the assertion of an absolute opposition between Philosophy and Science, Thought and Nature, Reason and Experience: it is, as Mr.Huxley candidly admits, simply the philosophy of David Hume, adjusted to the advances of modern science; and transformed, we may add, from a Scepticism into a Dogmatism. The contradiction here expressed is that which forms the special problem of Philosophy, and has demanded solution from the very dawn of speculation. So soon as man has satisfied his material wants, the sense of a contradiction between what *seems* and what *is* between the outer world of sense and the inner world of thought, begins to break upon his mental vision; and he awakes to the consciousness that there is an unexplored, suprasensual realm, transcending all that he has hitherto known. At an early period in the history of a nation this perception of a region higher than the phenomenal world expresses itself in the half-unconscious revelations of poetry, and in the proverbial sayings of men gifted with more than average insight; it is at a late period in the history of thought that it seems to embody itself in that systematic knowledge which constitutes philosophy. The whole history of philosophy is a record of repeated attempts to give an adequate solution of the problem to which we have referred. The earliest philosophers were unable to give any satisfactory reply, because they aimed at what was beyond the reach of the human intellect; attempting too much they ended by gaining nothing. They vainly strove to answer the question, What is the origin of all things? and it was only when Socrates directed his attention to man himself, seeking to discover the essential nature of thought, that philosophy entered upon its proper task; and although this point of view was afterward obscured and lost, it has been recovered in modern times, and philosophy placed upon a sure foundation. This result has not been effected in a day; it has been the slow and gradual growth of all modern systems of philosophy. Now, therefore, that it has been so emphatically declared that Philosophy and Science stand to each other in the position of irreconcilable enemies, the question as to how, by availing ourselves of the wisdom of the past, the contradiction between the phenomenal and the ideal, the world of nature and the world of thought, is to be reconciled, has become an all-important one. It is no solution of the difficulty to be told that it is insoluble; in this way the claim of reason to be heard may be suppressed for a time, but it will inevitably force itself again upon our notice and refuse to be dismissed. To give an adequate reply to this fundamental question would require the unfolding of a complete philosophy, and we must content ourselves with indicating in outline the solution we deem the only adequate one.

Those who tell us that Science and Philosophy lead to directly opposite conclusions, tacitly assume that both are *co-ordinate*, and that the results of the one are not less *ultimate* than those of the other. Science leads to Materialism, Philosophy to Idealism, and we must accept the deliverances of each as of equal value. But is this assumption tenable? or does not the apparent antagonism between the two spheres of knowledge arise from regarding them as co-ordinate, when in reality the one is subordinate to the other and finds its final justification in it? It will be our duty in the sequel to show that the latter is the true alternative: that a clear conception of the legitimate sphere of each will break down the hard opposition which is supposed to subsist between them, and that the asserted materiality of mind results from pushing the boundary of science beyiond its proper limits.

The special sciences are, from their very nature and method of investigation, *limited* in their range, and hence can never give more than a limited explanation even of the class of objects which form their province. They discover truth, but it is only relative truth. Their object-matter is the phenomenal, and whatever advances they may make, they must be ever restricted to the phenomenal. Thus far our scientific men are right in saying that knowledge is limited to phenomena, and that of things in their real essence we have no knowledge; for, properly viewed, the phenomenal world means one side of knowledge taken in abstraction from the other. Now — not to insist upon the evident fact that each of the sciences is restricted to a particular and limited sphere of investigation —even if we view all the special sciences in relation to each other and as constituting one organic whole, we can only discover relative truth, and we are therefore debarred from rising higher than phenomena, and, consequently, from finding an ultimate explanation. The starting point of science is the world as it appears in ordinary consciousness — the world as independent of thought and made up of a collection of individual and independent things, — and however great its discoveries may be it never abandons this point of view. But in so conceiving the world, Science has made one great abstraction: it has abstracted entirely from self-consciousness or thought, and ibn so doing it has implicitly *assumed* the materiality of the mind. For if the world is absolutely independent of thought, the latter must be purely *passive* in its apprehension of knowledge, and have no existence except in so far as it is acted upon from without. This, however, is merely another way of saying that the mind is material, for this proposition can have no other intelligible meaning than that all modes of consciousness are transformed forces of nature. It is very easy, therefore, for Mr.Huxley and others to shew that the method of science leads to the conclusion that mind is a manifestation of matter, for this is merely an explicit statement of that which is taken for granted at the outset. Thus we learn at once the proper sphere of science, and the necessity of a branch of knowledge which shall transcend it and carry up its generalizations into a higher unity. Unassailable so long as it keeps within its legitimate sphere, science inevitably falls into error when it seeks to bring consciousness, as well as the phenomenal world, within its grasp. While it keeps within the range of the material world, its materialism is just, for it is dealing *with* the material; when it applies to thought the same method it adopts in regard to nature, it necessarily falls into grave error. Mr.Huxley, therefore, commits a vital mistake when he assumes that the conclusions of science are as ultimate in their nature as those of a true philosophy; for, to be so, they must explain not nature alone, but also self-consciousness.

The failure of science to reach ultimate truth arises, then, we may say, from its assuming external nature at the beginning; for its very method implies the independent existence, or — what is the same thing — the absolute truth of the outer or phenomenal world. Now it is here where science fails that philosophy triumphs. To the question, What is Nature? philosophy is not content to answer with science, "There are such-and-such laws of nature," or even, "All material things are indissolubly united together." An ultimate explanation must tell us not only what are the forms or laws of a thing, but what it is *in itself*, in its essence, in its truth. Carry up your generalization of facts as far as you please, conceive nature as a congeries of laws, or, if you will, as a correlation of forces, and we must still ask, What is this unity of forces or laws? What is nature itself? and what is its relation to intelligence? It is only by an appeal to philosophy or pure thought that any adequate answer can be given to such enquiries. Philosophy, unlike the special sciences, does not deal with a particular section of knowledge, but with the essential nature of all knowledge, and hence it aims at revealing ultimate or necessary truth. The statement that knowledge is limited to the phenomenal is true only when applied to common consciousness and to science; it is the special business of philosophy to transcend the world of phenomena and to disclose the world of real being, by a discovery of the true bond of connection between thought and nature.

From the primary assumption of the absolute independence of the outer world flow other assumptions which essentially belong to the scientific method. Having abstracted from self-consciousness and thus vitally asserted that it is capable of arriving at the highest truth attainable by man, Science necessarily takes for granted a number of logical notions, without subjecting them to a process of criticism. It seems to be merely enquiring into the laws of nature and to be quite passive in its presence, while it is really guided and controlled by categories which are the common stock of the age to which it belongs. These categories it finds in common consciousness; it does not think of enquiring into their origin and testing their validity; nor, indeed, has it, *as* science, a perception that any such investigation is needed. Starting, as it does, with the opposition of subject and object, and concentrating its attention upon the objective world alone, it is the victim of the natural illusion that the categories it brings to nature it extracts from it. It makes continual use of such fundamental notions as *being, force, cause and effect,* without dreaming of making them an object of special inquiry. Such notions lie at the basis of all thought, and constitute "the diamond net" which envelopes all the material of thought and gives it order, coherence and consistency. The assumption of these categories is at once the strength and the weakness of science: its strength because without them it could not make a single step in advance; its weakness, because it is led to overlook their true origin and nature. So soon as we seek to discover, prove and concatenate these notions, we see that they must be referred to thought and not to nature, to the inner and not to the outer world; and thus the need of a science which shall exhibit the necessary relation and interdependence of the fundamental notions that underlie all thought and being — the science of *Logic*, the first department of Philosophy — clearly manifests itself to our minds.

It may seem, at first sight, to be of little moment whether we say that these categories belong to nature or to thought; and in one sense this is true. Speaking in an external way, we may say that they belong to both; it is not less true that the category of *causality*, for instance, is evolved by thought than that it is manifested in nature. From another point of view, however, it is of the last importance which of these alternatives we accept; for if these notions pertain to the external world alone — to Nature taken in abstraction from Thought — the mind becomes the mere sport of impressions acting from without, and is therefore materialised. Here again the imperfection of the view which would co-ordinate science and philosophy, regarding them as two parallel lines that never meet, becomes apparent. For it is manifestly a complete inversion of truth to conceive of thought as entirely dependent upon matter, when all that gives meaning to matter is resolvable into thought; it is to degrade self-consciousness by weapons furnished by itself.

We have seen, then, that the special sciences are limited to the relative and phenomenal, and that they contain a number of uncriticised notions, because of their primal assumption of the absolute independence of nature; and we now remark that, for the same reason, their list of categories is defective and incomplete. As Science always keeps within the limits of the phenomenal world, its categories are unmethodized and limited in number, because they are picked up at random, instead of being obtained by a careful elimination of all that belongs to the empirical consciousness. This uncritical use of these fundamental notions runs through all theories, such as that of Mr. Huxley, which confine themselves to the scientific method; but it is especially apparent in the reasoning of Mr. Herbert Spencer, chiefly because he has expressed, in a clear and logical way, the legitimate conclusions to be drawn from that method. Following out the result of the special sciences, he arrives at the conclusion that the sensations and emotions in consciousness are equivalents of material forces, and, by inference, that mind is a product of nature.

The main aim Mr. Spencer has in view is to shew that mechanical forces, chemical action, vital energy and the phenomena of consciousness are each resolvable by analysis into manifestations of force and transformable into any one of the others. Space and Time are evolved by a more and more perfect generalization of individual instances of *resistance* to our muscular energies, and are thus reduced to *force*. Matter, scientifically considered, is made up of resistance and extension, the former being the primary notion, the latter the secondary. Motion, again, involves the conceptions of Space, Time, and Matter, and as these have been already reduced to manifestations of force, it follows that it is also a mode of Force. We are thus driven to the conclusion that "Force is the ultimate of ultimates; Matter and motion, as we know them, are differently conditioned manifestations of Force; while Space and Time, as we know them, are disclosed along with these different manifestations of Force as the conditions under which they are presented." Now it is admitted by all, continues Mr.Spencer, that Matter is absolutely indestructible, *i.e.*, can never be either increased or diminished; and this admission, converted into scientific language, means that any given quantity of Force always remains the same. Again, it is an established law that, "when not influenced by external forces, a moving body will go on in a straight line with a uniform velocity," and this law properly means that Motion, as well as Matter, is "indestructible" Mr.Spencer, therefore, instead of saying that "Matter is indestructible," and that "Motion is continuous," would prefer to comprehend both statements under the one formula, that "Force is persistent." This formula implies that Force never either increases or diminishes *in quantity*; but as there are undoubtedly changes in force, whether manifested in matter or in motion, how is this position to be established? By the fact, it is answered, that the motion which in certain cases seems to be entirely lost, is in reality merely transformed into *equivalent* Forces. Motion that is arrested produces, under different circumstances, heat, electricity, magnetism, light; and all chemical changes are simply modes of Motion or Force. It is further apparent that vital actions are merely transformed chemical forces; and this holds good whether we speak of the plant or of the animal. Finally, consciousness is itself reducible to material Force. The sensations which affect our organs of sense are directly related to external forces, of which they are the equivalents, and are thus new forms of the Force which produces them. Nor can we deny a like genesis to emotions, for the relation between emotions and the physical effects produced by them is quantitatively as exact as that between external agents and the sensations they excite.

We have in this theory a conception of the universe, inclusive of man, in which no sphere is higher than another. Mechanical are transformed into chemical forces, the latter into vital energy, and this again reappears in equivalents of sensation and emotion. The world, to the eye of Science, is thus a vast level plain; to Philosophy, on the other hand, it is, like the celestial orbs in Dante's "Paradiso," an ascending series of realms, of which the first rests on earth and the last terminates in heaven. Beginning with physical forces, Philosophy ascends gradually upwards, through chemical energy and vital action, till it attains to the sphere of man, regarded as a spirit, from which the ascent to God, the first and the last, upon whom all the lower spheres are dependent, and whose nature alone supplies the key that unlocks the whole universe, is easily and necessarily made.

An examination of Mr.Spencer's reasoning will make this more apparent. His highest conception of the world is that of forces and correlations of forces. The proposition that the given quantity of force in the universe always remains the same, however it may change its outward manifestation, contains two notions, *change* and *identity in change*. Now this will be found upon examination to be simply the category of cause and effect in a concrete form. When a cause is transformed into an effect, it changes its form, but remains virtually the same. In the notion of cause, as of force, we have therefore change and identity in change. The heat of the sun is the cause of evaporation and re-appears in the form of vapour; the condensation of this vapour is the effect of the action of the winds; the rain which falls from the clouds, or, more accurately, the rain which *is* the clouds, is dispersed over a particular tract of land, and, as effect, assumes the form of a river-current. Our notion of cause and effect is therefore simply that of the unity of identity and change — identity of matter combined with the change of form; and we are thus entitled to assume that whatever holds good of the relation of cause and effect will also be applicable to the correlation of forces.

Now unless the category of causality adequately characterise the phenomena of life and of consciousness, as it undoubtedly does those of the inorganic world, the reasoning of Mr.Spencer will be vitiated. But no great amount of consideration can be required to prove that this category does not properly apply to the phenomena of the *organic* world. So long as we are speaking of material things, the category of causality is correct and appropriate; it fails when we rise to a higher sphere. In the phenomena of life, we have not simply to explain a relation of so loose and external a character, that one force is completely transformed into another force and ceases to exist in its first form. This relation is transcended even in *vegetable* life. We do not adequately express the nature of the plant when we say, with common consciousness, that it possesses leaves, stem, colour, or with Chemistry, that it is composed of certain elements, or even, with Mr.Spencer, that it is a manifestation of force. All this is truth, but it is not the whole truth; we have not yet pointed out what distinguishes the plant from a mass of inert matter. From one point of view, then, we may here, in strict propriety, apply the notion of cause; from another, a higher notion is required, which shall at once include and transcend this lower notion. For while the plant exhibits the action of chemical forces, and thus comes under the relation of cause and effect, it also displays phenomena of a much loftier nature. It is not held together *merely* by chemical relations; it cannot be broken up into parts,like a stone, and still remain a plant; for it is a unity which is continuously differentiating itself into manifold variety — a totality that is ceaselessly evolving itself into externality —and this it is which constitutes its Life. The plant, therefore, is inadequately conceived when it is subsumed under the notion of causality or force; its essential nature can only be expressed when it is referred to the higher notion of *life* — a notion which at once includes while it goes beyond the lower notion of causality or force. To view the plant solely under the relation of cause and effect is, in short, to leave out all that is characteristic of it as an organism, and therefore to degrade it to the level of inorganic things. Even if it could be shown that the plant has been developed out of inorganic matter, still, as in that case matter must have contained the plant, *potentially*, the latter is *ideally*, or in order of thought, primordial; and in attempting to reduce the organic to the inorganic, Mr.Spencer has eliminated the higher element to be found in the former, and has thus vitiated the whole of his reasoning.

Now what is true of vegetable life is true in a still higher way of *animal* life. The unity of the former is not so complete that it cannot be broken up into different parts without ceasing to be a unity. Each part of the plant is, to a great extent, a repetition of the other, and is capable of forming a new plant by being simply severed from its parent and placed in proper external conditions. This, indeed, is also true of the lowest type of animal, where the line of demarcation between the vegetable and animal world is so indistinct that what may in one way be classed as animal, may also be regarded as vegetable. With a more complex structure, however, this difficulty ceases, and we find an organism in which no part exists except for the rest, while the whole are gathered up into an ideal unity that is manifestly more perfect than that exhibited in the highest vegetable organism, and is in complete contradiction to the loose and external unity of inorganic things. It is in virtue of this presence of life in all parts that the animal has sensation; and hence Aristotle was justified in saying that "the soul (life) is all in the whole and all in every part." The animal is thus determined to evolution *from within* and not conversely, although the possibility of such an evolution is conditioned by the external world. Now exactly in proportion as the animal organism increases in complexity, and at the same time becomes a more and more perfect unity, the category of causality becomes less and less appropriate, so that in the higher organisms its inadequacy is forced upon our notice. For the category of cause, or, if you will, of force, implies as has been said the transformation of one phenomenon into another, and therefore the complete extinction of the former. In life, however, we have not simply one phenomenon ceasing to be, in its transformation into another, but a unity that continually differentiates itself into infinite variety, and by this very process maintains itself. Here, therefore, the notion of causality utterly fails. It is true, indeed, that as the animal is not only a vital organism but also exhibits mechanical and chemical forces, it may in one way be subsumed under the notion of cause, but it is only in so far as it is viewed *as* mechanical or chemical — only in so far as we abstract from what is *distinctive* of it, viz. its *vitality* — that this is legitimate. When we wish to designate what is essential to it as an organism, we have, explicitly or implicitly, to leave the notion of causality behind and employ a higher notion.

We have already said that sensation *as* sensation belongs to life and not to thought. A mere sensation is but an affection of the nervous organism, and exists in the animal without implying a *consciousness* of its existence. The animal is in complete unity with its sensations, and has no power of abstracting from them; it is affected by them for a moment, and then they vanish for ever. It is the power of abstracting from sensation, and making it an object of consciousness that distinguishes man from the animals, and renders him capable of thought. Even, therefore, if it could be proved, by the scientific method; that life depends upon a due proportion of certain chemical elements, and consciousness upon life, it would not follow that consciousness is a mode of matter. For consciousness includes the mechanical, chemical and vital forces, while it adds an element of its own higher than either. The notion of causality, which we found to be imperfect even when applied to the organic world, becomes much more inadequate when we reach the higher realm of consciousness. It is by abstracting from what is characteristic of it, that the dynamical philosophers are enabled to give plausibility to the theory that the phenomena of consciousness are but transformed material forces. It may seem, indeed, that little is gained by pointing out that the notions employed by the physicist in the explanation of nature are imperfect; for is it not a fact, it may be said, that consciousness is dependent upon life, and life on matter, and how then can it still be held that consciousness is not a mode of matter? But the answer is simple: as the conclusion that mind is material is based upon an imperfect use of categories, the whole conclusion is thereby vitiated. Nature is undoubtedly rational, but not *to itself*; it is only in so far as it is brought within the dominion of thought that it renders up its meaning, and the whole progress of thought is a history of the discovery and the deepening of categories. Now these categories science, from its assumptive character, can never prove, and hence its explanations, while relatively true, are not final. In its search for unity, it fails to perceive that no absolute unity can be obtained by simply leaving out all difference, and fixing upon agreement alone, for the differences are not less essential than the agreements. When, therefore, it asks, What are the points of agreement between consciousness, life, chemical action and mechanical force? it overlooks the fact that it has, by asking the question in this way, virtually *assumed* the identity of the highest with the lowest sphere; for what is common to the two extremes can only be that which is distinctive of the *lowest*. If, as we have shown, the various spheres of the universe form an ascending series, in which each higher realm includes while it transcends the lower, we can only adequately explain the highest by gradually descending to the lowest. To make consciousness dependent upon matter is to reason in a circle; for matter has no meaning apart from consciousness.

The bearing of these considerations upon the general question of the relation of Philosophy to Science will be readily anticipated. The dynamical theory of the world, which attempts to reduce all phenomena to manifestations of "the persistence of force," is found to be partial and imperfect, and to be inapplicable so soon as we attempt to apply it to the inorganic world. Legitimate when put forward in explanation of dead, inert matter, it totally fails when applied to animal organisms, with their wondrous power of continuous adjustment to external circumstances, and their indefinite power of preserving that unity in the midst of diversity which constitutes their life. And when we leave the phenomena of life and sensation, and seek to account by the scientific method for the phenomena of consciousness and thought, the imperfection of the scientific method becomes glaringly apparent. Its plausibility depends upon the assumption that pure sensation and thought are identical, whereas the one completely transcends the other; for, properly speaking, sensation does not belong to thought but to life. When, therefore, consciousness is viewed as a bundle of sensations, not only its true nature is overlooked, but the possibility of knowledge is destroyed. This will be best shown by a summary of the sensational philosophy.

Locke, like our scientific men, starts with the assumption of an external world, complete in itself, and composed of an infinite number of distinct and individual things. Hence thought or consciousness is regarded as a *tabula rasa* on which the world writes. When we ask, from this point of view, how we come to *have* the knowledge we possess, we obtain a wrong answer, because we have asked a wrong question. For if the mind is purely passive, all its knowledge must be got, as Locke held, from sensation, for this is merely another way of saying that all knowledge comes from *without*. But as a sensation is a perfectly immediate, simple affection, and contains nothing but itself, it was easy for Bishop Berkeley to show that Locke, in distinguishing between the primary and the secondary qualities of body — the former being regarded as existing in the external world in the same form as in sensation, and the latter as present only in *us* — laid down an untenable position. For as a sensation exists only as it is known, to speak of an external world beyond sensation is to make a gratuitous assumption. The external world of individual things, therefore, with which Locke started, has disappeared and left behind only a series of sensations belonging to the subject. All existence is now reduced to self and states of self; the objective world, just because it was assumed to be objective or self-dependent, has converted itself into a subjective world of sensations. Moreover, if, in the act of knowledge, the knowing self is purely passive, as Locke maintained, *it* also must be built up, if it exists at all, out of pure sensations. This is, however, but another way of asserting that self *is* this series of sensations — the conclusion deduced by Hume from the philosophy of Locke. All knowledge is thus reduced to a thread of sensations following each other in time. Hume did not, like his follower, John Stuart Mill, maintain this position dogmatically; but he asserted with perfect justice that it was the legitimate result of the Lockean philosophy. We have thus seen that Empiricism, starting with an external world, seemingly independent, ends with conceiving knowledge as a series of sensations without a self to know them and without an object in which they can be known. It is the contrast between what Sensationalism intended to do, and what it really did, that constitutes the Scepticism of Hume. The fact to be explained was a permanent and *objective* world; the theory propounded to explain this world converted it, instead, into a series of *subjective*, fleeting, simple sensations. It is this contradiction between theory and reality that Hume signalised when he spoke of the absolute opposition between common sense and reason, and which makes his philosophy one of the bitterest sarcasms on human knowledge that has ever been enunciated. It is this contradiction, in another form, that defies the solution of our modern Physicists.

It may seem that Hume, in reducing the philosophy of Locke to a series of sensations following each   other in time and spread out in space, had brought it to its utmost simplicity. But Empiricism has a still "lower deep," for there are two fundamental notions which Hume did not account for — those of Space and Time. Now, assuming for a moment that Time, as Locke argued, is generated by reflection upon successive states of consciousness, the idea of Space still remains to be explained. And if, as is maintained, all knowledge may be reduced to a series of sensations, and therefore to a succession in time, it is evident that the spatial must be evolved from the temporal relation — the position adopted by recent Sensationalists. The reduction of Space to Time must, indeed, be forever unsuccessful: whether we try to derive Space from the simultaneity of different sensations, with Mr.John Stuart Mill, or from the direction and intensity of muscular effort, with Mr.Bain, we attempt an impossible task; for sensations are from their very nature, fleeting and individual, and hence can never transform themselves into our conception of a world of permanent and co-existing objects. It is, however, of more importance to observe that it is quite in harmony with the Sensational theory to attempt this reduction, and to regard space as generated out of a temporal succession of sensations. We are thus left with nothing in the universe except a series of impressions, and it will not be difficult to shew that even this series is doomed to disappear before the test of criticism. Sensations, from their very nature, are incapable of mutual relation. The very idea of a sensation is that it is simple, individual, and contains nothing but itself; and hence it no sooner gives place to another impression than it must vanish into non-existence. It cannot exist in relation to another sensation, because relation implies *comparison*, and comparison could only take place if it were capable, as it evidently is not, of objectifying itself and then relating itself to another sensation. Thus, even the "series," which is always tacitly assumed by the Empiricist, involves an assumption he is not warranted in making — the assumption of the mutual relation of different sensations. We are thus compelled to speak of knowledge as a number of disconnected and individual impressions, existing out of relation to each other, and therefore out of time; and hence Time, as well as Space, has disappeared. It does not mend the matter to say, with Mr.Mill, that the sensations are related by *association*, for as *individual* they cannot relate themselves. Here then we lose the last hold upon the world of reality, for as consciousness can only exist as a relation, and the sensations are *ex hypothesi* out of all relation, they cease to exist; Nature and Thought alike disappear,

> And, like an unsubstantial pageant faded,
> Leave not a wrack behind.

Absolute Nihilism, then, is the legitimate and demonstrable result of Empiricism. Starting with the absolute independence of nature, and therefore virtually with the assumption that consciousness is entirely dependent upon the material world, it tries to build up the external world and the world of thought out of sensation. The disastrous result of this mode of procedure we have already seen: knowledge is brought into conflict with itself, and finally accomplishes its own destruction. where then is the fallacy of Sensationalism — for fallacy there must be — to be found? It lies in this, that the essential activity of *thought* has been overlooked. When it is said that nature and thought are evolved out of pure sensations, it is erroneously assumed that sensation in consciousness and sensation out of consciousness — or otherwise, that life and thought — are convertible. But reflection upon the nature of thought makes the fallacy of such a view obvious. A sensation, as soon as I think it, becomes more than a sensation. In doing so I transform what was before a particular into a universal. As a thinking being I have the power of abstracting from all modes of consciousness and concentrating my attention solely upon myself, the being who thinks. In all the varying operations of thought, therefore, the Ego or Self remains as the permanent factor. And, further, this abstract self, while it seems to be perfectly simple and immediate, is in reality universal, for each thinking being, like myself, is a self, and for this very reason capable of thought.   Now, this self, which is common to all intelligences, is not, like a sensation, perfectly simple; for, from the very fact that it can make itself its *own* object, it contains distinction or difference within itself. And just because I can think away from all my particular states, I am capable of having something as an object of thought; in the very act of apprehending self I apprehend a not-self. Hence the two are inseparably united, and in apprehending an object, I bring it under the dominion of thought, and infuse into it the universality or permanence that belongs to thought. Spirit, therefore, in virtue of Thought, destroys the assumed independence of Nature and assimilates it to itself. The permanence which we ascribe to the outer world is thus produced by the *activity* of thought, instead of being, as is assumed by the Empiricist, *passively* imprinted upon the mind; what we call experience or objectivity, is really the product of the universalising power of reason.

This exhibition of pure thought or the Ego, as the only possible explanation of objectivity is what the great German philosopher, Kant, designates, in his somewhat barbaric terminology, "the synthetical unity of Apperception (self-consciousness)." The process, that is, by which experience is gradually built up is essentially a *synthesis*, and the great imperfection of Locke, leading, as it did, to the Scepticism of Hume, was in regarding it as a mere analysis. We have before us, says Locke, experience, full-formed and complete in itself, and the only object of philosophy is to analyse it into its component elements. It was thus overlooked that all analysis implies a prior synthesis, and hence that no explanation of knowledge can be adequate which bases itself upon analysis alone. To Kant, on the other hand, experience was the result of the synthetical power of self-consciousness. Starting, like Locke, with sensation as one element of knowledge, he held that this of itself can never generate experience, and that the other element is supplied by thought. Experience is the product of two factors, the one *a posteriori*, or given from *without*, the other *a priori*, or supplied from *within*. Thought for its part has, as the essential and necessary heritage of its nature, the faculty of forming judgments, and in doing so it employs such fundamental notions or categories, as Unity, Reality, Negation, Cause and Effect. Into these categories thought *cannot but* differentiate itself, for they belong to its own inner nature, and to think is to employ them. Hence, also, they are *universal* and *necessary* notions, for otherwise we should have the contradiction of that which belongs to the very essence of thought being limited and contingent. We have thus, on the one hand, a ground work of sensations, and on the other hand, self-consciousness radiating into a number of necessary notions. Neither separately can give knowledge, for the sensations are nothing until they are thought, or, as Kant expresses it "sensations are *blind*"; and thought cannot come into exercise without the aid of the sensations, for as the categories are mere *relations*, thought can only use them when it has got something to *relate*, or, in the words of Kant, "the categories are *void*." But now, if thought bring the sensations into relation with the categories, shall we not then have knowledge? Yes, answers Kant, but for one thing: that experience is only possible, on the one hand as a succession of mental states, and on the other hand in the form of objects lying outside of each other; in other words, to complete our theory of knowledge we require to account for Space and Time, which are the conditions of all external or internal experience. Whether then do space and time belong to Thought or to Nature? Evidently to the former, is the answer, for they are necessary and universal, and necessity and universality are the criteria by which we discover what belongs to self-consciousness or is *a priori*. We can now explain how experience is possible. Thought differentiates itself into the categories, and, by means of the universal perceptive forms of Space and Time, gathers up into itself the sensations which form the material of knowledge. Thus we get a world with objects extended in space and existing in time, and viewed under a variety of necessary relations. To Kant, therefore, knowledge is essentially a synthesis, and a synthesis which is only possible because self-consciousness is the universal that lies at the basis of every experience, and reduces it to a unity. Kant has the honour of effecting a complete revolution in philosophy. Instead of attempting to explain thought by experience, he accounts for experience by thought. It is, therefore, with perfect justice that he regards himself as having done for philosophy what Copernicus accomplished for astronomy. Copernicus, when he found that the motions of the stars could not be explained by assuming them to revolve round the spectator, tried the effect of making the spectator revolve, and the stars remain at rest. Similarly, Kant, finding that Locke's assumption of the absolute passivity of the mind led to the complete overthrow of knowledge, was led to adopt the theory that the mind is essentially *active*, and was thus enabled to explain the fact of experience. He has, therefore, simply followed the method in which all great discoveries have been made — viz., by setting up a theory and regarding it as true or false according as it does or does not account for the facts it has to explain.

To Kant, then, belongs the high merit of pointing out the method which a true Metaphysic must adopt; but he has not himself followed out that method to its ultimate results. An ultimate explanation of knowledge must, as he perceived, be based upon the activity of self-consciousness in all its manifestations, for any other supposition leads to scepticism and, by an easy path, to Nihilism. But in the "Critique of Pure Reason" there is this essential imperfection, that it does not tell us *how* or *why* thought or self-consciousness develops itself into the infinite variety of experience. Thought, the Categories, the forms of Space and Time, and a groundwork of Sensations, are all, *somehow or other*, necessary to constitute experience, but when we ask *why* this is so, Kant has no satisfactory answer to give. *Why*, we may ask, does thought differentiate itself into categories, and what is their number, relative importance and interconnection? *Why*, again, has thought two and only two pure perceptions —those of Space and Time? *Why*, finally, does thought, by means of its categories and pure perceptions, transform sensations into experience? A proper answer to these questions will give a true system of *Metaphysic*.

To this conception of Metaphysic as the science which deals with the ultimate *ground* or *reason* of things, it may be objected that it is a purely supposititious knowledge. There are, it has been said, ultimate truths which, *as* ultimate, are incomprehensible and unthinkable, and which, therefore, from their very nature, cannot be proven. We know *that* they are, we cannot tell *why* they are ; for to do so would be to resolve them into a higher notion; which, *ex hypothesi*, is impossible. But this objection arises from a false notion of what proof is. We prove an *a priori* truth when we shew that it belongs to the essential nature of thought, and consequently that without it thought is impossible. The problem of Metaphysics is not simply to find unities in Nature *per se*, or in Thought *per se*, but to shew how, from the very nature of the case, the former must be resolved into the latter, and that only in this way can an ultimate unity that embraces both be obtained. To do this in a strictly systematic way is at present impossible, as it would require the unfolding of a complete system of metaphysic. We must, therefore, content ourselves with shewing that, looking at thought as a whole, and as displayed in the history of the race, it must necessarily pass through certain stages, culminating in ultimate truth. We say *must*, for it can be proven that thought is essentially *dialectic* in its nature, *i.e.*, that it is impelled on from one stage to another by the inner necessity of its own nature. These stages we shall briefly indicate, premising that they are not to be found by a mere inspection of the individual consciousness, but by an examination of the universal consciousness of mankind. The individual may stop at the first or some succeeding stage, without going through the whole cycle of thought; only in the infinite possibilities of the race is the full stature of the perfect man to be found.

The first and lowest stage of thought is that of the *Sensuous Consciousness*; the peculiarity of which is, not that in it alone the outer world affects the mind through the senses, but that reflection is at its minimum, and hence the object known and the person knowing it are each regarded as simple, immediate and individual. Whether the mind is filled with a number of external impressions or of internal feelings, it accepts either, without any enquiry into their real source or validity; thought is so little active, that it seems entirely passive. A number of sensations, supplied by the various senses, arise in consciousness, and seem to constitute all the truth attainable by man. We, who are at a later stage in the development of humanity, easily perceive that this was an illusion but it never occurred to those sunk in the sensuous stage of thought to question the truth of what appeared in their consciousness. If they had been capable of asking themselves, "What certainty have we that our immediate knowledge is real?" the only answer they could have given would have been: "We know it is real because it *is*, because we *feel* it to be real." But here, the mere *existence* in consciousness of anything is regarded, or would have been regarded if those at this lowest stage of thought had been capable of interrogating themselves, as a proof of reality and objectivity: the two senses of the word "being" — that of a mere predicate, and that of a developed experience of the objective world — being as yet inseparably interwoven with each other. It is in this identification of what is in consciousness and what is in reality, that the great imperfection of the philosophy of Berkeley consists. The lowest stage of consciousness is formalised, and in this, rather than in his denial of an external world, the great imperfection of his system is to be found. "There is," Berkeley maintains, "an absolute identity of sensation and the conscious self; the *esse* of things consists in their *percipi* — sensation and existince are synonymous;" and hence, because he deals with pure sensations alone, he fails to shew how objectivity, since it is not to be accounted for from without, comes into consciousness at all.

This first form of consciousness may be illustrated by the infancy of the race. The savage is dominated by the individual sensations which come and vanish from his consciousness like shadows. Like a child, he only sees or hears what comes directly before his notice. He has no interest in the external world apart from its subserving his material wants, and hence, when not engaged in hunting or fishing, or in war, he passes his time in a listless indolence, allowing impressions to move through his consciousness without an effort to retain them, compare them, and investigate into their source. Moreover, as he has no evidence for the reality of his impressions except that they *are*, that they pass through his mind, he is a prey to all kinds of superstitious terrors; even his rudimentary ideas of religion contributing to people the world with invisible enemies. As the only evidence he has for the objectivity of his ideas is the mere fact of their existence in consciousness, reality and fiction, the world revealed by his senses and the world conjured up by his terrors, are to him indistinguishable.

It is difficult for us who have advanced beyond this first crude stage of thought to divest ourselves of our acquired notions, and to put ourselves at the point of view of those who knew of nothing beyond it; but it may assist us in doing so if we compare it with analogous states of our own consciousness. In what, for instance, consists the illusion by which, in dreams, fancies seem realities if not in this, that we assume, without reflection, the validity of what passes through our minds, simply because it does pass through our minds? When we emerge from this realm of unreality the spell is destroyed, because we find, by comparing our fancies with facts we have established by number-less relations to thought, that the former are devoid of the reality or objectiv-ity of the latter. And so the victim of spectral illusions, in which imagination projects images that, at first sight, wear all the semblance of truth, may satisfy himself of their deceptive nature by employing the test of other senses besides sight, and thus converting his uncriticised impressions into definite knowl-edge. These illustrations may make more apparent the imperfection of the sensuous consciousness, and the logical necessity by which thought is impelled to a higher stage . The mind cannot rest satisfied with taking merely individual things, out of relation to each other, for in doing so it has, unknown to itself, implicitly related them; it naturally and necessarily regards reality, not as a chaos of isolated impressions, but as forming a cosmos in which each thing contains relations within itself, and is related to other things. Thought, excited to greater activity, reflects more carefully upon the objects presented to it, and discovers that they contain many qualities, and must therefore be expressed by manifold predicates. This second stage of thought may be called *Observation.*

The simple belief in the truth of any phenomenon that arises in conscious-ness has now given place to deliberate reflection upon individual objects and upon their mutual relations. Mediate has been substituted for immediate knowledge, experience for sensuous certitude. Higher categories are applied to objects than mere *being.* The observing consciousness advances beyond the fleeting impressions of sense to things in their concrete reality. On the one hand, it views objects as composed of various qualities — such as *solidity, extension, figure,* — and on the other hand, it soon discovers that it must view them in relation to each other, *i.e.*, as manifestations of such notions as *unity, plurality, cause and effect.* The plant I see, for example, may be viewed as a concrete object, made up of root, stem leaves; or again, it may be regarded as a unity, a plurality or a totality — as *a* plant, as possessed of certain definite parts, or as an object that is at once one and many; or finally, it may be referred to the category of causality, since it depends for its existence upon situation, soil and moisture. By the observing consciousness we thus come to regard things as possessed of various qualities, as gathered up into classes, and as interconnected with each other. Common consciousness, and the special sciences in so far as they merely generalise groups of phenomena from observation, belong to this phase of thought, and differ only in the greater or less accuracy of their results.

At this stage in the development of thought we have, then, an objective world, which is composed of individual things mutually related to each other, and which seems to be entirely independent of the knowing subject. To common consciousness and to science, nature has no deeper meaning than this; but to a philosophy explanatory of it the further question must be asked,

"What is the relation of the objective world to *thought*?" This is the question to which the "Critique of Pure Reason" seeks to give an answer. Kant assumed the world as it presents itself to ordinary consciousness, and, in the limited extent we have mentioned, to the special sciences, and, by a critical enquiry into the ground of experience, was forced to deny that absolute dualism between thought and nature, which led to Hume's Scepticism, and which has resulted in modern Materialism. Nature or experience, he argued, cannot be accounted for except on the supposition that thought brings a large contribution of its own to assist in producing and completing it. Neither in thought alone, nor in nature alone, can we find that permanence and objectivity which is assumed both by common consciousness and by science, but can not be proven by either; only by the union of the two — by an orderly interblending of *a priori* and *a posteriori* truths — can this be effected. As, therefore, the philosophy of Berkeley, and of all Sensationalists. interprets the first phase of consciousness, the deeper meaning of the second is revealed in the Metaphysical system of Kant.

Thought is, however, capable of a still further advance than that which is attained by the observing consciousness. It rises above that conception of the world which regards it as a congeries of objects, possessed of different qualities, or grouped together into classes, or related to each other by universal notions; for the very idea of a correlation between facts leads to a more intimate relation that that as yet attained. Thus thought is, by its own nature, impelled to seek higher unities than it has hitherto found and ends with conceiving the world as a system of *laws*. This stage of thought is the *Understanding*. The phenomena of nature are now transmuted by the action of thought into exemplifications of necessary laws, and thus half-subjective generalizations are raised to objective truths. Science, in so far as it is not a loose grouping of facts, but a collection of laws, belongs to this stage of thought. The special sciences, while they are still limited to the observation and classification of facts, belong to the observing consciousness; when they carry their inductions so far as to find the laws that regulate phenomena, they have come within the range of Understanding. The advance from the one stage to the other thus consists in finding greater permanence or objectivity in nature, in finding that it is not governed by caprice but by reason.

The philosophical consideration of this mode of thought reveals truth higher than that which is discovered by those who assume the absolute independence of nature, and therefore the passivity of thought in its presence. It is true the great object of scientific men is to eliminate all that is subjective, and to interpret nature from itself alone. But this, when examined more closely, only means that we must exclude our *individual* fancies or opinions and hold only that to be a law of nature which all intelligences or universal thought would recognise to be true; for law in its true sense means an inseparable unity, an indissoluble connection, of distinct relations. The Understanding, therefore, has penetrated into the inner soul of Nature and found it to be rational. What, however, is overlooked by those at this stage of thought is that in discovering the laws or necessities of Nature, we have at the same time found that it is a manifestation of *Thought* or *Reason* — the thought, not of this or that intelligence, but that which is participated in by all. And thus, in another way, we come back to our original statement that the special sciences are not fully conscious of the truth they reveal, because of the dualism they assume between nature and intelligence. Viewed from the higher platform of philosophy, the lesson taught us by the progress of science is the continuous discovery of a greater and greater unity between Thought and Nature; and, although Science does not perceive that in mastering nature it is at the same time revealing the thought latent in it, its unchecked progress is a prophecy of ultimate triumph — the reduction of the whole external world to a system of laws — the revelation of the absolute rationality of the universe. The progress of thought has been, as it still is, an ever greater assimilation of nature into itself, and thus to philosophy Thought and Nature are found to be but obverse sides of the same shield. We have occupied so much time with the logical and metaphysical sides of Philosophy, that we can only add a few words on the contradiction which it is the office of Ethics to solve — that, namely, of Freedom and Necessity. The metaphysical theory which reduces the nature of man to a bundle of sensations, naturally leads to the ethical theory that he is the slave of uncontrollable feelings and desires against which he is powerless. For if the actions of man are entirely due to natural impulses, any given action will be determined by that impulse which preponderates at the moment; and hence Hume but expressed in clear terms the result of this view when he said, in his incisive way, that "Reason is and must be the slave of the passions." It in no way mends the matter to explain that the basis of duty is to be found in the happiness of the majority; for although this idea, when systematically carried out, *may* lead to a course of conduct that will harmonize with the dictates of duty, it cannot serve as a substantial basis upon which a *system* of Ethics may be reared. The ultimate ground of action is pleasure, and no adequate reason can be given by the Utilitarian why the individual may not act in accordance with his depraved tastes, if they are depraved, whether his conduct will contribute to the happiness or misery of others.

We do not obtain more satisfaction, but rather less, by interrogating any of the Ancient Philosophers; for,as they had no appreciation of the glorious destiny to which man is reserved, they were unconscious that any reply was needed. Man was by them regarded not *as* man, but as a member of the State; and hence the sole method of elevating him was by adding to his natural advantages the endowments and privileges of the few. Aristotle's ideal of humanity, the magnanimous man, is a Greek citizen, possessed of the highest honours the State can confer upon him, and conscious that he is worthy of them; courageous, honest, cultured; contemptuous of the applause of the common mass of men, but pleased with the approbation of the more refined; born of a good family, and prosperous in his worldly affairs; asking favours of no-one, or only with the greatest reluctance, but rejoicing to confer benefits upon others. Such an ideal, it is evident, is only attainable by the privileged few, but by that few may be realised with comparative ease. Now Christianity, by recognising all men as equal in the sight of God, broke down the middle wall of partition between master and servant, cultured and uncultured, and contemplated man simply as man; while, in setting up an ideal of infinite purity, which embodied the essential nature of the human Spirit, it destroyed the self-righteousness of the Ancients and substituted an infinite despair of perfection by showing that "after we have done all we are unprofitable servants." Christianity, therefore, in unveiling the infinite possibilities of humanity, and demanding their realization, necessarily implied the freedom of man, for only as free can he work out his high destiny. How is this demand to be reconciled with the fetters of necessity by which he seems to be enchained?

Much unnecessary confusion has been introduced into this question by the way in which human liberty has been conceived. Freedom, it has been held by the majority of Moralists, can only exist if we can act independently of motives, and even in opposition to them. It requires very little consideration to see that if this is the only possible conception of freedom, man is a slave to the most absolute necessity. He finds himself at his birth restricted by position, circumstances and many other relations to others, which he cannot by effort shake off. He cannot, further, perform the most trivial act without having *some* motive for it, simply because he is a rational being and not a mere animal. Freedom, therefore, in the sense of exemption from all external influences and restraints, is a mere figment of the brain, invented by a scholastic subtlety and felt to be absurd by the common sense of mankind. But there is a truer and higher way in which freedom may be conceived, which at once secures moral responsibility, and allows for the influences of society upon the individual. The highest freedom is not that in which we act *without* motives —for that would be mere caprice — but that in which our action is regulated by the highest laws of our nature. The profligate man, who is under the dominion of sense, the capricious man, who is tossed to and fro by every wind of passion, and the wilful man whose only motives are to act in opposition to motives, seem to themselves to be free, but in the light of reason they are in the hardest bondage. He, on the other hand, who regulates all his actions by eternal principles of duty, may seem to be bound by the chains of necessity, but he really enjoys the highest liberty. For he is not subject to any external necessity, but only to the inner necessity of his own nature, in obeying which he purifies and strengthens his will and becomes a master where others are slaves.

The possibility of working out one's freedom through seeming necessity, may be seen in all relations into which man is brought. At first everyone is under apparent bondage to his superiors in the family relation, but in reality this is the means by which a measure of freedom is attained. It is true that he must render implicit obedience to those in authority over him, but in so doing he learns to free himself from an undue accentuation of his own individual desires, and to seek his freedom where alone it can be found — in the subordination of his own will to the good of others. By and by he is liberated from the restrictions of the family, but he finds that he has only thrown off one yoke to take upon himself another and a heavier burden; he is now a citizen — a member of the State —and as such he not only enjoys the rights of a citizen, but is also bound down by the duties of his new relation, which hold him as by adamantine chains. Here, again, he is free in so far as he voluntarily and cheerfully discharges his duties; he is a slave if he attempts to avoid them and to throw them upon others. He cannot, further, be a member of the state without being more than this; for a state is but one of the community of nations, and he who is a member of one is a member of the other also. He alone, therefore, is free who recognises in every man of whatever country or position that humanity which unites the race by the bonds of a common brotherhood, and who freely discharges the duties he owes to all. He is enslaved who shuts his eyes to this truth and seeks only the satisfaction of his own selfish inclinations.

We cannot conclude this lecture without remarking that the three departments of Philosophy of which we have spoken are intimately related to one of the most important subjects that can engage the attention of the human mind. It is not for us to intrude into the sacred realm of Theology; but this we may say, that Logic and Metaphysic and Ethics were incomplete if they did not, as their final result, lead us up to the Infinite and to God. Philosophy elevates itself above all mere opinions, above all untested assumptions, above all caprice and impulse — in short, above all that is peculiar to this or that individual — and lives and moves in the realm of necessary truth. It shews that man is able to free himself from all unwarranted beliefs and to unveil the secret of the universe, by discovering the essential rationality that, however it may be concealed from those who seek it not, shines through all the outward manifestations of Nature and of Spirit. All men, consciously or unconsciously, participate in universal truth, and thus there is a universal consciousness, given *through* the consciousness of the individual, but in no way *dependent* upon it. In thus revealing necessary truth, Philosophy at the same time reveals Him who is Truth itself. We do not affirm that every man, or any man, can fully comprehend the infinite fulness of the Divine nature, but neither, we venture to assert, need we raise an altar to "the unknown and unknowable God," in whose existence we may believe, but whose nature must be forever concealed from us. The human Spirit, made in the image of God, Nature, "the visible garment of God," and Duty, the voice of God speaking in the innermost depths of our moral nature, agree in pointing upwards to the Great Being whose essence they unfold. And thus the assurance which Religion gives to the individual man of the existence of a Supreme Being whom he must reverence and love, Philosophy endorses and supports. The fundamental notions with which it is the office of Logic to deal may not inappropriately be termed the plan of the universe as it existed in the Divine mind before the creation of the world; the long but sure path, by which Metaphysic ascends from the inorganic world to the world of living beings, and thence to the realm first of individual consciousness, and next of universal thought, at last terminates and loses itself in the all-embracing glory of God; and the highest lesson that Ethics has to teach is that only by unity with the divine nature, only by the elevation of his individual will to the high standard of duty, can man enter into the glorious liberty wherewith the truth makes free.

I should have preferred closing this lecture without making any reference to the feelings awakened within me upon the present occasion, did I not think it but just — not to use a stronger word — to express my public thanks for the honour which has been done me by my appointment to the chair of Philosophy in this University. Knowing the eminent success which has attended the labours of my predecessors, I feel that my position is a peculiarily arduous one; but this I may be permitted to say, that as the study of philosophy has been to me a source of exquisite pleasure in the past, so nothing could now give me more intense satisfaction than to be assured that I shall be in the future a successful teacher of Philosophy in Queen's University.

Section Two

JOHN CLARK MURRAY
(1836-1917)

2

John Clark Murray:
Religion Science and the Unity of Nature

Elizabeth Trott

When John Clark Murray had a piper pipe in the pudding to Christmas dinner in his home on McTavish Street in Montreal, he did so with the utmost reverence for his Scottish heritage. When one knows that through much of his philosophical career he suffered a hearing problem and required the use of an ear trumpet, one more fully appreciates the strength of his determination to pursue and share knowledge.

Murray did more than bring Christmas traditions to his home in Canada, he brought a well-trained philosophical mind, a mind shaped by the thought of Sir William Hamilton, and infused with the spirit of his predecessor, Francis Hutcheson. Murray, in new surroundings, felt free to subject his philosophical inheritance to rigid examination, something which may have been less likely had he remained at home in Scotland.

When he arrived at Queen's University in 1862 as the most promising young scholar Sir William Hamilton had taught, he joined a mere handful of philosophers in Canada who had assumed the enormous task of educating future teachers, clergymen and civil servants in a colony that was not yet a nation-state. There was little philosophical history that demanded his countenance and Murray was free to go his own way. The excitement of new horizons spurred him on to a productive career of over forty years, the publication of more than half a dozen books, several treatises, and numerous articles. Having learned the ancient trade from skilled masters, he set about to carve his own niche in the history of Canadian philosophical thought.

John Clark Murray was born in Thread and Tannahill in 1836 before the Great Disruption of the Scottish Protestant Church. His father, David Murray, became the provost of Paisley. Murray attended the local grammar school and Glasgow University (1850-1854). Glasgow had benefited from

Frances Hutcheson's reforms in the previous century and Murray attended a university that encouraged education for all, whether rich or poor, and one that provided adult education courses and special lectures for tradesmen and labourers. Murray experienced a Presbyterian university with strong sentiments of Calvin's protests against the theological class system of Catholicism. A more thorough study of Murray's work in Canada would illustrate these humanist and social influences.[1]

Murray's allegiances can be traced to his Edinburgh mentor, Sir William Hamilton, but the critical spirit he brought to Hamilton's common sense philosophy must have been somewhat inspired by his year at Heidelberg and Gottingen. The intellectual consistency that Hegelian thought demanded contributed to Murray's resilience during the nineteenth-century debates between scientists and theologues about the foundations of all knowledge, including Christian thought. Murray was a Christian and he was not about to let the current scientific discoveries of his era change his mind. Reason, he believed, would act as the mediator of all intellectual dissension, and science, for Murray, had no more claim to the ultimate standard of truth than theology. Each had a perspective to offer and each had its place in the rational scheme of knowledge. Murray's commitment to reason may have been inspired as well as reinforced by the Great Disruption in the Scottish Church in 1843. One of the issues involved was the role of the church in the state. The new Free Church of Scotland wanted to sever all ecclesiastical connection with the state, believing that "appointment to ecclesiastical office by lay lords and princes corrupted the Church and was an unholy compromise of the latter's divine commission" (Latourette, 1953, p.1192). The church was not to be considered a creature of the state nor subordinate to it. Thus the new Free Church of Scotland gave up all claims to state endowments, buildings, foreign missions, and declared itself no longer subject to political dictate. With Thomas Chalmers at its head, the new Free Church of Scotland embodied the spirit of Evangelical revival that was sweeping Europe and American Protestantism. In the spirit of democracy presbyteries regained the right to have only church officials that had congregational approval, not ones appointed by the store.

The revival of faith and Christian belief was also in reaction to the eighteenth century rationalism of Hume, Rousseau, Diderot, Kant, and other post-Cartesian philosophers. Some felt that too much rationalism had penetrated the church, weakening its centrality as a source of moral knowledge. Murray was a graduate student when the impact of revolutionary scientific theories about evolution was beginning to be felt. Darwin made his historic voyage in the H.M.S. Beagle and his findings were published in 1859 (though the intellectual way had been paved by Spencei, Leibniz, and French geologist and botanist, Lamarck). Murray had returned from Germany and was studying theology at Edinburgh when Marx, having fled from Belgium to London and the British Museum Library 10 years earlier had finished his preface to the *Critique of Political Economy* in 1859. Even the world of arts was severely reeling from the revolutionary spirit. Wagner finished writing *Tristran and Isolde* in the summer of 1859. The Greek musical drama was reborn, and from that time on the great music halls of Europe and Britain sometimes willingly, sometimes reluctantly wrestled with Wagner's pervasive spirit, never quite ridding themselves of his ghost in the aftermath. Murray also studied and wrote during the rise of psychology as a discipline of science, not philosophy. Materialist accounts of the operations of the mind, as both source and processor of knowledge increased, supported by the experiments done in Leipzig by W.Wundt — a man four years Murray's senior. Wundt published his first books a year after Murray moved to Canada.[2]

In Scotland the Great Disruption of the Church precipitated its own flowering of scientific scholarship, philosophy and theology. The challenge to purge the Church of political patronage had been won. The new scientific discoveries required serious attention in order to be fit into a rational scheme with faith. Henry Drummond came to the service of the baffled Christians in Scotland with his works *Natural Law and the Spiritual World* (1884) and *The Ascent of Man* (1907). Churches became livelier with organ music; hymn writing flourished; and the church moved more to the people's world spearheading social reforms, demanding better housing and instigating programs to reduce drunkenness. The church reached out to embrace its parishioners. It was a world that produced men as different as Robert Owens (an originator of co-operative industrial enterprise) and George Matheson (blind scholar, mystic, preacher and hymn-writer), and John Clark Murray (1836-1917).

Murray took up the cause of accommodating science and religion in his own way. Through his articles he targetted individuals opposed to religion, such as British physicist, John Tyndall. He championed social causes with vigour. He continued to read the Bible (either in Greek or in Latin) in church when he could not hear the sermons, and he bicycled around on cold winter nights embracing his fold of interested young Canadians.

Murray's arrival in Queen's landed him in a setting already secure in its Presbyterian conscience. Queen's had been founded as "a university managed and staffed by members of the Presbyterian church in communion with the Church of Scotland" (Neatby, 1978, p.11). Founded October 16, 1841, a year and a half before the Great Disruption, it soon became prey to the controversies engendered by the uneasy partnership of the Scottish Church and State. Little sympathy came from the Canadian Scottish folk for the separated Free Church. Canada had no real equivalent to the Scottish State Church. In a sense the situation of Canadians already was that for which the Free Church in Scotland sought. Still, the schism was imported and in 1844 Canadian Presbyterians suffered their own separation. Queen's University lost students and lost support in the aftermath of spiritual revivalism.

During the ensuing years Queen's developed "an immense moral seriousness, a sense of mission" (Neatby, 1978, p.60) about its goals and survival. Survival meant hard work both for the university and for the students and promises of salvation meant continued hard work. There would be no coasting on graduation. Echoes of Calvin were heard in Convocation Hall, and messages of Calvinist theology seeped heavily into the life of the university. God had given the students a weighty and a life-long responsibility. During their years of fulfilling their duties they were to expect few rewards. (Perhaps CUPE has finally buried the ghost of Calvin).

Queen's remained small, struggling to survive with competition from Presbyterian colleges in Toronto and Montreal. Its conservative views and programs of intensive courses required diligence and faith in the educative mission. By the 1860s, when Murray arrived, one might have expected Queen's to be maturing after twenty years, but he arrived in the midst of an administrative scandal concerning ineffective teachers, inadequate supplies, misapplied funds and poorly educated students — all brought to public attention through articles in *The Presbyterian* in Montreal. Furthermore, the vice-principal philosopher James George, who had borne the brunt of the attack was accused of impregnating the sister of one of his most virulent attackers, Professor George Weir. The principal had resigned. James George had resigned. The college's reputation was in disarray. It must have been a heady shock to the young philosopher, Murray, hired to replace James George.

During the next decade, when Murray was learning the rigours and discipline of life in the colonies and life as a university professor, Queen's struggled to its feet. It was a time for healing academic wounds and regaining dignity. Murray was beginning to make his presence felt. At the time of the opening of Hitchin College for women (1869) in London, England, Murray, in Kingston, Canada, offered a special class in English for women at Queen's. Twenty-two arrived, enough to wedge open the door for an increasing stream of women students at Queen's University. His address to an opening class in 1871 was entitled "The Higher Education of Women."

The following year, 1872, Murray was offered the chair at McGill University in Mental and Moral Philosophy, and a fellow competitor for the McGill position quickly applied to Queen's for Murray's position. Thus John Watson took Murray's old job. Happily his support for the equal education of women was enthusiastic. It was at McGill that Murray's career began to flourish. Perhaps the thought of new causes to pursue inspired him. Perhaps he feared that the self-assuredness of Kingston Presbyterians who had survived the Disruption without the abandonment of tradition would breed a kind of academic complacency. Perhaps his sense of an increasingly industrial world in trouble, a sense to which no Glaswegian student could be oblivious (as no Glaswegian preacher would ever permit it) led him to depart the pastoral environs of Kingston for the factories and big city atmosphere of Montreal. Whatever the reason, Murray headed for McGill where he tackled the injustices wrought on the labouring class, the chauvinist suppression of women,[3] the threats to Christian virtue brought about by capitalism and the assault on theology by scientists in Canada and abroad.

Murray was not one to let the events of his time pass him by. The arguments of scientists and philosophers, such as Tyndall, Spencer and Huxley, which seemed to undermine the foundations of Christian faith posed a challenge for Murray. His concern, like those of other Canadian philosophers and intellectuals was to accommodate the findings of science with theology. Murray, of course, was not alone on this course. John Watson at Queen's[4] and William Dawson LeSeur at Toronto were filling the pages of *Rose Belford's Canadian Monthly* with articles in defence of the compatibility of science and theology — articles designed to diffuse, for example, the assaults on evolutionary theory by the Bishop of Ontario, John Travers Lewis, and designed as well to remind people that "science... is simply the intellect of man, exercising itself in a certain direction" (LeSeur, 1877, pp.22-28).

Murray's efforts to grapple with the post-Darwinian scientific revolution were focussed initially on the debate between the new mechanistic or materialistic view of nature and the Christian humanist view that was shorn up by idealism and the primacy of rational thought. His arguments in the two articles following are directed specifically towards the claims of British physicist and natural philosopher John Tyndall (1820-1893), about the primacy of matter as the stuff of the universe, including the mind. Tyndall set forth his ideas in the Presidential Address to the British Association for the Advancement of Science in 1874. This paper later became known as "The Belfast Address." In it he suggested that science in his day was beginning to confirm the atomistic speculations of early pre-Socratic natural philosophers. He also asked why science had been so slow to do so. "Why was the scientific intellect compelled, like an exhausted soil, to lie fallow for nearly two millenia, before it could regather the elements necessary to its fertility and strength?" (Tyndall, 1903, p.18) Tyndall then placed much of the blame on the rise of Christianity. "... the political and theological strife between the Church and civil governments... must have done much to stifle investigation" (Tyndall, 1903, p.18).

In "Atomism and Theism" (1875) Murray identifies Tyndall as an atomist. Atomism was a particle theory about the universe that found its origins with pre-Socratic philosopher Democritus. The determinism associated with atomism (there seemed to be no way of accounting for free will) led Tyndall to be an agnostic and to deny all supernatural phenomena. Tyndall was, however, not oblivious to the implied phenomenalism of his own views. In affirming that the exercising of thought had a correlative in the physics of the brain, he was positing two sets of phenomena — mental processes and physical processes. Thus, according to Tyndall, all we can know of atoms comes through sensations. Tyndall wanted a revised concept of matter, one that included the phenomena of mind and that made possible evolving life forms. Thinking of matter as essentially inert or dead made little sense in face of the expanding knowledge of biology and the corresponding field of psychology — scientific examination of the material counterpart of mental phenomena in the brain. Still he was convinced that "it may be doubted whether wanting this fundamental conception, a theory of the material universe is capable of scientific statement" (Tyndall, 1903, p.25).

Tyndall conceded that we can never know the ultimate cause of the universe, or our experience, but he would not make the inference that in positing an ultimate cause he was supporting Christian belief. He also agreed that science could not explain the ultimate connection between mental and physical phenomena, suggesting that "[m]an the object is separated by an impassable gulf from man the subject..." (Tyndall, 1903, p.40). Science could not answer every question but given the present state of knowledge atomism was the most reasonable theory for interpreting experience. Tyndall, toward the end of "The Belfast Address" stated:

> We claim, and we shall wrest from theology, the entire domain of cosmological theory. All schemes and systems which thus infringe upon the domain of science must, in so far as they do this, submit to its control, and relinquish all thought of controlling it.

These were strong words.[5] Murray was puzzled. Believing that a unified theory of knowledge was preferable to a dualistic one (he had, after all, been educated and lived through enough disruptions), Murray suggests in "Atomism and Theism" that Professor Tyndall has no way of making any claim about knowledge of atoms, if one cannot know the ultimate cause of experience or the causal process that gives rise to mental phenomena. Thus he lists and responds to what he believes are a series of inconsistencies in Tyndall's thesis. The suggestion that the source of consciousness is not conscious he finds suspicious.

> Now, if there are any means by which we can know that the Supreme Power in the universe is not a conscious or intelligent being, then there is no ground for the assertion that Power is absolutely unknowable. (Murray, "Atomism and Theism" p.37)

Secondly, the suggestion by Tyndall that atoms are the end of a chain of divisibility seems spurious, because whatever can be thought of as divisible must be able to be thought of as infinitely so. Thirdly, the argument that the forces of the universe depend on the motion of molecules and atoms doesn't account for thought and feelings, and Murray suggests that motion and force themselves are still concepts of the mind. Thus he concludes that we have no greater reason to believe a physical force to be a worthier or truer conception of the cause of the universe than a human force stripped of all human imperfections. Reason itself cannot be explained by the motion of atoms, rather, it is the source of all explanation.

Murray is offering a form of rational theology, and one cannot help sense the serious impact of his exposure to German idealism. Reason, for him, is not physical. It underlies all concepts and system building, and has no imperfections of its own. God, for Murray, is Reason as absolute, and through it we interpret the findings of science. Thus Reason, as the embodiment of the ultimate cause of conscious intelligence, is unassailable by Tyndall's phenomenalism.

Murray continued to pursue these ideas with the publication of "The Dualistic Concept of Nature" in *The Monist*, 1895. Murray begins by claiming science to be monistic by nature since it demands a single unified explanatory system. Whatever principle explains one thing must be transferable to all data of science. If such a system were not forthcoming, scientific explanations would always end with something unexplained. He takes the unity of nature as an implicit assumption.

Thus an illusion of dualism in science, the notion of mental phenomena and physical phenomena, appears odd. Murray's concern is to explain the presence of such dualism, and he locates its origins with the Stoics (although it also appeared, but with little significance, in Pythagorean doctrine). Stoic ethics distinguished between nature (essentially rational) and feeling (essentially non-rational). This distinction applied to an analysis of the character of people as being rational or irrational which, according to Murray, "corrupted Christianity" (1896, p.387). Such dualism has been represented in the moral antagonism between the senses and reason, or the flesh and the spirit. It also led to the postulation of two equal and opposed powers in the world — good and evil (typified in Manichaeism [Murray's spelling]). Christian thinkers kept the Devil as the evil power. The universe on such conceptions would be inherently irrational and unscientific. Hobbes, for example, affirmed its dualistic nature when he referred to man in a 'state of nature' as opposed to a 'state of grace.' But a strange inversion occurred in the history of philosophy after Stoicism, according to Murry. Religion became associated with the non-rational side of the Stoic division, and reason, with the state of nature. The state of nature, for Hobbes, had become the arena wherein reason was free to outwit the laws of nature, if so able. Thus the rational man was no longer thought of as orderly and in control of his passions. Rather his rational side made him part of nature and able to pit his wits against all others. The irrational side of man was thought of as having merged with a mystical view of religion. If God existed He could not be a source of rational morality.

Murray argues that the dualistic separation of man's life into spheres that the Stoics proposed originated in an imperfect conception of nature in general and of man's nature in specific. Idealistic monism seems the only possible solution. Both science and religion can be sustained in terms of idealistic ontology and scientific inquiry need not be misled.

Once again Murray is proposing the supremacy of Reason as the source of all human inquiry. Reason is the ground of both moral and non-moral inquiry. "Science therefore must give to the reality of this power a prominence equal to the reality claimed for the force of non-moral causation..." (Murray, 1895, p.395). A dualistic conception of nature will make moral laws as laws of reason impossible. Nature (as non-moral) may bring suffering. Nonetheless man's reason can recognize human misfortune and respond through human love. Reason can therefore stand as the ultimate arbiter and interpreter of all opposing forces in the universe.

Murray's work culminated in the publication of texts on psychology and ethics, and in manuscripts on social and economic philosophy. His rational theology is in line with Hegelian idealism and the work of Augustine.[6] For Augustine, eager to salvage theology from mystical fanatics, God was Truth. For Murray, respectful of the progress of reason as seen through scientific inquiry, reason was a form of truth and God the rational order discernible in the universe. Certainly science has gone far to resolve Tyndall's phenomenalist dichotomy. Ever refined pronouncements are made about the movements of electrons and neurons in the brain; the locations of feelings, emotions and language are being identified; the control of behavioural aberrations is being affected through drugs. In light of this Murray's early forays against the incoherence of Tyndall's atomism may seem naive. Still, the indivisibility principle behind particle theory continues to be challenged by new theories about the ultimate stuff of the universe — the latest being 'superstring theory' (*Physics Today*, January 1986, pp.5-31).

We are, it seems, no closer to the source of conscious experience than Murray was. His insistence on logical coherence and a unified field theory, however anachronistic his terminology, is in keeping with the spirit of scientific inquiry today.

As a Scotsman in Canada, determined, fiercely principled, and suspicious of sensationalist innovations, Murray was a paradigm case. Systematic rationalism and respect for learned inquiry would rule all novelty. In the face of intellectual adversity, extra-hard work and public debate would sort out the sense from the nonsense. There would be, during those turbulent years, no monkey trials at McGill.

Notes

1. One would need to explore his writings on labour, property, and capitalism (manuscript of 1887, published in 1982), his battles on behalf of women and higher education (1871) and his lecture notes on ethics, political economy and history of philosophy prepared for those who could not attend the university. Prominent among them were women who formed educational associations. Murray lectured to them in community halls, church basements and living rooms. He was a familiar figure in the streets of Montreal, bicycling furiously to fulfill his mission, even after a full day of teaching at McGill.

2. Murray's time in Germany enabled him to experience the foundations of the rising new experimental science and he responded to these developments with his own books on psychology, *A Handbook of Psychology* (1885) and *An Introduction to Psychology* (1904). Murray, forever the sceptical Scot, was not about to turn the treasures of the human mind into a warehouse of conditioned responses. Undoubtedly he would agree that when one studies rats, one learns about rats.

3. In spite of a long and volatile fight on their behalf by Murray, women gained access to mainstream classes at McGill only after Sir W.Dawson, principal, retired in 1893.

4. Watson published several articles on the apparent schism. In his paper "Professor Tyndall's Materialism" he referred to Tyndall's position as a "detected sham"(1878, p.282). In "A Phase of Modern Thought" he wrote "No scientific truths as such can serve as a substitute for religion, simply because science does not seek, and so does not find the evidence of intelligence in the world."(1879, p.477)

5. The reaction around the western Christian world was so severe that Tyndall soon published a rejoinder, "Apology for the Belfast Address, 1874" (1903, p.43-53). It was, however, an 'apology' in the original sense of the word, as signifying 'vindication' or 'defence.' he withdrew *none* of his original claims.

6. Murray was certainly aware that the dualism of Good and Evil that created a schism in concepts of man and nature was reinforced by the theology of Augustine, His affinities with Augustine come in comparing their concepts of God. Augustine's God was immanent and timeless. Before God there was nothing. God was creation and represented eternity. To know that was to know truth. (Bonaventure made the marriage of reason and faith a little too equitable for future Catholics). Murray's God was also immanent, but as a source of intelligible order in the universe He was manifested through reason. Truth, for Murray, was not anchored in faith, but evolved through our increased understanding of experience.

References

Armour, Leslie and Trott, Elizabeth. *The Faces of Reason* (Waterloo, Wilfred Laurier University Press, 1981).

Cox, Reverend James T. *Practice and Procedure in the Church of Scotland* (Edinburgh and London, William Blackwood and Sons Ltd., 1945).

Drummond, Henry. *Natural Law and the Spiritual World* (New York: Pott, 1884).

— *The Ascent of Man* (New York: Pott, 1907).

Latourette, K.S. *A History of Christianity* (New York, Harper & Bros, 1953).

Le Seur, W.D. "Science and Materialism," *Canadian Monthly and National Review* XI(January, 1877) (22-28). Reprinted in *Critical Spirit*, edited and with commentary by A.B.McKillop (Toronto, The Carleton Library, McLelland and Stewart 1977).

Marx, Karl. "Preface to a Contribution to the Critique of Political Economy," in *Karl Marx and Frederick Engels, Selected Works* in one volume (London: Lawrence and Wishart, 1968).

Murray, John Clark. "The Higher Education of Woman," An Address Delivered at the Opening of Queen's College, Kingston, Canada, 1871 (Kingston, 1871).

— "Atomism and Theism," *The Canadian Monthly and National Review* VII(January, 1875) 31-39.

— *A Handbook of Psychology* (London: Alexander Gardner, 1885 Montreal: Dawson Bros., 1885).

— "The Dualistic Conception of Nature," *The Monist* VI (April, 1896) 382-94.

— *An Introduction to Psychology* (Boston: Little, Brown, 1904).

— *The Industrial Kingdom of God*, edited and with an introduction by L.Armour and E.Trott (Ottawa: University of Ottawa Press, 1982).

Tyndall, John. *Lectures and Essays*, including "The Belfast Address," 1874 pp.13-43 (London, Watts and co., 1903).

Watson, John. "Science and Religon: Reply to Professor Tyndall on 'Materialism and its Opponents," *The Canadian Monthly and National Review* IX(May, 1876) 384-97.

— "Professor Tyndall's Materialism," *The Canadian Monthly and National Review* XIII (March, 1878) 282-88.
— "A Phase of Modern Thought," *Rose Belford's Canadian Monthly and Review* III(November, 1879) 457-72.

Atomism and Theism

John Clark Murray

The recent Address of Prof.Tyndall has raised anew the question: What progress has been made, in the light of contemporary science, towards an explanation of the universe on purely physical grounds? In the following remarks it is proposed to notice two prominent points in the Address: (A) The Atomic Theory; (B) the acknowledged impossibility of completely solving, by this theory, the problem which the universe presents.

(A) In connection with the Atomic Theory one is tempted to question some opinions expressed in the historical sketch, which forms a large portion of this Address. It was natural that a sketch of the history of speculation in such a connection should have touched with special lustre the names of those who have contributed most to the distinct conception and intelligible application of the Atomic Theory. Now there seems no doubt that the first achievement of importance in this direction was the work of Democritus. It is true that the other principles which Prof.Tyndall attaches to the philosophy of Democritus had been clearly thought out and enunciated long before his time; it is true that the way had been prepared for Atomism by the whole course of previous Greek speculation from the first conjectures of the Ionian physicists, and that an Atomic Theory of a cruder character had recently before been suggested by Empedocles; it is, moreover, possible that Leucippus, the companion of Democritus, has been unfairly jostled out of view by the crowd of subsequent Atomists. Still we cannot overlook the special greatness of Democritus in grasping a magnificent idea while yet unfamiliar, and shaping it, probably by many unrecorded years of fervid intellectual toil, into that luminous form which has made it a light upon the path of many a subsequent inquirer into the physical constitution of things. But it is not incomprehensi-

* First published in *The Canadian Monthly and National Review*, Vol. VII, No.1, January, 1875, pp. 31-39

ble that the fame of Democritus should have been eclipsed by that of Plato and Aristotle. Nor to comprehend this, is it necessary form the supposition which Prof.Tyndall adopts, that the heavier metal of his philosophy sent it to the bottom of that ocean of barbarism with which Europe was inundated during the middle ages, while the lighter stuff, composing the philosophies of Plato and Aristotle, floated with ease. Whatever may be the inanities of temporary popularity, the voice of the ages is, after all,

"the proof and echo of all human fame,"

and is never heard ringing from generation to generation the praise of what is worthless in preference to that which is of real worth. This is evidently the explanation of the subordinate position which Democritus occupies in the history of speculation on the ultimate origin of things. The haze of enthusiasm seems to make the Atomic Theory loom so vastly before his mental vision as to hide everything else from his view. Now, valuable as is that theory in the explanation of the physical universe, it brings us not a step nearer to the discovery of the primal origin of that universe. Yet to Democritus, Atomism apparently afforded the key to the solution of all problems; and it is precisely because we find in him no glimpse of that great region which his theory cannot touch, that, though he may rightfully claim a chief place in the history of science, he cannot take the highest rank among those who have inquired into the fundamental principle of all things.

To return from this historical criticism, we proceed to consider the Atomic Theory both from a scientific and from a philosophical point of view.

I. Even looking at the matter from the standpoint of science, we are tempted to demand whether the confident tone of the Atomists is justified by any results which can stand the test of scientic proof. For 1. the very existence of atoms is acknowledged to be a mere hypothesis. It is true that the hypothesis has proved marvelously fruitful in its applications. Still, in view of many recent utterances of physicism, it cannot be too earnestly repeated that the real existence of atoms has not only never been proved, but that, in the present state of knowledge, it is impossible to conceive any instrument of discovery by which their existence can be made evident. It is unnecessary to discuss whether this should not render the hypothesis illegitimate, which it would be considered by some of the most distinguished expounders of scientific method, (see Mills Logic Book III chap. 14.) but it is perhaps worth observing that the hypothesis would be discarded by the rigid application of a criterion on which Prof.Tyndall strongly insists for testing the value of scientific theories. It is essential, he holds, to a true physical conception, that it should be "capable of being placed as a coherent picture before the mind." Now this is precisely what the conception of an atom does not admit. It has long been pointed out that we cannot imagine (*vorstellen*) any quantity of matter which is absolutely indivisible. The minutest particle we are compelled to represent as into particles minuter still. Even when the Atomic Theory is applied to render intelligible processes which cannot be otherwise represented in thought, it is not absolutely indivisible, but only indefinitely minute particles, that are conceived. This is not urged as an insuperable objection to Atomism, for nature is not limited by the capacities of human thought. But the inability to form a mental picture of an atom ought to be a reminder of the purely hypothetical character of the fundamental conception, by means of which the Atomist pretends to unlock the most hidden mystery of things. However useful, therefore, the Atomic hypothesis may be for guiding the labours of scientific inquirers, it becomes a pernicious hallucination when it is applied, as if it were a known fact, to reveal the primeval constitution of all things. If the physicists would accept from metaphysical literature a term by which the scientific value of the Atomic hypothesis would be correctly expressed, it should be described, in Kantian phraseology, as a *regulative*, not a *constitutive* hypothesis. In other words, the hypothesis would be regarded as fulfilling its legitimate function in merely *regulating* the inquiries of scientific students, so that they may conduct their inquiries *as if the hypothesis were true*, while they avoid making the hypothesis a *constituent* fact in the real system of the universe.

2. Still, supposing the existence of atoms to be demonstrated, one is forced to ask further, whether all the phenomena of the universe have been, or are likely to be, interpreted in terms of Atomism.

(a) Even when this question is limited to the physical world, it reminds us of the incompleteness of Atomism as an explanation of physical phenomena themselves. It is in the region of chemistry that the hypothesis has been especially applicable. When it is found that a composite substance, however often analyzed, yields invariably the same constituent elements in the same proportions; when it is found that the quantity of any body which combines with others bears a uniform proportion to the quantities of these others, as estimated by their weights; these and other rudimentary facts of chemistry become more intelligibly represented to the mind by the supposition that all bodies are composed of indestructible particles which remain unaltered amidst all possible combinations. But in other departments of physical investigation the theory does not admit of an equally obvious application. To take only one example, the phenomena of light become intelligible, by the Atomic hypothesis, only when that hypothesis is subsidized by the additional hypothesis of an ethereal form of matter, the relation of which to other matter cannot be established by weight, the existence of which cannot be made evident to any of the human senses; which is, in short, imagined to exist merely to make the agency of light conceivable in harmony with the Atomic hypothesis.

These remarks are not intended to invalidate the Atomic explanation of the physical world, or to cast doubt upon the service which it has rendered in physical science. Our object has been merely to show that, even in reference to the physical world, Atomism is as yet only an hypothesis — an hypothesis, indeed, which renders a large number of physical phenomena more clearly imaginable, and which may perhaps render all physical phenomena equally intelligible. But while admitting all legitimate value to the hypothesis, we protest against accepting it as an established fact — as if it were a fact which has been already applied to all physical phenomena, and has already explained all their mysteries. And much more do we protest against the assumption that such an hypothesis can dispel the mystery of *all* phenomena, whether physical or not.

(b) For it seems as if it were necessary to remind our physicists that there are other than physical phenomena in the universe. Occupied exclusively, in their professional researches, with physical phenomena, many of them seem to become incapable of appreciating phenomena of any other order, or they interpret them by the ideas and terms of physical science. Surely nothing but this professional tendency could lead any man to suppose that the phenomena of our conscious life can be explained in the language of Atomism. It is quite possible, every year seems to render it more probable, that all the phenomena of organic and inorganic bodies may be due to the various combinations of atomic particles of which they are composed. The physiologist may yet explain on the Atomic theory every process in the human organism, every tremor of a nerve about the periphery, through the spine, in the brain; but what do all his explanations to render intelligible the simplest act of consciousness? Can a thought or a feeling, can the memories and reasonings, joys and griefs, the loves and hates of the human soul be represented, without absurdity, as formed by any combinations or movements of material atoms? My thoughts and feelings may be — there is good ground for believing that they *are* — uniformly related to certain molecular movements of nervous tissue; but a thought or feeling — *is* it a molecule, or any combination or movement of molecules? And yet these phenomena of the inner life *exist*; our feelings and thoughts are, to us all, realities of the most stern character. Nay, are they not, in truth, the only realities which we know at first hand; while your atoms, and compounds of atoms — are they not known merely at second hand — hypothetically assumed to exist in order that we may account for those feelings and thoughts whose reality we cannot doubt, and which, we suppose, cannot be accounted for except on some such hypothesis?

II. But we come to look at the Atomic Theory from a philosophical, rather than from a scientific point of view. Now, what is an atom? To the mere physicist this may seem a question to simple to be asked. But, unhappily for physical science and for all science, this question brings us face to face with the radical defect in all purely physical theories of the universe.

What, then, is an atom? For the use of physical science a definition of atoms is easily enough obtained: — An indivisible particle of matter! Yes; that definition will carry you through all the uses of atoms in physical science. Give it unlimited opportunity to open the doors by which the light of human knowledge may flood every cranny in the material universe, to show that it is governed by the law of a divine order, and by no demon's caprice. But your key snaps in your hand when you put it to the lock of any other mystery, even the ultimate mystery of the material universe itself. For an indivisible particle of matter is something definite enough for him to whom matter forms a starting point of inquiry — a *datum*, a given fact which he need not question. But to the metaphysician the nature of matter is the most perplexingly problematic of things. Do you attempt to dispel this perplexity by defining matter as *a substance occupying space*? True; but what is substance; and what is space? If we can tell what substance is, we shall hesitate to say whether matter is a substance or not; if we can tell what space is, we shall question whether it is imposed by things upon our thoughts, or imposed by our thoughts upon things. So that, instead of supposing that the mind has been beaten into the fire of emotion and the light of thought by substances in space, it is likely that we shall, with more truth, see the forces of the universe fashioned into substances in space by the fire and the light of the human soul.

Yet again, what is meant by an atom, supposing such to exist? It is implied that, if the minute nerve-network of the retina were subdivided into infinitely finer threads, we should be able to discriminate sensations of light, I don't know how many millions of times more minute than the present *minimum visible*; while a similar intensification of tactile and muscular sensibility would enable us to discriminate correspondingly more minute contacts and pressures. Perhaps also — though this "perhaps" is not encouraging — some fact, of which at present we can form no conception, might enable us to discover that minuter points of light or touch or pressure are absolutely incapable of being discriminated. Perhaps, we have said; but our physicists are the very men who refuse to let us look on anything as absolute, as absolutely necessary or absolutely impossible. Suppose, however, that we could make evident the existence of atoms, all that we should make evident would be that, under the supposed circumstances, the supposed immeasurably refined sensations of light and touch and pressure would take place. But would this bring us a whit nearer the solution of the problem how these sensations are produced? It is, after all, only the sensations that we know immediately: the belief that these sensations are produced by any particular means is only an inference from the sensations; and it is a very big stride which steps to the inference that these sensations are produced by indivisible particles of a thing called matter, which is prior in existence to the sensations it creates. I know that these sensations are produced by no voluntary effort of my power: I recognise, therefore, the presence of powers, forces, wills, or of a Power, Force, Will which is not I. But that these forces reside in an unknown thing like an atom or a combination of atoms, is what no philosophic or scientific principle compels us to suppose, is perhaps but one of those guesses, with regard to the origin of things, which scientific thought has not been able to emancipate from the vulgar notion of a material world, and which may be relegated by a subsequent age to the limbo of crudities into which have been packed the theories of the early physicists among the Ionian Greeks.

(B) To the narrow specialists in physics these objections might be no novel, if intelligible; but Prof.Tyndall is too profound a thinker to be blind to the fact that Atomism, even if admitted for the explanation of the physical world, can carry us but a part of the way to the fundamental principle and origin of things. Accordingly, although, "abandoning all disguise," he confesses that he "discerns in matter the promise and potency of every form and quality of life," yet he entreats us to avoid haste in the interpretation of his words, lest we misunderstand his "materialism." Let us, therefore, wait for his explanation. "We can trace," he says, "the development of a nervous system, and correlate with it the parallel phenomena of sensation and thought. We see with undoubting certainty that they go hand in hand. But we try to soar in a vacuum the moment we seek to comprehend the connection between them. An Archimedean fulcrum is here required which the human mind cannot command; and the effort to solve the problem, to borrow an illustration from an illustrious friend of mine, is like the effort of a man trying to lift himself by his own waistband. All that has been here said is to be taken in connection with this fundamental truth. When 'nascent senses' are spoken of, when the 'differentiation of a tissue at first vaguely sensitive all over' is spoken of, and when these processes are associated with 'the modification of an organism by its environment,' the same parallelism, without contact, or even approach to contact, is implied. There is no fusion possible between the two classes of facts — no motor energy in the intellect of man to carry it without logical rupture from the one to the other." Another explanation is also worth quoting: "All we hear, and see, and touch, and taste, and smell, are, it would be urged, mere variations of our own condition, beyond which, even to the extent of a hair's breadth, we cannot go. That anything answering to our impressions exists outside of ourselves is not a *fact*, but an *inference*, to which all validity would be denied by an idealist like Berkeley, or by a sceptic like Hume. Mr.Spencer takes another line. With him, as with the uneducated man, there is no doubt or question as to the existence of an external world. But he differs from the uneducated, who thinks that the world really *is* what consciousness represents it to be. Our states of consciousness are mere *symbols* of an outside entity which produces them and determines the order of their succession, but the real nature of which we can never know. In fact the whole process of evolution is the manifestation of a Power absolutely inscrutable to the intellect of man. As little in our time as in the days of Job can a man by searching find this Power out. Considered fundamentally, it is by the operation of an insoluble mystery that life is evolved, species differentiated, and mind unfolded from their prepotent elements in the immeasurable past." After this, if we were allowed to put our own interpretation on it, not only do we agree with Prof.Tyndall, that "there is no very rank materialism here," but we wonder why he should have "discerned in matter the promise and potency of every form and quality of life," or indeed any promise or potency at all! Let us, however, examine more closely this explanatory concession to the anti-materialists.

I. This concession admits that the only *facts immediately known* by us are certain mental impressions, all our notions with regard to the source of these impressions being mere *inference*. It admits, however, or rather it concedes, that there *is* something beyond these impressions — something by which these impressions are produced. In this admission or contention Prof. Tyndall is the mouthpiece of the whole school of recent philosophical physicists. Mr.Herbert Spencer, for example, is never weary of repeating that this is the one point at which the otherwise diverging lines of religion and science inevitably converge, the ultimate teaching of both pointing to a Great Reality behind all phenomena. We are, therefore, not asked to face an extreme Phenomenalism, which is recognises nothing beyond phenomena, is content with the fact of mental impressions, and declines to assert whether there is or is not anything besides.

This, indeed, is the only consistent doctrine for the Positivist, as was long ago pointed out — *implicitly* by Hume, *explicitly* by Kant. For the theoretical philosophy of Kant, as represented by the "Critique of Pure Reason," is truly the most systematic Positivism ever taught; and according to its teachings the Causal Judgment — the judgment by which we assert that every event must have a cause — is valid only within the limits of experience, but wholly impotent to leap beyond; valid to connect the different phenomena which experience presents, but invalid to connect the totality of these phenomena with any cause. Even the recognition of a mere Reality, as Spencer and others call it at times, without asserting any causal connection of that Reality with phenomena, implies still that we know *some* thing of It, that we know at least that It *exists* — is *real*; unless we make no difference between existence or reality, and non-existence or unreality.

But, in truth, thorough Phenomenalism is a position in which no human thought can find rest. All the Phenomenalists, from Heraclitus and the Sophist down to Comte and the Positivists, have explicitly or implicitly refused to admit the possibility of the phenomenal universe being produced by fetishes or the beings of mythology, by an antagonistic Ormuzd and Ahriman, by the gods of an Olympus or an Asgard, or by any other "mob of deities." But we cannot be wholly ignorant of the source from which the universe has sprung, if we know that it is not the manifestation of any of those causeₒ which are assigned to it in the polytheistic creeds.

At all events the Phenomenalism of Prof. Tyndall does not prevent him from admitting the existence of something beyond those mental impressions, which he recognises as being the only facts that are immediately known. Let us see what further assertions he ventures with regard to the origin of our mental impressions.

II. From the general drift of the address we should have expected to be told that these impressions which make up our conscious life are due to the operations of material atoms. But the ultimate cause of this phenomenal world, which floats in the consciousness of man, is declared to be only "the nature of which we can never know" to be "a Power inscrutable to the intellect of man," to be an insoluble mystery. Now

1. After this, what meant all the talk about atoms and the potency of matter? If the external cause of the world of consciousness is absolutely unknowable — if the endeavour to connect that world with a cause outside of itself is like "the effort of a man to raise himself up by his own waistband" or the attempt to "soar in a vacuum," — then what are we to understand by the greater part of this address, which assumes not only that matter is known to exist, but that it is known to be composed of atomic particles, and that in it may be "*discerned* the promise and potency of every form and quality of life?" The dilemma is unavoidable: either there is no meaning in the solemn phrases in which Prof. Tyndall describes the irremovable mystery which veils the source of our conscious life; or it is inconsistent to speak of discerning in matter the potency in which life has its roots.

2. But, further, if the origin of consciousness be beyond human ken, what right have we to speak of it as the manifestation of *Power*? Prof. Tyndall and others, who represent the philosophical position of pure physicism, never hesitate to use language of this purport. It is seldom, indeed, very clear what meaning they attach to the terms *power, force, cause* and the other expressions by which they represent the same idea. But whatever their meaning — and it would be unworthy to charge them with attaching no meaning at all to their words — then to the extent of that meaning at least they must hold that the

source of life is known; they must admit that this at least is known regarding the Great Reality behind all the phenomena, that It is related to these phenomena as their producing cause. It is not necessary to weaken this argument by any such slight attempt as could here be made to settle the delicate metaphysical problems connected with causality. But settle these problems as we may, it must be acknowledged that an important step is taken beyond mere phenomenalism, in the admission that there is a POWER of which all that appears in the consciousness of man is a manifestation.

3. But there is yet another contradiction of the assertion that the source of consciousness is absolutely inscrutable, in the doctrine which is implied in thorough-going physicism, that the POWER which originates consciousness is not itself conscious. Prof. Tyndall, indeed, does not make this assertion in so many terms. His most explicit declaration on this point is to be found in a couple of sentences near the close of his address. "On the one side," he says, "we have a theory (if it could with any propriety be so called) derived, as were the theories referred to at the beginning of this address, not from the study of nature, but from the observation of man — a theory which converts the Power whose garment is seen in the visible universe into an Artificer fashioned after the human model, and acting by broken efforts as man is seen to act. On the other side we have the conception that all we see around us, and all we feel within us, — the phenomena of physical nature as well as those of the human mind — have their unsearchable roots in a cosmical life, if I dare apply the term, an infinitesimal span of which only is offered to the investigation of man." Whatever objections may be taken to the statement of the first theory here described as an expression of modern philosophical theism, the drift of the second theory, interpreted in the light of the whole address, seems evidently to exclude the conception of consciousness or intelligence as an attribute of the "cosmical life" which evolves all phenomena, at least in any sense in which we can think of a being as conscious or intelligent. Now, if there are any means by which we can know that the Supreme Power in the universe is not a conscious or intelligent being, then there is no ground for the assertion that that Power is absolutely unknowable.

Mere Phenomenalism, therefore, or absolute Positivism, breaks down on every side. In refusing to attribute the phenomena of the universe to the "mob of deities" by whose operation they were explained to the popular mind of the heathen, the Positivist claims to know so much with regard to the region beyond phenomena, that it is not peopled with such a mob. In recognising a Reality beyond phenomena, he admits that knowledge transcends phenomena so far as to discover at least the *existence* of something besides. In calling this Reality a Power, Force or Cause, he assumes the further knowledge of the relation between this ultimate Reality and the phenomena which It produces, or in which It is manifested. And, last of all, in the vehemence with which it is contended that this Power does not act with intelligence, a vast but wholly unjustifiable claim is put forth of acquaintance with the nature of this Power, and with Its mode of operation.

It is impossible, then, to maintain that the Primal Cause, from which this universe originates, is absolutely unknowable; and the question is obtruded on us by the recent physicists themselves, whether that Cause may be known to be an unconscious force or thing? Let us consider the grounds on which this daring knowledge is claimed.

I. It is maintained that all phenomena are found to be due to movement —to the movement of masses or the movement of molecules. It is further maintained that all this movement is the result of force drawing or pushing in the line of least resistance, and it is consequently inferred to be unnecessary to suppose that the production of phenomena has been directed by plan, by intelligence. In reply to this,

1. It is worth while to be reminded that the whole phenomena of the universe can*not* be interpreted in terms of motion — that, while nervous and cerebral action may be merely the play of the molecules of which the nerve-tissues are composed, our thoughts and feelings cannot be so described. But it is unnecessary to dwell upon this again. It is also unnecessary to dwell upon the fact that it is impossible to represent motion and force except as conceptions of some mind, and that we only delude ourselves when we suppose that they can be imagined, except as apprehended by some mind.

2. Let it be supposed that everything may be explained as resulting from the tug of a force "in the line of least resistance," does that render it inconceivable that everything is directed by intelligence? It certainly excludes the conception of a capricious will, guided by no permanent principle; it certainly excludes, moreover, the conception of a defective intelligence or a feeble will, incompletely acquainted with, or incompletely master of, the forces at his command; but are we thus prevented from attributing the universe to an Omnipotent Will directed by an Omniscient consciousness — a will and a consciousness limited only by the reason of things? Are we to suppose that such a Will should select clumsier processes in preference to the simplest means for the attainment of His ends? There is, in fact, but one conception with regard to the movements of the universe, which is in harmony with their direction by Supreme Reason, and that is the conception of these movements as following "the line of least resistance."

II. It is held by some, though apparently by but a small number of recent philosophical physicist, that the Universal Force, though following the "line of least resistance," produces results which are incompatible with the guidance of Perfect Reason. We shall not dwell upon this, as Prof. Tyndall does not venture such an assertion, and the strongest replies to the assertion have come from the materialists themselves. Prof. Tyndall, too, would probably affirm the explanation which has been generally accepted by theists in reference to those otherwise inexplicable phenomena, that only "an infinitesimal span" of the great cosmical life is offered to our view and that, if we could see the whole, we would probably discover the harmony of every part with a Supreme Reason.

III. It is commonly contended that the theistic explanation of the universe is one of those anthropomorphisms which the progress of science has been gradually eliminating from our views of things. This is a favourite line of argument with Mr. H. Spencer; and it is this argument that is indicated in Prof.Tyndall's description of theism as "derived, not from the study of nature, but from the observation of men," and as involving the conception of "an Artificer fashioned after the human model, and acting by broken efforts as man is seen to act." We feel justified in taking these words as intended to describe explicit theism. At least they express the only alternative offered from the creed of "Know-Nothing," in reference to the source of the universe. Now, in the explanation of nature, human nature as well as physical nature, must be taken into view; and it does not necessarily follow that mere physical force is a worthier or a truer conception of the Universal Cause than human force stripped of all human imperfections. Such a conception does not involve what is usually understood by anthropomorphism; for an anthropomorphic representation of the Supreme Being implies the ascription to Him of human attributes which are incompatible with perfection. But there is no such incompatibility in Perfect Reason; nor is it Perfect Reason that the progress of science has been gradually eliminating. What science has gradually dispelled from our views of the Supreme Cause is the idea of that caprice which we ourselves rise above the more we learn to govern ourselves by Reason alone; and we come to recognise more fully the perfection of the Reason which governs the universe, the more we discover what the old Hebrews expressively styled "the faithfulness" of God in evolving similar results from similar antecedents.

Modern physicism, therefore, has adduced nothing to interfere with the ancient faith of man, that the Lord of all "by wisdom hath founded the earth, by understanding hath established the heavens." This does not contradict, but rather implies, the belief that it is impossible for the finite understanding of man to fathom the plans of that Infinite Understanding; and therefore, many of the expressions used by modern Positivists to describe the inscrutability of the Supreme Being, have formed familiar commonplaces in the language of theism. It is true that the common talk of religious men implies much impious assumption of familiarity with the intentions of the Universal Mind in the minutest details of His administration. But we cannot insult the philosophical physicist by supposing that he is unable to separate these immaturities of popular thought from the fundamental faith of the theist. It may be questioned, indeed, whether any literature surpasses the Bible of Christendom in the variety and oriental splendour of imagery with which it describes the "unsearchable greatness" of the Power that "worketh all in all;" while the Inscrutability of the Divine Decrees" has formed a prominent article in all Christian theologies worthy of the name.

Still there is one region in which all theistic systems must contend that we *do* know the Supreme Will which governs the universe, and that is the only region with which all men in common are essentially concerned — the region of ethical practice. The demand that we shall do to others what we would have them do to us — the Moral Law, as it is called, in whatever terms expressed — is meaningless if there is any doubt of its unconditionally imperative obligation; and there is doubt if our knowledge is limited to what has been and is likely to be, if we do not know what *must be* by the very nature of the Will which rules through all things. It would take us too far to enter on the theme which is thus opened up. Let it be enough to point to the light with which it illumines the faith of those who look to Jesus of Nazareth as the Word of God to men, because He revealed, not great scientific or philosophical truths, but that harmony, after which ethical practice endeavours, of the human will with the divine. He, too, recognises the unfathomable secrets of the Supreme Will which directs the processes of the phenomenal universe. "Of that day and that hour knoweth no man, — no, not the angels which are in heaven, neither the Son, but the Father." And yet He does not hesitate to declare that the great problem of modern philosophy, as to the possibility of knowing the Infinite Being, is solved so far at least as the blessedness of human life requires a solution: "Blessed are the pure in heart, for *they* shall see God."

The Dualistic Conception of Nature

John Clark Murray

In one form or another, monism is a necessary concept of science. For scientific research is essentially the effort of human intelligence to bring all facts into intelligible connexion with one another; and that object can be attained only when all facts are comprehended as parts of *one* intelligible system. The unity of nature therefore is implicitly assumed at the very dawn of scientific intelligence, and it becomes an explicit concept as the work of science gains in perspicuity. Accordingly, on first reflexion it must appear somewhat startling, that this monistic assumption of science should, from a very early period, have been traversed by an illusion of dualism; and in the interests of science itself, not to speak of the general interests of humanity, it becomes important to trace this illusion to its source, and to point out the injurious influence it has exerted upon human life in practical as well as in speculative activity.

The conception itself of nature involves the conception of its unity. The term *natura* expresses admirably, because literally, that eternal process of birth, to which it has come to be applied. By its grammatical structure in fact it conveys the idea more pointedly than *physis*, which it was used by the Romans to translate. Of neither word does there appear to be a philological history of any value for the history of scientific ideas. The use of *physis* goes as far back as the Homeric poems. In *Od.* x.303, the word if used to denote the "nature" of the mythical herb *moly*, which Hermes gives to Odysseus as a counter charm against the spells of Circe. The force of the word here is indicated by the fact, that a few lines before (vs.288) the word *kratos* is used as an equivalent to denote the "power" of the herb.

In this use of *physis* there is already implied the idea of some quality in a thing that makes it what it is, and cannot therefore be altered without the thing ceasing to be. In other words, the *nature* of things is conceived to be determined by the very power which makes them what they are, and thus to be

*First published in *The Monist* Vol 1, No3, April, 1879, pp. 382-394

independent of human will. Accordingly these phenomena, which are products of nature, come to be contrasted as unalterable with those which, being products of man, can be altered or abolished at any time by his efforts. This contrast had already become a familiar commonplace to the Athenians in the second half of the fifth century B.C., as a result of the primitive philosophical movements of the preceding century. In the speculations of Sophist and Socratic alike the antithesis is quite marked between *physis* on the one hand, and *nomos* or *thesis* or *techne* on the other. In fact the great problem of that period was to find out whether the principles of man's moral life are based upon distinctions in nature, or are merely regulations of human enactment, institutions of human society, artifices of human ingenuity.

But along with this idea of nature being unalterable there runs the idea of its unity. The one fact indeed is made the corollary of the other. The essential nature of things is conceived to be unchangeable just because all their phenomenal changes are supposed to be temporary modifications of some principle which remains forever the same. To find this principle was, from the outset, the problem of all scientific inquiry. In the language of the early Ionic thought this principle came to be spoken of as *arche*, at least from the time of Anaximander who is said to have first used the term in its philosophical signification.

Among the Ionics monism was thus implicitly assumed. But it became an explicit feature of speculative thought among the Pythagoreans, who may thus be regarded as the first true monists. The monad indeed became with them *the arche* of all things, and that in a far more rigid sense than with Leibnitz. For the Pythagorean monad is really nothing but the abstract idea of unity, — the abstract unity whose repetition constitutes all number, and constitutes thus also the very essence of all things.

But the Pythagoreans evidently felt the perplexity of the problem which this rigid monism imposed upon human thought. "How can the whole of things be for us a unity, and yet each separate?" *Pos de moi hen ti ta pant'estai, kai choris hekaston;* is a question which the Orphic poems, though spurious, yet with a certain historic truth, represent as being forced upon human intelligence at the very dawn of reflective thought. In the effort to solve this problem the monism of the Pythagoreans collapsed into a fateful phase of dualism. Among numbers they detected two forms, even and odd; and recognising number as the essential constituent of all things, they were forced to find the same duality throughout the universe. With a curious, at times even pathetic illustration of the limitations of human intelligence, they followed this dualistic idea into fantastic analogies of odd and even with male and female, right and left, good and evil, etc., — mere conceits which have long ago lost all meaning and interest. But it is only fair to this old school of thinkers to bear in mind the incalculable service which they rendered to primitive science by their essentially monistic conception of nature. It was they who laid the first foundations of exact science by their efforts, fanciful though they were at times, to trace through the universe proportions calculable in definite numbers. They also, alone among ancient thinkers, rose above the sensible appearance of stellar movements, and conceived the earth as merely one of the planets revolving around a central point. It was in fact a fragment of the Pythagorean Philolaos, that suggested to Copernicus the heliocentric explanation of celestial phenomena. It remains, in fine, a significant fact, that the word *cosmos* — the general Greek term for any orderly arrangement — was first applied by the Pythagoreans in the use which almost displaced its primitive meaning, to denote the universe of things *dia tes en auto taxeos*.

Dualism therefore is, at worst, merely an unessential feature of the Pythagorean philosophy, and its influence is practically neutralised by the intrinsic monism of the system. But this is not the case, or at least by no means so completely, in the Eleatic philosophy. Here appears, for the first time, in rugged prominence, the most obtrusive dualism of popular thought and of science. The first discovery of common reflexion, as well as of scientific inquiry, is the fact, that "things *are* not what they *seem.*" It is therefore one of the earliest results of reflective thought, to distinguish things as they really are from things as they appear to the senses. As the real nature of things is revealed by reason forcing us to go beyond their sensible appearance, the former comes to be distinguished as *that which is thought by reason (noumenon)* from *that which appears (phenomenon).* This antithesis is the most prominent feature of Eleatic thought. But the explanation of the antithesis remains a problem unsolved by the Eleatics. It is a knot which they cut rather than untie. They fancied the problem solved by the simple explanation that that which is demonstrated by reason — the noumenon — is the sole reality (*to on*) while the sensible phenomenon is a non-entity (*to me on*). But this is no solution of the problem. Sensible appearances *are* sensible appearances. They *exist* as such. Reason is therefore called to explain their existence, even if it be merely as sensible illusions. But reason cannot be satisfied with any explanation that is not based on a reasonable principle, that is, a principle in harmony with itself. Phenomena, therefore, and noumena, are to be explained on the same principle, and the Eleatic dualism vanishes in an inevitable monism.

Perhaps the first to see this clearly was Anaxagoras, and it is this fact that makes Aristotle speak of him as if he had uttered the first sensible word of a sober mind on the problem of philosophy. Anaxagoras saw that every principle offered by earlier thinkers as explaining the essence of all things —water, air, fire, earth, number, or whatever else it may be — always implies something more primordial. For every such theory always appeals to reason in vindication of itself. The true principle, therefore, Anaxagoras held, must be reason. This is the ultimate explanation of all things. Accordingly, from this time forward is became impossible to leave reason out in any attempt to give a reasonable account of the cosmos.

But naturally for man it is of prime interest to vindicate a rational unity in his own life rather than merely in the external world. In this direction no service has been rendered greater than that of the Stoics. No school has ever grasped more clearly the conception of all nature and all life as created and controlled by Perfect Reason. In fact the conception of nature (*physis*) was itself elevated and expanded. Prior to the Stoics the term had been mainly used, as it is perhaps mainly used still, in reference to the external material world. It was the Stoics who seem to have first applied the term to the phenomena of man's internal life; so that his moral nature and the nature of the external world came to be represented as governed by the same laws, and these the laws of Perfect Reason. Natural Law, therefore, — the law of nature, — was no longer conceived as merely the mode of operation in the physical world. Henceforth it came to be thought of rather as that unalterable principle of consummate reason which finds its highest expression in the laws of man's moral life, and its lower expressions in the laws of the physical world.

But in spite of this apparently all-absorbing rational monism an unfortunate dualism crops out in the Stoical system. It is the old dualism of sense and reason, which had been the prominent feature of Eleatic philosophy. no longer, however, does it signalise an antithesis in our views of nature in general; it is especially centred upon an antagonism in man's moral life, which is declared to be irreconcilable. Following Plato and Aristotle, the stoics divided off the sensibility with its passions as a function of the soul's life totally distinct from, and even opposed to, reason. Passion, for the Stoic, became explicitly what it was implicitly for Plato and Aristotle, an embodiment of the abstract essence of irrationality — *to alogon*. It is thus the moral enemy of those activities of reason which form the essence of rationality — *to logistikon*; and rationality, as we have seen, is, for the Stoic, the very essence of nature, the governing principle of all things. In its practical applications, therefore, the Stoical ethics would make no terms with passion; all kinds of sensibility must simply be suppressed. For the excellence — the virtue (*arete*) — of man is to be found only in a life that is in accordance with nature; and as reason is the essence of nature, a life in accordance with nature must be a life in accordance with reason. But a life that is to any extent controlled by sensibility, however gentle and amiable the sensibility might be, is to that extent irrational; and, therefore, the ideal of human excellence is a state of apathy in which life is completely controlled by passionless reason. As a result of this, Stoicism drew a painfully dualistic division between men, in its estimate of their actual characters. All men, in this estimate, must be either rational or irrational. That obvious intermingling of virtues and vices in actual life, which must be recognised in all just estimate of human character, was stubbornly ignored by the Stoic. For him that man is completely sunk in vice who indulges his passions to the slightest degree, just as, — to use a common illustration, — the man whose head is one foot under water is drowned as completely as the man who is covered by a thousand fathoms. No doctrine of the narrowest sectarianism in the Christian Church ever drew a harsher division between converted and unconverted.

The dualism of Stoical ethics has thus suggested the dualism which has corrupted Christianity. The indebtedness of Christian theology and ethics to the theology and ethics of Stoicism is a commonplace of intellectual history. The whole conception of the universe, as developed in the Christian doctrines of creation and providence, drew largely from the writings of the Stoics. This conception, which represents the universe as being in every nook and cranny under the ceaseless operation of Supreme Intelligence, might be supposed to exclude the very possibility of any irremovable dualism. Yet a painfully prominent dualism distorts the characteristic features of the Christian conception of the universe. It is in some respects based on the moral antagonism of sense and reason, in New Testament language, of the flesh and the spirit. The very excellence of Christian ethics tended to accentuate this antagonism. For by holding forth a peculiarly noble idea of life as the fruit of the spirit, Christianity degraded into a more violent contrast the shortcomings of man's actual conduct, to which the flesh drags him down. This deeper consciousness of sin, evoked by a higher conception of righteousness, has undoubtedly given a sharper antithesis to the ideas of God and Devil, of angel and demon, of heaven and hell, which make up a large portion of distinctively Christian thought. The grotesque imagery of horror which has been evolved out of this dread dualism, is indeed one of the most repulsive regions in the popular mythology of Christendom, yet it is not without a certain terrible fascination which has attracted the poets of Christendom to it as offering a fit material for the highest tragic art.

The source of a great deal of this imagery is still a problem for historical research. In the history of the subject prominence has not unnaturally been given to Manichaeism. But the connexion of this system with Christianity has often been misunderstood. Manichaeism is not properly a Christian heresy; that is to say, it did not spring out of the circle of Christian thought. It is not even to be regarded as a phase of Parseeism; for the Parsee creed is not, any more than Christian, dualistic in its true interpretation. Manichaeism indeed draws certain ideas from the Parsee creed as well as from the Christian; but in its essential drift it is independent of both. Recent researches seem to prove that Manichaeism grew out of an old Babylonian religion modified by some elements of Parsee and of Christian thought, possibly of Buddhist as well.

Though Manichaeism is thus to be considered as a religion outside of Christendom, it probably contributed, with the general Semitic influence which it represented, to accentuate the dualistic ideas of Christian demonology. The Devil of Christendom, though created by God, is still conceived as His successful enemy, marring the perfection of his work by a factor of evil which is maintained in existence, not only throughout the whole history of earth, but for ever afterwards in Hell — irremovable by all the power of divine wisdom and love.

This influence of Manichaeism upon Christianity seems to be implied in the prominence it receives in the writings of Augustine, the man who did more than all the early thinkers of Christendom to shape the theological system of the Christian Church. It was in fact rather in Latin than in Greek theology that Christian thought tended to the dualistic conception of the antagonism between evil and good. Under the influence of the juridical ideas predominant in the Latin mind, the universe came to be conceived often after the analogy of the Roman Empire, and the Supreme Being mainly, if not exclusively, as an infinite monarch, whose laws must be vindicated at any cost. To minds dominated by such a conception of God it seems a sufficient vindication of divine law to inflict an infinite penalty on its violation — a sufficient triumph of goodness if the will to evil is balked by banishment into some dim chaos of eternal suffering, beyond the confines of the divine cosmos. Such representations were extremely natural for minds to whom the problem of human life was mainly such jural organisation of society as it was the mission of the Roman people to work out. These representations are also, of course, useful in their place for popular illustration. But the concept of God, which they imply, is a very inadequate category on which to construct a philosophical theology. The finer speculative genius of the Greek Fathers was untrammeled by the peculiar concepts of Roman jurisprudence; and therefore it is not surprising that Origen, the most brilliant of them all, shrank from an eschatology which did not ultimately eliminate hell, finding the true triumph of good only when all evil is finally subdued.

But the theology of Augustine, with all its dualism, became that of Western Christendom, and has continued to influence Western thought, both in and out of the Church, even to our day. His dualistic influence, like that of the Stoics, has been very marked in the separation of man's moral life into two mutually exclusive conditions or spheres. The state of nature and the state of grace are two concepts, the antithesis of which has been peculiarly distinct in all theological speculation moulded by Augustinian influences. The early history even of modern philosophy can scarcely be understood if we fail to note the fact that the Augustinian definition of these antithetical concepts formed a prominent subject of controversy about the dawn of modern speculation. In the Catholic Church Jansenism was substantially a revival of Augustinianism; and though the Jansenist doctrines were condemned by a papal bull enforced for political purposes by Louis XIV, yet they formed the creed of the finest minds in the Church of France. They were specially associated with the eminent men who lent the lustre of their learning and literary power, as well of their piety, to the Oratory and Port Royal during the seventeenth century, and it is a fact of some import in the history of philosophy that it was among these men that Descartes found his most enthusiastic disciples and his most brilliant expositors. In the Protestant section of Western Christendom, too, the essential drift of Augustinian teaching was revived in Calvinism; and Calvinism became the predominant phase of religious thought among the most distinctive representatives of the Protestant movement. It drew out all the passions of intellectual as well as of religious life among the Huguenots of France, among the Anti-Remonstrants of Holland, among the Puritans of England, Old and New.

But here, as often elsewhere in the history of human thought, extremes meet. For. while Jansenism and Calvinism represented the most intensely religious movements of human thought in the seventeenth century, on the other hand, in that century at least, probably speculation never took a more blankly anti-religious direction than in the philosophy of Hobbes. That philosophy is an attempt to construe all the phenomena of the universe, including the phenomena of man's life, by eliminating all the essential ideas, not of religion only, but even of morality, and reducing nature to a play of purposeless, non-moral agencies. Hobbes' conception, therefore, of the state of nature in human life is fundamentally that of Calvinist and Augustinian. His cool, callous exposition of this concept — his description of man's natural state as a *bellum omnium contra omnes*, caused by all men being naturally actuated by egoistic impulses alone — all this is not only paralleled, but even exceeded in its repulsiveness by the language of eminent Calvinistic divines.

A similar meeting of extremes is found in the comparison of Calvinism with another system of philosophy, which was almost as great a horror to orthodox thought as the system of Hobbes. The system of Spinoza seems indeed in many ways a complete contrast to that of the English philosopher. Yet beneath the apparent antithesis of the two systems there is a profound affinity. Though Spinoza starts with the idea of God, which is an adventitious adjunct to the system of Hobbes, yet his definition of the idea, reducing it to that of mere substance or being, scarcely carries us beyond the agnostic concept of the Supreme Being, which is all that Hobbes allows. Moreover, Spinoza's identification of will and intelligence in God simply means that all we understand by intelligent activity disappears in mere will. The volition of God is therefore explicitly denied to be an act of purposive intelligence. Creation is a purposeless evolution of the eternal substance, a necessary modification of its attributes in accordance with its own irresistible laws. Under such a concept of creation there is no room left for independent activity or personal responsibility on the part of the finite individual. Consequently all the ideas of moral life are relegated by Spinoza among the illusions of "imaginatio," that is, the intellectual activity from which all error arises, and which is therefore carefully distinguished from the genuine knowledge to be attained only by *ratio* and by *scientia intuitiva*. As a result, Spinoza explicitly coincides with Hobbes in his conception of man's natural state. In this state man is declared to be void of those ethical *imaginationes* which grow only out of the soil of civil life.

The conception of nature by Hobbes and Spinoza was in a way thoroughly monistic; but it attained this character only by confining the term to the lowest class of phenomena, and ignoring the phenomena of intelligent moral activity as artificial conventions of society. It requires no very subtle argument to show that, under this analysis, the obligations of social union themselves disappear. For if there is no obligation *a priori* — no obligations *in the very nature of things* — to observe a contract, then the so called social contract itself is left without the support of any such obligation, and it simply remains a question whether the individual cannot outwit by superior astuteness, or resist by superior power, any governmental machinery that may be devised to enforce the contract. A similar issue is inevitable under Hobbes' analysis of religion. If the very nature of things, as unfolded by science, does not involve the essential ideas of religious life, then it is impossible to create a religion by artificial enactments of any civil authority. This fact is overlooked by Hobbes and by Comte as completely as by the agnostic champions of ultramontanism in the Church of Rome. It is not therefore surprising that Hobbes's philosophy of religion and morals should have met with strong opposition from men who were in earnest about the obligations of moral and religious life. Their opposition commonly took the form of a return to the larger and nobler conception of nature which had distinguished the ancient Stoics. A long line of writers, especially among the moralists of England, sought to trace, either in the nature of man or in external nature, if not in both, the foundations of his moral and religious life. Again the old Stoical conception of the law of nature became familiar in ethics and jurisprudence, and all positive enactments of human societies were viewed as merely imperfect embodiments of the law of nature. Accordingly men became accustomed to conceive the problems of moral and social activity as implying an endeavour to break through the artificial trammels by which civil society was cramping the life of man, and to get back to the simple requirements of nature, of natural law.

It is not difficult, and it is profoundly interesting, to see how this conception of life's problems represented the drift of the great historical movements by which the last century was characterised. The claim of individual freedom against unreasonable restrictions of social law had become inevitable, partly under the trend of speculative thought, partly under the impulse of social conditions themselves. For never perhaps in the history of civilization had human life entangled itself in such a complicated net-work of exacting regulations. Every sphere of man's activity from the highest to the lowest, — religion and literature, morality and etiquette, military and political and industrial life, — all were subjected to minute and often petty and even vexatious restrictions that prevented the natural and reasonable expansion of the human spirit which it was their proper function to develop. Never had the clothing of custom, in which of course human life must always invest itself, become so outworn, so ill-adapted to the wants of growing humanity. The great revolution, which shattered the old life of Europe as the century closed, was an outburst of passionate impatience on the part of European society to get rid of its outworn clothing before it had well considered in what fashion it was to be clothed anew.

This memorable movement is commonly regarded by historians as having found its most characteristic literary expositor in the writings of Rousseau. There we find the reactions against the social philosophy of Hobbes and Spinoza carried to its extreme. The contrast, which these philosophers had drawn between man's natural state and his civil state, is by Rousseau completely reversed. The state of nature he conceives to be one of innocent social equality, which has simply been corrupted by the artifices and restrictions and divisions which political institutions have introduced.

But the extravagance of this theory as well as of its opposite arises from the fact that the state of nature, as defined by both, is a pure fiction of abstract thought. It is an attempt to conceive what man would be if we were to eliminate all those factors of his life which are derived from social organisation. It does not matter that in one case these factors are supposed to be the virtues by-which human life is adorned, in the other the vices by which it is corrupted. In either case the error is the same. It consists in taking a fictitious abstraction for a reality in nature. It ignores the only human reality that nature knows, that is, man living in the social state. The absolute solitary is not a natural man. As Aristotle said long ago, he is either a god or a brute.

It is evident then that all the dualistic separations of man's life into spheres that are mutually exclusive originate in an imperfect conception of nature in general, but of man's nature in particular. This imperfection continues to mislead scientific inquiry. Human nature is still at times defined by concepts which imply a merely animal existence; and an attempt is made to interpret human actions simply as effects naturally resulting from impulses of pleasure or repulsions of pain. On such an interpretation of human life science must of course pronounce all morality of a spiritual or disinterested nature to be not only impossible as a matter of fact, but even incapable of any rational vindication. In like manner if nature in general is defined by similar narrow concepts, if nature is understood to mean the universe with all the rational purposes of human life eliminated, then it may be perfectly consistent to assert that there is no morality in nature, or even that nature is profoundly immoral. But the evolution of the universe with the history of man eliminated is the drama of Hamlet with the part of Hamlet left out. It is the life of man that at once forms the most essential part of the problem of all science, and furnishes the most essential data for its solution. The truth is, therefore, that scarcely one eminent thinker has fallen into this narrow conception of nature without at the same time protesting more or less explicitly against its inadequacy to satisfy the demands of scientific thought. More than one noble passage might be cited from recent literature, in which the scientific thinker rises to the part of a modern Prometheus, defying the non-moral omnipotence that he seems to see ruling in external nature, and asserting the power of man's internal nature to act upon a moral law of love in spite of any suffering which the non-moral laws of external nature may bring about as the result of his action. Nor is such Promethean assertion an abandonment of the scientific attitude of thought for an idle bravado of fancy. It is rather a recognition of the fact that there has always been in the universe a power adequate to sustain the man

> Who trusted God was love indeed,
>   And love creation's final law,
>   Though nature, red in tooth and claw,
> With ravin, shrieked against his creed.

Science therefore must give way to the reality of this power a prominence equal to the reality claimed for the force of non-moral causation, and it can escape from an incomprehensible dualism only by advancing to a conception of nature which embraces both in intelligible harmony.

Section Three

JAMES BEAVEN
(1801-1875)

3

James Beaven and the Argument from Design

Leslie Armour

A Stupid Dry Old Stick?

James Beaven was the first professional philosophical writer in English Canada, and the author of the first full length fully-philosophical book written in Canada outside Quebec. There were other philosophy teachers before him — notably Thomas McCulloch[1] — but the others mixed a little philosophy with a lot of theology or, like McCulloch, made their philosophical points in stories and essays. Though Beaven's main philosophical work, *The Elements of Natural Theology,*[2] has a theological title, *natural* theology based on philosophical principles and on the examination of the empirical evidence is what interests him. He was also the first "secular" professor of philosophy in English Canada, a popular writer on travel and on the Indians, and a religious controversialist.

Very likely he was the first Christian philosopher to predict the success of and to welcome what long afterwards was named "the unity of science" movement — the doctrine that there is one and only one set of laws which governs everything in the objectively knowable universe. Such notions have usually frightened Christian believers who see in them overtones of materialism, but Beaven saw them quite differently.

He was a genuinely original mind, and yet Thomas Daniel Wilson, a one-time president of the University of Toronto, called him a "stupid dry old stick that we would well be rid of."[3] But for this remark Wilson might well have been forgotten long ago (though he lived to serve philosophy by preserving some of Paxton Young's manuscripts). Dry, perhaps, but Beaven, the first man to write a full-length work of philosophy in English Canada, was hardly stupid. Wilson, it should be said, was not entirely alone in his opinion: Ernest Hawkins, the Secretary, no less, of the Society for the Propagation of the Gospel, remarked that "the worthy Dr. B. rather bored me."

Truth to tell, Beaven, a Wiltshire royalist, born in 1801, but still defending Charles I in the middle of the nineteenth century, probably could be a bore. On his high horse defending some tasty bit of Anglican high church practice against the generally very low church clergy in Toronto, he may sometimes almost have been a figure of fun.

He had at least two other characters in his repertoire, and he could play both of them to the full. One was the raconteur whom we have known as the narrator of *Recreations of a Long Vacation*,[4] who describes his travels around Ontario amongst the Indians; the man who gradually comes to prefer Indians to Americans if not always to Englishmen, who makes us laugh at the "lined and cushioned pews" of a Church in Detroit and describes with equal delight and great detail the scenery and the horses. *Recreations* sold well and made his name with the larger public.

It is his third "persona," that of the serious, tolerant and creative philosopher which concerns us here. This "persona" was not very evident before Beaven left England in 1841. He had written a book on St. Irenaeus — the late second century Bishop of Lyons who, in our time, has been revived by John Hick as the source of our most up-to-date theological ideas. Adelaide the Queen Dowager, (who would now be called the Queen Mother), and the future Cardinal Newman signed up for copies before the publication, but though *An Account of the Life and Writings of S. Irenaeus*[5] should now be restudied with care, one's first impression is that Irenaeus was very useful as a source for scoring Anglican points against Roman Catholics. Chiefly, however, Beaven's works appeared under such titles as *A Help to Catechizing*, *A Manual for Visiting the Sick* and *On Intercourse with the Churches*[6] — worthy works, no doubt, but not such as to set the world afire.

His first extended, serious book of general philosophical interest appeared nine years after he arrived in Canada. Clearly, *Elements of Natural Theology* was different in tone from his earlier works. These had been — even, I think, *S. Irenaeus* — missionary works in the high Anglican cause. They tended to be dogmatic, or polemical, or both. One does not expect the author of *A Help in Catechizing* to be anything but dogmatic, of course, and one must look at these works in their context. They more often expressed the kind of certainty which one associates with closed minds and dubious causes than the reflective assessment which a philosopher might be expected to show in the presence of important truths.

One must, therefore, say something about the two sets of circumstances in which Beaven found himself. In England, as a high Churchman — that is as one who believes that the central concern of Christians and the centre from which truth emanated was the Church and that Anglicans, therefore, should preserve as much as they could of the traditions of Catholicism — he was fearful lest old certainties be lost. The "low church" party despised ritual and tended toward Calvinism while the "broad church" party, the party of Thomas Arnold and the reformers, was prepared to allow within the church any doctrine which was not specifically anti-Christian, and they were willing to compromise with modernity and to replace theology as much as possible with a universal and rationalist philosophy. Outside the Anglican church were a small number of Roman Catholics and a large number of "dissenters" or "non-conformists." Beaven's views were very much like those of Pusey and Keble who formed the Oxford Movement. He was too much a monarchist to follow Newman into Catholicism. He deplored the "regicide" and would gladly have had on the throne another Charles I who perhaps would have made the country Catholic again, but, things being what they were, he supported the monarch. It is unimaginable that he would ever have become a "dissenter."

In such a circumstance, it did not seem unreasonable to devote himself to the consolidation of the accepted certainties. There was, after all, an established church, in England, and the main thing to do was to make certain that it did not lose its message. The philosophical task of exploring the underpinnings of that belief and the task of defending it against the encroachment of unbelief, scientific belief and heretical belief could be left to others. There *were* plenty of others.

In Canada the situation was quite different. The idea of a state church had already been abandoned, though it was not until 1854 that the associated question of "clergy reserves" was settled. There was no possibility of Anglican dominance, even in Upper Canada. The immigrant population, apart from the United Empire Loyalists, many of whom were Anglicans, came chiefly from the Celtic fringe of the British Isles, above all from Scotland and Ireland. Though, in fact, there were more "Irishmen" than Scotsmen, a great many of the Irish were from Scottish-settled Northern Ireland and very often considered themselves Scots.[7] Hence the cultural dominance of the Scots in Canada. These peoples, however, brought a variety of denominations with them. There were large numbers of Presbyterians, (never a single body from the beginning, and, after 1844, further divided by the "Great Disruption" in Scotland), and Baptists, and two distinct groups of Methodists as well as Anglicans, Roman Catholics and a few Congregationalists.

Various efforts were made to mix them — along the road from Arthur to Owen Sound, for instance, Catholic and Protestant villages alternated with one another. But each denomination had established its own institutions of higher education and Beaven himself was in the thick of the attempt to create a federal University of Toronto with a "non-denominational" University College at its centre. There, he came to be the first non-denominational Professor of Philosophy.

A Rational Basis for a National Consensus

The need was for a core of rational belief in which everyone might share and from which each might go his own way. If such a core could not be found, it was reasoned, there would be no basis for an ultimate settlement. The problem is still with us. There is, perhaps, a rolling consensus, a world-picture made up of fashionable conclusions from science and history; but we frequently face problems (abortion is a recent one) which have religious undertones and about which we confront one another across an abyss of conflicting belief or unbelief. But Beaven did contribute in his *Elements of Natural Theology* to the creation of a consensus which lasted through much of the nineteenth and early twentieth centuries and which was to provide the view of the world from which our social reformers most frequently worked.

There was, however, a more directly philosophical aspect to this project in Beaven's mind: on what basis could the foundations of such a rational belief be built? Beaven's own taste at home had been to build on the foundations of church history, for the principal threat to his kind of Christianity came from those who thought of the church as a purely social and religious institution or from those who believed that the continuity of Christianity from Jesus and the evangelists to us was a myth. But these very people were already, in all likelihood, a strong majority in Upper Canada in 1841. A related but different alternative would have been to build on the authority of Scripture. But quite a lot of what Beaven thought to be essential to Christianity was not to be found in Scripture, and Scripture, itself, at least since the upsurge of German "higher criticism" had come to seem dubious. Pure reason was an obvious choice, perhaps, for one who wanted *rational* foundations.

The surface of the earth was unique and quite special and unique processes took place on various parts of it. When the thought dawned on people that the atoms which made up rocks also made up pigs and that pigs coontained all and only elements which are found in the natural world, most theologians took fright at the idea and continued to look for something which would keep life and inanimate nature — above all *human* life and inanimate nature —quite separate.

It appeared to Beaven as we shall see, that the unity of science was the very best argument for the existence of God and he rejoiced in all such ideas. To be sure it was all a hypothesis. It could only be tested by experiential evidence and the evidence was by no means all gathered; but Beaven thought that the best bet was that the unity of science would hold. More surprisingly, Beaven was prepared to turn theological doctrines into scientific hypotheses. He was not *absolutely* sure he could explain all the evil in the world, that men were really immortal or even that God existed. But evidence there was. And he proposed to use it to show that theology was on as good ground as natural science.

Design and God

There are a number of approaches one could take if one wanted to lay the foundations for rational theology on the basis of experience. One might conduct scrupulous investigations into claims about miracles; but Beaven was skeptical. One might (as Matthew Arnold did a little later) point to the curious fact that men seem moved to reach for a best which is beyond them in poetry, in music, in painting, and indeed in moral conduct; but Beaven was never much impressed by the works of fallen man. Or one might, like Newman (who was Beaven's contemporary) see whether one could make a case for the claim that God speaks to us in conscience; but Beaven, I think, was fearful of stirring up a rabble of conflicting voices. Finally, one might seek for other complex phenomena of the inner life, but Beaven wanted to take his stand in the open public world.

He wanted to make a claim about something in the objective realm of public debate. And so he chose to defend a form of the design argument — the argument to the effect that a close study of the facts would show that the universe bore the hall-marks of a designer. But he started, in fact, by rejecting the most famous of all such arguments — Archbishop Paley's argument about the watch and the watchmaker.

Why the Watch and Watchmaker Argument Won't Do: Paley[8] had argued that design is an observable fact. He urged that, if you were out walking in the desert and came across a watch, you would at once know that it had been made by someone for a purpose. You would know this even, perhaps, if you had not grasped that it could be used to tell time. Certainly, as soon as you found that it could be used to tell time, you would no longer be in doubt. Paley had not invented the argument: it goes back to Plato's Socrates and to Cicero. But he was quick to exploit it in reference to various parts of the human body: surely the eye is made to see and the ear to hear and surely it is improbable that such organs would grow by chance.

Many people, however, were not convinced, and early in the nineteenth century Lord Bridgewater commissioned a series of expert treatises on various aspects of the subject. One of them, by William Whewell[9], plays a crucial part in any account of the matter, for it calls attention to the problem of natural law. This is important because, even supposing that there is evidence of intelligence and design in the world, this does not lead us to anything like the unitary Christian God unless certain other assumptions are made. One is that these events are law-like and the other is that all the laws form a unity.

Accidental and sporadic intelligence proves nothing except that there is intelligence in the universe. Paley's watch was made by a watchmaker. Perhaps human eyes were made by another spirit, greater, perhaps than us but no more God than a watchmaker. Perhaps, too, *we* might say the human eye was made in any little steps as a result of biological mutations and the ability of light-sensitive creatures to respond efficiently to their environment.

Whewell's Point: Whewell had grasped that what was important first of all, therefore, was that nature should be law-like. Whewell argues that one could make an overwhelming case for the claim that natural events display an order which can be expressed as natural laws even though Hume had urged that no finite collection of instances justifies us in believing that the next event will be like its predecessor.

It is Whewell's case that this is beside the point. It is the *form* of the laws which matters. They are not laws in the sense of rules which nature is ordered to follow; they are mathematical formulae which render the order and connection of the facts intelligible, and they rely on the exhibition of a common *principle* amongst a great variety of disparate factors. One principle explains both the movements of the planets and the fall of the apple though the facts are very unlike one another. And this *principle can* be found expressed in and through the facts. *If* there is a principle, it will hold if the future facts are of the same general sorts

Beaven's Extension: Whewell himself warns that principles are not exhibitions of will. One cannot go straight away from them to the idea of God. He however believed that one *can* argue from the fact that the laws we know seem well-adapted to the production of human life — the sort of life which naturally gives rise to the problems of theology — and may lead us on to the conclusion that God exists.

Beaven points out that there are still two more steps which are necessary. One is to show that all laws form a unity. If they do we can, surely, ascribe them to a diversity of principles even if those are spiritual.

He was willing to bet that the principles would prove to come together, for he could see already that biology and physiology must form a single science and that both would turn out to be related to physics and chemistry. Only in recent years, of course, has it become apparent how right he was. It is surely remarkable that there are not independent principles — that the physics and chemistry of life seem to follow precisely from the properties present in the physics and chemistry of inanimate objects. Many people would still hold that the case is not made, but they are becoming fewer.

If there is a unity and if that unity produces precisely those creatures — us — whose existence seems meaningful in terms of universal moral laws then, indeed, the argument carries weight. Beaven warns, however, that there is room for doubt, that by no means all the problems can be solved and that even in these terms there still remains another fundamental question.

Suppose, after all, that it is simply in the nature of matter that the fascinating phenomena of human and animal life should arise. Suppose, that is, that there is no alternative. The working together or the exhibition of a common *principle* amongst a great variety of disparate factors will explain everything: one principle explains both the movements of the planets and the fall of the apple though the facts are very unlike one another. And this *principle can* be found expressed in facts. *If* there is a principle, it will hold for the future facts of the same general sort.

Beaven's answer is that matter, by itself, is not predisposed more to one set of laws than to another. This may seem to make Beaven's argument old-fashioned. Do we not, by relating matter and energy so as to make them convertible, define matter in terms of what it does? And, if we do, do we not hold precisely the view that there is no other way in which matter can behave?

Modern Difficulties: No doubt the answer to these questions is "yes" if what is meant is that we cannot conceive of the universe which is talked about in physics and chemistry except in terms of some activity. But there are two questions involved here. One has to do with the framework — which *perhaps* might be different — and with what might be called the "activity type" which perhaps goes along with the different scientific definitions.

Middle sized objects (between the size of a molecule and that of a galaxy) tend to exhibit inverse square laws. Thus bodies attract one another directly as their mass and inversely as the square of the distance between them. This is because (as Whitrow explained following Kant)[10] the universe in which they exist is three dimensional and its space is uniform, continuous and non-interfering (there are no four dimensional bits and no "breaks in it" and space itself does not interfere with the diffusion of energy.) For force-diffusion phenomena, then, there are a finite number of dimensions in which the force can dispese and there is no more resistance in one dimension than in another If we had a four-dimensional space, we should have inverse cube laws and so forth.

Now it is true that we may say that the objects in a space define that space, for there is no current use for Newtonian "absolute space" which exists even when there is nothing in it. But we can not imagine the type of activity which is gravitation taking place in a four-dimensional space and producing inverse cube laws. Is there any real reason why the assembly of particles should have produced such a space? Failure to define such space has dramatic consequences. When we can deal with the components of a single atom, we seem not to have all the components of such space and quite different forces are at work. Perhaps the tendency to define spaces also plays a part in the curious phenomena of low temperature physics. *At any rate, if there are no good reasons to suppose that the present framework is somehow necessitated by matter, then Beaven has a point.*

We can easily imagine many ordinary things in a four-dimensional space — a radically different world in which we would not be here because two dimensions would not provide enough connections to make possible a human brain; and also the mathematics of orbit theory entail instability when one gets more than three dimensions. We would have alternatively fried and frozen during the long march of evolution. Beaven's point is that the framework *could* have been different. Why is it like it is? Bear in mind that we would not be here if there had been more than three dimensions —or if there had been less.

The possible number of dimensions is very large. Matter by itself does not seem to necessitate a three dimensional world. Many other hypotheses can be entertained.

It is frequently said that the design argument could not carry any weight because we do not know to assign probabilities to a world which doesn't yet exist. But *if* there is no reason to suppose that our three-dimensional space was necessary and if such a space is necessary for us to be here, does it not seem a little too much to suppose that it was fortuitous — that we drew the only winning ticket in an infinitely large pot of tickets? Doubtless different answers will commend themeselves to different people; but Beaven's argument would seem, still to justify inquiry.

Notes

1. Thomas McCulloch, (1777-1843) is best known for *The Letters of Mephibosheth Stepsure* which originally appeared in the *Acadian Recorder* (Halifax) of 1821-22. He was the first principal of Dalhousie College.

2. James Beaven, *The Elements of Natural Theology*, London: Rivington, 1850.

3. Cited in the *Dictionary of Canadian Biography*, Vol. 10, Toronto: University of Toronto Press, 1972, p. 40.

4. James Beaven, *Recreation of a Long Vacation*, Toronto: H. and W. Rowsell, 1846.

5. James Beaven, *An Account of the Life and Writings of S. Irenaeus*, London: Rivington, 1841.

6. For an account of (and reference to) Beaven's minor works see Leslie Armour and Elizabeth Trott, *The Faces of Reason, An Essay on Philosophy and Culture in English Canada, 1850-1950,* Waterloo: Wilfrid Laurier University Press, 1981, Ch.2.

7. The best recent discussion of the demography of Upper Canada in the mid-1840's is in Donald Harman Akenson, *The Irish in Ontario*, Kingston and Montreal: McGill-Queen's University Press, 1985. Many people are surprised to discover that nearly a quarter of the population of Upper Canada in 1842 were of "Irish" origin, against only an eighth for the Scots and another eighth for the English and Welsh combined. But most of the migrants came from the northern half of Ireland (Belfast was the most used port of sailing). They were also often Protestant than Catholic, and so very many of them were evidently from the "Ulster" communities which were Scots in origin. The problem of distingushing the "Celtic fringe" is compounded by the fact that the data, at any rate as reported by Akenson, do not distinguish the Welsh from the English. But it is certain that the "Celtic fringe" predominated. One might note that the figure Catharine Parr Traill gave in *The Backwoods of Canada*, London: Charles Knight, 1836, p. 339, also lumped the Welsh with the English. Her figures for the years 1829-1834 showed that the Irish immigrants always outnumbered the combined Scots and English/Welsh immigrants in all but one year by atleast two to one.

8. William Paley, *View of the Evidences of Christianity*, 2 vols., London: Faulder, 1794.

9. William Whewell, *Astronomy and General Physics Considered with Reference to Natural Theology*, London: George Bell, 1833.

10. G.J. Whitrow, *The Structure & Evolution of the Universe*, New York: Harper, 1959.

The Elements of Natural Theology

James Beaven

CHAPTER VII
That the Design Evident Throughout Creation Proceeds From Only One Being

In the course of our inquiries we have been brought to the conclusion, that we have throughout the universe traces of some intelligent contriver or contrivers. As Christians, we of course know that there is but One; but our mere evidence from nature, whilst it must have impressed upon the mind more and more the feeling of the oneness of the creating power, has not actually been shown to prove it. So far as our argument has yet carried us, it is quite possible that all the various portions of the universe may have been designed by a multitude of intelligent beings; just as all the houses, and ships and articles of furniture, and implements, and tools, and machines, have been designed by thousands of mankind. If, therefore, we could proceed no further than this, we should still be far from proving from the works of nature (as the Scriptures teach us we can prove) the existence of one God; for, in the very idea of God, we require a first and final cause of all we see. In order, therefore, that we may be able to evince that there is such a being, we must be able to connect together the scattered indications of design, and we must be able to show that one chain passes through the whole. We must prove that they are all parts of one great plan, proceeding from one master mind.

In order to establish this point, let us go back to the solar system. We have seen that the fourteen planets move around the sun. Now this connexion of all these bodies with the sun, and their dependence upon him, of course connects them with each other; and thus proves, that the whole system, so far as it is a piece of machinery, was contrived by one governing mind.

*First published by F. and J. Rivington, London, 1850. Selections by Leslie Armour

There is, however, a remarkable set of facts in connexion with this subject, which places the argument in a point of view so irresistibly convincing, that the statement cannot be complete without them. (See Paley, XXII.iii.2 and Whewell's *Bridgewater Treatise*, Book II; ch.3).

If each planet were to revolve round the sun without being affected by the other planets, there would be a complete regularity in its motion; and this regularity might continue forever. But it is discovered (as I have already stated) that the law of gravitation is universal. The planets, therefore, do not execute their movements unaffected by each other: each of these is acted upon by the attraction of all the rest; and this produces a derangement of the regularity of their motion. All the planets indeed are very small compared with the sun; and, therefore, the derangement they can all together produce upon any one will be extremely small, in the course of one revolution. But this gives no security that it may not become very large in the course of many revolutions; the cause is perpetually acting, and it has the whole extent of time to act in. Is it not then quite conceivable, that in the lapse of ages the derangements of the motions of the planets may accumulate; the orbits may change their form; their mutual distances may be much increased, or much diminished? Is it not possible that these changes may go on without limit, and end in the complete subversion of the system? If, for instance, the result of this mutual gravitation should be that the earth's orbit should become less and less circular, its course might lead it by degrees to interfere with the motions of some other planet. Or if it were to cause the moon to approach nearer and nearer to the earth, it might finally fall to the earth's surface. In either case the result must be an awful catastrophe. We should have "years of unequal length, and seasons of capricious temperature; planets and moons of portentous size and aspect, glaring and disappearing at uncertain intervals; tides like deluges, sweeping over whole continents; and perhaps the collision of two planets, and the consequent destruction of all organization on both of them."

On a common examination of the solar system, it is not at all clear that there is not a tendency to this ultimate disarrangement. Changes are continually taking place in the motions of the heavenly bodies, and have been taking place since the first dawn of science. The earth's orbit has been becoming more and more round, from the earliest observations to our own times. The moon has been moving quicker and quicker from the time of the first recorded eclipses. Will these and similar changes go on without limit or reaction? If so, we tend by natural causes to a termination and breaking up of the present state of things: if not, by what adjustment or compensation are we secured from such a tendency?

The answer to these questions is far from easy; and it belongs to mathematics to give a complete reply. (See La Place, *Expos. du Systeme du Monde*, p.441.) But the question has undergone a regular and close mathematical investigation, and it has been proved, by a process completely satisfactory, that we have nothing whatever to fear. The orbits of all the planets deviate from regularity to a certain extent; they continue to deviate more and more until they reach a certain point, and then they begin to return; they reach a maximum height of deviation and then diminish. The periods which this restoration requires are enormous; reaching to thousands of years, and, in some instances, even millions: and hence it is that some of these apparent derangements have been going on ever since the beginning of the history of the world. But, if the world shall endure sufficiently long, the restoration will be in the sequel as complete as the derangement: and meanwhile, the disturbance never attains a sufficient amount seriously to alter the adaptations of the system.

There exists, therefore, in the solar system, a provision for the permanent regularity of its motions, arising out of the dependence of every one of the globes which compose it upon every other: which proves still more completely, the unity of design in the system; and consequently the unity of the mind which at first devised and created it.

If we go beyond our system, amongst the fixed stars, we ascertain that, wherever we can discover motion at all, the same rules of motion are adopted; and thence, by an inevitable inference, we conclude that the same mind devised them which devised the more limited system of which we ourselves form a part.

But it might have so happened (so far as natural reason could enable us to judge *a priori*), that our Creator may have devised the magnificent and grand in the universe, and others the smaller details. This indeed was in a degree the theory of Plato, who taught that the inferior parts of creation were performed by the gods, in subordination to the supreme Intelligence. (See Chap.II. p.10.) Let us, therefore, examine what evidence we have that the same mind appears throughout.

It is well known that the changes of the seasons and the alternate succession of day and night are caused by the motion of the earth, either around the sun or on its own axis. It is likewise well known that the constitutions of man, of animals, of birds, of insects, and of plants, are connected more or less with the interchange of day and night, and of the seasons. For instance, night is the period of rest for man, and for most animals and birds: and if with some that is not the case, it is with equal regularity the time of motion. The owl and the bat as regularly come abroad by night and withdraw by day, as the other creatures come abroad by day and rest by night. Plants again disengage oxygen gas by day, and carbonic acid gas by night; whilst some of them mark the change more strongly, by closing their flowers in the evening and re-opening them in the morning. Connecting these facts with the circumstance that day and night are caused by the alternate presenting to the action of the sun, and withdrawal from it of the various portions of the earth's surface, we perceive an intimate connexion between every thing which lives and grows upon the earth with the sun, the centre of the system. Here then is another link in the chain.

Let us now contemplate the relations which things on earth bear to each other. We have already noticed how exactly the wings of the bird and fins of the fish, are suited to the elements in which they move. Put the bird into the water, or bring the fish into the air, and (with a few remarkable exceptions) their organs of motion are useless. If we compare the greater part of animals together, we shall find that their structure bears a mutual resemblance, (see Paley's chapter on *Comparative Anatomy*,) which shows a comparison in the mind of the Designer, and a variation of one idea to suit different circumstances. Man, quadrupeds, and birds, all have four limbs each; and the bony structure of all (as we have already noticed, Chap. VI.) is extremely alike; but varied in relative proportions, and variously clothed, to suit the modes of life to which different classes of creatures are subject. Thus the bat is a mouse, furnished with wings instead of fore legs; the long slender bones, which serve to expand the wings answering exactly to the toes of the fore feet of the mouse; and the claws actually remaining at their extremities, but applied to the use of supporting the bat during his hours of rest, by enabling him to suspend himself against walls, etc., by means of them.

And the mention of the bat leads to the remark, that the gradation from one scale to another in creation is very remarkable. From man we do not pass at once to quadrupeds proper, but first to the orang-outang or chimpanzee (whose structure is almost like our own), and thence to apes and monkeys. From quadrupeds we pass off in various directions to birds and fishes. For instance, there is a quadruped in New Holland which has the beak of a duck, and forms a link between quadrupeds and fowl. The whole tribe of lizards forms a link between quadrupeds and reptiles on the one hand, and quadrupeds and fish on the other; the land lizards connecting the former, and the water lizards the latter. So again, seals are a link between quadrupeds and whales; and whales themselves, in bringing forth their young alive, and in giving them suck, makes the transition more gradual from quadrupeds to other fish. Lobsters and crabs and other crustaceous fish, form a link between fish and insects; for, like insects, the osseous part of their structure is external, whilst their flesh resembles that of fish. Oysters, polypes and sponges, adhering to the ground and having no power of locomotion, — and yet having more or less of voluntary motion and of animal fluids, — connect together fish and plants. The sensitive plant and the pitcher plant of Upper Canada connects plants and animals: for their nutriment is composed in part of animal substance (feeding on flies); and the latter [sic] shrinks from the touch.

One of the most remarkable signs of this mutual connexion is the resemblance in one branch of creation to another in external form. For instance, the flowers of the orchis tribe frequently resemble some insect, as the bee or fly; and, again, there is an insect in Southern Africa and a caterpillar in Western Canada, either of which is scarcely distinguishable from a leaf.

Take again the structure of the stomachs of animals in regard to their food; and you have another connexion between animals, plants, and insects: for the stomachs of some animals will digest only vegetable substance, and those of others only insects and animal matter; whilst some are constructed with a view to both. Consider, again, the manner in which plants are nourished, by carrying up mineral substances from the earth, and imbibing other portions from the atmosphere, and you connect together minerals and air; and that mineral substances are carried into the plant is shown by the fact, that the outer coat of straw, and sometimes as a grain of wheat, is as perfectly flint as any flint-stone you can dig out of a bed of chalk.

The more minutely, therefore, we extend our inquiries, the more clearly we perceive that there is a connexion throughout nature, — no one thing stands by itself. Everything is related or adapted to some other thing; and this relation and adaptation is carried on from the stones in the bowels of the earth, and the scarcely perceptible insects throughout all vegetable and animated nature, — by the air we breathe, and the light by which we see, — up to the planets and stars, and by them to the utmost verge of the universe.

Nay, is there not one thing in nature which is connected with them all? Is there not the intelligent spirit of man, united to an animal structure, and capable of perceiving, contemplating, and reasoning, upon whatever exists throughout the universe?

Can there remain, therefore, a shadow of a doubt, not only that there are traces of intelligence every where, but that every where we perceive the operation of *ONE* governing Intelligence, viewing all his work together, and adapting every portion of it, more or less directly, to every other portion?

This doctrine of the unity of God is, moreover, in one way or another, recognised even by pagans.

Thus Philolaus, already cited, quotes Pythagoras as saying, "God is the director and ruler of all things, One, always existing, permanent, immovable, like to Himself and differing from others." And although we learn from Cicero, confirmed by Justin Martyr, (*Cohort. ad Graecos*, 18,) that Pythagoras taught Pantheism, yet these words are direct in their testimony to the unity of Deity. Socrates again, although he believed in a multitude of gods, recognised one as distinct from the others, and as *alone* the Being who arranges and holds together the whole world (Xen. *Mem.*IV.iii.13), and the wisdom that pervades all things. (I.iv.17.) Plato believed in one First Cause of motion, whose nature is spiritual.(*Philoebus*, § 56.) The opinion of Aristotle was similar. Zeno and his followers, although they likewise taught polytheism, and maintained that even deity could not exist unless embodied in matter, yet held that there is one supreme God, that is, the universe, the Author of the existence of all other beings (Cic.*Nat.Deor.* II.8.11); and he taught (if we may trust Diogenes Laertius, *de Vitis Philosophorum*, vii.137), that, as all beings sprung from Him, so they would all again be absorbed into Him, to be again produced in other forms, and again absorbed, to all eternity. Besides this Cicero attributes to him the opinion (II.32,33), that there is one moving, regulating power, which he calls nature; which is rational, and proceeds by orderly methods, and causes everything to act and grow in its proper manner, and connects it with every other thing. Now, although it is not absolutely certain what place he assigns to nature, nor whether he regards it (as he appears to do, ch.34) as the soul of the universe, yet it is clear that he teaches a unity of causation and action at the head of all existing beings.

To leave the philosophers, Justin Martyr, both in his tract on the Unity of God (*Peri Monarchias*), and in his *Exhortations to the Greeks*, quotes many passages from the poets, Sophocles, Euripides, Diphilus, Philemon, and Menander, to show that their language recognised one Creator, one God, above the ordinary objects of popular worship; even though they did not know Him as He is. And in this line of quotations he is followed and sustained by Athenagoras and Clement of Alexandria. Indeed it is remarkable that the arguments advanced by the early Christian controversialists to prove the Unity of God, proceed upon the virtual recognition of that doctrine in the popular mind. Thus Athenagoras (*Legatio pro Christianis*, ch.7) argues that there could not be two gods, because, as we know that One governs the universe, and comprises it within Himself, we must place the other in some other portion of space, which cannot be found, because the Creator of this world *fills all things* and *comprises all things*. Such an idea of God confesses his unity. So again Tertullian, reasoning against the doctrine of two First Principles, goes on the assumption, that God is *the Great Supreme* (*adv.Marcion*, I.3), and argues that there cannot be two such beings.

CHAPTER VIII
On the Operation of General Laws;
And on the Onmiscience, Infinite
Wisdom and Omnipotence of God

In drawing out the argument, by which we proved that there is one designer and contriver of ourselves, and of all things which come under our knowledge, it was necessary to view Him as acting in a number of isolated cases, selected almost at random from every part of nature to which our observation has extended. In so doing, however, we were led to see that (in some cases, at least) he acts, not only by the exercise of intelligence in particular instances, but also by the establishment of laws, ruling and including an indefinite number of instances. For example, in the solar system, where the twenty or thirty globes of which it is composed are moved, not each by a separate agency, but by general laws of motion, applying to all at once. The same must be the case with regard to all those things, whether animal, vegetable or mineral, which the mind is led to form into classes. We can as little doubt that the facts, that ostrich eggs never produce geese, nor the seed of the carrot the plant we call mustard; but that the egg of the ostrich and the seed of the carrot invariably produce bodies resembling the parent, are the results of general laws; as the fact that a printing-press produces books, and does not produce woollen cloth, is the result of general laws.

We may extend the same observation throughout nature. Events are brought about, not by insulated interpositions of Divine power, exerted in each particular case, but by the establishment of general laws. God, therefore, is the Author of the universe as it at present exists, and its Governor and Preserver likewise; through the laws He has given to its parts, the properties which He has impressed upon its constituent elements —through them He shapes, moves, sustains, and guides the visible creation.

This mode of operation requires, perhaps, some attention on our part to understand it with proper clearness. One reason of this is, that it is a mode of operation altogether different from our own. Man can construct exquisite machines, can call in vast powers, can form extensive combinations, in order to bring about results which he has in view: but in all this he is only taking advantage of laws of nature which already exist; he is applying to his use properties which matter already possesses: nor can he by any effort do more. He can establish no new law of nature, which is not a result of existing ones. He can invest matter with no new properties, which are not modifications of its present attributes. His greatest advances of skill and power are, when he calls to his aid forces which before existed unemployed; or, when he discovers so much of the habits of some of the elements as to be able to bend them to his purpose. He navigates the elements by the assistance of the waves, which he can neither raise nor still. And even if we suppose him able (at some future day) to control the course of these, it can only be by studying their characters, — by learning more thoroughly the already subsisting laws of air, heat, and moisture. He cannot give the minutest portion of the atmosphere new relations, a new course of expansion, new laws of motion.

But the Divine operations, on the contrary, include something much higher. They take in the *establishment* of the laws of the elements as well as the combination of those laws, and the determination of the distribution and quantity of the materials upon which they shall produce their effect. We conceive that the Supreme Power has ordained that the air shall be rarefied by heat, and water turned into vapour by it, — no less than that He has combined air and water so as to sprinkle the earth with showers; and determined the quantity of air, and heat, and moisture, so that the showers shall be as beneficial as they are.

And this leads us to a view of some of the *attributes* of God, as they are called, the habitual properties (if I may so speak) of his nature. In all our investigations throughout nature, we find traces of one governing and guiding mind. That mind shows an intimate acquaintance with the materials of every kind with which it has to work, so as to know in what way it may be applied to every conceivable purpose; not only that, but as actually impressing upon matter its properties, it shows a knowledge of all conceivable properties with which it can be impressed. Now of this knowledge we find no limit. Wherever nature is, there is that knowledge; and, therefore, we conclude that God's knowledge is unlimited, — that He is *omniscient*.

So again, we find not only knowledge of all the possible resources of creation, but the most exquisite skill in the use of those resources, in the adaptation of them to the end intended to be answered. Instances of this skill are furnished in abundance in the *Natural Theology* of Paley, and in the *Bridgewater Treatises*, particularly those of Whewell, Kidd and Roget. New skill in the adaptation of means to ends, and in the discernment of the ends to be aimed at, is what we call *wisdom*: and that wisdom we can trace every where; in the smallest insect, imperceptible to the naked eye, and in the arrangements of the vast system of worlds, of which we are a minute portion. We conclude, therefore, that the Being of whose skill we can find no limit, must be possessed of *infinite wisdom*.

So again the utmost knowledge and the most unlimited wisdom would be unavailing, were there not a *power* of using nature and applying it to the ends intended; were there not, in short, an unlimited command of the resources of the universe; and even were there not a power of augmenting these resources at pleasure. But, so far as our observation reaches, we find no limit to the power of God. We find Him not only having an unlimited command of the resources of nature already existing, but even impressing laws and properties upon nature. We conclude, therefore, that his power is unlimited, that he is *omnipotent*.

The idea, however, of these properties as pertaining to Deity was not left to be obtained by the results of modern inquiry. So sensibly is it impressed upon creation, that the ancient Greeks of every theistic school attributed those qualities, or at least the attributes of omniscience and omnipotence to the gods in general; not however as supposing that each of them independently possessed these attributes; but that they pertained to their nature, and were possessed by them as a society. (See Chap.II.)

CHAPTER IX
That God is a Spirit, That He is
the Author of the Existence of Matter

We have hitherto contemplated God as the former and fashioner of matter, as impressing laws upon it, and using and adapting it in every way to his purposes; but we have not distinctly considered Him as the Author of the existence of every thing. The question then arises, is God the Author of that matter which He has so wrought and fashioned? And that leads to another question, viz. What is He in Himself? Is his nature different from that matter upon which He has wrought?

Before we answer these questions, let us recall to our remembrance what we mean by matter, and let us consider what evidence we have that there is something besides matter. Matter, then, is that which has length, breadth, and thickness; which can be compressed and extended; which is light and heavy; which has no power of motion in itself, and never does move (so far as we can trace) except when impelled by some other power. Now what is there besides matter? We know that we ourselves, our inward self, are something different from matter. We are conscious that we perceive, and reflect, and reason, — that we invent, and contrive, and discover, — that we feel hope and fear, desire and aversion, joy and grief. We have abundant proof that some of the creatures around us possess some of these qualities (for example, the dog, elephant, bee, and ant); and that other portions of nature (as plants and minerals) possess no such qualities. We know that the thinking portion cannot be seen or heard; that it is not capable of being measured or weighed; it has no length, breadth, thickness, or gravity. It may be connected with substances which possess these qualities; but it is itself distinct from them, and appears capable of acting without them. Here, then, is another existence besides matter; and that existence, that substance, we call *spirit*. We know, further, that our spirit animates, and impels, and guides the matter of which our body is composed; that something similar happens even to brute animals; and that when the spirit is separated from the body by death, the matter of the body can no longer move. We know that spirit can move the body and matter in general, and modify and change them by its own will and art; but that if body does act on spirit, it is not by its own will and act, but in such a manner as to show that when a portion of matter acts upon any individual mind, it is only under the influence of general laws, impressed upon matter itself by some unseen controlling intelligence. We have, moreover, strong evidence in the case of dreams, that the mind is capable of being very active, when the body is reduced as nearly as possible to a state of inactivity.

Moreover we have evidence, that the Creator does resemble the intellectual part of ourselves, in the contrivance visible throughout nature, which is analogous to the operations of our own minds; and in the fact, that (like our own minds) He operates upon matter without making Himself visible to the bodily senses: and we have no evidence whatever that He is, like ourselves, compound; *i.e.* composed of matter and spirit. We therefore conclude that God is, in his nature, a pure spirit.

Some writers, as Lord Brougham (in his *Discourse upon Natural Theology*, Part I § 4) and Mr.Crabbe (Part I. ch.v. § 2), have entered into the question, whether we can prove the existence of the supreme spirit without premising the human mind to be spirit: and others, as Locke (Book IV. ch.iii. § 6), followed by Crabbe, whether it is necessary to assert the absolute spirituality of the human mind. These writers assert, and no doubt justly in a certain sense, that we should be limiting the omnipotence of the Creator, if we denied his power to communicate to matter the power of thought. But, after all, what do we know of matter, except by its properties? No one has shown better than Locke, that general terms do not represent actual essences, but only aggregation of qualities. And so, with regard to *spirit*, it is merely a general term to describe a distinct aggregation of qualities. To assert, therefore, that matter may have the properties of spirit, is strictly a contradiction in terms. We know nothing of either except by their qualities. We believe intuitively that these qualities are attached to individual beings, and that the individual man is more closely connected with the spiritual qualities than with the material. This belief on our part is altogether involuntary. (See Brougham, Note 4.)

And with regard to the question, whether we could prove the existence of a supreme spirit without premising the human mind to be spirit, the case is simply this: — We discern many effects produced throughout nature by causes, or by one cause, similar in operations to our own minds; and we conclude, upon further examination, that all these effects originate in one Being. We therefore conclude, that there is one Supreme Being, the Author of all nature, whose mode of operation and whose qualities resemble those of our own minds. It is, therefore, certain, that it was *in point of fact*, by analogy from the operations of our own minds, that the First Cause was at first concluded to be intellectual. And even Crabbe, who contends that we are sure (previously to all inquiry as to the precise nature of our own minds) that a supreme intelligence alone could have caused the phenomena of nature, says, "In calling that cause spirit, we give a name to something above matter, and distinct from matter;" and subjoins, "It is not necessary that we should know any thing positive of the nature of that cause, but that it *contrives*." This, however, is one of the very points of resemblance to the human mind, from which, from the time of Socrates downward, men have argued that the First Cause is of the nature of mind: nor can it be shown that they would ever have had any notion at all of a First Cause, as different from matter, except by analogy from qualities possessed by the human mind, which show it to be "above matter and wholly distinct from matter." It is true that we, having already this notion, can view it apart from ourselves, and argue respecting matter and its Author, without reference to ourselves; but that is only because we have an habitual notion of spirit and matter, and are not constrained to be constantly referring to the source from which we derived this notion.

There remains the question, Whether He who fashioned and arranged all matter into its present shape, was the Author of matter itself.

To this inquiry Natural Theology cannot return so distinct and positive an answer, as to our former inquiries. We know nothing of matter, in the abstract, as a real existence. We know not whether there is one substance, out of which all material substances are made. All we know of matter is in the individual substances we find subsisting, and the elements into which chemistry has resolved them. But those elements are still so many, that we can form no conclusion whatever, whether there is or is not one substance, out of which they are all made. All the evidence, therefore, which we possess for the existence of any of them, rests in the qualities they exhibit; in the powers they possess of acting upon other substances or beings, or being acted upon by them. The feeling of the Platonic school upon this point was so strong, that they actually denominated the various bodily substances by the name of *poiotetes*, which in Latin is *qualitater*, the word from which our word *quality* is derived. (Cic.*Quaest. Acad.* I.6.)

Now all these qualities, of whatever kind, are means prepared to accomplish given ends, or at least adapted so as to produce them. Wherefore the whole of the evidence we have for the existence of matter, resolves itself into the evidence of design or adaptation throughout all material substances;

and all these, as such, must necessarily have sprung from the mind of that great Being, who designed and adapted them. The result then is, that all the phenomena of matter, every mode in which matter makes itself known to us, owes its existence to Him; that in this sense He is the Author of matter, as being the Author of all its phenomena. And thence it is a fair conclusion, that, if any such universal substance exists, it likewise must owe its origin to Him.

This, however, is a conclusion which none of the ancient philosophers reached. Some of them, as the Platonists (Cic. *Qu. Ac.* I.6), thought it impossible that a spirit should exist without a body to operate with; and thence concluded that matter is the body of the soul of the world; and all without exception regarded matter as equally eternal with its great fashioner and governor. They maintained it as an indubitable truth, that it is impossible to bring any thing into existence out of nothing.

The conclusion at which we have arrived, however, still more clearly follows, from a consideration of the origin of our own being.

We have seen that there must have been a time when the first human being or beings began to exist; and, therefore, there must have been a time beyond which we cannot trace the existence of a single human spirit. Indeed we have no evidence whatever for the existence of the mind of any one of us, beyond the time when we were born into the world. There is indeed a probability, from the resemblance in character, as well as in person, between parents and ancestors, and their children or descendants, that the mind of the child is in some inconceivable manner derived from the parent, as we know the body is. But there is no proof that this is the case; and the phenomena may be accounted for by supposing that the bodily constitution is capable of moulding the mind to such and such a character. At all events we have not the slightest evidence, that a single human spirit existed in any form or mode of existence before the formation of the first man; and if any such did exist, as its powers and faculties are of the same nature as those which subsist in God Himself, it must either have owed its existence to Him (as Socrates and his followers concluded it did), or have been itself eternal, *i.e.* self-existent, which is the very idea we have of God Himself. Moreover, the very circumstance that every human spirit which ever existed was, by its union with a material body, subject to God, completely negatives the idea that any human spirit can be self-existent. It therefore follows that every human spirit derives its origin from Him.

If, therefore, every human spirit must have its origin from God, it appears to follow, that as all material substance is acted upon by spirit, and is consequently inferior to it, matter likewise must derive its origin from Him.

Section Four

WILLIAM LYALL
(1811-1890)

4

Rationality and Intuition in William Lyall's Philosophical Method

Peter Smale

Introduction

"William Lyall, or to give him his full style and title, Professor the Reverend William Lyall, Doctor of Laws, Fellow of the Royal Society of Canada, was born on the 11th of June, near Paisley, about ten miles more or less southwest of Glasgow."[1] For a time after graduation from college, he was a pastor in Scotland and then he emigrated to Canada to become tutor at Knox College, Toronto, in 1848. "In 1850 he was appointed professor of Classics and Mental Philosophy, 'to give instruction in the ordinary subjects of the Arts course,' at the Free Church College. . . Halifax. . .. Lyall taught Latin, Greek, Logic, Rhetoric, Moral and Mental Philosophy and Mathematics. He was, in fact, the whole Faculty of Arts (*Gazette*, 20 December 1893, 136)."[2] At thirty-nine, Lyall was still possessed of considerable energy and maintained this schedule for ten years, during which he wrote and published his major text, *Intellect, the Emotions and the Moral Nature*. It is interesting that although he taught for nearly thirty-five years longer this was his only large philosophical work. "The work. . .' was favourably noticed by the reviewers at that time (Rose, 233)'. It was to serve as a textbook in his classes for many years to come and was also used for the same purpose 'in several other colleges.' (*Gazette*, 30 January, 1890) . . .. Lyall was a man of simple, transparent goodness: kind, gentle, genial, generous, patient, 'not easily ruffled and easily pacified.' (*Morning Herald*, 20 January 1890). . .. He was a man who not only praised, loved and preached goodness, but lived it."[3] We might ask why Lyall's book is not, to this day, a staple of philosophy in Canada? According to Professor F.Hilton Page's examination, it is mostly Lyall's style that discourages us from reading his 600 page text:

Lyall's book is very much a period-piece. I do not say this to belittle it as I am myself rather partial to period-pieces, especially those of Lyall's own period. . . anyone reading Lyall's book now has to be aware of the conventions and attitudes of the time; otherwise his attention will be distracted from the matter to the manner of writing. . . There was a time when almost every Scottish professor of philosophy published his lectures. Volumes of lctures were almost as popular as volumes of sermons. To understand Lyall it is necessary to understand the peculiarities of the Scottish philosophy lecture of this period, on which his own lectures were, if unconsciously, stylistically modelled. . .. [For Lyall,] . . . eloquent passages; taste, culture, moral and spiritual elevation. . . [were important].[4]

Lyall as a Rational Metaphysician

Most philosophers of the time were committed to taking the tenets of "rationalist philosophy" seriously. Lyall believed that reality was absolutely "rational," that "the" explanation for all that happens in the world and beyond can be found. Such confidence does not appeal to most of us in the 1980s — we think that such a view is naive. Perhaps it was not for Lyall's time, but even in 1850 Lyall was aware that there was a philosophical leap-of-faith necessary to go from the ability to think rationally to a rational world and the personal ethical requirements to follow this belief.

Lyall's text title, *Intellect, the Emotions and the Moral Nature*, expresses the sequence of his reasoning. *First* he is fully committed to the demands of rational reality; that is, when it is all said and done, reality is rational and if we attempt to deny that we must suffer the consequences of our ignorance — chaos. *Secondly*, he realizes, as a matter of fact, that we are emotional creatures, and reference to his biography shows without doubt that he does not see himself above others in understanding and "wisdom" — he, too, is emotional. *Thirdly*, he recognizes that until we have reconciled the emotions, which are first in importance to us, with the absolute demands of reality, it is impossible for us to *be* moral. There would be no *reason* to be so. This all sounds very plausible and, of course, Lyall is a common-sense philosopher of the Scottish bent. We cannot discuss here important figures in common-sense philosophy, like Thomas Reid, other than to assert that they were, in a sense, anti-intellectual — their primary assumptions were based on ordinary experience. For example, most believe that experience is of a regulated, external world, not of changing imaginations. Therefore, no proof of the external world seems necessary. Fortunately, Lyall presents arguments for the details of his position, while at the same time making the most of good "sense." Belief in *The World* is justified by being well thought out by us. Essentially, he sees moral feelings (a compulsion in important cases to do the right thing) as the drive for right actions and results. Ultimately, right action is justified by reason. According to Lyall's reading of the Augustinian philosophy, the "love of Being" is founded in the intuitive grasp of our fulfilling place within God's creation.

Outline Of Lyall's Philosophy

Experience and Reality: for Lyall, the basic principles of philosophical reasoning, for both the common-sensical and the metaphysical are evident. What is not clear, and what is of interest to him, is how emotion predominates in motivation and action and can lead to constructive or destrcutive behaviour. In the first steps of his analysis, he makes assumptions about the process of reasoning which give away a Christian optimism and affirm rejection of extreme skepticism.

> The idea of *existence*, of course, is a simpler idea than that of *personal* existence, but we do not seem to obtain the one without the other. The idea of *existence* comes with that of *personal existence*.[5]

Thus, Lyall undercuts the Cartesian skeptic. Lyall does not prove *an* existence (his own subjective thought processes) but affirms the relation of consciousness *to* existence.

> Every feeling of internal consciousness would be referred to self, as belonging to self, to the "me." By and by, however, feelings of a *peculiar kind* would be experienced. The senses would not only convey sensations to this internal Being -but sensations so modified as at last to awaken the idea of *something distinct from self*, something that was *not self* — and hence the idea of *externality*.[6]

We must not be misled by philosophers who use a logic which gives an exclusive ontological status to personal consciousness, for it is obvious to Lyall that we can definitely distinguish personal sensations from those with an external source. He argues, however, however, for an absolute distinction between the *experience of ideas* of the world and the "causal" relation between the mind and brain, which we believe makes these ideas possible. This is a clear experiential distinction used by Lyall to defend the mystery of the relation of mind and external matter.

> God has so willed it, and we can and need go no further. Matter communicates with mind, and mind with matter by a law, or after a mode, of which we can give no account.[7]

Lyall's claim is coherent enough if we stick strictly to the content of experience; his faith is that this world is an ordered one despite some notable appearances to the contrary.[8]

Although he is a thoroughly committed rationalist, it is important, for an appreciation of his honesty of observation, to note that Lyall seriously considers the role of feeling and emotion in the human processes of thought and action. This proves to be the key to moral behaviour and the faithful *commitment* to rationality, both of which justify the above epistemological and ontological clarification.

Coherence and Self-Identity

Rational "deliberate" consciousness is the basis of knowledge of self-identity and its place in rational order.

> The *identity of the soul* is owing to its immateriality, while, again, its immateriality may be inferred from *the feeling of identity.*[9]

Of course, all he can really claim here is that there must be coherence for there to be extended thought. The total personal coherence, Lyall, assumes, is unproved.

> But to deny identity to self, whether to our organic or our thinking self, is to put an end to dicussion by making it useless to discuss. What is it to any one how any question is settled, if he is not, or if he does not know, that he is the same person, the same conscious being that he was twenty years ago, or even an hour ago? Could any seriously call this in question?[10]

Fortunatley, Lyall softens the seemingly naive commitment to a continuing, conscious self by noting that he does not deny obvious changes in the organic person or personality. The core of the individual is to be discovered in the spiritual aspect of the mind which is unchanging according to traditional Christian doctrine on the nature of the soul.

Lyall is preparing the way for an enthusiastic acceptance of the role of feeling and emotion in human nature and its action. Essentially, man's design is a rational one, and the best emotions truly serve this design, in the desire to love "Being."

The Role Of Emotion in Human Nature

Unfortunately, Lyall does not make a clear, conceptual distinction between feeling and emotion, necessary to demonstrate the connection of emotions and rationality. This distinction is prevalent in current discussion and is helpful in realizing that emotion *concepts* cannot simply refer to explicit feeling states. (There are many emotions and a fairly limited range of felt responses.) "Emotion" concepts and the states that precipitate their use are as much evaluative as descriptive in nature.

Strong feelings can result in emotional responses and evaluations, but, as well, human situations can result in emotional "interpretations" which then cause the felt response. Lyall initially argues that we "fell" (a type of intuition) the significance of all our emotional responses. This cannot be the case with highly developed moral emotions; nevertheless, Lyall does make an important point about the natural tendency that man has to be emotional and that this is the impetus to rational behaviout. It seems unlikely that basic emotional (felt) intuitions direct our behaviour in complex (moral) situations.

For example, Lyall relies heavily on an intuitive appreciation of the emotion of love which to a secular mind often demands complex analysis. However, the appeal to direct comprehension of love (of Being) is needed in a system where intuitions about the inherent rationality of things must be strong as a compensation for limited argumentation. In all fairness to Lyall, the assumption of rationality in this systematic philosophy is not any greater than any other wholistic or absolutistic metaphysical philosophy. And Lyall never claims to prove this traditional philosophical goal. He claims to discover it within his ordinary experience. I believe he makes as strong a case for his practical conclusions for this very reason not only by generalizing our understanding of emotions, but by distinguishing key instances of human emotional response which tend to make it possible for specific (and positive) human actions. He has seen the problem of a strictly rationalist assessment of the worth of human feeling. In Plato, for example, the emotions must always be subservient to reason which is the final arbiter in decisions about actions. For Lyall, without emotion as a general disposition, there would be no moral action and, at the same time, these emotions nurture our tendency to be rational.

Lyall's claims that emotions are somewhere between thought and feeling is descriptively helpful in establishing the relation between thought and feeling but it must be elaborated further.

> There is a region of feeling in the mind, or the same spiritual substance which thinks can feel, which exhibits the phenomenon of intellection, exhibits the phenomenon of emotion. It is the same spiritual substance in all, but now it thinks, and now it feels, —now it is an intellectual, and now it proves itself an emotional nature; and it may be both at once, while sensationalist impressions of pain or pleasure may be racking or transporting it. And here we take no account of the strictly moral or spiritual departments than either the sensational or intellectual, or purely emotional. Of all is man composed, but we have now to do with the strictly emotional. We view man as capable of emotion — *mental feeling* it may be termed.[11]

"Feelings" are the motivators of human action.[12] And a person devoid of "feelings" is incapable of personally committed action.

> Emotion is a higher state than pure intellect; not this or that emotion, but the region or susceptibility of emotion. . .
> It is his emotions that make any one person interesting to another. These are life and life giving, and ideas are important only as the minister to these.[13]

Lyall distinguishes carefully between emotion, in its purest state, and the elements of emotion: desire, affection and passion. Strictly speaking:

> an emotion is. . . any feeling of the mind suddenly inspried or produced; it is the feeling either in its first and sudden excitement, or the same feeling considered in relation to that first or sudden impulse or excitement.[14]

> Emotion is generic; Passion is specific. The passions are not the emotions, but the emotions include the passions.[15]

Thus, basic emotion is a general state of attunement or the tendency to respond spontaneously with desire or aversion. "Desire is an essentially peculiar state of mind, and the different desires are the same feeling only directed to, or set upon, different objects; whereas every [explicit] emotion is distinct from every other."[16] An extended emotional response, such as being in love, becomes an affection with continuing influence.[17] "The first essential condition of emotion would seem to be one of calm and placid enjoyment. That might be taken as the first essential state of emotion."[18] But situations demonstrate that emotions are often in conflict with reasonableness. We are reminded again of Plato's reservations about emotional responses in the "just" personality.

> The phenomenon of man's present emotional nature therefore cannot be regarded without attention to the moral derangement which prevails, and which must affect more or less all the emotions and feelings.[19]

Lyall's task, then, is to emphasize those emotions which are partners and instigators in rational moral behaviour. These are spontaneous dispositions to action, non-rational when contrasted with the description of moral dispositions or in a spiritual sense, supra-rational. In the final analysis, his commitment to love as the penultimate emotion is spiritual in nature.

> *Love* accordingly, is an emotion which has more directly for its object our fellows of the same species, after that great Being who gave to ourselves being, and whom it is our first duty at once supremely to love, and reverently to adore.[20]

This part of his analysis avoids a problematic identification of each emotional response with a specific feeling. Rather, I believe he wishes to say that specific emotions and the actions taken on these "emotions" are the result of the refinement of the more generalized tendency to see or intuit the value of Being in an ultimately rational world. His expression of this is mostly religious, but in many respects Lyall's common sense scheme makes a general concern with Being more comprehensible than detailed "metaphysical" accounts. Perhaps Lyall's analysis should have moved from his experiential-ontological commitments to the specifics of emotional responses and *their* appropriate rationales. This would have been the place to develop specific moral standards; however, for reasons of his place in the history of rationalist philosophy, it seemed evident to him that the strongest and most fundamental emotional response is to an underlying ontological order. For a modern perspective Lyall too quickly sought an absolute satisfaction from "love" as the ultimate justification for rational behaviour.

The love of the race will be restored, and it exists in some degree in every renewed heart. The gospel is the true regenerator of our species; for it is its object to implant anew that principle of universal love, which is consistent only with a state of **unfallen innocence**.[21]

We are to love our neighbour as ourselves; as we love ourselves, so we should love others, — not in equal degree, but *because we love ourselves,* and *others are the counterparts, as it were of ourselves.*[22]

And yet as a rationalist, he fears that emotions can be dangerous because they are forces ideally directed to Being, but not, in themselves, predictable. We may be led by them into choices of evil.

It is thus that *love* and *hatred* are distinguished. *Being* is indeed the proper object of love, and we love being *absolutely*. It must be allowed, therefore, that the absolute emotion, love, or love in its absolute state, has not *directly good* for its object, but *still has its object in good. . Being* is *good*; we invest being in itself with an attribute of good.[23]

Conclusions

For some Lyall's common sense philosophy will be no more than a cover for a vast number of rationalist assumptions. He assumes that the human personality has a basic core of rational coherence. He assumes that the original or primary emotions are life affirming and he assumes that man is free to understand and pursue rational moral goals. In fairness to him his common sense solutions to fundamental philosophical problems do sometimes undercut serious problems in historically important philosophical theories. For example, he realizes that the rationl nature of man must not be treated in separation from his physical, worldly and emotional capacities. He sees emotion as the key motivator of human action. His insights in the area contribute much to the idea of a (moral) "good will." However, his full analysis never fails in its enthusiasm for a rational universe and though his system is coherent, it seems a bit too easy and confident at times. Certainly he is not fully aware, to say the least, of many of the conceptual problems that beset contemporary philosophers who work with the concepts of "individuality," "externality," "emotion" and "freedom." However, as we have shown he makes a valuable clarification in the case of emotion. By introducing an ontological component in his fundamental analysis of the experience of emotion, he brings together the rational and the felt componenets of human consciousness more effectively than have other philosophers. He is wrong, as we have said, to identify each emotion with a specific feeling but he is not wrong, I believe, to assign a hierarchy of emotional responses. There is, it seems, a fundamental emotional disposition which inspires all others. Without the encompassing emotion of love of Being (and it is clear for Lyall that this is not a mere physical desire or enthusiasm), the individual is condemned ultimatley to an amoral or disinterested existence. Lyall is equally committed to the tenets of rationalist philosophy and to elements of spontaneous response to Being that he argues are necessary for a morally fruitful existence. From the perspective of the individual, spontaneous creative action comes first; this is obvious to Lyall's intuitive nature, but the indivicual creativity possible for man is dependent on the rationality that underlies the workings of the universe.

It is Lyall's purpose in his book to emphasize the personal elements of philosophy, and he is a delightfully optimistic man, but a close reading of his text shows that the demands of coherent philosophical reasoning are not ignored even, if at times, they are not given sufficient, detailed attention. He does not prove his position but it is ingenious and his philosophical points are very often far from implausible.

The following selections from Lyall's text deal with his epistemology, philosophy of mind, categories of experiential explanation and his metaphysical intuitions of the "love of Being." For the student of philosophy and, in particular, the student of Lyall's period of philosophy of science and its connections with theology, these selections should give a comprehensive understanding of his thought.

Notes

1. F.Hilton Page, *William Lyall in His Setting*, Dalhousie Review, 60 (Halifax, Dalhousie University, 1980), p.51. The following background material comes from the above article published by Dr.Page which establishes Lyall's book, *Intellect, The Emotions and the Moral Nature* as the first major work of philosophy produced in the Maritime of Canada. Dr.Page's thorough research of Lyall's life and philosophy, and his generous support of my work in Canadian philosophy has influenced these pages more than I can properly express.
2. *Ibid.*, p.52. (*Dalhousie Gazette*, Halifax, referred to as *Gazette* in text).
3. *Ibid.*, p.53 and p.58. G.M.Rose, *A Cyclopedia of Canadian Biography*, Toronto, 1888.
4. *Ibid.*, pp.59-61.
5. William Lyall, *Intellect, The Emotions and the Moral Nature* (Edinburgh, Thomas Constable and Co., MDCCCIV), p.17.
6. *Ibid.*, p.19
7. *ibid.*, pp.27-28.
8. See Lyall's text p.92 for further discussion of the difficulty of deciding the nature of material reality through rational analyses.
9. *Ibid.*, p.127.
10. 11. *Ibid.*,p.282.
12. *Ibid.*,p.286.
13. *Ibid.*,p.284-285.
14. *Ibid.*,p.286.
15. *Ibid.*,p.287.
16. *Ibid.*,p.287.
17. *Ibid.*,p.286.
18. *Ibid.*,p.291.
19. *Ibid.*,p.292.
20. *Ibid.*,p.391.
21. *Ibid.*,p.398.
22. *Ibid.*,p.557.
23. *Ibid.*,p.421

Intellect, The Emotions and the Moral Nature

William Lyall

The Self

[18]The mind thus awakened, the idea of its own personality, or of personal existence, once obtained, the mind would probably for a time be occupied with this idea: — it would not be immediately let go, and every subsequent feeling or impression would be referred to *this personality — this personal self.* *It* would now be the centre of reference — whether in the case of external or internal impressions — impressions from without or[19] impressions from within. All would be judged of from this point of reference — this stand-point of the German philosophy. Every feeling of internal consciousness would be referred to self, to the "me." By and by, however, feelings of a *peculiar kind* would be experienced. The senses would not only convey sensations to this internal Being — but sensations *so modified* as at last to awaken the idea of *something distinct from self*, something that was *not self* — and hence the idea of *externality.* The *in*ternal feelings were now such that the idea of something external is awakened; The mind receives the idea or impression of externality. It is impossible, perhaps, to trace minutely how this idea is awakened, but that it is awakened at a very early stage of Being is undoubted. At least, of *the idea* of an external world, not all the efforts of philosophers could deprive us; although they might endeavour to rob us of an external world itself, and have accordingly attempted to reason us into the persuasion that there is no such thing. This was the gigantic, we should rather say Quixotic, effort of Berkeley and Hume; and it is what most of the German philosophers of the present, and recent times, although by a different process, not only essay, but, as it seems to themselves, triumphantly accomplish. They arrive at the conclusion, they think, by the most absolute demonstration. So did Berkeley, so did

*First published by Thomas Constable, Edinburgh; Hamilton Adams, London, 1855. Selections by Peter Smale. Original page numbers are reproduced in the text in square brackets.

Hume, granting them their premises. But with so much of truth in their reasoning — starting with a right principle, they erred in not admitting what was equally a principle, and should have been recognised, — viz., that authority is due to all the depositions of consciousness; and that though consciousness is strictly the court of appeal in all our questions, and *mind* is therefore ultimate in the judgment, or in the question, we are not warranted to reject any plain intimation of consciousness; while mind may undoubtedly testify of what is diverse from itself, as well as of what is itself, or of its own nature, if God has so connected the two as to act and react upon each other. Consciousness is a simple feeling, and its testimony to self, or to a being in which that consciousness resides, is no more direct than its testimony to what is not[20] self: the feeling in either case is but a feeling, and the ground of a conviction. The question as to the existence of an external world depends altogether upon the constitution of that mind which, as being ultimate in the question, is thought to deny the existence of an external world, or at least to render it impossible that we can ever attain to the knowledge of its existence. The full discussion of this point, however, does not belong to this stage of our inquiry.

The idea of something external to *self*, then, has been awakened. The exact process of this we have not stated. That this idea should arise, however, very soon after the idea of self, it is natural to suppose. The very consciousness that would awaken the one idea, would negatively testify of the other. The feeling of *self* would testify of what was *not self*. The positive supposes the negative. If there were feelings or impressions which awaken the idea of self, every other would of course be referred to something *else, and hence something external*. It must have been by the simplest process possible that the idea of something different from self, something not self, something *external*, arose. *Externality* was next in order, or process of time, to *personality*. They were co-relatives — that is, if there *was* anything distinct from, and external to self. And the idea of an *external world* being one of our ideas or impressions, as much as that of self, or of our personal existence, it must have been something distinct from, and external to self, that awakened it. Everything pertaining to self would, by an unerring consciousness, be referred to it; and whatever did not pertain to it would be excluded, or would by an unerring alchemy be rejected, and consequently referred to something else. Self being the centre of reference, everything that did not crystallize with it, or belong to it, would fall off....

[21]So early is the idea of an external world — *that idea disputed by philosophers* — attained. There is a time when the infant seems to lie passive, taking in its lessons, receiving perhaps those very ideas which we do our utmost to trace; but soon the notion of an external world seems to be gained: the little philosopher has first been strengthened in the idea of its own existence: it has come to be a believer in its own existence, for it has felt its own wants: it is not long till an external world, too, dawns upon it, and now it can look with understanding when before it only looked with mystery, and its gaze is not only with a half intelligent smile, but with intelligence beaming

from every feature, expressive of anger or joy, gratification or disappointment, aversion or love. It is now a denizen of this world, for it has recognised it: it has been made free of it: it is now one of ourselves, and it is left to learn its other lessons as it best may, having learned this much, that there is a world upon which it has been ushered, and whose fights and conflicts it must, in common with its elder fellow-combatants, sustain....

[29]The idea of *externality* is not yet that of an external world. There is much that goes to make up the latter idea that is not in the former. We derive the former from an interruption to a wonted series of feelings which are referable to self, or to a state of simply self-consciousness — the new feeling being something altogether different from any which had either hitherto been referred to self, or could be referred to self as its origin: it is therefore attributed to something else. Whether it be, according to Dr. Brown, a feeling of resistance to *muscular action* — or it be some feeling among the many which the [30]external world may awaken in the inner self-conscious Being, it at once leads the mind to an external object as its cause, — and this by an original law of the mind, which is infallible. We have already seen that if there was not such a law, the new feeling, however peculiar, would still be but a feeling of the mind itself, and would never lead to anything without as its cause. It must be by an intuitive process that the mind passes from a state of consciousness to the certain conviction of an external world — or just from an inner consciousness to an external cause. No *mere difference of feeling* would awaken or justify such a reference. It is by an intuitive law of the mind that that reference is made, as much as when we conclude that an effect must have a cause, or when we refer an object possessing certain properties, or exhibiting certain characteristics, to a class to which it belongs. The law or constitution of our minds leads to the reference or conclusion in both cases.

Externality, however, as we have said, is not an *external world*. The idea of externality, however, having been obtained, other ideas follow, which, combining with that of externality, make up the idea of an external world. All the senses of the child are open to impressions from without. The eye takes in the colours of the landscape — the ear the sounds which salute it — the smell the fragrance of the fields — the touch the texture, the hardness or softness, of bodies, while the taste is regaled by the sweets which are offered to its palate, or offended by the nauseous potion which affection administers for its benefit. Here are plenty of intimations, impressions or sensations, all coming from an external world. But the child is *philosophic* in its procedure, or rather the mind does not operate but according to its own laws. Colours, sounds, taste, smell, might all affect the several senses, and not one idea, or the faintest intimation of *matter* would be created, or conveyed to the inner thinking being. It is perhaps impossible to determine whether the idea of *externality* might not be excited. According to Dr. Brown, it is resistance to muscular action which excites this idea — first awakens it: but this it may be impossible [31]positively to determine. There is certainly a greater arrest given to the mind by a feeling of resistance to muscular action, or by the interruption of a

series of muscular feelings than can be conceived in any other way; but still it is no more than an interruption of a series of feelings — it is no more than a feeling of resistance, — as a feeling of colour is one of colour, or sound is one of sound. There can be no doubt, however, that we owe the first idea of *matter* to the sense of *touch*, and that none of the other senses could ever have awakened it. With the sense of taste the sense of touch is combined, so that we must separate what is peculiar to the one from what is peculiar to the other. With the sense of sight, however, with that of smell, with that of hearing, we can have no difficulty: it is obvious that from none of these — nor from all of them combined — could we obtain *the idea of matter*. With respect to the sense of seeing, for example, it can be demonstrated, and has been demonstrated, by writers upon this subject, that light or colour is the only proper object of that sense. The eye is really affected by nothing but light or colour. This is at first very startling, and can hardly be believed — in opposition to all the varied solicitations that now affect, or seem to affect, the eye from without, the varied qualities or objects of which it seems *now* to be the organ of perception. Yet startling as this may be at first, it has been demonstrably proved by Bishop Berkeley in his Theory of Vision, and has been a settled point in philosophy ever since. *Magnitude, figure, distance* — which seem to be objects of sight — *to be seen* — it has conclusively shewn, are acquired by the *sense of touch*, and are now, apart from the operation of that sense, mere *inferences of the mind* in connexion with certain states of the visual organ....
[34]The first idea of *matter* would be that of something *tangible* — something that could be *touched* — external to *self*. A greater or lesser degree of hardness or tactual, *not muscular* resistance would be implied in the idea. We oppose tactual to muscular resistance, [35]the latter being more violent, the former being the mere resistance which matter, in a more or less solid state, offers to the touch. Dr. Brown was the first, we believe, who took notice of muscular resistance as a distinct kind of sensation, different from mere tactual sensation. But there is a certain amount of resistance in every tactual sensation, even when it is a fluid body that is met or encountered. In physical philosophy, there is such a doctrine as the *impenetrability* of matter, that is, matter may be displaced but cannot be *penetrated*. Matter is composed of infinitely small particles — we can set no limits, by our understanding at least, to the divisibility of matter, to the minuteness of the particles of which it is composed. Each of these, then, may be displaced, but cannot be penetrated. When we pierce a solid body, we only set aside, or remove from their former place, its constituent particles, but each several particle is unpenetrated, and remains in all its integrity. Even in fluid bodies, then, there is resistance. Matter, then, as first apprehended by the mind, would be something that offered a resistance, however faint, to the touch. By and by, hardness and softness would be distinguished, solidity and fluidity — and these several ideas would be acquired by the mind. Matter would be something that was hard or soft, solid or fluid. Hardness and softness, solidity and fluidity, would be *properties* of *matter*. *And here the idea of substance would arise*. It would be

to the mind that in which those qualities of which the mind had obtained the idea, or an intimation however faint, inhered. *The mind obtains the idea of them as qualities*; but qualities imply a *substratum*. The substratum would be the substance, the qualities being no more than *qualities*: *matter would be that which possessed, or was the subject of, the qualities already named*. In like manner, the qualities of mind would be referred to some substance or being in which they inhered, some spiritual substance or essence of which they were only the *qualities*. In this case the idea of the Being, although not apprehended as *mind* — for it is not so apprehended till it is distinguished from *matter* — the idea of this Being — [36]the self, the inner self — would be first, and the idea of the qualities would be after. But it would be at this time, probably, that the ideas of *substance* and *quality* would be obtained, discriminated; and the mind and its qualities would be seen to be distinct — the mind the substance — the qualities the properties of that substance. So simultaneously, and yet in so orderly a manner, would the mind's ideas arise. We can but give a conjectural view of that order. It is impossible with positive certainty to determine the exact order, in point of time, of the mind's ideas. But it is probable that it was as we have traced it. It is well that no question of importance depends upon the precise order in which our ideas arose, or our knowledge of that order, — that no valuable or vital decision is risked by the nicer distinctions of metaphysics. It is interesting, however, as well as useful, to trace, as far as possible, the development of mind — of that inner-thinking Being, which, in truth, constitutes the whole of ourselves. . . . To determine the limits of mind and matter, and to mark their entire and essential difference, and yet, in our present state, their mutual dependence, is what is [37]necessary, the very desideratum, in the *philosophy* of the present day, the surest safeguard against the scepticism which would confound mind with matter, or, as in German metaphysics, resolve all into mind, nay, annihilate mind itself, and leave nothing but "the dream of a dream." We are forced to be metaphysicians whether we will or not; not if we would not be sceptics, but if we would be able to meet the sceptic. False philosophy can be met only by that which is true or sound. The materialist can be successfully refuted only by him who has examined well the separate limits of mind and matter; the idealist by him who has discriminated well the *laws* of the mind, and is in no danger, therefore, of being carried away by an absolutism, which will allow no force, and no reality, to anything which is not mere consciousness. Mind, and *the laws of the mind*, are what must be held up in the face of that infidelity which would reduce man himself to a mere *organism*, somewhat superior to a *shell-fish* — or that which would take away all certainty from our beliefs, and allow nothing to those laws of our mental constitution which demand our submission, as much as our merest consciousness, authoritative as that consciousness in reality is. Are we not conscious of these laws? *Are we conscious only of consciousness*? If *consciousness, at least,* is to be trusted, does it not depone to these laws? Nay, what is our consciousness, at any particular moment, but, as we have seen, the state of our mind at that particular moment? — and what is our consciousness when it exists in the state of a sensation, and what is it when it exists in the state of an internal feeling? There are two separate states of consciousness, pointing to two separate sources or quarters from which these states are derived, pointing to matter and to mind. The one state of consciousness informs us of matter, the other informs us of mind. Are both not to be believed? It is in vain that the materialist or idealist endeavours to escape, according to his own favourite tendency, from the beliefs of the mind — the beliefs of consciousness, or our conscious beliefs. . . .

[40]The next quality of matter that would develop itself would probably be that of *extension*. The feeling of tactual resistance would be prolonged or continued over a surface; and hence at once the idea of extension would arise, and the *quality of extension* be discerned or apprehended. The feeling of resistance would be multiplied in a continuous direction, and the idea of extension would be the result. We had first the feeling of resistance itself, producing the idea of hardness and softness, solidity and fluidity — the primary ideas, no doubt, of matter. Consequent, perhaps, upon these — the first intimations of *qualities* — or, *contemporaneously, in the very ideas* — we obtained the idea of substance, as that in which the qualities resided or inhered. This would, if not immediately, yet ultimately, lead to the distinction between mind as a substance and the qualities of mind. *Matter* as a *substance*, and *mind* as a *substance*, would both now be apprehended, and that probably, or possibly, upon *the first knowledge of qualities, or suggestion of these as qualities of a substance.* But the idea of *extension* would follow upon the possession of the idea of hardness or softness, and in connexion with the continued feeling of resistance. *This substance without* would now be perceived, or learned, to be *extended*. It would be ascertained to be *an extended substance.* The idea of *magnitude* would follow — dimension — that which was contained within the limits given to the feeling of resistance. The term *manitude* must be taken, in the sense of dimension or size; and greater or lesser magnitude would be a subsequent idea, and the result of a comparison. The idea of *figure*, again, would be awakened, and while the abstract idea of *figure* would be obtained, *matter* would be discerned to be something *figured*, as well as possessing *dimension, magnitude, extension, hardness, softness..* The idea of *matter* would now be pretty complete — those qualities which are *essential to it* being now ascertained. *Extension, figure, magnitude, hardness, softness, would now enter into the conception of matter. . . .*

[41]*Magnitude* and *figure* are obviously but modifications of *extension*, but they are distinct ideas. Magnitude is the degree of quantity of extension. Figure is extension in different directions, and in each direction considered relatively to another. A cube, for example, is equal extension in all directions — an oblong, greater extension in one direction than in another — while a circle, perhaps, may be said to be extension *continuous* in *no one* direction, and every part of which is equidistant from a common point. Now, although the mathematical definition of these figures is not part of the information acquired at this early period, there can be no doubt that the figures themselves are appreciable, and are laid hold of by the infant mind. How soon will the

ball be distinguished from the surface on which it rolls! How are the solid dimensions of the cubes, and the flat surface of the cards, which are respectively to construct its airy mansions, ascertained; while the table on which the mansion is to arise is pretty well known to be higher than itself, or the scaffolding by which it is reached. A long is soon distinguished from a short body, a high from a low, a narrow from a broad. . . .

Essential Properties of Matter

[47]We have thus, then, arrived at the essential properties of matter. These are extension, divisibility, solidity or fluidity, hardness or softness, and figure. Motion does not seem to be a property of matter: it is something communicated to it, not belonging to it. But the qualities enumerated enter into our very conception of matter. It is by these qualities that matter becomes known to us. The properties of fragrance, heat or cold, sweetness or bitterness, are not essential to matter — they do not enter into our idea of matter. We can conceive matter totally destitute of them, as indeed it often is. But matter without extension, or some degree of resistance to the touch, would be a contradiction. And there is more than our having given the name, Matter, to that which discovers itself to us by these properties which, according to Dr. Brown, seems to be the amount of a quality or qualities being primary, or essential to matter: they are so, according to him, because we have called that matter which possesses these qualities. If we had given the name of matter to that which excited the sensation of colour, of fragrance, of heat or cold, of sound — these, according to Dr. Brown, would have been the primary qualities of matter. But these must first have been capable of intimating the existence of matter to us, which they are not. They do not seem to be capable of intimating even anything external to us. It is not to them that we have traced either the idea of externality, or that of matter as a substance without us. Besides, they are fluctuating, varying qualities. They may be possessed, or they may not. They are possessed by some bodies — they are not by others. To give the name of *matter*, then, to them, would be but to assign another name to qualities, or rather to sensations, for they could not themselves intimate that they belonged to an external substance. Or if they could intimate this, there would be as many kinds of matter as there were qualities, for none of them were essential to all matter. But there must be some permanent or invariable qualities before we can employ a name significant of them all, or of [48]which they were significant. According to Dr. Brown himself, extension and resistance are the only two qualities which can invariably be predicated of matter; for figure and magnitude are modifications of extension, — as solidity and fluidity, hardness, softness, are of resistance. *Both* solidity and fluidity, *both* hardness and softness, are not essential to matter; but either of them must be — that is, matter must be either solid or fluid, hard or soft. We cannot conceive the absence of both at one and the same time, but we can conceive

the absence of one of them. The same with roughness and smoothness. But extension and some degree of resistance must always be possessed — must always be present, and therefore it is that Dr. Brown himself has reduced the primary qualities of matter to these two. They may be reduced still further, viz., to *resistance*; for extension is rather a property of *space* than of *matter*. Matter, even a monad, is *resistance in space*. What is essential to matter, what enters into our very idea of it, is called a primary quality. All the other qualities of matter are called secondary.

[Secondary Qualities] The non-essential, or secondary qualities of matter, are those which are not invariably possessed by it. We could not give an unvarying, or one, name to that which was itself varying and more than one. The two qualities which are always possessed by matter, never separate from it, and *one of which is that which intimates its existence*, these two qualities are extension and resistance. Under extension we include magnitude and figure; under resistance hardness, softness, solidity, fluidity, smoothness, roughness. And these are objects of the sense of touch. The qualities which are the objects of the other senses may be possessed or may not; and hence they are called secondary. The colours of bodies, their fragrance, their sonorousness, or, again, their sapidity or insipidity — these vary with the object. Some objects possess them, and more or fewer of them; others may possess none of them, or some of them in so small a degree as hardly to be the object of sense. But every object is extended, and has the power or property of resistance. The material framework by which we are surrounded including this world and these globes, far into the [49]boundless regions of space, but presents these two essential qualities — extension and resistance. Weight or gravitation is a law of matter, rather than a property. Weight is but the action of gravitation which pervades all matter — a law which preserves the universe in order, and but for which everything would rush into original chaos. No particle of matter would cohere to another: no planet would seek its centre, or rather a planet or globe could not exist. We would have Epicurus' dance of atoms, — and yet why that dance? — why motion at all? — and if stationary, by what law? The truth is, it is impossible for our minds, at least, to conceive any other state of things than that which prevails; and we are led inevitably to a presiding mind, the author, and upholder of all the order and all the harmony that obtain in the universe...

Space

[52]The account which Locke gives of Space, or the idea of Space, is this: speaking of solidity he says, — "This is the idea which belongs to body, whereby we conceive it to fill *space*. The idea of which filling of *space* is, that where we imagine any *space* taken up by a solid substance, we conceive it so to possess it, that it excludes all other solid substances." Locke thus traces our idea of *space* to *solidity filling it*; the idea of a solid substance gives us the idea of space, as that in which it exists, or may be said to be. Dr. Reid's account of the idea is the following: — "We are next," says he, "to consider our notion of

space. It may be observed, that although space may not be perceived by any of our senses, when all matter is removed, yet, when we perceive any of the primary qualities, space presents itself as a necessary concomitant, for there can neither be extension nor motion, nor figure, nor division, nor cohesion of parts, without space. There are only two of our senses," Dr. Reid continues, "by which the notion of space enters into the mind, to wit, touch and sight. If we suppose a man to have neither of these senses, I do not see how he could ever have any conception of space. Supposing him to have both, until he sees or feels other objects, he can have no notion of space. It has neither colour nor figure to make it an object of sight; it has no tangible quality to make it an object of touch. But other objects of sight and touch carry the notion of space along with them; and not the notion only, but the belief of it; for a body could not exist if there was no space to contain it. It could not move if there was no space. Its situation, its distance, and every relation it has to other bodies, suppose space."

[53]Such is the origin of the idea according to these several philosophers. Locke separates the idea of space from that of solidity, by supposing a body moving out of its place, and no other coming into it. Reid says, — "A body could not exist if there was no space to contain it. It could not move if there was no space; its situation, its distance, and every relation it has to other bodies, suppose space." The two things which suggest the idea, therefore, are solidity, or body occupying space, and motion. Dr. Reid says, — "There are only two of our senses by which the notion of space enters into the mind, to wit, touch and sight." In this he rather defers to an opinion of Berkeley than adopts it. Berkeley held that there was a *visible* extension, and a *visible* space, as well as a *tangible*, being that extent of the visual organ that was affected by the outward object or space. . . .

But when we have got the idea, what is the amount of it? Perhaps, we may in vain put the question. We quote again the words of Dr. Reid: — "But, though the notion of space seems not to enter at first into the mind, until it is introduced by the proper objects of sense, yet, being once introduced, it remains in our conception and belief, though the objects which introduced it be removed. We see no absurdity in supposing a body to be annihilated, but the space that contained it remains; [54]and to suppose that annihilated seems to be absurd. It is so much allied to nothing or emptiness, that it seems incapable of annihilation or of creation."

"Space not only retains a firm hold of our belief, even when we suppose all the objects that introduced it to be annihilated, but it swells to immensity. We can set no limits to it, either of extent or of duration. Hence we call it immense, eternal, immovable and indestructible. But it is only an immense, eternal, immovable and indestructible void or emptiness. Perhaps, we may apply to it what the Peripatetics said of their first matter, that whatever it is, it is potentially only, not actually.

"When we consider parts of space that have measure and figure, there is nothing we understand better, nothing about which we reason so clearly, and to so great extent. Extension and figure are circumscribed parts of space, and are the object of geometry, a science in which human reason has the most ample field, and can go deeper, and with more certainty, than in any other. But when we attempt to comprehend the whole of space, and to trace it to its origins, we lose ourselves in the search."

Perhaps there is not one of our ideas that is so puzzling as that of space, unless it be that of power, and even it is more capable of being grasped than that of space. "An immense, eternal, immovable and indestructible void or emptiness!" Is that an idea that we can take hold of? or is it the idea of anything? And yet, it is perhaps as good a description of the idea as we can have while space itself may be susceptible of no better definition. Kant and the German metaphysicians deny its reality, and make it a mere form of our sensibility. This, however, is about as intelligible as space itself. It would be as easy to understand the one as the other. Nay, I have some idea of space, however puzzling the idea, but I have no idea of what a form of sensibility is, distinct from the sensibility itself; and if space is to be resolved into a mere state of our own sensibility, then it is nothing. The mind will not give up its ideas in that way. An idea must have something for which it stands. It is true the mind may conceive of what [55]never existed: it may have the idea of a centaur and a golden mountain. But these are mere combinations of ideas, and the ideas of which they are composed must have had their prototypes in reality. It is not of such ideas that we speak, but those simple ideas that are forced upon us in spite of ourselves, which we cannot divest ourselves of, and which seem to retain possession of the mind only because there is that of which they are the ideas. We must be content with the idea at least, and believe that there is so much as the idea goes for.

Dr. Samuel Clarke makes it an *attribute*, and contends that as an *attribute* must have a *subject*, and we cannot conceive the time when space did not exist, we have an argument for the existence of God. . . .

[58]The peculiarity regarding space is, that it is not a substance of any kind, and yet it cannot be called merely an attribute, as Dr. Clarke regards it, while it is an "objective reality." What can that be which is neither a *substance* nor an attribute, and yet has an objective existence? *But what is a substance?* Can we give any other description of it than as that which reveals qualities? May it not, then, be as *intelligible a description of space that it is that* in which a substance exists? Substance is that in which qualities exist — space is that in which substance exists. It is not a quality or attribute of substance, but it is that in which substance exists, but which itself again might exist without substance. Farther our ideas cannot go. There is one difficulty connected with it, that it is eternal, and infinite, and necessary, and has an existence. Are not these the very attributes and description of Deity? and are we not thus making something distinct from God co-eternal with him, and possessed like himself of infinite and necessary existence? But although we make it an *existence*, we do not make it *Being*; and our idea of it is, *that* in *which Being exists*. We say, *farther than this* our ideas cannot go. We know it, at least, as that in which

matter exists, and in which matter moves. Whether it be equally necessary for spiritual beings to exist, and expatiate in, it is impossible for us to say. In one of the most metaphysical and profoundest of our poets, we find the expression, "placeless as spirit." We cannot, at all events, [59]conceive it not existing, and we believe it to be one of the attributes of God, that he fills space. It is a sublime thought to conceive *space infinite*, space not as being, but as that in which being exists, and God filling it with his presence, and yet so filling it as that he does not exist in parts, and is not divisible as space is. And it is a thought of Foster's, apart from astronomy altogether, and to which he ascends by one reach of his own great intellect, or which he arrived at by a subtlety peculiarly his own, that while we cannot speak of matter as infinite, yet *in infinity* there may be *space* to allow worlds *for ever multiplying*, so that go where we will there may be no limits to creation; and it may be part of the occupation of blessed spirits hereafter to explore the universe, and to find no end to their discoveries and their ever enlarging contemplations. We give this thought of Foster's merely from memory; but we think we have accurately conveyed it. The thought supposes a reconstruction of the universe after its final destruction, or as some have regarded the dissolution of the universe, plainly foretold in Scripture, to be no more than itself a purification or reconstruction, both this world and those worlds that people immensity may remain to afford that glorious field for actual observation which Foster has pointed at or suggested in one of his writings.

Time

Time must always have been as well as space. We do not believe in time, however, as objective, as having objectivity. It is a very different idea from that of space. Space is without us: time is neither within us nor without us. Shall we say that time is merely a form of thought? And yet, what is time? Let it check the vanity of speculatists that they cannot define that of which they have yet so clear and distinct an idea.

Locke refers the origin of this notion to the succession of ideas in the mind, that succession marked by the mind, and with it growing up or arising the idea of time. [60]Dr. Brown, again, thinks that it is in acquiring the idea of extension that we acquire the idea of time, and he supposes that the latter is necessary to the former. He supposes it is by the fingers of the child closing upon a circular body, as a ball, or some body of different dimensions, in the hand, that the idea is awakened. The *fingers reach the different parts of the body in different times: this is marked by the child, and the idea of time grows up.* This, according to Dr. Brown, is even before the idea of an external world, or indeed of externality at all. It is the interruption merely of certain series of feelings at different points, giving different lengths, and the co-existence of the series awakening the notion of breadth; and thus the ideas of time and extension are simultaneous. The idea of extension is thus, according to Dr.

Brown, before that of a body that is extended. But is it not possible that in some, nay in many, out of the millions of cases, such a process as is supposed was never gone through; and how did the ideas of time and extension arise in these cases? It is necessary to Dr. Brown's theory that every infant has gone through this process. Now it is quite supposable that many an infant never had a ball placed in its hand, or any body of different dimensions. Or if Dr. Brown were to peril his theory upon the obstruction of other objects — its own limbs, for example, when it moved its hand, is the supposition at all probable that the idea of time *in every instance came into the mind in this way*? This may have been one of the ways, but even as one of them, it seems a fanciful source for the idea, — rather a precarious hold for such an idea to depend upon. It seems far more likely that the idea arose from a *series of feelings of whatever kind*, or even, according to Locke, the procession of thoughts in the mind. The idea of the inner self, repeated in the mind, frequently borne in upon it, and thus duration or time occupying every such idea or act of memory — for there is memory in every feeling of self-consciousness, otherwise how could there be a reference of any, and particularly, every new feeling to self? — we say duration, or time, accompanying every act of memory, implied in self-consciousness, the idea of time would necessarily arise. [61]We would trace, therefore, this idea to a *series of feelings* of whatever kind; it is not necessary to condescend upon the particular series. *Prolonged self-consciousness*, or *ever-recurring self-consciousness*, seems enough to give us the idea. . . .

[64]While the notion of time is derived from *succession*, it is not itself *succession*. Succession only *measures* time: *time* is itself absolute. *Events* in time in no way affect *time: it* remains absolute.

Time is therefore necessary, as space is. We are not able to conceive *no time*, or *time not existing*. And thus we are led to the idea of Eternity — for, as it is impossible to conceive time *not to be, it must always be*. The two Eternities meet in God; for as He has existed in the one, it seems impossible to conceive the other has not somehow its existence also in Him. The name, *"I am,"* "Jehovah," accordingly, is the peculiar title which he challenges for himself. Amid such mysteries are we situated. They touch — they press upon us on every side — we cannot escape them.

"Si non rogas intelligo" was a wise answer to what, except as an inquiry connected with history and philosophy of our ideas, [65]is an idle question. We cannot explain time, as we cannot explain space. But we can understand it if we do not seek an explanation.

Power

Another of our simple elementary ideas is that of *power*. It appears, like those already considered by us, to be very early acquired. It would seem to be naturally suggested by the observation of change, whether within us or without. The succession in the mind's own ideas of states, or the succession in the many instances of it in the external world, might awaken the idea. Perhaps it is not necessary that the succession be one which has been frequently observed, and which is invariable in its operation; it may be enough that there is succession. Just as the idea of time arises with the succession of ideas in the mind, it being, perhaps, impossible for the mind to mark its own ideas, referring them always to the same internal self, without acquiring the idea of time, so may the idea of power; as it would be natural to refer to some source, or power of producing them, the changes in the mind's states, whether of thought or of feeling. Some mysterious power of awakening or producing those thoughts or those feelings, which the mind had present to it, or even before they were referred to mind as such, would be felt, or conceived of, in the very thought or feeling present for the moment. It would, perhaps, be a very early question, — Whence these thoughts — whence these feelings —what power has produced them? It is an intuition of the mind that every effect must have its cause. *How soon would the feelings or states of the mind be recognised to be effects?* The idea seems to be implied, at least, in the reference of certain internal states to an external cause. How could there be such a reference without the idea of cause? For what does the reference amount to? Is it not this? — *There is something without me which produces this state or feeling.* The development of our ideas is something like the opening of the leaves of a flower. [66]The one is involved in the other, and hardly separable from it; it is like a part of it; it opens as the other opens. The idea of power would brood, perhaps, over the mind at its earliest dawning. It would be involved almost in its earliest consciousness. It would be felt to be a *power* that was stirring in that first consciousness. At all events, it would undoubtedly accompany the first act of reference by the mind to something without. It would thus be before the observation of external changes. The idea would not be very definite, certainly, but still it would be possessed as soon as the mind made a reference of one of its feelings to something without. Cousin seems to argue that the idea, or the principle of causality must be possessed in order to the reference. So it must, but in this sense, that the idea, or the principle, may be developed contemporaneously with the reference, or in the reference. Something must obviously call the principles of the mind into play; and the principle of causality — the principle that every effect must have a cause, which is just the idea of power, may be awakened by that which calls for the reference of a feeling or feelings to something without. The idea of *power*, or causality, is, that an effect must have a *cause* — that there is something to *produce* the effect, some "je ne sais quoi," as Cousin phrases it, which produces the effect. That idea, then, in virtue of a law or principle of the mind, — that principle or law itself, now for the first time called into play, — that idea may be begotten in the very appeal to the inner consciousness by something without, and the answering reference of the inner consciousness to the external cause. The principle is called into play — the idea is begotten — and externality is marked — all at the same instant. Our ideas, we have said, expand like the leaves of a flower, one in the other. But the idea may be before this, and, in virtue of the principle or law to recognise power where there are effects, power may have been recognised *in consciousness itself*, or in virtue of consciousness — consciousness the effect of some power. . . .

Hume on Causality

[67]But here, again, the origin of the idea is distinct from the idea itself. What is the idea? What is implied in the idea of power? What do we mean by causality? What is implied in the principle that an effect must have a cause? This is one of the most vexed questions in philosophy. It gave birth to Hume's famous Essay on Necessary Connexion, and Dr. Brown's Essay on Cause and Effect, or 'Inquiry into the Relation of Cause and Effect." Cousin calls the idea of power, or, "l'Idee de Cause," one of the most important belonging to the human mind, and that which plays the grandest part, both in human life and in the works of the philosophers. The opposition which the General Assembly of the Church of Scotland offered to Sir John Leslie's appointment to the mathematical chair in the University of Edinburgh, because of his views on this question, apparently espousing the doctrine of Hume, which seemed to lead to Atheism, was what gave occasion to Dr. Brown's "Inquiry." Every philosopher, perhaps, has expressed his views on the subject; and it is not confined to philosophy, but theology reckons it of sufficient importance, to demand its notice at least; while science, too, has its theories on the engrossing question.

If we consult our own consciousness, we have no difficulty in determining what power is, or causality. But it is singular enough, that strong as the testimony of consciousness is upon the subject, the tendency was early exhibited to deny the existence of anything more in the relation of cause and effect than a constant or invariable succession. It was contended that, in secondary causes, at all events, there is no efficiency, and that we in vain try to find out the efficient cause of any phenomenon; that we merely arrive at a certain connexion between two events, the one invariably preceding, and the other invariably following. Dugald Stewart says, that the supposition of a real efficiency "has misled the greater part of philosophers, and has had a surprising influence upon the systems which they have formed in very different departments of science." It is interesting to remark, that in these very words of Dugald Stewart he recognises the very efficiency which he is at the same time repudiating or denying; for he speaks of a doctrine or view entertained by philosophers having a *surprising influence* upon the systems which they have formed in very different departments of science. What is this influence but efficiency? Barrow, and Hobbes, and Butler, and Berkeley, are all quoted by Dugald Stewart as denying efficiency in cause, and resolving it into an order or connexion established among the events in nature. It is in vain that we look for the efficient cause in any event; we but see an order, or law, or connexion which God may be supposed to have established, but which is in itself nothing more than a certain order, or law, or connexion. Barrow, for example, says, —"There can be no such connexion of an external efficient cause with its effect, (at least, none such can be understood by us,) through which, strictly speaking, the effect is necessarily supposed by the supposition of the efficient cause, or any determinate cause, by the supposition of the effect." Butler contends that [68]we but see *effects*, that we know nothing of *causes*. Berkeley and others, again, contend that attraction and repulsion and suchlike supposed causes are nothing more than certain rules or laws according to which Nature proceeds in a uniform course; they are the order that we observe, and are themselves phenomena to be accounted for. Almost every work on philosophy contains similar statements. They are always careful to remark that what we call laws or causes are nothing but a certain order or arrangement which God has adopted, and the names we give them should be to us significant only of that order. Thus even for pious purposes the doctrine has been held and insisted on, that the efficiencies in nature are no real efficiencies, and that the will of God is all. Butler says that we but see effects, we do not see causes; and he would lead us to the Great First and only cause, operating in and through all. This undoubtedly was the purpose of Barrow also; and we know that Berkeley's whole system was intended to lead us away from material causes to mind and to God. It was the best bulwark he thought to erect against Atheism. This was the design also of Malebranche's doctrine: with him everything which appeared to be a cause was but an occasion on which Deity himself operated; and hence his doctrine is called the doctrine of "occasional causes." He went so far as to hold that our very ideas were seen in God, and that our very minds were present, as it were, in the divine, as body was in space. . . .

[74]Scientific investigation was for the most part directed to the discovery of occult qualities — hidden powers — instead of observing the circumstances in which these powers operated, the only proper subject of investigation. Are we to deny powers, or efficiencies, however, in these circumstances, merely because we cannot detect them, and because we must limit our inquiries to the circumstances themselves in which they operate? This was not what Bacon meant, or Barrow, ...in the respective statements quoted by Dugald Stewart, in what Lord Brougham calls "a valuable and learned note." But whether the opinion could fairly be attributable to them or not, at all events they would never have proceeded the length of Hume and Brown, and denied energy or efficiency in the Divine Being. It is quite possible to allow, and to contend for, the absence of efficiency in the agencies in nature, and yet hold to its existence in God. This is quite possible, and it may be done for [75]the purpose of exalting the efficiency of the Creator, or calling our attention to it, more devoutly marking its presence, even when we would be apt to suppose that a secondary or inferior agency was all that was at work. It is but a more pious degree, as it were, of the sentiment that would discover God in the powers which he has conferred in creation. To "look from nature up to nature's

God," has long been a canonized sentiment, as the act itself was the delight and occupation of the poet who gave it birth. And to heighten the sentiment or the devout feeling implied in it, it is not uncommon to notice the absence of all true efficiency in the phenomena around us, and to refer all to the direct presence and operation of God. Accordingly, Dugald Stewart overlooking, as he must have done, the Atheistical tendency of Hume's view — for what is the denial of all energy in the divine will but Atheistical? — what have we left in the place of God, if efficiency is denied and mere antecedence is predicated? —overlooking this tendency, Dugald Stewart says, even of Hume's doctrine, that "it seems to be more favourable to theism, than even the common notions upon this subject (the subject of cause and effect); as it keeps the Deity always in view, not only as the first, but as the constantly operating efficient cause in *nature*, and as the great connecting principle among all the various phenomena which we observe." Scripture itself seems to point to this view in the words already quoted, — "In him we live, and move, and have our being," and in the innumerable passages which refer the operations of nature to him, recognise him in the minutest as well as the greatest events, whether in creation or providence. "He maketh his angels spirits, and his ministers a flame of fire," the clouds are his chariots, and he walks on the wings of the wind: he makes darkness his secret place; his pavilion round about him dark waters, and thick clouds of the sky. Nay, Job rises to the sublime anticipation of the very doctrine of these modern days, and of the law of gravitation itself: "He hangeth the earth upon nothing, and stretcheth out the north over the empty place." This seems to refer the retention of the earth in her [76]orbit directly to God himself, and there is almost an implied allusion to the law which modern astronomy has discovered as that which holds the planets in their spheres. But how far is all this from denying energy to God; and who will cordially own such a doctrine as makes the Divine will but the first link in a chain of sequence? We might now speak of the primitive ideas of motion and number; but it seems enough to mention them as among our primitive ideas. It were as vain to attempt any explanation of them as we have seen it was to explain time, power, space. We must content ourselves with the ideas we have of them. We may now, however, refer to Whewell's classification of the sciences, as based upon or springing out of these several original or primitive ideas we have noticed, including those of motion and number. It is in proposing to treat of these ideas in his "Philosophy of the Inductive Sciences," that he enumerates the sciences severally connected with them.

"I shall," he says, "successively have to speak of the ideas which are the foundation of geometry and arithmetic, (and which also regulate all sciences depending upon these, as astronomy and mechanics,) namely, the ideas of *space, time, and number.*

"Of the ideas on which the mechanical sciences (as mechanics, hydrostatics, physical astronomy) more peculiarly rest; the ideas of *force* and *matter*, or rather the idea of *cause* which is the *basis of these;*

"Of the ideas which the secondary mechanical sciences (acoustics, optics and thermotics) involve, namely, the ideas of *externality* of objects, and of the *media* by which we perceive their qualities:

"Of the ideas which are the basis of mechanico-chemical and chemical science, *polarity, chemical affinity* and *substance*."

The remaining sciences which Whewell enumerates, crystallography, mineralogy, botany, zoology, physiology, and palaetiology, depend upon derived, and not primitive ideas, which we have not yet traced.

[78]It is interesting thus to see the *roots of the science*, or their basis, in the ideas of the mind. All science may be said to have to do with the properties of space, of number, of time, of matter, of substance, of externality, of cause —to consist in tracing the forces of bodies, their resemblance, their affinity, their power of assimilation, their age, their history — or historical causation, as Whewell calls it — their final cause or purpose.

It is in this sense that metaphysics supplies a kind of "prima philosophia," of which Bacon gave the hint, although he became the legislator for science rather than the scientific investigator himself, either in the department of matter or mind.

Whewell seems, with Kant and the other German metaphysicians, to regard the ideas we have traced as forms of understanding, or ideas merely affixed to, or superinduced upon, the materials given to the mind by sensation. Of space, for example, he says, "Since there are such truths applicable to our experience, and arising from the nature of space, we may thus consider space as a *form*, which the materials given by experience necessarily assume in the mind, as an arrangement derived from the perceiving mind, and not from the sensations alone."

If Whewell meant merely that we are indebted to the mind as well as to the materials furnished by sensation, (as by the presence in space of a solid body,) for our idea of space, this would be an important truth; but his meaning rather seems to be that space is nothing but an idea, nothing apart from the mind — a *form* superinduced by the mind upon matter existing in space. For, after a statement to which we would not object: "Thus this phrase, that space is a form belonging to our perceptive power, may be employed to express that we cannot perceive objects as in space, without an operation of the mind as well as of the senses, without active as well as passive faculties": after this very intelligible and correct statement, he adds, "This phrase, however, is not necessary to the exposition of our doctrines. Whether we call the conception of space a condition of perception, a form of perception, or an idea, or by any other term, it is *something originally inherent in the mind perceiving, and not in* the objects perceived." Whewell thus plainly holds space to be in the mind perceiving and not in the objects perceived. It is an important truth to mark, that space and time, and suchlike ideas, owe their origin to the activity of the mind itself, and that any share that sensation has in any of them is but an occasion, and not properly as a cause. This is an important truth, one which is being more distinguished at the present day, [79]though we do not believe it to have been overlooked by those who are assailed as being to sensational in their philosophy; we allude particularly to Locke. The mode in which Locke traces the ideas shews plainly that he understood the part which the mind itself has in originating the ideas. But because the mind is thus active in producing these ideas, have the ideas no counterpart for which they stand? are they ideas merely? is Whewell's representation the right one when he speaks of space being something originally inherent in the mind perceiving, and not in the objects perceived? Is this a correct representation? We do not think so, and we see the justice of Dr. Chalmers's stricture upon Whewell, that he "expresses himself as if carried by the prestige of the German philosophy and its outlandish nomenclature." "We shall persist," says Dr. Chalmers, "in regarding the whole of the intermediate space between ourselves and the planet Uranus as an objective reality." Space, time, figure, cause, are not forms of thought merely, or forms of the perceptive power, but are realities, although it is the *mind* which gives us the idea of them. It is true, therefore, that our ideas are the very essence or the material of science itself; but then these ideas have something for which they stand, and are not solely ideas. It is of the very essence of the idea that there is something without the mind of which it is but the idea. In obtaining the idea the mind obtains it as the idea of something which has a real existence, or as Dr. Chalmers calls it, an "objective reality." It seems the greatest absurdity to resolve all into *forms* of thought, or of the understanding, or belonging to the perceptive power. At this rate, what is there between us and the boundaries of the universe? The car of the aeronaut is but a clumsy contrivance, when the whole of space is within our own ideas. What need for *railways* — the grand invention of modern times? and how comes it that ships have been traversing the ocean so long, that from the time of the Argonauts to that of Columbus, and till the present hour, the sea has been the highway for voyagers and adventurers of every kind, and many a noble triumph of nautical skill and personal enterprise....

[82]Power, or causation, is not *in* the idea, or *the idea itself*, but something of which we obtain the idea, in virtue of the principle existing in the mind which assures us that every effect must have a cause: in other words, such is the nature of the mind, that we no sooner see an effect than we recognise it as such, and refer it to a cause. It is not the observed instance of causation, however, which gives us the idea, but the mind itself, on the occasion of the observed instance. How unlike is the idea of space to the occasion of that idea, a body existing or moving in space! — as unlike as possible, and yet it is thus that the idea is acquired. Where is the similarity between the idea of time and the succession of ideas, or feelings, in the mind? The mind's own activity or spontaneity is thus to be marked in all its original and primitive ideas. We have endeavoured to trace it in its spontaneous action from its earliest state of [83]consciousness to the point at which we arrived, when it is now in possession of all its original and primitive ideas. The progress from this stage onward must be a very different one from all before. Hitherto, the mind was truly as if in Plato's Cave, or like the chrysalis exploring its way, as it were,

into being, but very different from the chrysalis, as not a mere organism, but an intellectual principle. And, hitherto, it is not to us now a subject of memory or observation; we can but speak of its progress or processes at this period from what we come to know subsequently of its mode of operation and laws. By and by, the mind turns in upon itself, and reflects on its own operations. It can make itself the subject of a double consciousness, as it were. It can become conscious of its act of self-cognizance or reflection. It can, in short, take notice of its own acts, and inquire into its own phenomena and laws. There is a great difference between the mind in the one, and the mind in the other of these two states; and yet we can have no hesitation in asserting that the former is the more important stage of its history or progress. We confine our view, in this remark, of course, to the simple intellectual development. That can bear no comparison to its subsequent moral and spiritual development. But all its most important ideas are acquired at the early period — unconscious period, we might call it, (if the mind could ever be said to be unconscious,) — of its history through which we have traced it. Now, however, it advances rapidly upon its acquired ideas. It proceeds upon these, upward or onward — combining, multiplying, modifying — every subsequent idea being a mode, as Locke phrases it, or a mixed mode of the former.

Let us remark, however, again, the part which sensation, and which the mind itself, have respectively in our original and fundamental ideas. The mind's earliest consciousness, as we see, would be one of sensation. How do we know this? Not from any report which the mind itself brings from that early period, but from the obvious fact that the mind is dormant at that early stage, while we can perceive from the very nature of sensation, that *it* can at no time [84]be dormant — except during what physiologists call a state of coma or entire suspension of the physical as well as mental powers.

Sensation is that which connects the mind with the outward world — that which binds us to matter under the present law of our being. It is partly a mental, and partly physical state or phenomenon: what part is mental, and what part is physical, it is impossible to determine. All that we can say and that seems to be ascertained, is, that by the different senses, and by a part of the nervous system, which seems reducible to none of the senses — that, for example, which gives the sensation of pain or weariness — impressions from external objects are conveyed to the brain, while it, again, communicates with the mind, either as more immediately resident there, or as having more immediate communication with that organ. That there must be communication with the brain before there can be sensation, and that the nerves are the medium of communication, is seen from the fact that if the nerve which communicates with any part of the body is cut, there is no sensation in the part to which the nerve no longer extends; that when a limb is amputated, a sensation at the extremity of the remaining part of the limb is often referred to the part which has been amputated, as if the limb was yet entire — a sensation at "the extremity of the shortened fibres is referred to the member which in their perfect state they supplied"; and that when the brain is in a comatose state all sensation is suspended.

[102]*Intellection* is the word we would be inclined to adopt as "expressive of the action of the *mind* as *mind*, and in antithesis to *sensation*, which is partly a corporeal and partly a mental function or state. On the presence of certain sensations, we have seen a mental act takes place, and our ideas of externality, of matter, substance, mind, space, time, power, are obtained. These are purely the products of a mental operation, this is by no means to say that they have not their counterparts for which they stand, or of which they are the ideas. So wonderful is the connexion between the external and internal worlds. The objects of our ideas, or their prototypes, are without us — but these ideas are purely mental, or given to us by mind. But for this power of fashioning its ideas, the external world would appeal to us in vain; and figure, distance, magnitude, everything about which *science* is conversant, and with which taste and morals have to do, would be a nonentity, at least to us: other faculties, other minds, might apprehend them, but to us they have no existence. It is a marvellous connexion which exists between the world without and the world within. While all about which the mind is conversant is a kind of creation, *even as if it had no independent existence, and the Germans were right in making everything phenomenal and subjective*, we believe and cannot question that there is that without which is more than phenomenal, and is *objective*. God has created a material universe, he has endowed it with certain qualities, or it possesses those properties which are essential to matter: he has placed mind in this material framework or universe, as he himself is a Spirit or Mind of infinite perfection, — that created mind must learn those qualities or properties of the universe in which it exists, and it does so in a manner which is characteristic of itself, by an act or acts purely mental, so that the ideas are its own, while at the same time they have their counterpart without. This independent action of the mind may be denoted generally [103] *Intellection*, or *the action of pure mind*. We think it is of importance to employ a term by which *this action of the mind* may be designated, both as opposed to sensation as the first law or state of the mind, and to any view that would stop short of recognising the operation of *mind* purely or simply, even in the formation of our most rudimentary ideas. We know that in the account of the origin of our ideas, in any intellectual system, except in those sensational; ones in which our ideas are regarded but as transformed sensations, mind is recognised; but it is not enough marked that mind bears the whole part, and that sensation but acts as a prompter, or as the occasion of the mind's operations, — is the suggestive stimulant, if we may so speak, not itself approaching to the remotest resemblance of an idea. The grand point to be noticed is the distinction between a sensation and an idea — the one partly a corporeal, the other strictly a mental product. We vindicate the separate integrity of mind, its distinct nature, and its independent action. Having obtained its simple ideas, which are the rudiments of its other ideas, saving those which belong to taste and to moral duty — what happens after that? but that the mind regards its simple ideas under different modifications, thus forming its complex ideas, or its ideas variously related.

It is usual to represent the mind as possessed of certain faculties, to account for its ideas, and its varied phenomena. The *operations or states* of the mind are represented under the description of different *powers*, and thus we have — Sensation, Memory, Judgement, Perception, Conception, Abstraction, Generalization — what Locke calls Composition — Imagination. Discernment, and Comparision, are also names in the vocabulary of the faculties, and seem to be employed by Locke for the more generic term Judgment. Judgment is the faculty which, presiding over even our remembered sensations, discriminates, or forms them into ideas. A name is nothing, if we really understand what we express by it. But would we call that process or operation by which our simple or elementary ideas are obtained by the name of judgment? [104]Is it not better to refer all to *mind simply*, acting spontaneously and independently, but in a manner altogether inexplicable, and not to be accounted for by any name or names? In like manner, shall we say our complex ideas are obtained by a faculty which we term judgment, or comparison. or composition? For all practical purposes there is no harm in speaking of the faculties of the mind, and of the mind operating according to certain faculties, in the way of discernment, comparison, composition, or, more generically, judgement. But more philosophically and simply the view properly is, that the mind, first by its own spontaneity and activity, and then according to certain laws obtains its simple ideas, such as self, externality, matter, substance, with their various properties, — space, time, power: then these ideas are *modified*, and we have the idea of *universal* space, *Eternaty*, causality *under all its phases*: we can limit or extend our idea of space *ad libitum*, —consider it as circumscribed by lines, and thereby derive the properties of figures, and construct the science of geometry — divide time into periods, or consider it according to the observed motions of the heavenly bodies —regard the laws of motion and of force, and so obtain the mechanical sciences: and all this is just mind, one and indivisible in all its operations, regarding its ideas under those aspects in which they may present themselves to it, or may be capable of being considered — it is, in short, *intellection* operating in various ways, or *intellection* affected variously by limiting circumstances, supposed or actual.

[105]The mind, however, is guided or influenced by certain laws and principles: it acts under these laws or by these principles: its faculties are rather mind itself acting under or according to these laws or principles.

For example, there is the law of identity, the law of diversity, the law of resemblance, the law of contrast, the law of analogy, the law of proportion.

Then there are the *principles* — Causality, to which we have traced the idea or belief of Externality; Generalization, or the principle by which our generalized ideas are formed; Deduction, the principle on which all *reasoning* properly speaking depends.

[106]Then we have the voluntary actions of the mind, such as attention, to which again may be referred what is called the power of abstraction, which is nothing more than the mind applied steadfastly to one of many subjects or

ideas or qualities, and attending to it apart. Imagination is just the laws of mind above enumerated, with a *state* peculiar to itself, and which may be called the ideal or imaginative state. Memory is a property of mind by which the past is recalled, or reproduced: it is neither a law nor a principle. There is, lastly, the circumstance or property of association in our ideas.

The moral and emotional part of our nature does not come under our present review, although this may be mentioned as a separate source of ideas; for we could have no idea of emotion, unless we were capable of emotion, and we could have no idea of duty — of right and wrong — but for the law of right and wrong, or unless we were capable of perceiving this distinction; while it is the aspects of emotion and of principle which go to the formation of character, and all the variety of disposition. Actions, too, may be variously contemplated, as characterized by such and such emotions, or exhibiting such and such moral principles, or violations of principle. It may be seen what a wide range of ideas is thus opened up, or given to the mind.

We may specify here, too, the idiosyncrasies of the mind — a term for which we are indebted to phrenology — by which is meant some predominating bias or faculty, mental or moral, according to which one mind is distinguished from another.

We thus consider the mind possessed of a *spontaneous activity and inherent power*, by which our simple ideas are framed, products of the mind solely, and not indebted to sensation farther than as the prompter, or stimulant of the mind: *that activity still in operation* gives us the modifications of our simple ideas, in which extended operation we see the laws above enumerated, and those principles of mind — causality, generalization, deduction. We have the voluntary actions of mind, attention, abstraction. We have the state of Imagination, and the properties of memory and association.

[107]Memory, though mentioned so late among the phenomena which mind presents, comes first under our consideration. We mentioned it so late because it does not belong to any of the more general phenomena to which may be referred many of the mental characteristics. We have called it a property of mind, for it is altogether distinct from the spontaneous action of the mind by which we obtain our primitive ideas, the modifying laws of the mind, the principles of the mind, and even its voluntary actions; for although volition may exert an influence upon memory, so that we may set ourselves to recall any past event, this is not so much a voluntary *act of memory*, as influenced by an act of volition. All voluntary acts of mind, indeed, are just *mind under the influence of volition.*

Memory

Memory is undoubtedly something unique, or distinct from any other phenomena of the mind. Nor do we call it a faculty, as we have restrained from designating any of the phenomena of the mind *faculties*, inasmuch as the only thing pertaining to mind which we can properly apply the name *power*, is the will, the seat of moral power; and hence it is, that what are strictly regarded only as phenomena of mind take the aspect of faculties, because they may be under the influence of volition. A volition may be so present and operative as to give to what is nothing more than a succession of ideas in the mind the aspect of a faculty. Even what are called our judgments, are but ideas variously combined or related, but when *we set ourselves* to compare our ideas, or invite their presence in their relations and connexions, we are said to exert an act of judgment. In the same way, when we set ourselves to recall a past idea or event, we are said to exert an act of memory. But what truly takes place in each of these instances? In each instance we have but ideas arising in the mind according to certain laws, or according to a certain characteristic or property of the mind, under the influence of volition, or an act of will....

[341]If we look at the final causes of our emotions, we find none for those which supposes a previous perfect state. They were their own end. Every end was subserved in that state by things as they were, and of each by itself. It were vain to ask for the final end of any of the virtuous emotions, or of the emotions growing out of these. Each was its own end; but the Glory of God was the end of all, or God's glory in the happiness of the creature. Man was created in the image of God, and just as the attributes of Gods subserve no end, can subserve no end, but must be considered as absolute in their nature; so was it with the attributes with which God endowed man. They, too, were an end to themselves, but God's glory shone in all, as his own perfections were reflected or illustrated. There was nothing beyond that perfection. It could not be a means it shone absolutely, and in the lustre of those glorious qualities, even in the fair form in which God placed these, His image was displayed. It might be said that the proper end of love, or gratitude, was, that God might be loved, and all sinless beings, and that the sentiment of gratitude might rise in return to God for His benefits. Undoubtedly that was the very nature of the sentiment or feeling, — was it the end? Were they not proper in themselves? And was not God glorified in the very feelings or emotions? It was to subserve an end, however, that man was rendered capable of the other emotions — the counterpart or antagonistic emotions — for they could never be an end — just as evil could never be an end. Evil was permitted in the universe of God for some purpose, and those counterpart emotions were necessary to, or inevitable in a state of evil, or where evil existed. A final cause can be seen in these counterpart emotions. In a perfect state no end is needing to be accomplished; *all* is accomplished, except in the case of the physical part, which was to subserve the spiritual in man. The intellectual, too, might be regarded as subservient or ministerial to the spiritual: not when considered as created in the immediate image of God: viewed thus, it was an end itself; its only end could be God's glory. But as inferior, and actually ministerial to the spiritual or moral part of man, [342]the intellectual did and does subserve an end, but its *proper* end was not *that it might subserve that end*, but it too was a part of the Divine image. It is *now* that we see the subordination of means to

purposes in the region of man's nature. Before, to reflect God's perfections was the only end. God created the whole of man's spiritual nature for this purpose. It was in God's entire image that man was created, and as a perfect image of God one part was not to subserve another, but all was the expression of God's nature. Now, when man is no longer the reflection of God's nature, when that is no longer accomplished, and other objects are to be accomplished, adaptation and subserviency come into view. Matter is subservient to spirit — must always be — and there *are adaptations* in matter; for matter, although bearing the impress of God's perfections, was not the image of God — was not an end. The state of the soul now admits of adaptations, and subserviency of one part to another — of final causes, because the original design of God has been disturbed, and man no longer reflects his image.

[384]We are in the presence of the Creator, not of His works merely. We realize an uncreated Being, whose works we contemplate — these works so marvellous, so stupendous, so striking in their exhibitions of wisdom and power. We adore: Adoration is the sentiment we offer to this Being. A complete prostration of our faculties, of our hearts before Him, is felt to be called for — nothing less can we render. Mysterious, unseen, uncreated, eternal, having no limits to any of His attributes, by which any of His attributes can be bounded, incomprehensible therefore to us, except in so far as nature, though not the infinitude of His perfections, may be scanned or conceived of! We know the former, because we ourselves have been created in the possession of the same attributes, though limited, very limited in extent — capable however of endless progress. Man is the priest of God, because he can know God. It is the priest's function to adore, to offer worship. All should be priests to God. Sin has interrupted the priestly functions — the worship is not offered. Christ makes us again priest unto God.

Besides subserving the purposes of devotion, to what gratification does not this emotion minister in the constitution of our nature! But was it implanted in our nature for this purpose? or was it not absolute? Was it not an essential part of our emotional being? Does it not belong to our position as creatures in the universe? Could a creature, created with an emotional capacity, contemplate either its own creation, or that of any other being or object, without this sentiment? Could it be possible to be brought into contact with this great fact or idea, without being filled with-wonder? There is in it, and must be in it, to the creature, what can never cease to call forth this emotion. Creation! How wonderful! Grant an intelligent and emotional nature, and wonder could not but be experienced. We might indeed have been created like the stone, or any of the lower creatures, insensible, incapable of emotion, and incapable even of thought, but we would not then have been what we are, rational and moral beings. [385]We say so far as we were made intelligent and

Editor's Note: In sections of the text not provided here, Lyall connects his rational view of experience with his intuitive belief that this world mirrors God's perfect rationality. Man connects with this higher order, emotionally.

capable of emotion, there was what was absolute in our nature, what could not but be, what belonged to our nature, what was not intended merely to subserve an end, what was final, except that His own glory was what God proposed to Himself in all creation. We do not say that any part of our constitution does not subserve this or that end, but that the final end was God's glory, while there was what was *absolute*, and not merely provisional in our nature. Our faculties have all an absolute character, created in the image of God, and their grand design was, besides being an end in themselves, that God's glory might be reflected in them. That they accomplish subordinate purposes is somewhat different from these being the purposes for which they were created.

The emotion of wonder does then minister to the gratification of the creature in a high degree. It is accompanied with high delight. It produces a refined, in some instances a very lofty pleasure. No gratification is purer than that which is felt in the presence, or in the contemplation, of some great phenomenon — some very interesting manifestation of the Divine power, or wisdom, or goodness — some stupendous or beautiful; law of creation — some mark or evidence of God himself — in the possession of some interesting truth, some fine conception, some happy or admirable expression of such conception in language or art — greatness or excellence anyhow seen, contemplated or appreciated.

[390]We have considered those emotions which connect us with events and with objects generally, which do not allow us to be uninterested spectators of what is occurring [391]around us, or to survey unmoved the scenery of earth and heaven, or find no pleasure in the objects which meet with our view every day, and gather around them our familiar loves and hatreds, awaken delight or produce disquiet, or it may be unhappiness, — which, on the contrary, are alive to every event, and are awakened by almost every object — which pervade life as waters the channel of the stream, and invest everything with a kind of atmosphere, coloured by the emotion which prevails — which fill the heart with serenity, stir it with joy, excite it to wonder, exalt it to admiration, prompt it to devotion, or make it the victim of the disquieting emotions, from sadness or melancholy to the profoundest sorrow, or leave it the prey of weariness and ennui. But there are more powerful emotions than any of these — emotions which take a stronger hold of the heart, move it more deeply, are still more influential as springs of action, and more directly concerned in the production of happiness or misery. We refer to the emotions of love, of sympathy, of benevolence, of gratitude, and to the emotions which accompany our desires, which are distinguishable from our desires, and may be called the emotions of the desires.

It was not intended only that we should be partners in, or mixed up with, the events of life, and be capable of feeling emotion in connexion with every object that met the eye, and that solicited the regard; we were to be more intimately associated with our fellows, to have, in every way, a greater interest in them, and in their fortunes, and be capable, therefore, of stronger emotions as respects themselves, and what concerned them. *Love,,* accordingly, is an emotion which has more directly for its object our fellows of the same species, after that great Being who gave to ourselves being, and whom it is our first duty at once supremely to love, and reverently to adore. Love is by far the most important principle or emotion of the soul. It excels every other in value as in kind. Its object, if we may so express ourselves, *is more directly its object,* than is the object of any other emotion the object of that emotion. Cheerfulness has not properly an object at all. An event *produces* joy, an object *awakens* our delight; but the object of love is the object *of* our love. We love the object. Pleasure or delight *in* an object: joy *at* an event: is very different from the [392]love *of* an object, or from that object's being the direct object of love. Not only is the emotion in this instance produced by a cause, or, at least, awakened by an object, it terminates on that cause; it has *it for its object.* Even admiration does not so directly terminate on its object as love. We admire something about the object; we love the object. The emotion, like every other simple emotion, is incapable of analysis. We may state certain circumstances regarding it; but the simple emotion itself cannot be described. Every one's feeling of the emotion is its only interpreter or described. The last retreat of any emotion, it is impossible to reach; there is something in the emotion at last — the very essence of the emotion — that baffles all attempt at description or analysis. The emotion remains yet to be described. Nothing more has been done by all the efforts to bring out the emotion itself from its retreat or concealment, than if no attempt of the kind had been made. What do I explain when I say, that there is in *love,* or connected with it, "a vivid delight in the contemplation of its object?" or further, "a desire for the good of that object?" Do these two elements make up the emotion? The whole peculiarity of the emotion consists in the *kind of delight* which is felt, or *there is something beyond this delight,* while desire for the good of the object is an *effect* of the emotion, not a part of it. The kind of delight felt in the contemplation of the object, or in the object, is the very mystery. Delight and love as resting on an object are not far separate, but love is rather the delight in this instance, than delight the love, — that is, the emotion is rather love than delight.

[404] We carry questions of general interest into our family as we would into another household, or among the greatest strangers. Friends are nothing to us ultimately, but human beings; the greatest, the most important, interests affect them not otherwise. But does this destroy the other relations? Are these lost? By no means; but the love of our fellow is the greater. It is the more absolute — it is first, as it were — it is prior in our supposition. God had respect to it before He consulted for the other, or provided for the other. This may [405]let us into the meaning of some of the statements of Scripture: "In heaven, there is neither marrying nor giving in marriage, but all are as the angels of God": — "All ye are brethren": — "Ye are all one in Christ"; while the larger relation swallowing up the lesser will make the sad separation of friends in the next world hardly appreciable. The more limited relation,

however, is still a very important one, and it secures the most beautiful exercises of affection, and the most admirable results. It begins with that provision which was established at first for the continuance of the race. In that law which God constituted, by which a peculiar attachment is formed between the man and the woman, we have the origin of the family relation. This undoubtedly was a subordinate law; and the source of so much happiness in itself, it was connected with the mode which God took with our race for its continuance and propagation. [405]The love between man and the other sex is altogether peculiar. It is the same emotion we are speaking of, however, still in its essential characteristics. *It is love*, though love of a special and peculiar kind. The properties that inspire it account in part for its special and peculiar nature; but this will not all account for it. Let it be considered that love in itself *is absolute* — is a part of that emotional nature with which, as we were created in the likeness of God, He was pleased to endow us. Love may be contemplated as an absolute emotion existing even apart from an object to exercise it or call it forth. It is a state conceivable prior to the existence of any being to call it forth. God was love in this absolute sense, from the very eternity of His being, except as we may consider the reciprocation of this affection between the persons of the Godhead. Love is the necessary condition of a perfect moral nature. Hatred would be the opposite of this. Nothing could be the object of hatred but moral evil, or being so identified with evil as to be its impersonation. God had only then to call beings into existence to have objects for His love. His love would be complacency with all that He had created — every being, every object, the object of a complacent regard. But that complacency becomes higher according to the object contemplated. [406]We feel that we can regard with a kind of affection even inanimate objects; that our love, the absolute emotion, rests upon them. All creation would thus at first lie in the smile off God's love; but in proportion as the being rose in the scale of creation, the complacency, the love, would be of a higher character, would rise too. Intellectual and moral beings would be the objects of its highest exercise. Now, when God created man at first, just such would be his nature — the very condition of his being — he would know nothing but love — hatred would be foreign to him — and his love would take a higher exercise according as its object rose in the scale of being, until God himself was its object, who would draw forth its supreme and undivided regards. But God adopted a peculiar procedure with respect to man; He did not create the race at once, and He made the law of its continuance the source of a new aspect of this peculiar emotion. Undoubtedly there was something arbitrary in this. It was not absolute, it was not necessary, as in the case of the other aspect of the emotion already referred to. The new aspect of the emotion was something special. It depended upon a particular fiat or arrangement of creation, — upon an arbitrary but beautiful provision on the part of the Creator. Can we give any other account of the affection which sprang up in Adam towards the helpmat˯ which God provided for him? Can we give any other account of the emotion now? It is the love of our fellow; but it is modified by the constitution or arrangement which God adopted, and depends upon the will of the Creator. What account can be given of the influence which female form and beauty have upon the mind? It is not accounted for by the influence which beauty has upon the mind wherever seen. That does not affect the mind at all in the same way. [406]No doubt we are affected by the one beauty in many respects as we are by the other. Many elements enter into the conception of the one that go to the conception of the other; but why love at last in the one case, while there is nothing of the kind in the other? What is love in this instance? It is the love of a being — it is the love of a fellow-being — and that being is the [407]woman whom God gave to man. We can say nothing more of this love than that it is a law of that nature or constitution which God originally conferred upon us. It is the same with parental love or filial love. Both depend on an arbitrary provision or arrangement on the part of God in creation: It is more than love absolutely — it is love, but it is love again modified. It may be said to depend upon the peculiar proximity of relation in which the parties stand to one another. But how does this produce the effect? We can say no more of the matter than that God has ordered it so. The love of a parent to a child, and of a child to a parent, and again of the members of the same family one to another, — how shall we account for this but by a peculiar will or fiat of God in creation, or in those arrangements which He was pleased to adopt with respect to our race? The most admirable effects are secured both by this and the other arrangement alluded to, which is a condition again to the family relation. It is from such springs that the social economy is conducted — it is in accordance with these that it works. The effect could not otherwise have been secured; and how otherwise could it have been secured with such happiness to the species? Of what delightful feelings, of what amenity, of what order, of what virtue, are the arrangements we have alluded to the source or the cause! The love of the sexes is as peculiar as it is strong. The happiness it inspires is perhaps the most exquisite which God intended His creature to possess on this side of time.

[408]But the emotion increases with the object: the higher the being, the higher the emotion. When God is its object, it is the highest character conceivable of the emotion. We might suppose angels next; and, doubtless, were we as conversant with them as we are with our own race, and were the relation of race lost in the one great relation of being, this would be so. We see a modifying law even in the case of the race as distinguished from other races. Our love of the race, however, is the love of being; just as the love of family may be considered the love of being, apart from the modifying circumstance; but it is then not the love of family but *the love of being*. The love of race is the love of being, take away the distinction of race. The truth is, *being* is ultimately the object of love, and *being* should properly be regarded only as higher or lower, apart from every other distinction. It will ultimately come to this, or if the modifying circumstances or arrangements connected with this emotion continue [409]in a future world, being will then form the grand relation, and the love of holy beings will be a far higher and intenser love than any other.

If *being* is thus properly the object of love, there is a sense in which a being may really be the object of our love, in spite of moral qualities the opposite of excellent. This may be affirmed, that a malicious being cannot be the object of our love; and those beings, accordingly, in whom malice has its climax are, and must be, the objects of our hatred. Hatred to being can be met only by hatred. The malice of Satan, and the other wicked spirits who fell with him, as we are taught to regard their nature, excites our hatred even towards the beings in whom such malice lodges. Direct enmity to good can be met with nothing but enmity. It is the distinguishing circumstance of God's love, that it loved not only its enemies, but sinners. In what other case has such a love been exhibited? This is made the very marvel even in Scripture of God's love. Here we speak in ignorance, and can only wonder. "Herein is love": — "Herein God commendeth His love toward us"; these are expressions which magnify God's love to our conception. But where malice is not discerned, as it is by God even in man, or where it is not seen in such distinct and palpable form as in the case of the fallen angels, a being may be loved though otherwise morally depraved, or destitute of those excellencies that may be supposed necessary to awaken our love. That being has not forfeited our love by a disposition that cannot but call forth hatred. Towards God he may have exhibited all the qualities of enmity, of hatred; but it has taken no active shape against all that is good, and the love of being, therefore, has still room to operate. That state of love is not repelled by what is in direct opposition to itself. The absolute emotion, love, still rests upon its object; wherever it finds being it finds an object on which it terminates. It is here that we perceive the nature of that command, "Thou shalt love thy neighbour as thyself."

NOTE: Lyall refers to numerous philosophers, few of which will be familiar to the reader. Most were prominent in Lyall's time or before and directly related to his interests in common sense philosophy, science and theology. The following information about some of these philosophers should provide valuable background for the reader.

Thomas Reid (1710-1796) born near Aberdeen. He originated the Scottish school of common sense philosophy and argued that common sense beliefs are imposed upon us by the constitution of our natures and are 'the inspiration of the Almighty.'

Thomas Brown (1778-1820) born at Kirkambrech, Scotland. He was on the periphery of the common sense school of Reid and appealed to intuitive truths and the procedures of philosophical analysis. Brown wrote a defence of Hume's account of causal relations. He attended lectures by Reid's close adherent, Dugald Stewart, who is referred to in the Lyall text.

William Whewell (1794-1866) born at Lancaster, England. He was a philosopher of science who espoused a view of induction — test various hypotheses in turn until by a 'happy guess' one hits on the relevant idea. He incorporated ideas into the facts.

Victor Cousin (1792-1867) born at Paris. Influential philosophically and politically, Cousin was in personal contact with Schelling and Hegel. He followed Thomas Reid as interpreted by Royer-Collard. Combined the empiricism of sensationalism in epistemology with the spiritualism of religion.

Samuel Clarke (1675-1729) born at Norwich, England. A convinced Newtonian, admired preacher, and he was known for his complex proof of God's existence: 'one argument in a chain of propositions.' The above biographical information was taken from *The Encyclopaedia of Philosophy*, editor in chief Paul Edwards, New York, 1967.

Section Five

GEORGE PAXTON YOUNG
(1818-1889)

5

George Paxton Young: Sceptical Fideist

J. T. Stevenson and Thomas Mathien

George Paxton Young (1881-1889) — mathematician, theologian, philosopher and educator — exercised a considerable influence on the intellectual life of Canada West (later Ontario) over a period of some forty years.[1]

He was born in Berwick-on-Tweed in Scotland but attended high school and the University in Edinburgh, where he acquired an M.A. degree. After teaching mathematics for a time at the Academy in Dollar, he entered the Free Church Theological Hall, was ordained, and ministered to charges in Paisley and London. His call to the ministry was inspired by Thomas Chalmers (1780-1847), mathematician, theologian and preacher, who led the 1843 disruption of the Established Church of Scotland—a schism largely about the method of appointing ministers. It was not the last time Young had difficulty accepting the orthodox position in ecclesiastical polity or theology.

In 1849 he emigrated to Canada, taking a call to Knox Church, Hamilton in 1850. In 1853 he was appointed to a Theological Chair at Knox's College (as it was then called) in Toronto. He is reported to have lectured at one time or other in almost every department in the College, teaching amongst other things logic, mental and moral philosophy, and the evidences of natural and revealed religion.

In 1864 he resigned from Knox as he found he could no longer subscribe to the Westminster Confession, which had been adopted in 1647 by the General Assembly of the Church of Scotland. It expounded all the leading articles of the Christian Faith from the creation of the world to the last judgment and had quickly established itself as a definitive statement of Presbyterian doctrine in the English-speaking world. Although both Young and his commentators are reticent about the grounds of his dissent, some things are tolerably clear.

As an independent thinker and a man of great rectitude, Young would not retain his position under false pretenses. In his reply to an address presented to him on his seventieth birthday he said:

> The address has spoken of me as a truth-seeker, and such I am. I have
> sought with all the earnestness of my nature to find truth for your sake
> and my own. I have had no other purpose but to know the truth and make
> it known.[2]

That his independent spirit brought him pain and a certain amount of
isolation is indicated by the fact that one of his favourite poems was Whittier's
"The Eternal Goodness." We are told that those "who heard him read it
could not fail to realize that in the words of the poet he found the expression of
his own deepest feelings and firmest convictions." The first three stanzas of
this rather banal and sentimental poem by a minor American poet might well
speak to a shy bachelor who had to steel himself to the consequences of his
search for truth:

> O FRIENDS! with whom my feet have trod
>   The quiet aisles of prayer,
> Glad witness to your zeal for God
>   And love of man I bear.
>
> I trace your lines of argument;
>   Your logic linked and strong
> I weigh as one who dreads dissent,
>   And fears a doubt as wrong.
>
> But still my hands are weak
>   To hold your iron creeds:
> Against the words ye bid me speak
>   My heart within me pleads.[3]

Secondly, he retained his fundamentally religious views in spite of rejecting what he regarded as secondary standards such as the Westminster Confession. On this point we have the assurance of his memorialists, as well as the
fact that he entered into a renewed fellowship at St. Andrew's Church in 1878.
A clue that his dissent may have turned on fine points of doctrine is contained
in his letter to this Church. D.J. MacDonnell in his funeral sermon for Young,
"Death Abolished," summarized the letter thusly: "If you and your Session
will allow me to come to the Lord's Table, putting my own construction on
the act, I shall be glad to profess in this way my purpose to live soberly,
righteously and Godly." Yet he apparently maintained some credal position,
for one of his students tells us that when (probably in the 1880's) a divinity
student interrupted one of Young's lectures

> ...to suggest that such and such a line of reasoning would lead at the last to
> atheism. Young pushed his spectacles up on that majestic dome of a
> forehead, looked at him in silence for a moment, then stood to his full
> height while his chest swelled out, and with extended hand and closed eyes
> he gave this confession of faith:

'I believe in God, the Father Almighty, the Maker of Heaven and Earth.'[4]

(Whether he went beyond theism to trinitarianism and other orthodox doctrines is not clear from this account.)

Upon leaving Knox College, Young became inspector of high schools, under Egerton Ryerson in the Ontario Department of Education, charged wih reorganizing the grammar schools of the province. His three reports on these schools were influential and he remained an advisor to the Department until his death.

In 1868 Knox College invited him back to its faculty under the understanding that he not be required to teach theology. In 1872 he was appointed to a philosophy chair at University College, University of Toronto, which he retained until his death.

Young's greatest influence was on his students, a small but influential group in a conservative colonial society. (As late as 1887, two years before his death, the University of Toronto had but 891 students, as compared with some 40,000 in the 1980's.) Yet most students at the University of the time would come in contact with him, and they included influential figures: Chief Justice Sir Lyman Duff; a later University of Toronto President, the Reverend H.J. Cody; and intellectuals such as Archibald MacMechan of Dalhousie University. That he was a revered figure is evidenced by tributes in the *Varsity* (the student newspaper) and memorials offered years after his death. A marble bust of him in the University of Toronto Library depicts an imposing figure with balding brow and large beard. The impression we have from testimony is of a man who was kindly and serious without being solemn, who could provoke laughter with his sallies against intellectual opponents, who impressed his audiences with the breadth of his erudition, and who had a special gift for logical analysis and lucid exposition. He tried to combine disinterested inquiry with a deep religious conviction.

What were his views? It is not easy to say. He published relatively little on philosophical and theological topics. In fact, most of what little he published was on mathematics.[5] With the exception of six critical reviews of or commentaries on the works of other philosophers, Young published but one book of sermons, an essay on the phīlosophy of natural religion and a lecture on freedom and necessity.[6] There are several sets of lecture notes by students extant, but how reliable they are in depicting Young's own views may be an open question.[7] His former pupil and successor, James Gibson Hume, published in 1911 *The Ethics of Freedom, Notes Selected, Translated and Arranged by his Pupil, James Gibson Hume*, which reprints the lecture on freedom and necessity together with notes on related topics and a brief biographical comment—a slim (76pp) volume.[8]

Young's later commentators—John Irving, Thomas Goudge and Armour and Trott—agree on denominating him an objective idealist, but they do not agree on when he became one, nor is the evidence adduced unequivocal.[9] Irving has him become an objective idealist in 1883, just six years before his death; Armour and Trott read this tendency into his work as early as 1856; Goudge is less definite, but says that he arrived at the tenets of objective idealism after "studying Kant and especially T.H. Green." (Here Goudge may be relying on Irving; in any case, the reference to Green probably dates the views to 1883.) The influence of J.G. Hume, who seems anxious to claim that the views of his master were similar to but antedated those of T.H. Green, seems to have been a decisive one on these commentators. In fact Hume is relying, at least in part, on a brief note by Young's collegue, Sir Daniel Wilson, and what he says is "that Young and Green came to very similar results in Ethics." A disinterested reading of Young's own words suggests that he may have been, for the great bulk of his career at least, a kind of direct (or presentational) realist, and, as such, perhaps a more interesting and independent theorist than he has hitherto been depicted.

Young sums up his positive position on science and religion in 1862 at the end of his "Lecture on the Philosophical Principles of Natural Religion" with these words:

> Intellectual science teaches that in the universal and necessary conception of cause we have a direct manifestation of God in the exercise of His Almighty sustaining (virtually, creating) power; and Ethical science teaches that in our moral conceptions properly interpreted we have a direct manifestation of God in the glory of His eternal and unchangeable moral excellence.

(We focus on this lecture because it expresses his own positive view on religion and our knowledge of the natural world. Unless otherwise noted, quotations are from the 1862 lecture. Earlier and later works are referred to insofar as they throw light on this lecture.)   He begins his lecture by, following Kant, claiming that all the possible arguments for "the existence of an intelligent Creator" can be reduced to three: "the argument from the contingency of the world, the argument from final causes, and the argument from our subjective conception of God." Again largely following Kant, he claims that these arguments are not deductively sound and hence do not provide a logical refutation of atheism.

The first argument assumes without proof that there cannot be an infinite series of contingent causes. Now Young himself believes that the universe was created and hence accepts the assumption on that ground. But, as he points out, that begs the question. Nor is the moot proposition self-evident. Therefore the argument fails.

The second argument, "that from final causes or from the general plan and special adaptations of the cosmical system," is not much better. He makes three criticisms. First, the order and adaptations we find in the universe may *suggest* an Author or Designer of it, but suggestion does not constitute proof. Second, any inference in the argument is merely probabilistic, for order is a matter of degree; hence "the argument concludes nothing with certainty," and Young evidently craves certainty on the matter. Third, and perhaps most telling from his point of view, the argument at its best can conclude only that there is probably an *arranger* of the universe, not a *creator* of it — and Young will settle for nothing less than a self-existent, necessary, morally perfect Creator. (Young takes essentially the same position in his 1856 review of *Typical Forms and Special Ends in Creation*.) Where Kant had treated the second of Young's arguments as the one most deserving of respect, Young accords most respect to the third. (He also strongly disagrees with Kant's treatment of the idea of God as a regulative one, for he regards the Kantian position as altogether too subjectivistic.) Nevertheless, Young readily agrees that the Cartesian argument (i.e., the ontological argument as expounded by St. Anselm, Descartes, Leibniz and Clarke) is not a sound deductive argument. He concludes that "some sharp logician" could accuse him of arguing in a circle, if he were using the 'argument' as an argument:

> ...for you to take your certainty of the Divine existence as proof of the assertion that the conception of God involves the actual relation of God to the mind; while at the same time you derive your assurance of the Divine existence from the existence of the conception viewed as involving the actual relation of God to the mind. A manifest circle...

Young's defense is simple: "I am not reasoning in a circle for I am not reasoning at all. I am merely seeking reflectively to interpret my consciousness." As an argument, the ontological argument is as logically worthless as the other two.

What then is Young's own position? He claims to know with certainty that God exists. How does he know this? He claims to have direct knowledge of God. And his reply to the atheist is the same as his reply to the Pyrrhic sceptic who would deny that Young has knowledge that he himself exists or that Young has knowledge that there is a material world.

The sceptic and atheist get their purchase on us from an assumption commonly made:

> It is a common opinion that all our thoughts — using that term in the widest sense to include sensations, representations of objects in the phantasy, abstract conceptions, moral convictions and the like — are modes of thought pure and simple. In other words, any given thought is held to be nothing but the mind itself in a particular state — no existing object but the mind itself being involved in the thought as a constituent factor, or indispensable element, thereof.

It is this assumption that leads to scepticism, and Young says, "just because my whole nature, intellectual and moral, revolts against the conclusion, I reject the dogma that leads to it." If he rejects this dogma, what positive view must he accept?

Young avers (with David Hume) that "*no real fact admits of being proved.*" It must be cognized in consciousness, for example, it must be perceived. That is, "we could not be absolutely certain of the existence of any object, unless it were in direct manifestation to the mind." But Young rejects, as we have seen, the view that *what* is manifest to the mind is a mere mode of mind: "with me it is a principle past question that there is never a thought in the mind which is purely a subjective mode." Young holds a form of direct realism in a startlingly sweeping form: "With Plato, I hold, generally, that *all conception is the knowledge of a present reality.*" Thus, in particular, our perception of the material world is "*the mind in conscious relation to the material world*" and our conception of God is "*the mind in conscious relation to God.*"

It is clear that Young is asserting here, as he had earlier (in 1856) in a review of *Philosophy of Sir William Hamilton Bart.*, the "principle that consciousness is infallible." He held that "...in no intelligible sense...can the veracity of consciousness be even proposed as a question for debate." In addition to a negative ground — that a denial of the principle would lead to scepticism — he had a positive ground for his conviction. It lay in his very conception of consciousness as essentially relational: "The consciousness realized is nothing else than the Ego and the Non-ego existing in relation to one another..." Any claim that there was consciousness without a Non-ego would be a contradiction in terms — as would the converse claim of consciousness without an Ego. His chief objection to Hamiltonianism was Hamilton's fallibilism, and it was this objection that was the main burden of his review. (As we shall see, he also rejects Hamilton's views on causation and creation.)

It is a mistake, we believe, to divide Young's intellectual life into three phases — the first, in which he was a Hamiltonian until he rejected this philosophy "root and branch" in 1862, the second, in which he became a sympathetic student of Kant under the influence of Edward Caird and John Watson, and the third, after 1883, in which he identified himself with the objective idealism of T.H. Green — as John Irving would have us do. On the only direct evidence we have in the form of his own publications, Young was criticizing Hamilton at least as early as 1856 and had early on studied Kant, too, for Young's teacher, Hamilton, was the very one who introduced Kant to the English world.

It may also be a mistake to read objective idealism into Young's doctrines in the 1850's and 1860's about the nature of consciousness. Consider the following passage from the Hamilton review:

> In an act of sensitive perception (it is said) we are conscious of self, the subject knowing; and of something different from self, the object known. Now, let it be understood, that though a two-fold object may be discriminated in an act of sensitive consciousness, the act itself, the consciousness, is not two-fold but is single and indivisible. By one indivisible act of consciousness, *Ego* and *Non-ego* are apprehended in their mutual relation. The *Ego* is apprehended, not absolutely, but in its relation to the *Non-ego*: the *Non-ego* is apprehended, not absolutely, but in its relation to the *Ego* — the latter apprehension not being a distinct cognitive act from the former, but being identical with it.

Young is not saying that the Ego and the Non-Ego are identical or merely two aspects of the same thing. He is saying that the relation of conciousness, the *act* of apprehension,is *one relation* whether we express it by saying "The Ego apprehends the Non-ego" or "The Non-ego is apprehended by the Ego." If we have converse relations [1] aRb and [2] bR*a, then Young says the following identities hold: *a* in [1] = *a* in [2], *b* in [1] = *b* in [2] and *R* in [1] = *R** in [2]. (Some later logicians, e.g., Bertrand Russell, wondered whether R = R*, because their senses or directions are different. If we assume Leibniz's law applies to properties, including relations, and the sense of a relation is a property of it,then this would be so.) For Young, at least in his published thought, consciousness was *one* relation (apprehension) with *two* relata (Ego and Non-ego). There is no evidence that he thought Ego and Non-ego are two aspects of *one thing*. It is, moreover, unlikely that Young held, at this period at least, the very heterodox view that in apprehending God he was apprehending one thing (Young/God) of which God was merely an aspect. For him, God might not be epistemologically transcendent (for He can be directly apprehended) but He was still ontologically transcendent (for God exists independently of our apprehensions of Him).

Nor did Young hold Berkeley's form of idealism. In his review in 1856 of Ferrier's *Institutes of Metaphysics*, he points out that Hylas gave in too readily to the arguments of Philonous. From the fact that we cannot be *conscious of* or *have a conception of* Non-ego without a relation to Ego, it doesn't follow that it is impossible for Non-ego to *exist* out of relation to Ego. The test of possibility or impossibility does not lie in *our* capacities to imagine or conceive.

Of course there are glaring problems with Young's epistemology. Among them is the problem of accounting for the existence of errors. If consciousness is infallible, how can we ever be mistaken? For example, how could anyone ever be an atheist?

Young had earlier attempted to deal with this question in his last sermon to his congregation at Knox, "The Gospel Judged to be Wisdom by Them that are Perfect," on 1 Cor. ii. 6. There he claimed that a "certain peculiar state of mind and heart, a peculiar faculty, or whatever you choose to name it, is necessary to our judging of the Gospel." He uses three analogies to make his point: those who are blind, or who lack artistic taste, or who lack moral conscience are incapable of perceiving visual phenomena, artistic excellence and the viciousness or impropriety of actions respectively. Likewise those who lack the capacity for spiritual apprehension are incapable of knowing that God exists. This capacity, while a specific one, is not esoteric: "...the capacity for judging of spiritual things, depends not upon one's natural intellectual gifts, but upon his being enlightened by the spirit of God," hence "persons of very ordinary mental powers" may have it. He makes the same point in the lecture of 1862: religion "does not after all need high scientific culture, nor a library of painful treatises." The details of how we acquire and develop this capacity will not concern us here, but some indication of Young's views can be found in the aforementioned sermon and an earlier one, "The Mirror," on 2 Cor. iii. 18.

Given that we have the requisite capacity, we can see God in nature. The opinion was not uncommon in the nineteenth century, as, for example, in this little poem:

> Your Garden is a lovesome
> thing, God wot!
> Rose plot,
> Fringed pool,
> Ferned grot —
> The veriest school
> Of peace; and yet the fool
> Contends that God is not —
> Not God! in gardens! when eve
> is cool?
> Nay, but I have a sign;
> 'Tis very sure God walks in
> mine.[10]

But sightings of God are not limited to cool, peaceful Manx gardens. He can be seen in the Bush Garden of convoluted, red granite and blasted pines —indeed anywhere and everywhere, under all conditions. (Death at an early age, for instance, was an omnipresent reality in 19th century Canada. In his sermon, "The Fear of the Lord: A sermon Preached to Children," — a curious mixture of presbyterian admonishment, didactic clarity and avuncular kindness — he says to the children, "most of you must have seen the little coffins that from time to time are carried through the streets.") For Young is not appealing to any particular order of nature or to special and beneficial adaptations in nature. He has rejected the probative force of the cosmological argument or argument from order.

We apprehend God, according to Young in 1862, in apprehending any change *as caused*. Our conception of a cause is of a sufficient as well as a necessary condition; it involves the conception of *power*. But we are not conscious of power in change as mere succession. Nor are we conscious of physical causes: "some people talk of physical causes...This is a mere vulgar figment unsupported by a single consideration worth looking at." So our notion of cause involves an apprehension of "the actual present sustaining power of God," in whom we live and move and have our being. Or as Young puts it again: "...the conviction we at any moment have that the change of which we are conscious is being caused, or brought about by power, is nothing else, in my humble opinion, than our immediate apprehension of the Supreme Power..."

(In Wittgensteinian terms, which may be partly helpful here, in seeing events as caused — in the full-blown sense in contrast to causation as mere regular succession in time — we are seeing the world as sustained by God from moment to moment — and this is tantamount to seeing a continuing act of creation. In the 20th century John Wisdom's influential essay, "Gods," made use of the notion of 'seeing as' to explain how two persons observing the order, and disorder, in a garden could arrive at different conclusions as to whether there was a gardener. Young's view is importantly different, for it does not depend so much on seeing the *world as beneficently ordered* as it does on seeing *events as caused*. And, for him, those who fail to see them as caused are suffering from a defect in conscious capacities.)

Young is walking a narrow line. He is, in effect, accepting David Hume's analysis and critique of causation without accepting his attribution of the notion of power to the operations of the human mind. Likewise, he wishes to avoid Kant's conception of God as a regulative idea, a God of whom we can have no knowledge. Moreover, although God is that in which we live and move and have our being, and although "believers beholding the glory of the Lord in this mirror (the face of Jesus Christ) are progressively transformed into Jehovah's image,"[11] he wishes to avoid Spinoza's "hideous pantheism." In his last sermon at Knox he also recognized that he might be charged with mysticism for claiming to see God directly. He replied that his view was not contrary to Scripture and was not obscurantist. His whole position involved a delicate balance.

Yet it had its advantages. It was proof against the vagaries of scientific discovery, for it did not depend on natural science, only on 'intellectual' and 'moral' science. As new doctrines in natural science were advanced Young could accept them. Indeed, in a note transcribed by J.G. Hume on T.H. Green's *Prolegomena* Section 98, and therefore dating after 1883, Young says, "I have not a single word to say against the theory of evolution...I am willing to regard it as though it were established."

But, because he accepts evolution and its principle "that no changes take place '*per saltum*' in the organic world," he refuses "most decidedly to admit that the earliest dawn of consciousness may have arisen from the non-conscious elements." Intellectual science is supreme:

> Material forms whether organic or inorganic can have no possible existence — at any time whatsoever — except in relation to and dependence upon self-consciousness — as Kant has demonstrated.

By the time of this note, then, Young may have changed his views radically.

The problem of error plagued his position. Even if we grant that some errors can be explained by the absence of the capacity for a certain kind of consciousness (e.g., vision or religious sensibility), it is still difficult to claim infallibility for forms of consciousness. For we make visual errors: two *sighted* persons can disagree about what they see. In general, it is difficult to sustain a simple identity between appearance and reality. (As the American new realists of the early 20th century, who were direct realist, quickly discovered, their views required them to ascribe contradictory properties to objects.) It may be that consciousness always has an object that is not to be confused with any mode of mind, but this object is an *intentional* object. Even though consciousness may bring with it a conviction that its intentional object is real and is as it appears to be, the fact is that it may be neither. The question of a criterion for separating veridical from nonveridical consciousness remains.

Young was no fool and certainly recognized the problem in connection with morality. He thought that there is "an essential, eternal, immutable distinction between right and wrong." He rejected the view that our moral conceptions are "pure subjective modes, states of mind." But the problem is: "Does my conviction of the absolute and unchanging distinction between right and wrong possess validity?" He rejects the Hamiltonian (and Cartesian) argument which claims that a benevolent God would not deceive us, for this assumes God's existence — and that is the point at issue. "Without dogmatism, in great humility, stretching out lame hands for the truth," he suggest that right "is apprehended by us in its reality, only in so far as a manifestation of the nature of God is made to us." It appears, then, that, if we have the required sensibility, we apprehend God and His qualities, including moral ones, in apprehending the power that sustains all the events of our experience.

As early as his Knox sermons in the 1850's, especially in "The Mirror," he stated the principle of "the progressive sanctification of believers" "the image of God transfers itself in a progressive manner to believers." He agrees with the Psalmist that "the pure in heart shall see God," but the converse is true, too:

> The perfect possession of a holy character is indispensibly requisite to the full vision of God to be enjoyed hereafter; while, at the same time, it is through means of the vision of Him enjoyed now, that the holy character of believers is gradually brought to its perfection.

And in the transcribed note, "Conscience," which must date much later, perhaps the 1880's, he says:

> ...the view that Conscience furnishes an immediate unerring assurance of the validity of certain moral principles unconditionally and without exception valid, cannot be maintained.

He disagreed with Calderwood's moral intuitionism, because it is "simply indubitable, that men differ...in their moral judgment (and) in the principles on which their moral judgment proceeds." His own view was that

> ...there is no contradiction in saying that Reason, while not revealing to any man any moral principles unconditionally and without exception valid, does reveal to all men in whom its light has begun to shine, the existence of a better and a worse, in other words, the fact of Moral Law, though what the law in a particular case is, may not be so clearly apprehended by one man as by another. It may not be apprehended with equal clearness by the same man at different times.

We may sum up all this in the following hypotheses.(1) It is likely that Young maintained his views substantially unchanged for a period of some thirty years (from the 1850's to, perhaps, the 1880's). This doctrine comprised both a lively religious and moral conviction and a general theory concerning the grounds of the conviction. (2)The grounds lay in experience rather than in argument or inference. (3)It is likely that Young maintained throughout his life a doctrine of the primacy and irreducibility of consciousness. Knowledge (i.e., certain knowledge, for in his opinion probable knowledge is not knowledge, properly so-called) is a matter of being conscious. Consciousness is in general infallible as regards its having an object, but fallible (yet progressive or capable of correction) as regards details. It is unique and is not reducible to, nor does it arise out of, material or organic states-of-affairs, its sometime objects. (4)In conscious experience — an Ego apprehending a Non-ego, two relata in one relation — we know with certainty (a) that we ourselves as conscious beings exist, (b) that a material world exists, (c) that a moral, self-subsisting Creator exists, and (d) that there is a moral law, an objective distinction between right and wrong. Consciousness is a self-presenting or reflexive state. Consciousness brings with itself self-consciousness. It reveals both a direct object and the act of consciousness itself as a relation between a self and an object. (5)Those who deny the basic claims of consciousness are in error, and they are so because either (a) they lack the capacity or sensibility for the required kind of consciousness, or (b) are befuddled by the subjectivistic opinion that the objects of consciousness are mere modes of mind. (6)Regarding these basic convictions, positive consciousness, is infallible. (The absence of a form of consciousness, such as moral or religious sensibility, is an imperfection or defect.) (7)But, within a form of consciousness, there is the possibility and fact of disagreement about the detailed nature of the object of a particular form of consciousness. (That there is an objective material world is certain, but there is a disagreement about its nature, qualities and order; that there is an objective distinction between right and wrong is certain, but there is disagreement about exactly what is right or wrong; that a perfect creator, God, exists is certain, but there is disagreement about points of doctrinal detail.) (8)There is a progressive development of the powers of discernment within a form of consciousness, so that consciousness is capable of self-correction or advancement. (9) The foundation of revealed religion is in natural religion, for the latter is required as an assumption of the former. (10)Natural religion should be experiential rather than argumentative. (11)But natural religion does not depend upon the particular order of nature, as in the argument from the order of nature, with its general beneficence and special adaptations within that order. (12)The doctrines advanced require for their explanation, but not for their truth, a general system of metaphysics and epistemology.

It is on this last point that Young seems to have exhibited considerable diffidence about his own powers. He was too well-read, too acute an analyst, too sharp a deductive reasoner, perhaps too modest, to suppose that he could easily "hold in an iron creed" the fundamental, vivid and sustaining experiences of his life.

That he sought a philosophical system is clear; that he spent time carefully studying the systems of his day is certain. But that he ever found one in which he could repose full and complete confidence is very uncertain. Consider the period in the 1860's when, it has been claimed by Irving, he was studying Kant's system under the guidance of the work of Caird and (later) Watson. In a letter to D.H. MacVicar, August 18, 1866 he says that he has been restudying the modern German systems "very minutely and with great care."[12] He doesn't want to "reject them simply from their consequences, because they contradict revelation," for he wanted to take "the higher ground" of philosophical criticism. He says, "Understanding now thoroughly and minutely all the modern German systems, except Hegel's (on which I am not quite clear), I feel perfectly satisfied that they are utterly baseless." And a little later with specific reference to Spinosa (sic), Fichte and Schelling: "...I believe I can point out objections of a purely philosophical kind, fatal to these systems." Perhaps he eventually did become clear about Hegel and could embrace without reservation his doctrines or those of some member of the eccentric British school of objective idealists. But given the general evidence we have of his intellectual temperament, one is permitted a certain amount of doubt in the absence of direct evidence.

Whether he never did develop a full-blown metaphysics and epistemology that satisfied him as an explanatory and justificatory framework for his personal experiences and convictions —or whether in late life he found that some other philosopher had independently discovered and pre-emptively published the views he had developed — is unclear. What is clear is that a shy Scottish-Canadian bachelor remained faithful to the depths of his own experience, while maintaining an intellectual independence and scepticism; that while serious he did not take himself too seriously; and that, while leaving virtually no mark on the history of philosophy on a larger scale, he left an important mark on his students and their nascent community.

Notes

1.The biographical material was drawn largely from the following sources: H. Calderwood, "Professor George Paxton Young LL.D.," *The Knox College Monthly*, Vol 10, No 1, May 1889; John Campbell, "Reminiscences of the Late Professor Young," *The Varsity*, Vol 9, No 17, March 23, 1889; William Caven, "Professor Young," *The Knox College Monthly* Vol 9, No 5, March 1889; John MacDonald Duncan, "George Paxton Young LL.D.," *University of Toronto Monthly*, Vol 2, No 3, December 1901; Henry Rushton Fairclough, *Warming Both Hands*, Stanford University Press, 1941; J.G. Hume, "Professor George Paxton Young," *University of Toronto Monthly*, Vol 28, No 1, October 1927; A MacMechan, "George Paxton Young.An Acknowledgmentof a Debt," *University of Toronto Monthly*, Vol 8, No 5 March 1907 W. E. MacPherson, "George Paxton Young, Inspector of Grammar Schools," *Ontario Education Association*

Proceedings, 1916; D.H. MacVicar, "Professor George Paxton Young: An Appreciation," *The Westminster*, March 3, 1900; J.F. McCurdy ed., *Life and Work of D.J. MacDonnell*, Toronto: William Briggs, 1897. Also consulted were: L. Armour and E. Trott, *The Faces of Reason*, Waterloo: Wilfrid Laurier Press, 1981; S.E.D. Shortt, *The Search for an Ideal*, Toronto: University of Toronto Press, 1976; and Ramsay Cook, *The Regenerators*, Toronto: University of Toronto Press, 1985.

2. Quoted in Duncan, *op.cit.*

3. J.G. Whittier, "The Eternal Goodness," *The Complete Works of John Greenleaf Whittier*, Boston: Houghton Mifflin, 1894. His love for this poem is attested to in Duncan *op.cit.*, and confirmed by Sir Daniel Wilson.

4. Duncan, *op.cit.*

5. Young's mathematical or quasi-mathematical papers that we know of comprise 18 items. Two are continuations, reducing the number to 16. One is a review of George Boole's *Laws of Thought* and thus is on mathematical logic. Three might be said to be on mathematical physics. Of the 12 purely mathematical papers, two were published in the *Quarterly Journal of Mathematics*, five in the *American Journal of Mathematics*, and the remaining five in *The Canadian Journal*. The earliest of these papers is from 1856 and the latest 1888, the year before his death, so he was a productive mathematician pretty well throughout his adult life. A proper evaluation of this work in its historical context by a professional mathematician remains to be done.

6. Young's philosophical or theological works, in chronological order, are:
   (a) *Miscellaneous Discourses and Expositions of Scripture*, Edinburgh: Johnsone, 1854.
   (b) "An Examination of Professor Ferrier's Theory of Knowing and Being," *The Canadian Journal of Industry, Science and Art*, New Series, Vol 1, No 2, February 1856.
   (c) "The Validity of Consciousness," a review of *Philosophy of Sir William Hamilton Bart.*, *The Canadian Journal*, New Series, Vol 1, No 4, July 1856.
   (d) Review of James McCosh and George Dickie, *Typical Forms and Special Ends in Creation*, *The Canadian Journal*, New Series, Vol 1, No 6, November 1856.
   (e) Review of *Reid's Works* (ed. by Sir William Hamilton), *The Canadian Journal*, New Series, Vol 2, No 10, July 1857.
   (f) Review of Alexander C. Fraser, *Rational Philosophy in History and in System*, *The Canadian Journal*, New Series, Vol 3, No 16, July 1858.
   (g) "Lecture on the Philosophical Principles of Natural Religion," *The Home and Foreign Record of the Canada Presbyterian Church*, Vol 2, No 2, December 1862.
   (h) "Notes on Passages in the Platonic Dialogues," *The Canadian Journal*, New Series, Vol 7, No 42, November 1862.
   (i) *Freedom and Necessity: A Lecture*, Toronto: Adam, Stevenson, 1870.

7. One set is in the possession of J.G. Slater, Philosophy Department, University of Toronto; the others are in the University of Toronto Archives.

8. This book was published by University Press, Toronto, in 1911.

9. Irving's account can be found in "The Development of Philosophy in Central Canada from 1850 to 1900," *Canadian Historical Review*, Vol 31, No 3, September 1950. See Thomas Goudge, *Instruction and Research in Philosophy at the University of Toronto, Part I: 1827-1969*, 1977 (mimeo.). See Armour and Trott, *op.cit.*, Chapter 4.

10. Thomas Edward Brown (1830-1897), "My Garden."

11. "The Mirror" in *Miscellaneous Sermons*.

12. See MacVicar, *op.cit.*, where the letter is quoted. MacVicar also quotes another letter (no date given) in which Young says that he could "preach the simple gospel with unqualified satisfaction." What Young seems to have had difficulty accepting was intellectual systems, however sophisticated, when they conflicted with his own religious experience and his reading (perhaps heterodox in terms of credal Christianity) of scripture.

Lecture on the Philosophical Principles of Natural Religion

George Paxton Young.

(The following lecture was delivered by Professor Young, at the opening of the Session in October. It is published in accordance with the request of several ministers of the church. — Editor, *The Home and Foreign Record of the Canadian Presbyterian Church*).

As the subject of lecture which has been announced, *the philosophical principles of natural religion*, may, perhaps, be thought ambiguous, I may explain that the special question to be brought before you is: does unassisted reason warrant the assertion of the being and moral perfection of God? The subject is extensive, and I must only occupy a short space of your time; I will therefore dispense with preliminary remarks, and at once address myself to the main inquiry.

Leaving aside in the meantime the question of the Divine perfection, and limiting ourselves to the question of the existence of an intelligent creator, —all the possible arguments to prove the affirmative can be reduced, according to Kant, to three; which may be described, not exactly in Kant's phraseology, as the argument from the contingency of the world, the argument from final causes, and the argument from our subjective conception of God. "Besides these arguments," says Kant — and my impression is that he is right in his judgment — "there are, and can be, no others." The first, from the contingency of the world, contemplates the world simply as a world, — of what sort is immaterial. Taking no account of the general plan or special adaptations of the cosmical system; disregarding all considerations of order, harmony, and beauty; it seeks, from the bare datum of nature as a reality, to infer a self-existent necessary Being. The second, from final causes, proceeds upon the view of the world as such a world — one, namely, full of order and beauty; and the inference is, that these features have not been the offspring of chance, but that the system which presents them must have had an intelligent author. The last, from the perception which we have of God, or of the Perfect Being, seeks to deduce the objective existence of God from our thinking. All

*First published in *The Home and Foreign Record of the Canadian Presbyterian Church*, Vol II, No2, December, 1862

these arguments are valuable; the last specially and preeminently so; yet I wish it to be clearly understood, that I do not regard them as by any means *demonstrative* of the being of God. They are fitted to produce a legitimate conviction — I go so far as to think, an absolutely valid conviction — of the great truth which they are employed to establish; but not as logical processes. Let us look at them in succession, and mark, as rapidly as possible, the weakness inherent in them as logical processes. This would indeed, had I nothing ulterior in view, be an ungrateful task; but the brief criticism I am to give is intended to lead up to, and terminate in, a statement of what seems to me the proper way of treating the subject.

I notice, first, the *argumentum a contingentia mundi,* which, from the bare datum of nature as a reality, infers a self-existent necessary Being. If anthing exists (I give the syllogism in the words of Kant), a necessary Being must exist. Now I at least exist. Consequently there exists a necessary Being. The only difficulty here lies in the Major Premise, which itself needs proof. The proof given for it is, in substance, as follows: On the hypothesis that something exists, it must, if contingent, have had a cause, if that cause be contingent, it also must have had a cause; and so on, until the series of contingent causes runs out, when we arrive at a great First cause, self existent and necessary — But (the skeptic will say) *must* the series of contingent causes run out? Why may it not go ad infinitum? Impossible (you exclaim). Yes, but the question is why impossible? For my part, I am satisfied that such a thing is impossible, but simply because I believe that the universe was created. I know of no law of the mind rending it imperative on me to deny the possibility of an infinite series of causes, except in view of the truth considered as already established, that, in the beginning God created the heavens and the earth. Instead therefore of inferring the existence of a supreme Creator from the impossibility of an infinite series of contingent causes, I would rather be disposed to look upon the latter doctrine as a corollary from the former. At all events, any person who can be supposed to need proof of the Divine existence, may be equally supposed to need proof of the assertion that a chain of contingent causes can have only a finite number of links. As an instance in point the late Professor Baden Powell, one of the authors of the well known "Essays and Reviews," indicates, in his contribution to that work, his opinion, that the universe has existed during all past time under necessary laws of physical causation, beyond which he suggests,rather than expressly affirms, that there is no God. Now, suppose you undertake to give a logical refutation of this form of Atheism; and that, in the course of your reasoning, you lay down as self evident the principle that there cannot be an infinite series of contingent causes; what is this but to assert, without proof, and as self evident, the impossibility of the very thing which your opponent holds, and which it is the object of your argument to disprove? In this way, of course, you succeed in refuting the Atheist; but you do so simply by averring that he is in the wrong.

But suppose the syllogism quoted from Kant to be admitted: what then? A necessary Being exists. This is only a small part of the doctrine of Christian

Theism. *Pantheists* believe that an absolutely necessary being exists; and they call this Being too by the sacred name of God —though their God is not ours — not he Author of the universe, nor even distinct from the universe, but merely the complement of actual existence. The whole line of reasoning followed in the *argumentum a contigentia mundi* is compatible with the idea that nature is God. For, recall the steps by which the reasoning proceeds. Something exists; for I, at least, do. Now, on the hypothesis that something exists, it must, if contingent, have had a cause; and so on. *If* contingent. But is anything contingent? This essential question lies wholly outside of the argument now under consideration. To *assume* that *the universe* is contingent, is plainly illegitimate — that is, if the existence of a Divine Creator requires to be logically proved; for, the subtlest form of Atheism, the only form indeed which has sufficient plausibility to give it importance, is precisely that which teaches that nothing is contingent, but that all so-called contingent existences are phenomena of the One necessary All.

This brings me to the second argument — that from final causes, or from the general plan and special adaptations of the cosmical system. Some state the argument as follows: whatever indicates design is the work of a designer (this is laid down by Dr.Reid as a first principle of necessary truth), but the universe indicates design; therefore it is the work of an intelligent cause. This is evidently quite unsatisfactory; for the Major Premise, Dr.Reid's first principle of necessary truth, is a mere truism. The veriest sceptic would admit that whatever indicates design implies a designer — the word *design* meaning nothing else than *what is in the mind of a designer*. If the argument be made to start from such a Major Premise — an irrefragable, because an identical, proposition — the sceptic challenges the Minor. For what (he says) is the assumption, that the universe exhibits marks of design, in other words, exhibits marks indicating that it is the work of a designing cause, but the whole thing at issue? Some writers, seeing this, have constructed the syllogism more judiciously: laying it down as their Major Premise, that, when we observe objects disposed in the manner which we describe by the term *order*, an intelligent Author of the arrangement is suggested to the mind. This is a true, and unspeakably important proposition. Its full significance we shall afterwards have to investigate. But meanwhile, looking at it as the major Premise of an argument, it seems plain that the argument so constructed does not possess any force of logical demonstration. It is sufficient to remark the three following particulars. *In the first place*, granting that an intelligent Author of the universe is suggested to the mind in the manner alleged, suggestion is not proof. *In the second place*, the conclusion deduced, if viewed as reached by logical inference, cannot be held to be absolutely certain. Order is a matter of degree. No-one will deny that some measure of order might be brought about by unintelligent instruments, a degree somewhat greater is less likely to have so originated, and, as the order still continues to increase, the idea of its having been produced otherwise than by an intelligent agent soon becomes so utterly unlikely as to be, in fact, unbelievable. Yet, even when probability is indefinitely heightened, it never grows into certainty. Hence the argument under review concludes nothing with certainty. Let no one say that this is needless refinement. The distinction between what is only conceived as immensely probable, and what is known as absolutely certain, is one of the most vital in philosophy; and no where is it of more proper or obvious application than in the case before us. *In the third place* — what is the most fatal weakness of all — the argument, regarded simply in a logical point of view, does not touch the notion of creation. It merely concluded that the materials of which the universe is composed must have been arranged by intelligence: which no more implies that God created the universe than the circumstances of a watchmaker having arranged the parts of a watch implies that he created them.

Here let us for an instant pause, and take note of our position. We have seen, that could a person be supposed seriously to hold the position of an Atheist, it is impossible, proceeding upon a view of the world, either as a world simply, or as such a world in particular, to dislodge him from it by logical process. But you will observe that I have not denied that the universe bears testimony to its Author. I have not denied that the lesson of the Divine existence may be learned from the fact alone even of the existence of the universe. Still less have I denied that the arrangement of the universe, its marvellous beauty, its endless and perfect harmonies, have power to elevate us beyond themselves to Him who produced them. I believe, on the contrary, that the existence of a Creator is hymned forth by every object in heaven above, and in the earth beneath, and in the waters under the earth — and hymned forth in such a manner as to convey to intelligent creatures a legitimate conviction of the truth that God exists. Only *the hymn is not a syllogism.* Between nature and the Divine existence there is no logical connection. What nature does, whether considered in its bare reality, or in its marks of design, is simply (as we found the argument from final causes affirming) to stimulate the conception of its Author in the mind — to wake the soul, too apt to slumber on in heavy forgetfulness of an ever-present God, to the thought and conviction of his presence. I do not understand, that, at bottom, I differ much, if at all, from those Christian apologists who are accustomed to present that argument, as well as the argument from the contingency of the world, in full bristling syllogistic array. The only difference, if difference there be, is this: agreeing with them in the weighty positions which they begin by laying down as, for instance, the position now before us, that, when objects are observed disposed in an orderly manner, an intelligent cause is suggested to the mind — I cannot admit the success of their endeavours to proceed logically beyond such Premises. We *can* proceed further, as I shall presently attempt to illustrate, but it must be reflectively not logically.

The true function of nature, in respect of the question of the Divine existence, being what I have described, you will see why I have assigned the place of eminence, among all the arguments for the Being of God, to the third

— that from the conception of God in the mind. *The others are merely its forerunners.* All that they accomplish is effected through means of the conception of God which they arouse. *How* the universe awakens the conception of God is a question which need not now be discussed. Enough that it does so, or is fitted to do so, and that not exclusively, nor even in a special degree, to the men of science; for, though it is proper that Science, here as elsewhere, should consecrate her acquisitions to religion, it does not after all need high scientific culture, nor a library full of painful treatises, to satisfy us that the world is full of order and beauty. We see it at a glance, though we may be neither astronomers nor botanists, in every golden fire that frets the vault above us, and in every veined and tinted leaf which the winds of autumn scatter at our feet.

The Cartesian argument for the being of God, in which the value of the conception of God, inspired in the mind through the contemplation of the universe or in any other manner, is sought to be determine, is called after the name of the illustrious father of modern philosophy, because it was first regularly developed by him — though as Leibnitz remarked, its germs had previously been thrown out by Anselm, Archbishop of Canterbury. It was afterwards advanced in a very inferior form by Dr.Samuel Clarke, the friend of Sir Isaac Newton, in his discourse concerning the being and attributes of God. This argument, whose two great steps are, that the conception of the Perfect Being is in the mind, and that our conception implies the actual existence of the Being conceived, I adopt, as involving everything essential on the subject to which it relates;. only claiming to be allowed *in the first place*, to dismiss the notion of its being an argument, in the strict sense of the term, and *secondly*, to interpret and develop it in my own manner. Its weakness as an argument is sufficiently apparent. For, granting that the conception of the Perfect Being is in the mind, what are the logical forms by which we pass to the conclusion that a Being corresponding to the conception really exists? A necessary connection between what we think, and what really is, though it may subsist assuredly cannot be proved. I believe that such connexion does in every case subsist, but I believe also, that, in the case before us, we are assured of this only in actually knowing God; so that it is incompetent to use the fact of the connexion as the Premise of an argument intended to remove doubts regarding the existence of God.

Lest any student hearing me should fancy that the circumstances of our having found Logic to be quite unfitted (its last arrow now being spent) to establish the being of God, brings the doctrine of the Divine existence under suspicion; and as silly persons are sometimes met with, who insist upon having proof for everything, and who contend that you are not entitled to affirm as certain what you admit yourself unable to prove, I think it proper to remark that *no real fact admits of being proved*; so that the insufficiency which had been discovered to be inherent in the arguments we have had under discussion, is no more than might have been predicted beforehand. I distinguish between real facts, and abstract truths like those of geometry. The propositions of geometry can be demonstrated; that is, the conclusions which Euclid crowns with his triumphant symbols Q.E.D. can be shown to be absolutely certain, supposing the definitions, postulates, and axioms to be accepted. But when you pass to specific matters of fact, logical demonstration, from the nature of the case, fails; for Logic, as the science of the laws of the forms of thought, merely serves to shew that such and such notions are in harmony with, or contradiction to, given notions. The profoundest thinkers, therefore, have been unable to prove the existence of the Divine Creator, just because that truth lies beyond the range of logical proof.

In what sense then (it will be said) do I attach value to the Cartesian argument? Before answering this, I must ask you to consider what philosophy is competent, in a question of real existence, to do. Take, for instance, the question of my own existence. I cannot prove that I exist, but I can philosophically assert the fact as one immediately known, and I can point out in what circumstances the knowledge is realised. So in the case before us. God can be immediately known by his intelligent creatures — (such at least is the opinion which I humbly and reverently entertain) — and an exposition can be given of the circumstances and manner in which the knowledge is realized. And (to answer now the question which was put) I value the Cartesian argument as furnishing in substance the exposition required. As an argument to prove a fact conceived to lie beyond the range of our immediate knowledge, it is worthless; but let its propositions, instead of being considered steps in a logical process, be viewed as expositions of the manner and circumstances in which God is known by the mind, and I am mistaken if it be not found to contain the solution of our problem. DesCartes may not have put his case exactly in the form which I think best; in particular, I demur to the horrid Procrustean syllogistic arrangements into which he has tortured his thoughts; but when I attend to the thoughts themselves, he seems to me like a musician touching the very keys of truth.

I assume that we have the conception of the Perfect Being in the mind — to be more precise, that we have the conception of a self-existent holy God, the Creator of the Universe. And, if you please, observe here that I have passed beyond the fact of the existence of an intelligent creator, and have again brought into view what was referred to in the opening part of the lecture, but was allowed for a time to fall out of sight — the moral attributes of God. For, the Cartesian argument is of no narrow and limited reach. Deducing the objective existence of God from the conception of God in our minds, it infers that God is a self-existent necessary Being, because necessary self-existence is a part of our conception of God; it infers that God created the universe, because the notion of Creator enters into our conception of Him; and (I add) it infers that he is a perfectly holy Being, because moral perfection is an element in our conception of him.

That we have the conception of the Perfect Being, such as has been described, I must, without even an attempt at illustration, assume. The point is an extremely interesting one, but as I must study brevity, and as this is the step in regard to which my hearers are least likely to find difficulty, I do not dwell upon it. Let it be conceded that the conception is in the mind. Our task then is, to examine the conception, and to discover what elements of real existence it involves.

It is a common opinion that all our thoughts —using that term in the widest sense, to include sensations, representations of objects in the phantasy, abstract conceptions, moral convictions, and the like — are modes of the mind, pure and simple; in other words, any given thought is held to be nothing but the mind itself in a particular state — no existing object but the mind itself being involved in the thought, as a constituent factor, or indispensable element, thereof. Now, so far is this from being true, that, with me it is a principle past question, that there never is a thought in the mind which is purely a subjective mode. Take the case of perception through the senses; and suppose you say that the perception of an external world is a pure subjective mode. The sceptic at once is down upon you. A purely subjective mode (he insists), a mere state of the mind, a state in which the mind might conceivably have been though a material world never existed, cannot be a proper ground for asserting the existence of a material world. This "cavil," as some will call it — this "play of reasoning," as Dr.Brown does call it — is both legitimate and unanswerable. Of course we laugh at the sceptic who scruples to admit a material world; and our laughter is legitimate, for it is merely the confident hilarious expression of our knowledge. But this shews that the doctrine which makes our sense perceptions to be pure modes of the percipient mind cannot be true. If we are to continue to laugh, *we must change our base* (as they say now-a-days), and take the position, that perception involves two factors in one indivisible relation, namely, Self on the one hand, and Not-self on the other. In like manner, if the conception of a supreme Creator we (as it is too apt to be considered) a pure subjective mode, it would be hopeless to attempt founding a doctrine of Theism on it. As an instance in point, consider the position of Kant. Our notion of God is (he holds) simply regulative; that is, it is altogether an expression, after a certain manner, of the nature of the Ego; and hence he infers that we are not warranted, frrom this notion, to assert that a Divine Being actually exists. Christian writers have stigmatized this doctrine as it deserves; but I am not aware that any one has ever struck hi dart through the heart of what is (in my judgment) its primary falsehood, namely, the idea that the conception of God is purely subjective. Did I accept this dogma, I should feel myself shut up to Kant's conclusion; and just because my whole nature, intellectual and moral, revolts against the conclusion, I regret the dogma that leads to it. With Plato, I hold, generally, that *all conception is the knowledte of a present reality*; and specially, that *our conception of God is the knowledge of a present God.* God, in the glorious attributes of his nature, is not far from every one of us. We are, as a matter of fact, at every moment in the most intimate relation to Him, so that it is not impossible that he should be immediately apprehended by us. And why should it be deemed incredible —incredible that the relation which subsists betwixt God and his intelligent creatures should make itself felt? Under the very same species of compulsion which obliges me to regard the perception of the material world as *the mind in conscious relation to the material world*, I feel to regard the conception of God as *the mind in conscious relation to God*, and not a bare circumstance of myown thinking, a mode of Self which might conceivably have existed even had there (as the fool hath said in his heart) been no God.

I hope, after our previous discussions, that no one will ask me to prove the doctrine which I am delivering. Proof has been proved — I am half afraid *ad nauseum* — to be impossible. All that can be done is to set the doctrine forth in such a manner, that, if it be true, the mind which seriously reflects upon it, may become convinced of its truth. With this object in view, I ask youto consider at your leisure, more carefully than can be done during the delivery of a lecture, the principle on which a good deal of what I have been saying proceeds — that *we could not be absolutely certain of the existence of any object, unless it were in direct manifestation to the mind*. If not in direct relation to the mind, the object might be hypothesized —it might be set down as probable in this or that degree — it might be set down as probable in so high a degree, beyond the power of language or numbers to express, as to be, for all the practical purposes of ordinary life, certain, but it could not be felt to be certain, in the strict sense of the term. The mind is certain (in the strict sense) only of what it is actually apprehending —in other words, of what form a constituent element, or necessar factor, of its consciousness. Of this metaphysical maxim, I have not the shadow of a doubt. Suppose that you are, or that, on careful reflection you become, satisfied of it too. What then? Either we are capable of immediately knowing God, in which case His existence is absolutely certified to us; or we cannot be absolutely certain of His existence at all. Well (the Atheists will reply) I adopt the latter alternative. —It may be so (I answer); but that is what I cannot do. Before you are reasoning in a circle (methinks some sharp logician interposes); for you take your certainty of the Divine existence as a proof of the assertion that the conception of God involves the actual relation of God to the mind; while at the same time you derive your assurance of the Divine existence frm the existence of the conception, viewed as involving the actual relation of God to the mind. A manifest circle! — Nay, friend; I am not reasoning in a circle, for I am not reasoning at all. I am merely seeking reflectively to interpret my consciousness. I find within me a conception of the Perfect Being. I seek to render an account of it to myself. The conception is such as to impres me, from its intrinsic nature, with a feeling of its validity; just as the thought of my own existnece is such as to impress me, from its intrinsic nature, with a feeling of its validity. Now (I go on not to argue, but to reflect) absolute validity cannot possibly belong to the conception, unless the conception imply a direct knowledge of God. And so I come (not inferentially, but reflectively) to rest inthe conclusion that my conception does imply the direct knowledge of God, and is to me an absolutd assurance of the fact — just as my thought of my self, implying the knowledge of my self, is an assurance of my own existence.

But what could be said, were an Atheist to take the position of denyingthe views which have been expressed? I answer: what can be said when a Pyrhonist takes the position of denying the existence of a material world? In neither case is argument possible; in both cases an appeal can be made, fitted to arouse the mind to that action in which it shall aprehend the truth. You can call upon the Pyrrhonist to open his eyes and look upon nature. You can blow a trumpet in his ears. You can knock his head against a wall. Perhaps thus you will bring him to his sensew. If not, you can do nothing more. So with the Atheist. You can point him to the heavens which declare the glory of God, and to the firmament which sheweth His handiwork. You can bid him listen as day unto day uttereth speech and night unto night teacheth knowledge. an call You call upon him to mark how fearfully and wonderfully the members of his own body have been fashioned. You can ask him, as his spirit dances in the contemplation of the ever-changing numberless laughter of the happy billows on a sunlit summer sea — whence all this beauty and delight? You can whisper to him as the thunder-cloud is bursting overhead: "He looketh on the earth and it trembleth; He toucheth the hills and they smoke." Who sends the springs into the valleys, which run among the hills? Who causes the grass to grow for cattle, and herb for the service of man? Who has clothed the neck of the war horse with thunder, made leviathan to sport in his deeps, tuned the linnet's throat, and given power to the wing of the eagle? Thus you can frame your appeal. Still further, you can send the man you are dealing with into the chambers of his own soul. Does he never, it may be in the silent watches of the night, feel himself alone *with God?* Does no consciousness ever come home to him of his dependence on a Higher Power? Is he really in earnest in supposing that his existence is uncaused? that there is not a Creator in whom he lives and moves and has his being? Does he never, in reflecting upon his life, awake to the conviction that he is under the moral government of a Being who is absolutely holy, and who will render to every one according to his deeds? By such questionings and representations you may endeavour to stir the Atheists' soul to the apprehension of God; but if you fail, if his intellectual and moral energies still continue dormant, he must be left to his delusions.

Here I might let the matter rest. And indeed I am conscious that the points to which I am about to refer cannot be discussed in detail to any good purpose before a mixed audience — cannot be satisfactorily discussed at all, except on the basis, and as the ultimate results, of a complete system of metaphysics. Hence I shalll not inflict a discussion of them upon you; yet, as you will naturally expect me to be somewhat more explicit regarding the notions of *creation* and of *moral perfection* involved in our conception of the Perfect Being, I will endeavour to state — merely to state, and that as briefly as possible — the conclusions on these very difficult topics, in which, after the most earnest thought, I find myself resting. A single word of caution ere I proceed. Should the views which I am about to express be incorrect, the general doctrine that has been delivered will not thereby in the least degree be affected; except thus far — that it will be seen to be a doctrine which *I* am unable to work out. On these, as one the more special doctrines of revelation, may the Spirit of truth guide us into all truth.

The doctrine of Creation held by the modern Scottish (Hamiltonian) school, is that it is impossible positibely conceive creation, and therefore impossible, by any direct act of the mind, to realize the belief of it. I do not mean to deny that Sir William Hamilton denied creation — though his language on the subject is strange, and (as an utterance of a believer in the Bible) hard to be understood; but he certainly held that we cannot positively think or believe creation. Whatever thought or conviction of it we have, is negatice; which is just saying, in plain language, that we have no *real* thought or conviction of it at all. Now, adopting the Cartesian argument, I of course reject this doctrine — as indeed I reject the whole Hamiltonian system, root and branch. I think that I find, among the positive conceptions which my mind has in its possession, one to which no adequate interpretation can be given, except such as makes it to be the revelation of what is substantially an excercise of creative energy on the part of the Most High — I mean the conception of cause. Hamilton denies that we have any positive conception of cause. The notion (he would have us believe) is merely a negative impotency of the mind to think any addition being made to the sum of existence in the universe. According to this view, the notion of cause would take account simply of quantity of existence. This is assuredly not a correct statement of my notion of cause. When I speak of the power or efficient energy by the forthgoing of which something is caused, I am doing more than looking at, and comparing the mere quantum of existence in the universe at two different periods. Assuming that the mind has a positive conception of cause, I observe, next, that the conception is realized in connection with the thought of change. We necessarily think change as due to a cause; inother words, as brought about by power. Still further, the onlty change of which we ever are directly conscious, is a change in the system of beingof which we ourselves form a part. We cannot, for instance, be conscious of a change in the state of the celestial bodies, to which we are not in immediate relation. We are conscious while we contemplate the motions of objects in the celestial spaces, of a change in ourselves, and in the system of material existence to which we stnad proximately related. Our consciousness cannot possibly be severed from ourselves. These explanations having been made, I add that the conviction we at any moment have that the change of which we are conscious is being caused, or brought about by power, is nothing else, in my humble opinion, than our immediate apprehension of the Supreme Power, to which we, in the relation we bear to the material world, owe our continued existence from moment to moment. Some people talk of physical causes. The earth, by its attraction, draws bodies towards it; and so forth. This is a mere vulgar figment unsupported by a single consideration worth looking at. But, at any rate, if the Christian doctrine, which we all believe, be true, physical causes, granting them to exist — could not furnish the *entire* explanation of our conception of cause. For, cause is thought not merely as that without which the effect could not be produced, but as that which is sufficient to produce the effect. Now, no Christian believes that physical causes — admitting for a moment these purely imaginary agencies — are sufficient to account for the changes of which we are conscious, apart from what DesCartes terms the "concursus et cooperantia Dei" — the concurring power of the Almighty. Hence our notion of cause must involve an apprehension of the great First Cause — an apprehension, that is, of the actual present sustaining power of God. And what is the act of sustaining the world from moment to moment, but substantially a continued act of creation? Passing to the other point, our conception of God as a Being of moral perfection — I would *first* lay down the principle, that there is an essential, eternal, immutable distinction between right and wrong. *Next*, there must be some real ground for the distinction. And what is this? The ground and basis of a necessary and eternal distinction must itself be necessary and eternal, and hence, since there exists only one necessary and eternal Being, the ground of the distinction between right and wrong must be found in the nature of God. *Still further*, I possess a faculty, Conscience, by which I am capable of apprehending the distinction between right and wrong. The exercise of this faculty is accompanied (to use the technical expression) with the feeling of necessity; that is, I cannot resist the thought that right and wrong differ essentially. I can never think them confounded. For example, I can never think malice otherwise than as wrong; I cannot possibly conceive it becoming, in consequence of the mere command of any Being, or under any circumstances or conditions, a duty. Now here comes the knot of the problem: Does my conception of the absolute and unchanging distinction between right and wrong possess validity? of couse, all moralists who deserve the name answer in the affirmative; and they plead that an irresistible belief in he objective validity of our conception of right is, in fact, on of the features of the conception. I accept this plea, but with one vast and important departure from the ordinary theory. Our moral conceptions are ordinarily regarded as pure subjective modes, states of the mind not necessarily involving any real existence beyond the mind itself. On this theory, the doctrine just referred to, which finds in the intrinsic character of our moral thinking a guarantee of the objective validity of the conception of right, appears to be utterly inadmissible. Did I hold such a view, I should feel that the sceptic had me at his mercy. For, assuming the thought of right and wrong to be purely subjective — the sceptic asks: how can a purely subjective mode gurantee an objective reality? It is vain to urge — on such premises — that a persuasion of the objective validity of the conception is a feature of the conception, for, by hypothesis, this persuasion is still subjective. It is equally vain to urge, with Sir William Hamilton, that God could never have intended to deceive his creatures, nor framed them so as to be the victims of delusion; for, at this stage, while we are still enquiring whether the distinction which we think between right and wrong has any reality, we cannot be supposed to know anything respecting the Divine character, nor can we be entitled to assume that deception is worse than truth. What view, then, is to be taken of the conception of right, and how can the sceptical cavil, which has just been referred to, be evaded? Without dogmatism, in great humility, stretching out lame hands for the truth, and groping if haply I may feel after and find it, I suggest the following answer. May not our conception of the rightness or wrongness of what we are doing — in other words, of the moral state in which we are — be just the state of mind revealing itself as in accordance with, or in antagonism to, the nature of God? The nature of God is (as was explained above) the sole ground or basis of the reality of right. Right, therefor, is apprehended by us in its reality, only insofar as a manifestation of the nature of god is made to us. Since the creature cannot exist except in most intimate relation to the Creator, it is not *impossible*, and why (to repeat, *mutatis mutandis, the question which I put in regard to the power by which we are sustained) — why should it be deemed incredible*, that we should at each and every moment be capable of realising the absolute and uncghanging purity of God, set over against, and in relation to, the moral movements of our nature?

If the view now stated be correct, and the doctrine formerly delivered regarding the conception of cause be also admitted, it will be seen how Intellectual science and Ethical science together furnish the necessary foundations for a system of natural religion — and (I might add) for that of revealed religion too. All religion supposes the existence of a Divine Being, possessed of moral attributes, in conformity to whom our perfection consists. Now, with respect to the existence of God — if this were not infallibly certified to us by philosophy, it could not be certified to us at all. Revelation even could not certify it to us; because the possibility of revelation, and therefore the possibility of proving the Bible to be a revelation, proceeds upon the assumption that the question of the Divine existence is already settled. In like manner, if philosophy did not infallibly assure us of the moral attributes of God, and of the obligations under which we lie to be conformedto the Divine nature, revelation could not supplement its deficiency; for, a revelation, were its claims to be from God fully established, could not be felt to have authority, unless the perfection of the Being from which it emanates were already ascertained. Now how does philosophy fulfil the very high functions which thus fall to it. In the following manner: — and with this sentence, summing up the whole, I conclude. Intellectual science teaches, that, in the universal and necessary conception of cause, we have a direct manifestation of God in the exercise of his Almighty sustaining (virtually, creating) power; and Ethical science teaches, that, in our moral conceptions, properly interpreted, we have a direct manifestation of God in the glory of his eternal and unchangeable moral excellence.

Section Six

WILLIAM ALBERT CRAWFORD-FROST
(1863-1936)

6

Crawford-Frost:
Evolution and the Philosophy of Integration

J.Douglas Rabb

William Albert Crawford-Frost (1863-1936) was a Canadian born and educated Episcopal theologian who made his home in Baltimore Maryland where he served as rector of both the Memorial Church of the Holy Comforter in Baltimore and St.Mary's Church in Emmerton, a nearby town. Born in Owen Sound, Ontario, he studied philosophy and theology at the University of Toronto, B.A. 1884, M.A. 1886, University College. After gradua ting from Wycliffe College in 1887 he served successively as rector in St.Paul's Anglican Church, Charlottetown, Prince Edward Island, St.George's, New Glasgow, Nova Scotia and the Church of the Redeemer, Merrick, Long Island, New York, before moving to Baltimore.

Crawford-Frost's attempt to reconcile the theory of evolution with religious belief, to accept both science and religion, appears in a little monograph entitled *A New Theory of Evolution*. Published in 1925 by the University of Maryland "as a monograph edition of 1000 copies," the book consists of two guest lectures delivered at the University. The first lecture is entitled "Science, Philosophy and Religion." The second has the rather comprehensive title "From Amoeba to American." The book begins with the statement that:

> Philosophy, Science and Religion form a trio inseparable in many ways, but especially in this: that all three are necessary to understand evolution. Philosophy expounds the methods of evolution; science collects its details and religion explains the purpose of it.[1]

I do not wish to argue that Crawford-Frost is entirely successful in his attempt to reconcile religion and science. For one thing he seems to regard science as simply natural history. Its sole business is to describe and classify:

> When a scientist stops collecting and classifying facts and begins to theorize about them, he ceases to be a scientist and becomes a philo-

sopher. When a philosopher ceases to reason about facts and begins collecting and classifying them he ceases to be a philosopher and becomes a scientist. The philosopher is more productive when he attends to his own business just as the scientist is.[2]

In spite of this questionable division of labour Crawford-Frost does insist that "philosophy must build on scientific facts or it is nothing but cobwebby, hair splitting, mental gymnastics, running around in circles."[3] Given the importance he ascribes to science it is little wounder that Crawford-Frost insists on taking evolution seriously. However, in order to understand fully his attempt to reconcile religion and science it is important to realize that this attempt is made in the context of a fully developed system of idealism, which he called the philosophy of integration. Crawford-Frost's idealism is presented in two earlier books: *Old Dogma in a New Light* (New York, 1896) and *The Philosophy of Integration: An Explanation of the Christian Religion and of the Universe* (Boston, 1906). From the standpoint of the development of philosophy in Canada what is interesting about the idealism expounded in these two works is Crawford-Frost's claim that his idealism is, at least in part, a systematic working out of ideas presented to him by his mentor at the University of Toronto, Professor George Paxton Young. Armour and Trott's recent history of Canadian philosophy, *The Faces of Reason* describes Young as "the first of a long and influential line of Canadian idealists" but goes on to note that "his writings are mostly fragmentary and frequently known to us mainly through notes of his students."[4] In a "Biographical Sketch" attached to *Old Dogma in a New Light* Crawford-Frost, writing of himself in the third person, says the following about the influence of Young, not only upon himself, but also on the majority of the students at University College Toronto:

> At University College he [C-F] studied philosophy under the late George Paxton Young, LL.D., whose memory is still idolized by thousands of the brightest and most successful scholars in Canada. Dr. Young had a system of philosophy distinctly his own, but, through modesty, or for some other reason, he could never be induced to publish it. Consequently his theories live only in the minds of his students. It occurred to Mr. Crawford-Frost that if Professor Young's leading ideas were woven together and developed into a system, it would found not only an entirely new school of philosophy, but would open up a new line a reconciliation between science and religion. He [C-F] obtained the degree of Master of Arts by a thesis on this subject, and so strong a hold did the idea take upon him , especially in its religious bearings, that he felt it a divine call to relinquish his career as a journalist and enter upon a course of theology in the Protestant Episcopal School of Wycliffe College, Toronto.[5]

It is unfortunate that all copies of Crawford-Frost's M.A. thesis seem to have been lost. Although I have argued elsewhere that Crawford-Frost is not only an important idealist in his own right, but that his work also casts some considerable light on Young's thought,[6] care should be taken in regarding

Crawford-Frost's published work as an exposition, or even a development, of Young's ideas on every topic. We know, for example, that Young was vehemently against hedonistic utilitarianism in all its forms.[7] Crawford-Frost on the other hand not only held this type of utilitarianism but also believed that it had divine sanction:

> Hedonism that is rational and sanctified, not sanctimonious, is pure Christianity, for the object of Christianity is to make people happy... Our chief obligation to God is to be happy and to make other people happy. Duty is duty only because it leads to happiness, the greatest happiness of the greatest number.... And this same religion harmonizes also with the modern latest science, the sciences of psychology, psycho analysis, physiology and sociology. Whatever these sciences show to be conducive to the health and happiness of mankind and womankind will be found to be plainly in keeping with the teaching and example of Jesus.[8]

Still, the metaphysical theory from which both this ethical hedonism and the new theory of evolution are said to follow does seem to be consistent with at least the principle aim of Young's idealism. This Young outlines as follows:

> There is nothing in philosophy opposed to, but on the contrary all its conclusions are in beautiful harmony with , what revelation teaches.... The universe was not created once for all... but it is at every instant upheld by God. It is a continued product of the continued exercise of his power.[9]

Crawford-Frost's attempt to reconcile religion and science may well cast some light on Young's metaphysics. There is certainly more agreement between the two thinkers here than there is in the area of ethical theory. Crawford-Frost, in attempting to reconcile evolution with the notion of a creator God argues that "we may give a rational and understandable explanation of the theory of evolution as the persistent effort of the indwelling Divinity to find its way back to the centre of the Divine Personality."[10] In order to make this 'explanation' of evolution intelligible it is important to realize Crawford-Frost was influenced not only by George Paxton Young but also by Hegel and Herbert Spencer:

> Philosophically the theory is a union of Hegel and Herbert Spencer. Each of these has exhausted philosophy on his own line. No further advance is possible except by a union of them, and also by a synthesis of their united products with the facts of revelation. In other words they have explained the universe as far as an explanation is possible without the hypothesis of God and the Devil, and the truths of Christianity.[11]

One further source of influence should be mentioned. Crawford-Frost describes his position as "Modern Scholasticism" and argues that his attempt to reconcile Christian faith and philosophical reason is similar to that of

St.Thomas Aquinas, although Crawford-Frost expects a greater degree of success since he has at his disposal all the subsequent advances in science and philosophy:

> The mediaeval scholastics attempted to defend Catholic dogma from the standpoint of human reason, but they were hampered by false scientific hypotheses and wrong theories of the unvierse. We are at the beginning of a new philosophy —Modern Scolasticism — which shall have the same purpose as that of the Middle Ages, but shall possess, in addition, all the scientific and rational attainments of the world since the time of Bacon. Thus in defence of Catholic dogma the new scholasticism will have an immense advantage over St.Thomas Aquinas and the writers of the Middle Ages in that it will have the synthetic philosophy of Herbert Spencer to guide it.[12]

Crawford-Frost attempts to bring about this modern synthesis of faith and philosophy by accepting the Hegelian notion of God as absolute unity and arguing that this Divine Being is immanent in an evolving Nature which has as its *telos* absolute unity in a transcendent God: "...the mind of God is not only transcendent but immanent."[13] How God can in fact be both is explained by introducing the concepts of "integration" or "unity" and "disintegration" or "separation" based loosely on Spencer's concepts of "evolution" and "dissolution."[14] The principle of integration or unity is said to be a positive force which explains not only the origins of the universe but also the motions of the planets and the evolution of life on the planets as well as the social organization of the more highly evolved forms of that life. "This process of unification explains everything that happens on each planet, as well as the motions of the heavenly bodies in their totality."[15]

> In the evolution of human history, unity and order slowly triumph over disunion and disorder.... Every step in advance is only secured by a struggle of good and unselfishness against the primitive instincts of cruelty and greed, but a long view of the past shows clearly that these primitive impulses, although still strong and widely spread, and at times surprisingly powerful, are nevertheless being surely beaten.... There are temproary setbacks, no doubt, but the general progress in unmistakeable.[16]

Disintegration or separation, on the other hand, is said to be a principle of evil identified with Satan who is described as personification of the "disintegrating trinity of ugliness, evil and error."[17] Although religious thought conceives of Satan as a person, Crawford-Frost argues that philosophical reason shows us that the concept of evil or disintegration is in reality nothing more than the relaxation of the integrating force:

> Our contention is that the Devil is God's own limitation and relaxation of Himself. He is God's servant, and is allowed for God's own preordained purpose a succession of temporary triumphs. In reality God is Absolute Unity.. . . Yet he has chosen to relax himself into the Becoming by a conflict with a part of Himself, which is a mere negation of himself. The

Devil is not a real person but only an apparent or actual one. By actuality we mean the universe as we see it. By reality we signify the universe as God sees it to be in its true nature. The Devil is thus the foil for the attributes of an All-Wise and Beneficent Creator."[18]

Though we need not think of the Devil as a real person Crawford-Frost argues that we must conceive of God as a person since "complete intelligence implies personality":

...[T]he Creator must be a person, or something higher than a person. But anything higher than a person is not intelligible to us, because personality is a mark of the highest intelligence we can conceive. Therefore the Creator, from our point of view, must be a Person.[19]

Once he has established, at least to his satisfaction, the Personhood of God, Crawford-Frost then poses one of the most fundamental questions of metaphysics: "Why should this Person have created a universe? And why should he have created it by evolution? And still be creating it by evolution?"[20] After examining a number of possible explanations for the purpose of creation, including that of Augustine based on the nature of Divine Love, Crawford-Frost presents the following rather homely argument:

The answer I shall try to give has not, so far as I know, ever been given by anyone else... Suppose you were confind in a sick room for twenty years. You would come to know every crack in the wall paper, every detail of that room. You would be omniscient as far as that room was concerned. It would be unspeakably monotonous. It never seems to have occurred to anybody that omniscience for God would mean no variety, no adventure, unbearable monotony throughout eternity. Is it not a reasonable hypothesis, therefore, to suggest that as a relief from that monotony God should bury a part of himself in matter, so that the blind, or immanent part, should have a rest from omniscience, and be limited and blinded by its imprisonment, but, in septillions of ways, should struggle back again to the centre of the Divine Personality from which it had come? ...Evolution is the Great Game of eternity played between the Transcendent Deity on the one hand and the various parts of the Immanent Deity on the other, so as to pass through the ages with ever-increasing interest and happiness.[21]

In fairness it should be noted that this 'argument' or rather this analogy was presented in a lecture to a philosophy class, probably an undergraduate philosophy class, at the University of Maryland. Crawford-Frost seems to have presented his basic thesis at various levels of sophistication. For example in his book *The Philosophy of Integration* he argues that:

We are in the era of the gradual, but continuous, triumph of unity. When all the atoms in the universe are brought together ... our era will have ended, and the Destroyer will be annihilated, and there may begin the gradual triumph of separation which will end only when all the elements are distributed again throughout space into an imponderable, invisible and altogether imperceptible ether...[22]

Crawford-Frost seems to have accepted some form of the oscillating theory of the universe. It should be remembered that although he describes the universe as going through endless cycles of expansion and contraction it is not in fact a material universe that he is describing. Crawford-Frost is an idealist. Ultimately matter is explained in terms of mind, in this case the mind of God. Though Crawford-Frost does not say so, his cyclical theory is reminiscent of the Hindu view of the cosmos. Still, he leaves room for the Western belief in creation *ex nihilo*, though in reality this turns out to be a false belief, a mere appearance:

> The history of the universe is a succession of windings and unwindings. We are in an age of winding or condensation. Our era began when the whole universe was distributed throughout space in an imponderable, invisible, inaudible and altogether imperceptible ether, which nevertheless contained in itself potentially all the elements or atoms we know on earth. This is for us the nearest conceivable approach to nothingness. It is for man actual nothingness, though for God it is everything in potentiality. At this period God's self-relaxation had reached its climax of triumph over his unifying impulse. He now begins to conquer His self-relaxation. The impulse to relax yet exists in every atom but it is relatively weaker than the impulse to condense.[23]

Not only does this resemble the cyclical view of Hinduism but it is also, at least in general outline, compatible with the contemporary scientific theory of cosmic oscillation. Carl Sagan, for example, claims that: "The Hindu religion is the only one of the world's great faiths dedicated to the idea that the Cosmos itself undergoes an immense, indeed an infinite, number of deaths and rebirths."[24] After describing this Hindu view in some detail Sagan continues:

> These profound and lovely images are, I like to imagine, a kind of premonition of modern astronomical ideas. Very likely, the universe has been expanding since the Big Bang, but it is by no means clear that it will continue to expand forever. The expansion may gradually slow, stop and reverse itself. If there is less than a certain critical amount of matter in the universe, the gravitation of the receding galaxies will be insufficient to stop the expansion, and the universe will run away forever. But if there is more matter than we can see — hidden away in black holes, say, or in hot but invisible gas between the galaxies — then the universe will hold together gravitationally and partake of a very Indian succession of cycles, expansion followed by contraction, universe upon universe, cosmos without end.[25]

One of the major difficulties with Crawford-Frost's Christian cosmology is his erroneous belief that we are now living in a contracting, not an expanding universe. This is no mere minor setback for Crawford-Frost. His entire hedonistic moral theory and his optimistic social philosophy proclaiming the triumph of "unity and order ...over disunion and disorder" presuppose that the "Great Integrator" has the upper hand, that we do not live in an expanding universe. Crawford-Frost's attempt to reconcile religion and science illustrates the difficulty which any such attempt is likely to encounter given the rapid advance of scientific knowledge.

Notes

1. W.A. Crawford-Frost, *A New Theory of Evolution*, (Baltimore, 1925), p.3.

2. IBID., p.3.

3. IBID., p.3.

4. Leslie Armour and Elizabeth Trott. *The Faces of Reason: An Essay on Philosophy and Culture in English Canada* 1850-1950, (Waterloo, Wilfred Laurier U.P., 1981) p. 85.

5. W.A. Crawford-Frost, *Old Dagma in a New Light*, (New York, 1896), pp. 53-54.

6. J.D. Rabb, "The Fusion Philosophy of Crawford-Frost", *Idealistic Studies*, Vol. XVI, No1, 1986, p. 77.

7. OP. CIT., *The Faces of Reason*, pp. 98ff.

8. OP. CIT., *A New Theory of Evolution*, pp. 10-11.

9. George Paxton Young, "An Examination of Professor Ferrier's Theory of Knowing and Being", *Canadian Journal*, New Series, Vol. I, 1856, pp. 123-124.

10. OP. CIT., *Old Dogma in a New Light*, p. 13.

11. IBID., p. 9.

12. IBID., pp. 9-10.

13. IBID., p. 13.

14. See Herbert Spencer, *First Principles*, (New York, 1980), Section 97, p. 241.

15. OP. CIT., *Old Dogma in a New Light*, p. 13.

16. W.A. Crawford-Frost, THE WAY OUT, Sc. 11, "Evolution of an Organized Hnumanity", *Pamphlets on International Cooperation*, (Library of Congress), Vol. 12, 1931.

17. W.A. Crawford-Frost, *The Philosophy of Intergration: An Explanation of the Universe and of the Christian Religion*, ed. James Wilson Bright, (Boston, 1906), p. 3.

18. IBID., p. 3.

19. OP. CIT., *A New Theory of Evolution*, p. 9.

20. IBID., p.9.

21. IBID., p. 10.

22. OP. CIT., *The Philosophy of Integration*, p. 3.

23. IBID., p. 9.

24. Carl Sagen, *Cosmos*, (New York, 1980), p. 258.

25. IBID., p. 259.

Science, Philosophy and Religion

(Guest-lecture delivered before the Philosophy Class in the University of Maryland, December 14, 1925. The subject is as assigned by Thomas H. Spence, A..M., Dean Emeritus of Arts and Sciences)

William Albert Crawford-Frost

PHILOSOPHY, SCIENCE AND RELIGION form a trio inseparable in many ways, but especially in this: that all three are necessary to understand evolution. Philosophy expounds the methods of evolution: science collects its details and religion explains the purpose of it.

Neither philosophy nor science can explain the purpose of evolution. They can tell much about the how of things, but nothing about the ultimate why.

Science concerns itself chiefly with the collection and classification of facts. That is its especial business, and it is always most efficient and productive when it minds its own business. Consequently it always tends to emphasize the seen and mechanistic and to ignore the unseen and teleological. Scientists are expected to perceive rather than to reflect.

The philosopher, on the other hand, takes the facts that science has revealed and he reflects upon them. It is the business of philosophy to reason about the facts that science has apprehended, to ponder them and their relationships to each other, to suggest general laws, first as doubtful hypotheses and later, perhaps, as accepted theories.

When a scientist stops collecting and classifying facts and begins to theorize about them, he ceases to be a scientest and becomes a philosopher. When a philosopher stops reasoning about facts and begins collecting and classifying them he ceases to be a philosopher and becomes a scientist. The philosopher is more productive when he attends to his own business just as the scientist is.

But though each has his own sphere, and is better when he confines himself to it, yet each is indispensable to the other. When a certain number of facts'have been collected and classified one must begin to reason about them,

*First published as part I of *A New Theory of Evolution* by The University of Maryland, Baltimore, 1925.

else why go to the bother of collecting them? They must be reasoned about in order to apply them to practical use and in order to develop them further. They must be reflected upon in order to get some general law which will form the basis of a further collection and classification of facts. So each furnishes the material for the other to work upon. Science can go just so far without philosophy. Then it must stop till philosophy gives it a new life and a new impetus. On the other hand philosophy must build on scientific facts or it is nothing but cobwebby, hair-splitting, mental gymnastics, running around in circles.

But both science and philosophy deal with facts as they are perceived by the senses and reflected on by the understanding. They do not touch any source of motivation that may arise from faculties such, for example, as intuition or faith. Here comes in the necessity of religion as the foundation principle of enlightenment both for science and philosophy.

Which is of more importance in astromony, the naked eye or the telescope? The naked eye is all right as far as it goes. It shows us the sun, moon and stars and they form the basis of our knowledge. But how little they teach us compared with what the telescope reveals! Now when we come to deal with the problems of the universe as a whole, and man's part in it, faith is to knowledge exactly what the telescope is to the naked eye in astromony. Our science and philosophy are all right as far as they go, but it requires the telescope of faith to get any kind of a coherent and intelligible explanation of the whole and of the relation of the parts to the whole. Both science and philosophy fail us here. They have no answer to give of any kind whatever, bad, good or indifferent. Religion has an answer. It may not be the correct answer. It may be a very incorrect one, according to what kind of a religion it is, but at least it is an answer where both science and philosophy are speechless.

Some may say: What is the use of trying to answer a question that has no answer? Are we sure there is none? It does not follow that a problem is insoluble because it is difficult. If you will stop to consider how we deal with the small problems of life, you will see that we use what knowledge we have and when that does not carry us far enough we make the best guess we can and act on that. That is what faith is. It is merely making the best guess we can and acting on it. We have been doing this from childhood in regard to the little problems of life, why should we not do it in regard to the greatest problem of all? Life is a game and the chief interest in it is that it keeps us guessing. The romance of discovery is the greatest charm of our existence. As soon as we know a thing it loses interest. It is the finding out that is enjoyable.

Besides, if the answer to the Great Riddle could be found in science and philosophy then the scientist and philosopher would have an unfair advantage over the man in the street. If our future life and happiness depended on our knowledge alone, then the college graduate would have a better chance of getting into the Kingdom of Heaven than the garbage man would. But the Almighty in His wisdom has made faith, not knowledge, the main thing so that everybody has an equal chance. It is the only plan that could be fair to everybody. That is what the Scriptures mean by saying that He has hidden these things from the wise and prudent and has revealed them unto babes, and the only way a person can get into the Kingdom of Heaven is by becoming like a little child. So long as a man is proud of his knowledge, or proud of his riches, or his fame, or his power, he finds it hard to get into the gate. Only the humble can get in. It puts us all on the same footing. Anybody can enter who is willing to become simple, loving and trustful as a little child. This is fair for everybody. If a man is not willing to do this he bars himself out. Nobody keeps him out. He stays out of his own accord, and if he stays out he is not happy, whereas, the door being wide open, he could, if he would walk right in and be happy, because in this world and the next, only the humble are happy. I have made a great many discoveries in my lifetime, of one kind or another, but the greatest up to date is the discovery that pride is painful, and that the only way to be happy is to be humble. I cannot get a patent on this, because, sooner or later everybody else makes the same discovery. The trouble is that we generally discover it too late, or, if we find it out early, we forget about it and do not act upon it, and so we go on making ourselves miserable all our lives when we could have been happy all the time.

The province of religion is faith, but the right kind of faith consists not in believing every word of the Bible to be literally true. That is the greatest mistake of all. It is not "good news" to a man to tell him that unless he believes Jonah lived for three days in a whale's belly he will be burned forever in fire and brimstone. I do not see how anybody could consider this "glad tidings." It would not be good news to me, for I certainly do not believe it, and I do not believe that God expects me to believe it, or wants me to believe it, and I would not like to think that I should have to spend eternity swimming around in a scalding lake because I cannot believe it. It is not "good news" and, if it is not that, it is not the Gospel. I refuse to believe anything but what is Gospel.

The faith that supplements science and philosophy, and harmonizes with them, and explains them, is the belief that behind all creation is a personal intelligence, kindly and loving, that consequently, in spite of the temporary suffering, the whole scheme is a beneficent one, and that we, notwithstanding all our shortcomings, will ultimately be perfectly happy because the Creator is a loving father and cares for us as a father cares for his children, and we know that no earthly father, in his right mind, will be satisfied till his children are happy if it is in his power to make them so. This is good news. It is the gospel. That is why I believe it, and also believe that it harmonizes with both science and philosophy.

The old-time theologian was very contemptuous of knowledge as compared with faith. A man was supposed to take his religion as a child takes his medicine. The principle was "open your mouth and shut your eyes and I'll give you something to make you wise." Nowadays people are not satisfied with that kind of a religion. They want to keep their eyes open and see what they swallow. They want to use what reason they have as far as it goes, and they are right. Any religion that is afraid of science and philosophy is a losing religion.

Religion needs the facts of science and philosophy just as the astronomer needs his naked eye as well as his telescope, but for a person to stop short with knowledge and despise faith is just as futile in trying to solve the problem of the origin and destiny of man as it would be futile for an astronomer to use his naked eye and despise a telescope.

Listen to the parable of the blind man on the high rock.

Once there was a blind man who lived on the top of a high rock. It was a thousand feet high and a thousand feet across the top. Necessaries were brought to him in an aeroplane from time to time. Here he lived safely, although if he had once stepped over the edge he would have been dashed to pieces. Around his body was a strong belt to which was attached a wire, slender, flexible and strong, and the other end of this wire was fastened to a post in the center of the plateau.

He could go all over the top of his rock, work in his garden, do his chores, read his Braille and be happy so long as he was tied in this way.

Because he was tied he was free.

If at any moment he had been cut from his binding cord, in that moment he would have been afraid to move for fear of instant death. Only by being bound could he be free.

Now Religion, (from *re*, back; and *ligo*, to tie, or bind) as we all know, means a "binding back" to the "Great First Cause." Only by being "bound back" in this way can the scientist or philosopher be free in his thought to go wherever his investigations may lead him. The moment the line is cut that ties him back to the Great Primal Intelligence in that moment he is liable to be dashed to pieces on the rocks of absurdity.

When is a man a fool? By what standard shall we so harshly judge a man? We are all more or less foolish and ignorant. How can we who are all foolish give a good definition of a fool? I do not know what your idea of a fool may be, but mine is that anyone who can look around him at the works of nature and imagine that all these things have come about by chance, that they show no signs of a designing mind, is a fool.

An agnostic is not a fool. He is merely a stickler for correct expression and insists upon a certain definition of knowledge as something essentially different from belief. He may be both an agnostic and a believing Christian at the same time. He insists that he does not know, and cannot know, certain things which cannot be properly and logically proven in the Kantian sense, and he is technically correct in his use of the term knowledge. I am an orthodox clergyman of the Protestant Episcopal Church and consider myself more "fundamental" than most of those who call themselves "fundamentalists," but I would not be either afraid or ashamed to be called an agnostic.

The uneducated man, however, does not use the term knowledge in the Kanitan sense. He means by it belief of which he is very sure. When he thinks, but is not sure, he says he "believes." When he feels sure he says he "knows." This is the popular use of the word, and that deserves consideration because when ninety-nine men out of a hundred use a term improperly the hundredth man should not be too insistent upon his technical correctness. The whole question is only an academic one at best.

The chief objection I have to the word "agnostic" is that it is ambiguous. It may mean either a believer or an unbeliever. Even the word "unbeliever" is also ambiguous, because a man may believe some things and not believe others; but there is no ambiguity about the word "atheist." It means a man who says there is no God.

Even here there are two kind of atheists. One says he knows there is no God and the other says he believes there is no God.

No man could properly say he knows there is no God unless he had been all over space, and had visited all the suns, planets and moons in the whole universe, and had investigated every inch of them, over their surfaces and down to their centres, and also every inch of the ethereal medium, within the universe and beyond it. Even if he had done this he could not be sure unless he could prove that he had the faculties that would recognize a God when he saw Him.

The man who says he believes there is no God is not such a fool as the man who says he knows there is none, but he is a fool nevertheless, although, as I shall presently try to show, there is some excuse for his foolishness.

For example, what could be more foolish than to imagine that the orderly arrangement of central sun, surrounded by revolving planets according to "Keppler's Laws," just happened by chance when one star accidentally passed too close to another and drew off a nebulous cloud? What could be more foolish than to think that an arrangement so full of meaning should have had a meaningless beginning? Nebulae do condense into suns, but they do not do so only when one star accidentally passes too close to another. What is meaningful now was meaningful in the beginning. We must tie back to an intelligent First Cause or we are dashed on the rocks of foolishness.

To go back to the parable of the blind man on the high rock. We are all like that man and the cord that is light as aluminum, flexible as silk and strong as steel, is made up of three strands: Faith, Hope and Love. God is the centre to which man is tied by that three-fold cord, and so long as he is bound by that cord he is safe and free.

But everything depends on the kind of God a person is tied to. It is a terrible thing to be tied to a Tribal God, like the early God of the Jews, but it is all right to be tied to a Loving Father, for then the tie, on one side, is only parental affection and guidance and, on the other, filial affection and trust. That kind of a tie does not irk either party, but is a joy to each, a source of freedom and safety.

The trouble with the theologians of the past, and with many of the present, is that they insist that the scientist and the philosopher must tie back to the God revealed in the Bible, and the God revealed in the Bible varies according to what part of the Bible you find Him in. The God who was supposed to have told the Israelites to borrow gold and silver from the Egyptians, every woman from her confiding neighbor, in order to run off with them, sounds like Jacob talking through Moses rather than God talking through him. I cannot imagine God talking that way, but I can easily see how and why they would think it was God talking.

But God of the Jews gets better and better as the Jews themselves progress in enlightenment and ideals, and under the prophets God did indeed talk to them with unmistakable voice. It was God who said through Isaiah: "Wash you, make you clean; put away the evil of your doings from before mine eyes; cease to do evil, learn to do well: seek justice, relieve the opressed, judge the fatherless, plead for the widow." The first God was supposed to be a kind of being who would advise a mean and cruel theft. The second was a God of justice and compassion. He had gone far in evolution beyond the first, but even Isaiah's God of justice was far inferior to the Heavenly Father revealed in the New Testament.

It was better for primitive man to be tied to an imperfect conception of God than to no god at all, better still for the Jews to be tied to the God of Isaiah than to the God of Moses, but best of all is it for the whole human race to be forever tied to the God revealed in Jesus, because that tie is the only one that gives perfect freedom both for the scientist and the philosopher. The religion of Christ properly interpreted and understood, not as it is preached erroneously at present from most Christian pulpits, but as Christ himslf taught it, is the only satisfactory explanation of physical, mental and moral evolution.

When I speak of the relation between philosophy, science and religion, therefore, I refer to the Christian religion as I believe it to have been preached by Jesus, not to modern misrepresentations of it, and not to any other religion.

The religions of Confucius, Zoroaster, Buddha and Mahomet resemble Christianity in some respects, but not one of them except Christianity, properly presented, shows an ideal of the kind of a God people ought to tie to. The lower animals resemble man, but man is on the main line of evolution and the others are only on side tracks. Christianity is to the other religions what man is to the other animals.

What scientist and philosophers of the present day need is not to be tied to the God revealed *in* the Bible, but to the God revealed *through* the Bible. There is all the difference in the world between the preposition *in* and the preposition *through*. The God revealed by the Study of the Bible is a progressive conception reaching its climax and perfection in Christ and nothing true in either science or philosophy will ever be found to contradict the truth as it was taught by Jesus.

There is this to be said, however, in excuse for the atheism of some people: It has arisen from the false idea of many religionists regarding the government of the universe as being an absolute and not a representative government.

Most Christians, even in the present day, believe that everything that happens does so by the will of God. They ignore the free will of God's creatures. They do not recognize the inevitable sequence of cause and effect. When a person dies they say: "The Lord gave and the Lord hath taken away. Blessed be the name of the Lord." And they would say this even if the death were an atrocious murder. God does not rule this planet. He lets man rule it. All God can do under the present arrangement is to try to guide and persuade man to do right, and so avoid trouble. If man refuses to obey this guidance, man should not hold God responsible for the result. If it were otherwise God's government would be either mechanistic or autocratic. It is neither. God is a Constitutional Monarch. He allows his creatures to govern themselves. He tries to persuade them to do it properly, but if they will not follow His advice they must suffer the consequences, but, even then, He tries to mitigate, so far as he can, the suffering that is unavoidable, and to bring good out of it. But He does not interfere with the free will of any creature from the amoeba to man.

Now when a person has been brought up to believe that everything that happens does so by the will of God, and when he begins to realize the awfulness of what does happen in spite of frantic and pitiable prayers to God, he is apt to jump to the conclusion that there is no God at all. This is because he has always been taught that God is actually omnipotent. He does not realize that God's hands are tied by the free will that he has allowed to his creatures, and to interfere with that free will would be to spoil the whole course of evolution and ruin all interest in the game which we are playing as the most enjoyable way to spend eternity.

If you gave a man a power of attorney, you would not be actually omnipotent over your own property so long as you let him have that power of attorney. But you would be potentially so, because you could withdraw it. In like manner God is not actually omnipotent, but only potentially so as long as he allows his creatures their free will. The game of evolution consists of letting each creature freely evolve in its own way in response to its environment and to the material, or mental, stimuli which come to it. Free will is the essential part of the sport. Without it there would be no variety and no adventure. We would all be mere machines.

It may seem to one onlooker as if this game is not worth the candle, or to another that it is only a diabolical struggle of horrible cruelty, the invention of an evil monster, but we should remember that one cannot judge a game till he sees the whole of it, and all the good things it leads to.

I believe that every living thing, from the coral insect that lives but a day up to the man who lives a century, has far more happiness than misery, even in this life. If evolution means progress in beauty, goodness and intelligence, greater capacity for pleasure, and wider and more intense experience of happiness, who can deny that, even if in one stage of existence misery appeared to exceed happiness, it might not be so reversed in subsequent stages that the sum total of happiness for each creature would outweigh the sum total of misery to the nth degree? A religion that regards the whole game of evolution as good, and that sees in it the most delightful way in which we could possibly spend eternity, is the kind of religion that harmonizes with science and philosophy and explains everything, and it is the only thing that can do so. It alone can tell us the ultimate why of evolution.

How then, in detail, does religion explain the purpose of evolution? Since it ties back to a supremely intelligent and powerful First Cause, it ties back to a Person, because complete intelligence implies personality. The lower animals possesss intelligence, but they are not persons. A person possesses higher intelligence than a mere animal. If, therefore, there is, as Goethe supposed, at the centre of space a "monad of pure intelligence," it must, in order to be pure, i.e., free from the cloudiness of ignorance, be more intelligent than the most intelligent person we know, because the most intelligent person on earth is still very cloudy in his intelligence regarding many things. Therefore the Creator must be a Person, or something higher than a person. But anything higher than a person is not intelligible to us, because personality is a mark of the highest intelligence we can conceive. Therefore the Creator, from our point of view, must be a Person.

Why should this Person have created a universe? And why should He have created it by evolution? And still be creating it by Evolution? There are several answers to this question that religion has to offer.

In the first place, once we have accpted the idea of an Eternal Personal Being, it follows as a matter of common sense that this Personal Being would not be likely to spend eternity in idleness. He would be doing something rather than nothing throughout the ages, and, since, by our very hypothesis, He is a Creator, naturally the most logical thing for Him to be doing would be creating, thinking up new plans, devising new formulae, making new combinations, inventing new creatures, and not only designing their parts and functions, but experimentally calling them into existence and trying them out.

The great Austine has offered another explanation of the purpose of creation. It is of the nature of love, he says, to demand an object for it to expend itself upon. Only by creating a vast universe could the infinite love in the Creator find an adequate object for his love. This is the most satisfactory answer to that question, but it does not throw any light on why He should have done it by evolution rather than by a single and completed act, because, in either case, it could be an adequate object of his love.

The answer that I shall try to give has not, so far as I know, ever been given by anyone else. It may not be the true answer, but to me it seems reasonable and probable.

Suppose you were confined in a sick room for twenty years. You would come to know every crack in the wall paper, every detail of that room. You would be omniscient so far as that room was concerned. It would be unspeakably monotonous. It never seems to have occurred to anybody that omiscience for God would mean no variety, no adventure, unbearable monotony throughout eternity. Is it not a reasonable hypothesis, therefore, to suggest that, as a relief from that monotony, God should bury a part of himself in matter, so that the blind, or immanent part, should have a rest from omniscience, and be limited and blinded by its imprisonment, but, in septillions of ways, should struggle back again to the centre of the Divine Personality from which it had come? In this way God blinds a part of Himself in order that it may have the pleasure of learning to see, becomes dumb in order to enjoy acquiring the power of speech, becomes deaf that he may delight in hearing sounds and music, becomes insensitive that he may enjoy the pleasures of sensation.

Evolution is the Great Game of eternity played between the Transcendent Deity on the one hand and the various parts of the Immanent Deity on the other, so as to pass through the ages with ever-increasing interest and happiness.

You and I are parts of the Immanent Deity, and when we are having a good time it is God in us having a good time.

"But," someone will say, "is this not the philosophy of Hedonism?" I reply: "Certainly it is. Hedonism that is rational and sanctified, not sanctimonious, is pure Christianity, for the object of Christianity is to make people happy." "But, how about duty? Is not 'duty' our chief obligation to God?" No. Our chief obligation to God is to be happy and to make other people happy. Duty is duty only because it leads to happiness, the greatest happiness of the greatest number. If it does not lead to that it is not duty to God at all. What God wants, above all things, is for men to be happy. That is why He created man and why He is playing the game of evolution. Any religion that is a joy-killer is not from God but from the Devil. The Devil has all along been making men think that God is not happy unless men are miserable and make other men miserable. Aseticism and puritanism are the religion of John the Baptist, not the religion of Jesus. That is why Jesus said that he who was least ¬ the Kingdom of Heaven was greater than John the Baptist.

The religion of Jesus, not of John the Baptist, harmonizes with philosophy if it is the right kind of philosophy, the philosophy of liberty as against the philosophy of unnatural inhibitions and restrictions that have their roots in the jealousy, selfishness and ignorance of primitive man.

And this same religion harmonizes also with the latest modern science, the sciences of psychology, psycho analysis, physiology and sociology. Whatever these sciences show to be conductive to the health and happiness of mankind and womankind will be found to be plainly in keeping with the teaching and example of Jesus.

The young people of the present day have risen in revolt against what they call "conventions." Their real fight should not be against conventions as such, but only against false conventions which we have inherited from the past. Conventions are necessary. Restrictions are necessary. Self-control and temperance are necessary. But those conventions and restrictions must be only those which are rational and healthful and in accordance with what medical men tell us will best promote human happiness. What the world needs is not to abolish conventions, but to substitute proper conventions for puritanical, fanatical or superstitious conventions.

When we substitute the religion of Jesus, and the conventions of the Kingdom of Heaven based solely on the Golden Rule, for the religion of "Thou shalt not" which reached its climax in John the Baptist, we will find that it will harmonize perfectly with philosophy and science.

Here the parable of the bored king.

Once there was a king who was tired of everything. His crown was too heavy. It was a wearisome burden. The glitter of gold was distastful to him. He was satiated with nightingale's tongues, sweetbreads and plate de foie gras, and craved something different such as corned beef and cabbage. He was disgusted with others for their sycophancy, and with himself for always having his own way.

Then be heard of a substance which had the power to obliterate memory for a period of seven years. The person who took it forgot who he was and his past life was a blank to him, but at the end of seven years his memory would slowly return. He would begin to have flashes of his former life at intervals. These would gradually become clearer and at the end of a second period of seven years he would be able to recall everything. "Here," said he, "is the chance I have been looking for. I can forget my identity and all the things that now bore me to death. I can enjoy all kinds of adventures and new experiences. When I come back to my kingdom everything will seem different and I will rejoice in my position because of the contrast with the trials I have just gone through." So he began to look for a man who resembled him in appearance who could play the part of the king in his absence. At last he found one who was so like him that when he saw him he thought he must be looking into a mirror. The man was intelligent and was delighted to take his part in the proceedings. He was secretly drilled in the details of government, the personnel of the court, and all the duties he would have to perform, not the least of which would be to keep track of the real king in his wanderings and to see that he came to no serious harm.

The scheme worked. The king disappeared and nobody knew the difference. Everything went well in the kingdom and the substitute had the real monarch watched and assisted at every stage of his development.

The king awoke in a hovel in the slums of a large city. He worked as a stevedore on the docks, as a coal miner, as a driver of trucks. His intelligence grew rapidly. He started a taxi company and became rich. Then he found that he had talent as an inventor and soon became a multi-millionaire. Still he did not know that he was the king. The substitute reigned in his stead and watched over him and threw opportunities in his way until he became the most powerful industrial magnate in the world and had more real power than he had had as king.

Little by little his memory came back to him and he returned secretly to the palace and resumed his throne. The substitute was liberally rewarded and retained as a friend, but nobody knew the difference except that the king seemed happier and immensely wiser than he had been before.

Now a parable is only a parable. No human analogy could possibly represent the relations between the Transcendent and the Immanent Deity, but this allegorical illustration may serve to give us an inkling of why the Creator made the universe, and still continues to make it, by evolution instead of by a single fiat.

The history of the universe is a succession of Great Divine adventures. In each of these the Trancedent Deity buries a part of itself in electrones, atoms, molecules, suns, planets and moons. The adventure starts when there is nothing throughout space except what we call the ethereal medium. But the Transcendent God, acting on this ethereal medium by what we call electromagnetic force, makes electrons and atoms and buries a part of himself in each of them. The loving impulse, or impulse of condensation, then triumphs as chemical affinity, molecular cohesion and gravitation and the heavely bodies that make up the universe are formed by evolution. Everywhere the condensing impulse triumphs over the disintegrating, and, on each inhabited sphere, love in the form of beauty, goodness and intelligence, triumphs over disintegrating hate in the form of ugliness, evil and error; and when all the Immanent Deity has found its way back to the centre of the Divine personality, when all suns, moons and planets are back again into solid unity, or absolute being without admixture of non-being, that particular Great Divine adventure will have ended.

Each of these Great Divine adventures works out differently, just as in a single solar system each planet evolves differently, because each organism in which the Immanent Deity is buried has its own free will and responds to stimuli differently from any other. Hence the interest, the variety and the adventure in the great experiment.

And always this means progress in beauty, in kindliness and in intelligence, and consequently the greater efficiency and happiness of all sentient creatures.

Progress is the explanation of evolution. Progress is more enjoyable than perfection because perfection becomes monotonous. There can be no progress in beauty unless there is ugliness to progress from; no progress in kindliness unless there is cruelty to progress from; no progress in intelligence unless there is ignorance to progress from. Ugliness, evil and error are the antagonists in the great game. There could be no game without opponents except solitaire, and solitaire is dull.

This is the explanation of evolution that religion has to offer. Who can give a better one? "But," some one will say, "if you take this view of evolution, what becomes of the statement of Genesis: 'And God created man in His own image; in the image of God created He him. Male and female created He them'." Ezra, or whoever wrote these words, believed that God formed man out of mud, as a sculptor makes a model out of clay, and, when He had finished the statue, God breathed into the mud nostrils and man became a full-grown living person.

What other conception of it could we expect primitive man to have? Could we expect him to understand the theory of evolution? Yet, while it is not true that God created man in that way, it is true that evolution means the unfolding of the divine image latent in all living creatures and that this divine image reaches its highest expression, upon this planet at least, in man. God is still creating man in His own image. Of course, we cannot expect to be able with our present faculties to picture to ourselves what God is really like, or adequately to imagine His appearance, yet do we not in our hearts all believe that, if there is a God at all, a handsome man with a face that radiates kindliness and intelligence resembles God more closely than a snake does, or a fiery dragon, or a lion, or a bull, or a monkey, or an ugly Hottentot? It is more correct to say that a monkey resembles man than it is to say that man resembles a monkey. It is all right to compare the lower to the higher, because that exalts the lower without insulting the higher, but it is not fitting to compare the higher to the lower, for that degrades the higher without equivalent benefit to the lower.

Similarly it is all right to say that man is made in the image of God, but it may be absurdly inadequate, and perhaps blasphemous and irreverent, to say that God is the image of man.

The imperfection of a son may not prevent his bearing a striking likeness to a perfect father. So, in spite of man's imperfection, he is made in the image of God and his development, in beauty; goodness and intelligence, is really the evolution, or unfolding, of the divine image that is latent in him.

A man who smiles looks like God and a man who frowns looks like the Devil. Our passions engrave themselves on our faces. Anger, fear and hatred leave their marks on us, and nothing but love can iron them out.

At no time throughout eternity has the Transcendent Deity ever been angry, afraid, or full of hate. Therefore, His appearance must not contain any of the expressions which in man indicate these emotions. That is why I say that a man who smiles looks like God, and a man who frowns looks like the Devil.

Evolution means that throughout the universe in every organism there is a struggle between God and the Devil, and God is slowly triumphing over the Devil. This means that the image of God is gradually driving out the image of the Devil. But God, at the start, gave the Devil a handicap. In the beginning, the image of God was submerged and the image of the Devil was uppermost. Ugliness, cruelty and ignorance were triumphant. They had to be to start the game. That is what is meant by the Fall. A planet starts as a Hell of bararism and takes a long while in evolving into a paradise of beauty, kindliness and intelligence. All the way along, the Devil tries to make man think that the Devil is God and that the Devil's image is God's image. That is why the Hindoos worshipped the serpent, the Chinese the fiery dragon, the Babylonians the lion and the Egyptians the bull. The story in Gensis, where the Devil is represented as a serpent, is absurd in the supposition that a snake could talk, but it is a big advance over the idea that the serpent was God instead of the Devil.

All along the course of evolution you see the image of God progressing but slowly. The dragon is higher than the serpent. The lion is nobler than the dragon and the bull is more peaceful than the lion. So we see the image of God gradually triumphing over the ugliness and cruelty of Diabolism, and at last we reach the climax in the Man-God, Jesus of Nazareth, who alone can present   an image of God worthy of rational acceptance, and in whom we see the glory of the Godhead, full of grace and truth.

Yet even today the Devil still is uppermost. That is what we mean by original sin. Most men on this planet are still under the domination of Satan and are governed by envy, malice, fear and cruelty instead of love, joy, courage and gentleness. But the Kingdom of the Prince of Peace is spreading every day and in time the image of God will supercede the image of the Devil in the hearts and faces of men.

The progress is steady, but every little while the Devil accomplishes a throwback to Diabolism and people say the world is not getting any better. We saw it in the late War. We see it now in the contempt of the lowbrow for the highbrow, and in the scorn of the unscrupulous promoter for the plodding workman, or the arrogance of the millionaire bootlegger in his Rolls Royce towards the honest man on foot. We see it in jazz music, in the insane imaginings of cubism and in the freaks of futurism. We see it just now in the popular craze in England for turtles as pets. When a person begins to look upon a snake or a turtle as beautiful, it is a sure sign of diabolic obsession. It is the image of the Devil, triumphant in the earlier stages of evolution, trying to throw us back to the Mezozoic age.

Ezra no doubt believed that God made Adam from the dust of the ground and breathed into his nostrils and the mud figure became a living soul. Later on the soul was called psyche, a butterfly, by the Greeks. They represented life as a butterfly entering human lips and death as a butterfly flying out of the mouth. Such an idea was a natural one to people who did not understand the nature of respiration, or the circulation of the blood, or the functions of oxygen and carbon dioxide in relation to vitality.

I am not saying that God could not have created Adam full grown out of mud. I believe he could have done so, because all of our ninety odd chemical elements are really the same substance variously condensed by electro-magnetic force, and God could make a man out of mud just as certainly as he could make bread out of a stone, by the transmutation of substances, all in accordance with natural laws.

And similarly I believe that he could have taken a rib from Adam, with or without flesh adhering to it, and could have made it into a woman. Not long ago a physician told me he had a human jaw in an incubator and it grew so rapidly in the media that he had to keep cutting it down. God could easily make a woman from a rib without breaking any law of nature, but while he could have done it, I do not believe he did so and there are three chief reasons why:

First — We do not see God creating anything full grown in the present day. He does not make a hen, or a goose, or a turkey full grown. He makes the egg and the egg evolves into the chick and the chick develops into the full grown fowl. Development from the visibly simple to the visibly complex is the way of nature.

Second — The rocks tell the story of a long process extending over hundreds of millions of years. And the various strata contain different forms of live beings, beginning with what are comparitively simple organisms and developing always into more complex ones. Man, as we know him, did not appear among the fossils till about 500,000 years ago, and from that time on we see the image of God coming out in him more and more clearly all the time, but I believe the image of God was latent in him from the very first.

Third — The theory of a special and immediate creation of a whole man instanteously is not in harmony with the origin and progress of the universe as a whole. God does not create a sun all at once. He does it by the pressure of gases toward a centre, and as motion stops at the centre heat is generated there and an immense mass of burning gases forms a sun. So God does not make a planet all at once, but only by long ages of progressive condensation. And when God had made this planet He did not make the creatures on it all at once. He made granules, and single-celled organisms, and from these He developed all the different species including man, but each single-celled organism had in itself from the beginning a latent image of the creature it was intended to evolve into and the proper equipment of granules to develop that image.

Anyone who has ever hatched eggs in an incubator knows that the image of the hen is latent in a fertile egg from the beginning. At first there is no sign of it. Then a germinal spot is visible and this grows until, in less than a week, by holding it to the light, one can see the image of the chicken beginning to appear. It was there all the time. The heat just developed the latent image, and in due time the chick picks its way out of the shell and walks around a living image of its parents.

The same law applies to the human embryo. It is the latent image of its parents, and it is natural for people to ask: "At what stage in the development of man does the soul appear?" My belief is that the soul and spirit are latent in, or closely surrounding, the human organism from its beginning, and they bring about its development, but their action does not become manifest to us until the organism has reached a somewhat advanced stage in its progress.

A complete piano has seven octaves, and upon such a piano a skilled musician can play any piece of music adapted to the piano. You could play some music on it if it only had one octave, and much less if it only had three notes. But if it had three good notes, a limited melody could be played on those three, and two of the notes could be struck simultaneously and make a single harmony. Such a thing might be called a rudimentary piano. Likewise I believe that all the lower animals have what we might call rudimentary souls, but man alone has a complete soul and spirit capable of playing all the music needed for this stage of his existence and capable of infinite expansion.

The soul and spirit could not manifest themselves until man had developed a suitable brain, and I believe they helped to make the brain. The brain does not make the soul and spirit, but the soul and spirit make the brain. The soul made the cerebellum, pons, medulla and spinal chord because these are the instruments it plays on in order to keep the heart beating and the respiration going and to take care of the vaso motor system and all the vital processes of the body.

The spirit, however, has a higher duty. It has to regulate the relation of the person toward the things around it, toward its fellow men and toward its Creator. Its function is to receive the sensations and act as they require, to decide the conduct and to judge and think. It needs a larger instrument to play on and it builds for itself the two hemispheres of the cerebrum in which are all the higher centers of feeling, willing and thinking, of speech and voluntary action.

But, until the instrument was developed enough, neither the soul nor the spirit could manifest its existence. One might not think they were there, just as a musician might be waiting to play on a piano that was under construction but you could not tell he was there until he began to play on it.

The human amoeba presented little evidence of having a soul or spirit, but it was supplied in the beginning with the requisite granules to develop a human brain and to manifest spiritual music, while all the lower forms of creation were supplied in the beginning with only such granules as would fit them to play the inferior parts which the Creator intended them to play.

We express this essential difference when we say that man is a person and all the members of the lower creation are things. The most sagacious chimpanzee, the most industrious elephant, the most intelligent horse, or the most faithful and affectionate dog, is, after all, not a person.

When we talk of the immortality of the soul, we are not speaking correctly. We should speak of the persistence of the person, not merely the soul, after death, because the persistence of the person includes the immortality of the body as well as the soul and spirit, since a person consists of body, soul and spirit.

It is not true to say that the body is mortal, but the soul is immortal. The body is just as immortal as the soul, but it is the spiritual body, the ectoplasmic body, the formative shape, within our coarse bodies that retains the resemblances from year to year in spite of the continuous destruction and replacement of the cells of the outer body. It is a real body. In fact it is the only real body we have, because the one that seems real to us is only a lot of carbon, nitrogen and other chemicals that cluster around the real and spiritual body within us. The natural body is dying and being renewed all the time, every day, every hour, but the spiritual body, the image of God, is eternal, and ever grows more and more like God if we give it a chance.

From Amoeba to American

(Guest-lecture delivered before the Anthropology class in the University of Maryland, July 22, 1925)

William Albert Crawford-Frost

In 1816 a young professor of natural history in Jena, Lorenz Oken, published a little magazine called *Isis* in which he asserted that all living organisms were descented from a primitive slime. The authorities were horrified and he was promptly dismissed from his professorship. Oken did not give the primitive substance a name.

In 1835 a French naturalist, Dujardin, discovered the same substance and called it "sarcode" because all flesh was derived from it.

In 1846 Mohl also discovered it and called it "protoplasm" which meant "first creation." In 1850 it was proved that sarcode and protoplasm were the same, and in 1860 that it was found in both animal and vegetable cells.

Darwin and Herbert Spence both accepted the term "protoplasm" as the name of this substance which they regarded as not only homogeneous but continuous, that is, its parts were thought to be connected together, forming one substance. From that day to this scientists have been talking about protoplasm as if it were one substance.

I assert positively that there is no such substance in the universe as that which scientists now call protoplasm. It is only a name, a myth, an imaginary thing that does not exist, the result of a hasty conclusion from the imperfection of our microscopes. What scientists have considered to be a single homogeneous substance is in reality a disconnected and separated lot of primitive granules swimming around in a clear fluid. Some of them are beyond doubt endowed with motility and the power of response to stimuli, and each of them possesses either instinct or intelligence enough to do what the Creator intended it to do. The cell wall and nucleus look like solid protoplasm, but the cell wall is not solid because the granules pass through it

---

*First published as Part II of *A New Theory of Evolution*, by the University of Maryland, Baltimore, 1925.

and we see that the nucleus is not solid in the processes of reproduction. Where then is the substance known as protoplasm? It cannot be found. It does not exist. The granules in the cell wall and nucleus are more compact than the rest of the cell. That is all. Granules there are and organisms made up of granules, but protoplasm is a figment of the imagination.

It was this fundamental error that led Darwin to think that evolution could create species, and the same mistake made Herbert Spencer define evolution as a process of integration in which matter changes from homogeneity to heterogenity. The very definition is a contradiction in itself, because integration means the making of integers or units, or the condensation of scattered heterogeneous units into more unified and less heterogenous ones. What he should have said is that in evolution matter passes from invisible hetrogenity to visible heterogenity.

Even if there had been a single homogeneous substance as Darwin thought, it would not have been entitled to the name "first creation," because the first creation is the electron. Science must revise its terminology now that we believe in the electron.

When Sir Joseph Thompson of Cambridge, the discover of the electron, was passing through Baltimore several years ago, I called him up and asked him if he thought the electron was condensed out of the etheral medium by the Divine Will, using what we call electro-magnetic force. He admitted that something of this kind must be so. Now the ethereal medium is for man nothing, because it has no attributes. Therefore when an electron is made, something is called into existence that did not exist before. The electron is in reality the only thing in the universe, so far as we know at present, that has a right to be called "protoplasm," or "first creation." The electron does not evolve into the atom. Electrons are created into an atom. Therefore the atom is the second creation. Similarly the molecule is the third creation. Atoms, as far as we know, do not evolve into molecules.

These first three acts of creation are called inorganic. The fourth is the primitive granule and we call this organic. Out of molecules of carbon, nitrogen, oxygen, hydrogen, sulphur, and others less important, the Creator made primitive granules, and, as these were to fulfill many different functions, He made different kinds of granules according to the purpose each granule was to fulfill. And He made each kind by a different combination of the molecules mentioned. One kind was intended to evolve into, or to make, epithelial cells, so the right proportions of molecules were incorporated into that kind of granule. And so on, for the purpose of developing or creating plastids, cartilage-cells, bone-cells, muscle-cells, nerve-cells liver-cells, or what not. Each granule may therefore be looked upon as a primitive, or incipient, body cell.

We come now to the fifth and last creation: the creation of species, including man. Out of the primitive granules the Almighty made single-celled organisms to which we have given the name of amoebae. Darwin looked upon amoebae as all alike because they have the same appearance. In reality there are many kinds of amoebae — how many nobody on earth can even guess. There are supposed to be about a million different species of animals and plants. Even if there were a million kinds of amoebae we could not see the differences between them.

The Almighty made as many different kinds of amoebae as His scheme of creation called for and He made each kind by combining in the right number and arrangement and sorts of granules to evolve into the kind of creature He wished it to become.

Further He intended these kinds to be distinct from each other forever, because He so arranged it that when any two are crossed the result is an infertile hybrid. Cuvier tried to get the scientists of the world to give the name species to a kind of this nature. That would have been in accordance with the Divine plan. But scientists rejected Cuvier's definition and use the word species to describe animals that resemble each other in various ways. They say themselves that the term species has no fixed boundaries. There is no hard and fast limit between species and variety on one hand and species and genera on the other. That is the crux of the whole question. Each scientist makes his own classification and there is endless confusion, and all because the scientists have ignored God's evident intention. When scientists themselves cannot agree upon a definition of species, how can we expect the theologians and scientists to agree as to what a species is? If they will define it properly and authoritatively, through their International Association, and stick to their definition, theologians will promptly accept their definition and we will get somewhere in our debates regarding the origin of life and its relation to the Creator.

Now suppose we have two amoebae that contain exactly the same number and arrangement and kinds of granules with a single exception. Suppose that the muscle-cell granules, bone-cell granules, liver-cell granules, and all the others, are exactly the same in each with the exception of nerve-cell granules. Suppose that amoebae A has twice as many neuron granules as amoebae B. Do you not see that as the organism is gradually shaped by its environment A will respond more readily to stimuli than B? That it will adapt itself better to its environment? That it will go faster and further than B in its development? A is the amoeba from which man has been evolved and B that from which the monkey has come. Their development would of course in many respects be parallel. They would strongly resemble each other all the way through, but each is designedly and essentially different from the other in the beginning and throughout its entire evolution. Man was man from the first and monkey was monkey from the start.

In conclusion let us follow with our imagination the probable course of the two amoebae A and B in their development. They would likely go through the same stages of amoeba, protozoan, polyp, jelly fish, soft and cartilaginous fish, bony and scaled fish, fish with fins that developed into feet as A and B crawled on the bottom of shallow places, using their fins to push themselves along; lung fish, as they found themselves at times out of the water and the gills receded while the lungs developed. The next stage of both would be when, like the frog, they would be at home either on land or in the water but more at home on the land. From this they would go on through the stages of lizard, long legged reptile, quadruped, marsupial, mammal, sloth, lemur, loris, orang-utan and chimpanzee.

Thus far they might both go on parallel lines, but all the way through *A* is human and intended to be human, just as human as the human foetus in the womb of its mother. Does anyone doubt that the latter is human even in the stage when it has a tail? Their development would not likely be synchronous. *A* would reach the various stages sooner than *B*, and would keep on going when *B* stopped, because he had it in him to keep on going. He had the proper supply of neurons to do it with.

So *A* went on to the Java man 500,000 years ago, the Neanderthal man 100,000 years ago, the Cro Magnon man 35,000 years ago, the African dwarf, the Aztec, the Babylonian, the Egptian, the Greek, the Roman, the German, the Norman Frenchman, the Englishman and the American. The Roman Empire evolved into the old Germanic, which included the Gallic and Norman; the Norman absorbed the British, Saxon and Danish elements in England, and the English settled America. There were many admixtures in the process. The amoeba was multiple to begin with how multiple God only knows, and the chain of evolution is multiple all the way through, made up of an ever-increasing number of anscestors who were scattered units, but, though multiple and complex, the evolution goes ahead, as it were in a straight line, always toward greater beauty, kindliness and intelligence.

There is a right theory of evolution and a wrong theory of it, and it is as absurd to hold the right theory responsible for the sins of the wrong one as it would be to hold John Smith responsible for the failings of his brother James.

One wrong theory holds that evolution is without any definite aim or plan except the survival of the fittest, and by the fittest they mean the most cunning and powerful. Christian ministers are pointing out that this idea was prevalent in Germany and was partly responsible for the great War. There is some truth in the accusation. This theory leads to the most barbaric selfishness and cruelty, for it ranks man with the lower animals.

Another wrong theory is that evolution is just a blind groping after pleasure or self-consciousness and that it has no guide outside nature. This leads to atheism, or is atheism, pure and simple.

In opposition to this it is held that, while among the lower animals the fittest to survive is the one which is most cunning and powerful, when you reach the stage of manhood a different idea of fitness is found, and the man who is fittest to survive is the one who best combines efficiency with altruism. The objections to the German idea do not apply to this latter conception.

Against the false idea of evolution that it has no plan or guide, the truth is best expressed in the sentence: "For thou hast created all things and for thy pleasure they are and were created." In other words, the Deity, not wishing to spend eternity in idleness, and in order to obtain relief from the boredom of

Omniscience, buries a part of itself in matter, in electrons, atoms, molecules, suns, planets and moons, and the buried part is blinded and limited in order that it may have the pleasure and adventure of evolving into higher and higher forms, ever increasing in the consciousness of its divinity and ever experiencing the joys of discovery.

True evolution, therefore, may be defined as the persistent effort of the indwelling divinity to find its way back to the centre of the divine personality, being guided from without itself, i.e., from Heaven, by the transcedent will of God.

When a nebulous mass has condensed into a sun and the sun has condensed into a planet what we call life becomes manifest and the first form of it is the amoeba, a one-celled, thin-walled, little mass of granules that apparently has no stomach, heart or any other organs, and makes its way about by putting out "false feet" or bulges in the cell. The theory of evolution holds that these amoebae, coming by chance into contact with food matter, absorb it through the cell wall, and in time the influences of environment shape within them the stomach, heart, feet and other instruments necessary to their existence and development. From these amoebae all living things have been evolved.

There is a curious analogy between the fertilized ovum of the sea urchin and an amoeba in the way they develop from an undifferentiated mass into a highly complex organism having mouth, stomach, heart, eyes and legs. When the ovum of the sea urchin is fertilized, the two elements entwine and the cell duplicates and reduplicates until a certain number of cells are formed, each containing both the male and female elements. When the fixed maximum number of cells is reached the process of reduplication stops and the cells arrange themselves in two rows within the outer wall of the parent cell. From this they put out the folds, or processes, that afterward develop into mouth, stomach, and other organs.

Now the most remarkable feature connected with the proceedure is this: If the process takes place in sea water, containing a certain percentage of lime, the work of building up the young sea urchin goes right ahead to completion, but, if the sea water has not enough lime in it, instead of putting out the processes to form the various organs, the cells disband, and apparently in disgust, swim off, each by itself, thus forming hundreds of little miniature sea urchins that never come to anything, instead of holding together and building a young sea urchin the proper size. It would seem as if the cells had a sort of consciousness and knew that it is useless to try to build up an organism without the lime to do it with.

In the case of the sea urchin the cells are so large that all their actions can be clearly studied, but in the amoebae the granules are too small for us to see what they are like or what they are doing. They all look alike to us, just as the sheep in a flock look alike to a stranger, but, as each sheep is different from all the rest and easily recognized by the shepherd, so each granule in the amoeba may not only be a conscious living organism, but one possessing its own distinctive attributes, because from all we see in nature it would appear that no two organisms in the whole universe are exactly alike in every respect.

It is easy to believe, therefore, that just as in a single amoeba there may be many individuals of the same species, or even many different species, so in amoebae as a whole there may be an immense number of different species, that, in fact, the amoebae are really all created organisms in embryo.

It was natural for Darwin to jump to the conclusion that the amoebae are a species in themselves because all amoebae look alike and nothing else looks exactly like them, but to a person with a half-formed cataract trees and houses look alike. The lack of differentiation lies in the imperfection of our means of vision, not in the amoebae themselves. Darwin did not think of this.

Once adopting the premises that all amoebae are of one species, and that all living organisms are developed from that one species, then the question of evolution becomes entirely the question of the origin of species, as it was for Darwin, but if those premises are wrong and amoebae are really of many species then the question of evolution is merely one of the modifications of species by the action of environment and the process of natural selection.

Darwin's book, *The Origin of Species*, has given a wrong slant to the whole question of evolution. His contention was that the action of environment and natural selection brought about changes from one species to another, but that idea is not really necessary to the belief in evolution, and it may not be true. Evolution is true whether new species are formed or not.

There may be a million different kinds of amoebae for all we know, and if we had microscopes strong enough we might be able to separate them into a million different classes or species. Each of the little granules in an amoeba may really be a complex organism in itself and no two of them may be alike, although they look alike to us. Now that we know so much about the infinitessimal smallness of the electrons of which the granules, like all other forms of matter, must be composed, it seems highly improbable that the structure of an amoeba is homogenous throughout, or that all amoebae are of one species.

It is just as reasonable to suppose that God made one kind of amoeba intending man to be evolved from it, and another kind intending the monkey to be evolved from it, as it is to suppose that man is evolved from the monkey, or that the monkey and man have both been evolved from the same amoeba.

In any event evolution would be true, and it is true. The first eleven chapters of Genesis are inspired mythology, not history. The real history begins with the call of Abraham in the twelfth chapter. The first eleven chapters consist of Babylonian myths that were incorporated with the rest chiefly by Ezra after the return from the Captivity and represent the only presentation of the truth that man was then capable of understanding. That is why God inspired Ezra to write them. In due time God has given us a better realization of how it really happened. Truth can only be revealed by degrees. Jesus said of the Holy Spirit whom he promised to send: "Howbeit when He, the Spirit of Truth, is come, He will guide you into all truth, for He shall not speak of Himself, but whatsoever He shall hear that shall He speak." This means that Jesus did not consider truth a static thing, but something evolutionary and progressive. It must mean that or nothing. It is all right to attack the wrong theory of evolution, but the person who fights the true theory of it is an enemy of Christ, for Christ is the Way, the Truth and the Life, and evolution is the truth, and shows the way of life. Those who oppose the true teaching of evolution therefore are hurting Christ. They may not mean to do it, but they are doing it.

Section Seven

JACOB GOULD SCHURMAN
(1854-1942)

7

Schurman on Ethics and Evolution

Steven A.M.Burns

J.G. Schurman's book *The Balkan Wars 1912-1913*, is a marvellously lucid account of contemporary events by a man who knew Europe well (he had studied at London, Edinburgh and Heidelburg) and was on the spot as American ambassador to Greece, 1912-13. It begins:

> The expulsion of the Turks from Europe was long ago written in the book of fate. There was nothing uncertain about it except the date and the agency of destiny.[1]

Dare we begin an essay on science and religion with a quote from a book about political history? My answer is that this quote is typical of the thought of Jacob Gould Schurman on precisely those two issues. It promises us *science*: it will be empirical and historical science, and it will be careful, observant, detailed and up-to-date. It makes the promise in the language of *religion*: it is language in terms of which Schurman understood himself, too, for he was one of the agents of destiny.

It is true that his views of the Balkan wars were Euro-centric and Christian. he treats the Turkish presence in Eastern Europe (reaching the gates of Vienna in 1526, and still threatening Austria as late as 1763) as "purely military. They did nothing for their subjects, whom they treated with contempt, and they wanted nothing from them but tribute and plunder" (*Wars*, p.6). The expulsion of the Muslims from Christian Europe he regarded as inevitable for reasons of superiority of the European religion and civilization. He is, nonetheless, very careful to distinguish the various threads of national feeling — the racial types, the languages, territorial histories, religions, and political customs — which complicated the Balkan situation[2]. The penultimate sentence of the book perfectly captures Schurman's sensibilities: "For as an American I sympathize with the aspirations of all struggling nationalities to be free and independent"(*Wars*, p.131).

A reader of the sentence just quoted, however, may find it odd that it is the work of a Prince Edward Islander, educated there and in Nova Scotia (at Acadia, the Baptist university), before he left for study in Britain. Schurman's sympathies, however, clearly began as Canadian ones.

Schurman returned to the Maritimes to lecture first at Acadia, then at Dalhousie University. The latter made him inaugural holder of the George Munro chair in English in 1882,[3] but he married Barbara Munro in 1884, and soon left for Cornell University in the United States. He was hired there as Sage Professor and Head of the Philosophy Department in 1885,[4] and by 1892 was Cornell's President.

Shortly after moving to the U.S.A., Schurman wrote an article, "The Manifest Destiny of Canada," which appeared in 1889 in *The Forum* (fore-runner of *The Canadian Forum*). In it he argues that it is with good reason that "Canadians prefer their own political institutions to those of their neigh-bours" (p.10). He accuses the United States of treating us like a colony, of visiting "upon Canada the ancient sin of England" (p.16). His main theme is that the "destiny of Canada will be settled by the people of Canada. For them there is no manifest destiny but what they themselves decree" (p.2).

This theme is clearly echoed in the citation about the Balkans. Now if this began as a Canadian political perspective, it should not surpirse us if it ran into opposition among our southern neighbours. That is just what did happen. During his tenure at Cornell, Schurman was appointed President of the Philippines Commission. (The United Staes of America had just won the Spanish American War. The battle of Manila Bay, in 1898, left themwith some responsibiliyt for the Philippines, and the commission was to advise on what to do.) Schurman fought a losing battle against those Americans who had developed ambitions to have an empire of their own. Armour and Trott tell the story well[5]; essentially, Schurman failed to convince successive Ameri-can governments (he campaigned on this issue for decades) that the Philip-pines ought to govern themselves. The irony is fresh, as we have very recently witnessed further convulsions in the saga of American involvement in that nation. It is evident that Schurman's thought was permanently coloured by his early Canadian conviction that self-determination is important even for smaller national entitiies.

The Ethical Import of Darwinism

> Darwinism... is manifestly consistent
> with *any* philosophy, empirical or rational,
> spiritualistic or materialistic, theistic
> or atheistic.[6]

The political principle of national autonomy is deeply characteristic of Schurman's though. It would not be surprising, then, were it to show up in his thought about science and religion. It seems to do just that. The scientific work of his age — and Darwin's is just the most interesting of many examples — constitutes a series of new domains. but theology and metaphysics constitute other domains. It would be a kind of imperialism if philosophy were to dictate to scientists whether evolutionary theory could be true or not. Similarly, it would be a kind of imperialism if the establishment of Darwinism in biology were to dictate to theology what its laws were to be.

Schurman's four philosophical books were published between 1881 and 1896, long before *The Balkan Wars*, but the combination of scientific and religious concerns dominates these two works too. Indeed it was the theme of his doctoral research at the University of Edinburhg.[7] Of all his philosophical works, the most characteristic is *The Ethical Import of Darwinism*. We shall return to it shortly.

In 1890, *Belief in God*, his Winkley lectures at Andover Theological Seminary, was published.[8] This may be though of as the first book which Schurman conceived in and for the United States. It is no mere repetition of the themes of his early works, but extends the consideration of contemporary sciences to new areas. He is *au courant* with the latest Biblical scholarship, he invokes the new Freudian accounts of religious beliefs and the results of German laboratory experiments in perception. Always, though, his theme remains constant. The new discoveries do not contradict the truths of religion. We may discover, however, that Moses could not have been the author of all five of the "Books of Moses"; the Pentateuch, nonetheless, remains what it always was, the expression of "the ever-deepening religious... insight of the Jews, ...part of a religious development or revelation that found its culminating expression in the benign miracle of history, the truth and life which became incarnate in Jesus of Nazareth."[9]

In some circles, such views are still considered radical, secularizing humanism, yet we must acknowledge that Schurman is writing as a Christian. How can this be sustained? The sciences are subject to developmentand all human knowledge is a product of histroical aquisition and testing. Religions evolve and human morality, too, has a history. Must we not suspect that theology has been taken right out from under us? This question is most directly addressed in Schurman's last philosophical book, *Agnosticism and Religion*.[10] If knowledge is to be possible at all, he argues, there must be more than facts about the material universe which can be known. The sciences presuppose that there is order in the universe. If there is order, than there is a *prius* of all knowledge, a principle which is logically prior to any explanation and any understanding. This *prius* is a unifying principle and an eternal one, for if there are only diverse and temporary principles of order then randomness usurps the ultimate foundations, and knowledge is not really possible at all. It can be seen, then, that in the end Schurman maintains that belief in a divine first principle is justified, in spite of the 19th century pressures to believe that advances in the natural sciences had rendered such belief superfluous or impossible. The chapter which we have selected to represent Schurman's work is taken from *The Ethical Import of Darwinism*. This book stands at the threshold of his transition to a figure in American history. It received the praise of William James[11] and at the same time looks back to the preoccupations of Schurman's earliest studies, and looks forward to the later theological writings. Ours is the fourth of six chapters.

Chapter Four is the centre piece of the book, so it requires careful placing. What precedes it is an account of Darwin's theory of biological evolution, together with an assessment of its philosophical implications for science and theology. What follows it are a chapter about Darwin's own ethical speculations, and a chapter about the applications of his work to human morality, by some contemporary anthrpologists. Chapter Four, itself, deals with the proper understanding of the relation btween ethics and evolutionary theory.

I shall say something about each of these three parts of the book, beginning at the end.

The Import: Ethical Facts

[T]he man, in order to marry, had to move to the *craal* of his wife, promise constantly to provide the mother-in-law with wood, never undertake service elsewhere without her consent, and, in case of separation, leave all the children as the property of the wife.[12]

Darwin thought that there were direct implications of his biological results for our understanding of the human species, and particularly for one of the attributes which sets us apart from the other animals, our moral consciousness. He postulated the origins of human conscience in the combination of sociability (which 'lower' animals already exemplify) and intelligence (which humans have received in the normal course of evolution). Our having been selected for these two attributes, Darwin was led to conclude,is sufficient to explain our moral consciences. Schurman argues that evolutionary theory need not, and cannot, provide such an account. It need not, for it offers no similar account of human intelligence. That simply "appeared," and evolutionary theory merely explains why it had benn preserved. Schurman is prepared to treat conscience in the same way. It cannot, for reasons which appear shortly, in our discussion of chapter 4.

The impact of evolutionary biology on ethics is indirect. It does not tell us what ought to be — it does not provide us with a conscience to do the job, either — but it does tell us a great deal about how to study human affairs. In his final chapter, Schurman considers contemporary anthropologists who think that the evolution of human affairs proves the completely relative nature of human values. Societies had recently been discovered in which chastity was a virtue, and others in which it was not. There were societies in which men headed families, and societies in which women did. There were systems in which monogamy was practised, and others in which sexual relationships were more imaginative. These discoveries were popularly thought to threaten the belief that some things are right and others are wrong. Schurman found these matters fascinating, and thought them of great importance in the public reception of evolution. He claims that these anthropologists are not *replacing* moral philosophy, but are providing tools which can help moral philosophers to work properly. What moral philosophy ought to do is use the historical method which is so fruitful elsewhere. Ethical facts, as Schurman calls them, should be observed and classified as though they were biological phenomena.

This approach to philosophical issues is sometimes called "naturalizing" them. In moral philosophy, naturalizing the subject consists in setting aside attempts to discover by speculation or analysis what is right and what is wrong, and *looking to see* what people do in fact consider right and wrong. This scientific work will, he argues, throw light on the fundamental problem of ethics, the nature of moral law.

It will best illustrate what he means if I quote his conclusions at some length:

> [Our domestic morality] is despoiled of its absoluteness when the discovery is made that our own form of marriage is but one of several competing types, ...and that chastity and fidelity are so far from universal that many peoples have no conception of them, and when they have appeared they seem to have grown out of rights in women as property — adultery in Madagascar, e.g., having the same punishment as theft — and are consequently never, or seldom, required of savage men. The rights, duties, virtues, and sentiments associated with our idea of the family Cannot, therefore, be considered a part of the content of the moral law universal.
>
> This seems to me a result of considerable importance for moral philosophy. And it is a result that cannot be gainsaid by any school, since it is not a speculation, not even an inference, but an undeniable statement of actual facts. (*Darwinism*, pp.251-2).

All of this "history of ethical facts" has an important place in our understanding of Schurman's book. His first chapter makes clear that his general topic is the relation between science and ethics. He argued there that ethics had traditionally been a form of individual or philosophical speculation, an attempt to find eternal moral truths through the application of pure reason; on the other hand there are modern attempts to make ethics a corollary of natural science, and they, too, he finds wanting. His assessment is that human morality is a domain of its own, which deserves objective historical study. This will not preclude philosophizing, nor will it simply be a propaedeutic to it. It will be a part of moral philosophy, throwing light upon the nature of the moral law.

Still, there is the challenge of Darwin. Has not the science of evolutionary biology settled precisely the questions about which Schurman requests patience and historical research? Schurman's book should be seen as the long answer to this question. He thinks that in Darwin's own thinking, "historical ethics was forced into the service of a foregone conclusion," and that the work will not be properly done "as long as scientists are convinced of the finality of the ethical science... of Darwin" (*Darwinism*, pp.37-8). Accordingly, he must explain what Darwinism is, and how it is incompetent to settle ethical questions.

Darwinism: Science and Theology

It is a 'mean device for philosophers
thus to crib causation by hairs' breadths,
to put it out at compound interest
through all time, and then disown the
debt.'[13]

Evolutionary biology is, of course, a scientific study which is continually being challenged and refined. What we call its ethical import has been re-popularized in recent years by "socio-biologist." We cannot sketch all of this in a short essay, but we can say something about how it began.

What is evolution? In its simplest form, a belief in evolution is a belief that all things are constantly changing. With typical wisdom, Schurman reminds us that it is a belief with a rich pedigree; he cites the "legends of our Alquonquin Indians" (*Darwinism*, p.45), as well as pre-Socratic philosophers. The general view that the universe is constantly evolving supports the particular view that the forms of plant and animal life are also undergoing evolution. This is the idea of biological evolution; this idea also preceded Darwin. The French naturalist, Jean-Baptiste Lamarck, was already well-known for the view that living things are modified by their circumstances, by their habits and by breeding. Many biologists in the first half of the nineteenth century thought that species, themselves, were susceptible to evolution; simpler species might have given rise to varied and more sophisticated species. But if all of these ideas preceded Darwin, why is he so renowned?

Schurman's reply is masterful. He begins with well-known examples of selective breeding. Humans, over the generations, have improved the breeds of domesticated animals, have carefully selected the parents so that their offspring will be faster, or smaller, or give more milk, or be hardier in cold climates. This process of artificial selection takes for granted that the characteristics of plants and animals can be modified. What Darwin offered, was a demonstration of the mechanism by which such modifications could take place without human intervention. He called it *natural* selection.

The mechanism of natural selection is Darwin's explanation of the origin of species, of how, for instance, "from *one* ancestral species there could have descended, in the course of thousands upon thousands of generations, four species so distinct as the horse, the ass, the quagga and the zebra" (*Darwinism*, p.54). The mechanism depends on several premises. First, there is abundance. Plants and animals produce many more seeds, eggs or offspring than are needed. An appaling amount of death results, and the survivors who live and reproduce are a small selection fromamong the many who began the struggle to live. Second, there is variation. There are innumerable small but significant differences between the organisms produced. Now if the ones which survived were to be chosen at random, these variations would make no difference in the long run. But there is a third premise, that some variations are advaatageous to a being in its struggle to live, while others are disadvantages. Now it is clear how nature "selects." ("Selects" is, of course, a metaphor; nature does not deliberately make choices.)

Nature selects because those differences which are advantageous help an organism to survive. The result is the famous "survival of the fittest." There are many sources of evidence which supports a theory of biological evolution. Palaeontology studies fossil records of species which have died out, side by side with remains of species which have survived. This is our best source of information about the 'history' of living things on our planet. There is the evidence of embryology: when different species go through very similar stages in their early development it is natural to think that the species are related. Such considerations also arise from the study of comparative anatomy: similarities of structure may suggest that one species is a forerunner of the other, or that they have common ancestry. We have already cited the evidence of artificial selection. Finally, there is much to be concluded from comparisons of species persisting in isolation: the Galapogos Islands provided Darwin with evidence that species differ in different locales, as though they had adapted to local conditions.

From all of these sources the evidence for Darwin's theory is still much debated. Even in his own day, Malthus had believed that artificial selection could produce sheep with short legs, but could never produce sheep with no legs at all, or which had become goats.[14] Darwin, however, maintained that variation was potentially unlimited. More specific disputes arose, especially in genetics. This science was scarcely born in Darwin's day, and has continued to be a source of objections, as well as support, for his hypothesis. No geneticist will agree, for instance, that variations within species are random; it is the very point of that science to explain what determines the characteristics which are inherited, how the genes of the parnets are separated and recombined, for instance, to constitute the genetic inheritance of the offspring. As T.A.Goudge puts it: "There can be no doubt that the major limitation in Darwin's theory was due to his lack of knowledge concerning the factors and laws of heredity."[15] Schurman was already quite aware of this limitation. "The cause of this evolutionary movement in the history of organisms has not yet been established; though it is probable Darwin's natural selection is a part of the cause." (*Darwinism*, p.71)

Darwin's importance, then, stems not from his inventing the whole of evolutionary theory, nor from his definitive solution to the problem of how species change. Rather, his theory of natural selection, that advantageous variations tend to be preserved, brings together the various elements of biological evolution and completes them with a very general, "naturalized" account of the mechanism responsible, and thus sets the agenda for further scientific investigation.

To this admirably told story, Schurman adds Chapter 3. He "assumes for the sake of argument" that Darwin's theory is the whole truth, and considers the metaphysical implications of it. His view is that the new science's metaphors ("selection") too often get taken literally, that capital letters ("Nature") personify and give a false sense of permanence. As a result, enthusiasts fail to realize that survival of the fittest "does not explain the arrival of the fittest," as Schurman epigrammatically puts it. (*Darwinism*, p.78) Nor does it explain how advantages, once they have arrived, are passed on. The enthusiasts were willing to conclude that Darwin had shown that everything can be accounted for on mechanical and utilitarian principles. But the arrival of new characteristics cannot be totally fortuitous, or they would not be genetically reproducible. Schurman, opposing the metaphysics of design and teleology to the element of fortuitousness in mechanistic metaphysics, says, "there is no scientific warrant for this philosophy of chance" (*Darwinism*, p.112).

It is worth noting that this is not a simple case of denying that values can be derived from facts. As we showed in an earlier section, Schurman defends the view that certain facts about human scoieties do have consequences for the moral law. Nonetheless, he insists that a proper understanding of Darwinism as science shows that it does not have the sort of implications about God or about purpose that it was widely taken to have.

Darwinism and the Foundations of Morals

> No one influenced by the ethics of the
> school of Hume and Bentham would
> have ventured to interpret the evolu-
> tion of life as a continuous realiza-
> tion of utilities.[16]

We come now to the most ingenious chapter of *The Ethical Import of Darwinism*. It is set in a book which considers the fate of moral philosophy now that it is confronted by a new scientific theory; the theory has been explained, its claim to dictate a metaphysical position has been challenged, and later there will be recommendations about the proper way to make the study of ethics scientific. Chapter Four nonetheless is lambent; it is sufficiently self- contained that it is a joy to read on its own. Schurman's first ingenuity is the claim that Darwinian biology contains a principle of utility, a principle which it *borrowed* from the contemporary ethical theory of Jeremy Bentham and other Utilitarians. His first accusation is that it is circular to accept the utilitarian principles from one's social context, make them the central concepts in one's biology, and then claim that the biology explains why the original moral principles are true. His second is that although human morality may be useful to us, may be selected for preservation by the evolutionary process, it need not be the utilitarian ethics which get selected.

Special credit is given to John Stuart Mill's attempt to derive even non-utilitarian moral principles (absolute values, disinterestedness, obligation) from the process of evolution. Subtle uses of commercial metaphor in this exposition warn us of the deep connection between utilitarian ethics and the capitalist economy in which it flourished. The key manouevre is a distinction between something's being useful, and its existing only to the exent that it is useful. Even if goodness is an end in itself, and not just valued because of its useful consequences, "it still remains true that honesty is the best policy, that honest acts are the most advantageous acts, and that they will accordingly be rpeserved through natural selection in the struggle for existence" (*Darwinism*, p.134). A virtue may be useful, in other words, without its usefulness being its essence.

There are three hidden bases on which the "evolutionary ethics" rests, according to Schurman. The first is the notion, already criticized, that if morality gives us humans an evolutionary advantage, and is therefore preserved by the forces of evolution, it somehow follows that that morality ought to have usefulness as its central moral principle. The second false premise is that morality can exist without judgements of absolute value. Not only does Schurman think that one *can* be both Darwinian (in biology) and Platonist (in ethics), he holds a stronger thesis: that those who maintian that something is only valuable relative to some consequence have failed to recognize something which *cannot* be eradicated from human morality. A great deal of philosophical ingenuity has been expended over centuries attempting to show what Schurman puts in a sentence: "if man be merely a pleasure seeking animal, you but mock him when you enjoin him to promote the happiness of others" (*Darwinism*, p.137). The third false presumption is that a mechanical process could generate what requires intelligence and freedom. There is no original argument, here, but Schurman again insists that if these qualities do not exist in our biological predeccessors, then evolution will not provide them. Evolution is only a process which selects for preservation what has already been provided.

The central conclusion of this central chapter is that there are features of human moral life (our sense of absolute worthfulness, our sense of duty) which cannot be accounted for by the principles of evolutionary biology. These convictions are defended without compromising his enthusiastic support for the progressive contributions of the sciences, themselves. Although the human predicament has changed dramatically in the ensuing century, these issues still command the attention of moral philosophers, and Schurman's work still serves to focus them for us.

Schurman was honoured in his time by his American fellow citizens. He received honourary doctorates, for instance, from Harvard and Yale, from Dartmouth and Columbia. The University of Edinburgh also honoured him. He deserves more recognition form Canadians. He belongs among those Victorians who sought to combine faith and science to make the world a better place.[17] This is clear not only in his politics but also in his university life; he was dissappointed that Dalhousie of his day had abandoned the principles of religious tolerance on which it had been founded, and he worked to make a Cornell education of practical value for a wide diversity of students. He wrote, too, with a minimum of scholarly apparatus, holding that "the first duty of any philosophical writer is to make himself generally intelligible."[18]

Reading him, then, ought to pleasantly relocate us in the moral and intellectual atmosphere of an important part of our history.   It ought, too, to give us rigourous exercise in thinking about the most profound implications of our theories about biological nature. In this Schurman is in another sort of good company, for his are among the early responses to Darwin's work by thoughtful philosophers.[19]

Here I leave, and entrust you to the prose of Jacob Gould Schurman.

Notes

1. Jacob Gould Schurman, *The Balkan Wars 1912-1913* (Princeton: Princeton University Press, 1914), p.1. I shall cite it in the text as *Wars*.
2. See especially his account of racial propaganda, facts and fallacies in the claims of Bulgaria, Greece, Serbia and Romania to Central Macedonia (pp.79-91). Each group had claims to some of the local population, and had established schools, churches, etc. aimed at "nationalizing" the Macedonians.
3. George Munro was a great benefactor of Dalghousie University. He was a Nova Scotian who made his fortune in New York by publishing inexpensive editions of popular novels. He was indirectly responsible, too, for American copyright legislation, which was passed to protect the rights of other publishers in the works which Munro was so profitably republishing. In later American political life, Schurman was a vigourous oponent of such government interference in business freedom as anti-combies legislation. I do not know what he thought about copyright laws.
4. This is the date confirmed by Leslie Armour and Elizabeth Trott, in their invaluable study *The Faces of Reason: An Essay on Philosophy and Culture in English Canada 1850-1950* (Waterloo: Wilfred Laurier University Press, 1981). Schurman went on to Cornell in 1886, according to Henry James Morgan, ed., *The Canadian Men and Women of the Time*, first edition, 1898, according to the*Encyclopaedia Britannica*, eleventh edition, 1911, and according to Laurence Veysey, in the *Dictionary of American Biography*, Supplement Three, 1941-45.
5. Ibid., pp.211-215.
6. Jacob Gould Schurman, *The Ethical Import of Darwinism* (New York: Charles

Scribner's Sons, 1887), p.97. (I shall refer to this work as *Darwinism*).

7. Schurman received the D.Sc. in 1878. This research resulted in his first book, *Kantian Ethics and the Ethics of Evolution* (London: Williams and Norgate , 1881).

8. Jacob Gould Schurman, *Belief in God: Its Origins, Nature and Basis* (New York: Charles Scribner's Sons, 18man is citing Livingston, who described this case of mother-kinship, and the husband settling with the wife's family. These were the customs of an isolated tribe not far from Zululand.

13. *Darwinism*, p.98. This "happy observation" Schurman attributes to Dr.James Martineau. It is a perspicious commercial metaphor. R.C.Lewontin has pointed out that Darwin was an active player of the stock market; there is 6etaphor here, too, of the differential survival of the advantaged (*New York Review of Books*, Oct.10, 1985, p.20). There is an interesting chapter to be written on capitalism and Darwin's thought.

14. For a popular account of these debates, see Norman MacBeth, *Darwin Retried: An Appeal to Reason* (New York : Dell, 1973). The present example is discussed on p.30. Schurman takes clear note of the issue, quoting the reservation of Darwin's friend and defender, T.H.Huxley, that "it remains to be seen how far natural selection suffices for the production of species." (*Darwinism*, p.71).

15. T.A.Goudge, *The Ascent of Life* (Toronto: University of Toronto Press, 1961), p.21. Goudge, a major figure in the recent revivial of philosophical interest in evolutionary theory, is a fellow Maritime Canadian. He does not make 19th century citations, however, and so gives us no sense of a tradition of important Canadian contributions to the subject.

16. *Darwinism*, p.117.

17. See, for instance, a study of such figures by Ramsay Cook, *The Regenerators* (Toronto: University of Toronto Press, 1986).

18. *Darwinism*, preface, x. He is proud to be writing in the language of Locke, Berkeley and Hume, which, as they use it, is "in all three alike plain, transpaent and unmistakable."

19. Here we might note the continued industry of academics trying to measure Darwin and his impact just on the nineteenth century. See, for instance, the huge collection *The Darwinian Heritage*, ed. D.Kohn (Princeton: Princeton University Press, 1985). Schurman is a considerable figure in this Victorian story. See, too, Stow Persons, ed *Evolutionary Thought in America* (New Haven: Yale University Press, 1950).

The Ethical Import of Darwinism

Jacob Gould Schurman

It is important to fix accurately in mind what the subjet of the present chapter is. With Darwin's own ethical views and speculations we have now nothing to do, though the exposition and examination them (both in themselves and in relation to his natural science) must form the topic of a later chaper. Just at present, however, our inquiry is of a more general character. We want to know whether, the Darwinian doctrine of evolution being assumed, it entails any particular theory of morals. Or, since natural selection is the essence of the sienctific achievement of Darwin, we have simply to ask, Does natural selection involve or indicate a definite type of ethics, so that acceptance of the one logically necessitates acceptance of the other? This question, it is obvious, is not identical with an inquiry into Darwin's own moral system which, though dependent upon some philosophical principle, may be absolutely disconnected with the hypotheses of biology. Leaving Darwin the moralist, therefore wholly aside, we would fain settle whether Darwin the naturalist, in establishing the fuction of natural selection, thereby predetermined ethics to a particular form or invested its phenomens with a new cast of thought. And this point can be resolved only by ignoring the uncritical assumptions of the school and undertaking afresh an independent consideration of the facts and analysis of the notions which the Darwin theory involves.

   That theory, as already expounded, consists essentially of two moments — the struggle for life and the survival of the fittest. The former connects it historically and logically with Malthusiausm, and may be considered as an application of the famous doctrine of population to the whole organic world. That is to say, the struggle for life follows inevitaly from the enormous increase of living beings beyond the means of subsistence, as first pointed out in the case of man by Maltlus. This debt to the national political economy Darwin has openly acknowldeged. But it has not been observed that the other moment of his theory — the issue of the struggle — was conditioned by a

*First published by Charles Scribner's Sons, New York, 1887. Selections by Steven A.M. Burns.

conception borrowed from the national ethics. He remembered distinctly, as he wrote Haeckel, how on reading Malthus's "Essay on Population" the thought of a universal struggle for esxistence first flashed upon his mind. But he could not remember, so early, so gradual, so subtly pervasive is the entrance od ethical ideas, when he had become inoculated with the national utilitarianism. Yet it can scarcely be doubted that it was from this source he extracted the notion of utility as determinator of the issue of the combat for existence. No one uninfluenced by the ethics of the school of Hume and Bentham would have ventured to interpret the evolution of life as a continuous realization of utilities. And yet the survival of the fittest, by which, according to Darwin, development is effected, just means the preservation of the most *useful* modifications of structure or habit. "Any being, if it vary, however slightly, in any manner *profitable to itself*," says Darwin, "will have a better chance of surviving, and thus be naturally selected." Or, in other words, before the operation of natural selection there must be a ultility of some kind on which it acts. What is useful is preserved, what is harmful is destroyed. "Nature cares nothing for appearances, except in so far as they may be useful to any being." Thus, as you dig down to the roots of existence, you find it draws its vital sap from utility. "Natural selection acts solely by and for the good of each." It may "produce structures" for the direct injury of other species, but never for their exclusive advantage. With certain exceptions that can be explained, the structure of every living creature as well as every detail of that structure "either now is, or was formerly, of some direct or indirect use to its possessor." Similarly, the instinct of each species is useful for that species, and has never been produced for the exclusive benefit of another species. Could these propositions be refuted, "it would," says Darwin, "annihilate my theory," for structures and instincts could not in that case be the product of natural selection. The survival of the fittest implies an antecedent utility — a modification advantageous to the individual or, it may be, to the community of which it is a member, but never directly and exclusively to others beyond this pale. Natural selection rests upon a biological utilitarianism, which may be egoistic or communistic, but which cannot be universalistic.

Let us now apply this doctrine to man, with the object of discovering its bearing upon morals. We have, then,to admit that the human species has originated and developed to its present stage through the preservation and accumlation of a number of useful modifications which, whether of individual or social benefit, gave our semi-human, semi-brutal ancestors an advantage over other animals in the struggle for life. Of these modifications, one of the most obvious is an erect attitude. This peculiarity, which the orang, the gorilla, and the gibbon seem now on the way to acquiring, has manifest advantages. It enabled simian man, not only to hurl missiles at his enemies without forfeiting the power of simultaneous locomotion, but also to break and dress stones for definite purposes, thus beginning the career of that tool-using animal whose skill and ingenuity have changed the face of his physical environment. But this career, even in its commencement, would have been impossible without the emergence of a still more important factor in the development. Mind is infinitely more useful than mere bodily structure; and it is not necessary to deny intelligence to the lower animals when we aasset that the human mind is the most colossal and revolutionary of all the modifications any species has undergone. Such an enormous advantage would be preserved and perpetuated by natural selection. For it enables man to do at once what nature takes ages to accomplish for the other animals; it enables him to adapt himself to his environment without change in bodily structure and organization. Imagine a group of carnivorus animals suddenly exposed to a severer climate and obliged to capture more powerful prey; only those with the warmest natural clothing and strongest claws and teeth could manage to survive; and as the battle with their evil star grew fiercer, the group, if not altogether exterminated, must languish through the long course of aeons until their modifying organs and structures had become completely adapted to the new requirements through the play of natural selection. But the mental powers of man render him, in similar circimstances, independent of nature. He makes thicker clothing, and he fashions sharper weapons or constructs more cunning pitfalls. Simple as these performances seem, how infinitely advantageous they must have been in the struggle for life. When the intelligence which made them possible first appeared upon the scene, it effected "a revolution which [to quote the language of Mr. Alfred Russell Wallace] in all the previous ages of the earth's history had no parallel, for a being had arisen who was no longer necessarily subject to change with the changing universe."

Simultaneous with this revolution was another, scarcely less significant, due to the appearance and operation of the moral sentiments. The moral being lives for others as well as for himself. But the lower animals are at best gregarious, not social; they lead a life of individual isolation and self-dependence. Each is alone, in the battle for life, exposed to the whole force of the combat. The sick and the feeble fall victims to beasts of prey or die of starvation. There is no division of labor to relieve the one from directly procuring its own food, no mutual assistance to succor the other till health and vigor are restored. Accordingly, any group of animals endowed with the least tincture of sociality and sympathy would, through the internal union and strength which these qualities evoke, have a decided advantage over other groups not thus endowed. A tribe animated by these instincts contains in itself a principle of survival of scarcely less efficacy than the mental faculties themselves. If these check the action of natural selection on the body, and transfer it to the sphere of intelligence, the social and sympathetic feelings screen the individual and oppose to the play of natural selection the solid framework of a united and strengthened society. But sympathey and sociality imply fidelity, trustworthiness, truthfulness, obedience, and the like. And as these are useful in the struggle for life — being, in fact, means of social survival — not less useful are the other virtues which form the complex tissue of our morality. Hence it follows that the moral sentiments, as motors tending to the preservation of the tribe, must, like the mental faculties, be self-preserving and self-accumlating under the utilitarian sway of natural selection.

This view of the development of the simian quadruped into the moral person by means of natural selection seems to confirm the general impression that utilitarian ethics is the necessary implicate of Darwinian biology. We began by remarking that the biological theory borrowed the notion of utility from empirical morals; but we must now confess the loan has been so successfully invested that there is some ground for believing the proceeds suffice, not only to wipe out the obligation, but even to make ethics debtor to biology. In demonstrating the evolution of plants and animals, organs and functions, instincts and intelligence and conscience, through the preservation and accumulation of modifications useful for survival in the struggle for life, biology has led up to an ethical theory which places the governing principle of human conduct in utility; since, on its showing, utility has generated that conduct as well as the life and the species in which it is manifested. In the war of nature, nothing seems inviolate except what is useful. The stone which the intuitional moralists despised has become the head of the corner. In the evoluitiono-utilitarian theory of morals, the process which nature has blindly followed in the development of life comes to a consciousness of itself, and is recognized as the norm of human conduct. "The ideal goal to the natural evolution of conduct is," according to Mr. Spencer, "the ideal standard of conduct ethically considered." Moral life is held to consist in harmonious adaptation to that social tissue whose production through natural selection was a prime condition of the origin of a species of moral beings. Moral rules are regarded as the expression of those social adaptations which, on the whole, and after infinite gropings, proved most serviceable in the preservation of groups of human animals in the struggle for existence. They are the picked-up clothes which warmed and protected a naked social body and enabled it to vanquish all its rivals. Little wonder if, after the conflict, they have become a feitch to the victors — to all but the few who have tracked their fossil history!

Thus, then, this philosophy of human conduct has been merged in the wider philosophy of life. But the new utilitarianism wears an aspect somewhat unlime the old. They hold, indeed, the same fundamental position in regard to opposing theories; but as between themselves there is an obvious contrast. For, though the note of utility is as clear in the "Origin of Species" as in the "Principles of Morals and Legislation," there it means power-giving, here pleasure-giving; so that, far from running into each other, Darwinism and Benthanism might take their places respcetively under those opposing categories of activity and pleasure into which Schleiermacher resolved every difference of ethical systems.

Of course, if it could be shown that what brings pleasure is identical with what gives power to survive — what is serviceable in the struggle for life — the case would be changed, and the last residumn of the old utilitarianism would have been assimilated by the new. But for this identification Darwinian biology supplies no material. And though it has been speculatively attempted in Mr. Herbert Spencer's elaboration of Professor Bain's suggestion that pleasure is accompanid by an increase of some or all of the vital functions, his arguments are not so much deductions from evolutionary science as postulates of a foregone psychological and ethical hedonism. Even, however, where hedonism is theoretically held to, it is no longer the real vital moment of evolutiono-utilitarianism. Instead of the greatest happiness of the greates number, you have another standad; and morality, as with Mr. Leslie Stephen, is defined as "the means of social vitality," "the conditions of social welfare," "the sum of the preservative instincts of a society." In the last phase of its development, as in the earlier, utilitarianism retains the conception of morality as something relative, a means to an end beyond itself, and as a product of physical or psychological compulsion rather than the self-imposed law of a free moral agent. It has forfeited none of the essential attributes of a system of utility. But, in spite of the protests of its leading advocates, it is casting the slough of pleasure, which seemed a vital part of its earlier life. It still holds that the moral is identical with the useful, though when you ask, "Useful for what?" the answer is no longer "For pleasure," but "For preservation" — *i.e.*, for social vitality, for the well-being of the community. Of those pleasures and pains in which Mill found the sole motive of conduct, as well as the criterion and the sanction of morality, Darwin knows nothing; but, these apart, the essence of utilitarianism and the essence of Darwinism, the principle of utility and the principle of natural selection, have such strong elective affinities that to effect their combination nothing was required but to bring them together. Their union establishes the high-water mark of contemporary utilitarianism.

The transformation has given scientific completeness to utilitarianism. In the hands of Benthan, even, the phenomena of morals were held apart from all other phenomena, but through the common notion of natural selection they have been colligated with the facts of biology; and from the enlarged horizon a gain is expected similar to that which came to the sciences of heat, light, and electricity when they were recognized as merely different applications of the one general theory of motion. And already it is maintained, obscurities of the system on its lower plane are dissipated in the light of its higher altitude. Nor is this effected by the incorporation of elements foreign to the primitive doctrine, such as may be seen, for example, in that peculiarly noble and attractive exposition which the pre-evolutionary utilitarianism received from its last great exponent. In John Stuart Mill's presentation of it the ethics of utility teranscends itself, and the hedonism of Benthanhas has to be suppplemented by the moral law or categorical imperative of Kant, which appears under the form of a "sense of dignity," a reverence for the humanity in one's person, an abiding consciousness of an ideal and attainable worth which forbids dallying with lower ends however strong the attraction of their pleasures. But it is not by such an amalgamation of opposing conceptions that the evolutiono-utilitarian commends his theory. He holds that utility alone, under the action of natural selecion, takes on the appearance of morality, and he pledges himself to derive from this lowly source all those lofty attributes with which men have invested the moral law and glorified it as the oracle of God. Thus evolutionary ethics claims the field, not merely as a deduction from biology, but as a complete scientific explanation of the phenomena of morals. This aspect of it we have now to consider.

The moral law is popularly regarded as simple unanalyzable or ultimate. When it is said that justice is right, that benevolence is a duty, that stealing or lying is wrong, we do not attemp to demonstrate these propositions by means of others, but directly and immediately assent to them as carrying their own self-evidence. It is instinctively felt that no reason can be given for them, any more than for the axious of geometry. And the unsophisticated sense of the plain man is shocked by the suggestion that moral precepts stand or fall with their conduciveness to pleasure, and still more by the suggestion that virtue, which he takes to be the end of life, "is naturally and originally no part of the end," but merely a means to something else — to pleasure as final goal. And it was very difficult for Mill and his predecessors to explain how in theory men had been duped into accepting ethical precepts solely on their own credentials, and how in practice they had been hoodwinked into realizing them disinterestedly, for their own sake, and without the slightest reference to ulterior consequences. But the example of the miser did valiant service in their psychology; and it was argued that, if money, originally only a means to what it purchases, could through association of ideas come to be desired for itself, and that, too, with the utmost intensity, virtue might undergo a similar transformation, and through conduciveness to an end eventually become identified with the end. Nor is the musty example of the miser yet obsolete, as readers of Mr. Spencer will remember. It is, however, reinforeced with new arguments in the ethics of the evolutionists. They do not require the plain man to believe that the tissue of his ethical sentiments has been woven in his own lifetime. They show him how the warp and woof were spun in the brains of animals scarecely yet emerged as men, and then, following the movements of the shuttle in the roaring loom of time, they delineate the formation of a moral texture in our race — a texture inherited by every individual when once it has been acquired bty the species. And how precisely is it acquired? By the help of natural selection. The early societies that did not happen to hit upon the practice of justice, benevolence, etc., could not possibly hold together against groups observing these relations; and then the constant danger of extermination impressed the survivors with the indispensableness of the fundamental virtues, which flamed ever before them, as it were, in characters of blood. What we are familiar with seems simple, what we have always done we do again; and who can wonder, therefore, that our primitive ancestors, slaves of imitation and of habit, should have deemed moral precepts self-evident and the practice of them an end in itself? Equally with the simplicity and ultimateness of our moral conceptions, the evolutionist explains their innateness. Agreeing with the intuitionist that these notions are part of the original furniture of every mind that comes into the world, the evoluziono-utilitarian holds them to be ultimately derived from experience; and if he be a hedonist, like Mr. Spencer, he will add, from experience of pleasurable or painful consequences, though this experience is by him relegated to the past history of mankind. "Moral intuitions are the results of accummlated experiences of utility." Just as the emotion you feel in visiting the home of your youth seems unique and inexplicable, yet is manifestly due to a vague recollection of yoys formerly associated with the objects that surround you, so, it has been ingeniously suggested by Mr. Fouillee, the sentiments which accompany the performance of virtuous acts are the perfume of an eathy soil — a kind of recollection or indistinct echo, not only of our own pleasures, but of the joys of the entire race. And it is this reverberation over the ages of a utility for the race that we take for an innate tendency to disinterestedness. A similar account is given of the inmutability and universality of moral conceptions. Morality being the indispensable condition of social existence, it is coextensive with humanity. The primal virtues shine in every tribe and nation, for without them no section of the human family could have found its way through the struggle for existence. And as amid many smaller variations the general conditions of social life are everywhere the same, moral laws could not fail to be, if not eternal and immutable in the absolute sense of Cudworth, yet as unchanging and enduring as the human species and the universe it inhabits. The fundamental agreement in men's moral notions is thus explained without any assumption of supranatural revelation or *a priori* intuition.

Moral obligation presents a greater difficulty; and evolutionary moralists of the school we are now considering have had to fall back upon the answer of the ordinary utilitarians. They ascribe the sense of obligation to the effects of the legal and social sanctions with which certian kinds of conduct are visited. Moral motives being at first inseparable from political and social motives, they have been permeated with that consciousness of subordination to authority which naturally arises out of the relation of subject to ruler and of individual to tribe. The coerciveness which now forms so important a constitment in our consciousness of duty is a survival of the constraint with which primitive man was forced by external agencies into certain lines of conduct and deterred from others. And hence it follows that, as morality is differenitated more completely from the legal, political, and social institutions in which it originated, the feeling of obligation generated by them will gradually fade away. Thus the evolutiono-utilitarian account of obligation discovers it a transitional feature in the process of human "moralization," and this essentially is all that it adds to the theory of Mill and Bain.

This newest theory of morals, here too briefly outlined, embraces in its range the entire province of moral conceptions and sentiments. But from what has been said the general character of the system will be readily discerned. It is simple, intelligible, and even plausible. That it should have proved fascinating to all, and irresistible to many, of the generation that has so long listened to it with an ardor brooking little distraction from other theories, cannot be a matter of surprise to anyone who has duly considered the facts with which the theory is associated. Borrowed, as they are, either from observation or from well-established sciences, and fitted ingeniously into current evolutionary ethics, they seem to be an organic part of the structure; and the question of otherwise explaining them is not likely to be raised. Conversely, the full implication of the principles upon which they are here grafted has been left unexplored. And thus, while the new ethical philosophy has been widely accepted, a determination of the bases on which it really rests still remains to be made. This want we must now attempt to supply.

In the first place, then, evolutionary ethics, as hitherto presented, takes for granted the derivative character of morality. I say "as hitherto presented," because I hope to show in the sequel that there is nothing in the notion of development when applied to morals which necessitates, or which even warrants, the assumption. But our exponents of evolutionism happen to have been trained in the school of Epicurus, Hume, and Bentham, and it is not, on the whole, very surprising they should have carried the old leaven into the new teaching. What is surprising is the assumption, so coolly made, that the theory of evolution in some way vouches for the utilitarianism our moralists associate with it. As though a follower of Plato or Kant, for example, could not be a Darwinist in science! Is it forgotten that, even if goodness be an end in itself — the sole end worth living for — it still remains true that honesty is the best policy, that honest acts are the most advantageous acts, and that they will accordingly be preserved through natural selection in the struggle for existence? All that natural selection requires is that something shall be useful; *what else it may be*, what other predicates it may have, wherein its essence consists, natural selection knows not and recks not. Be virtue a proximate end or an ultimate end, natural selection tells us it will be preserved and perpetuated if it is useful; and it tells us no more. It is, accordingly, a gratuitous assumption which our exponents of evolutionary ethics make, when they decline to allow more than a merely relative value to morality. And as their position derives no support from evolutionary science, so is it exposed to all the objections which moralists, voicing the universal consciousness of mankind, have brought against it, from the time when Aristotle asserted that virtue has no extrinsic end (*Tov kalou Eneka*) to the time when Kant proclaimed the absolute worth of a good will.

In the second place, the current expositors of evolutionary ethics having made the radical assumption that moral laws are not categorical imperatives which command unconditionally, but hypothetical imperatives which prescribe means to the attainment of some end, they cannot escape the problem of determining wherein consists that ultimate end, conduciveness to which alone gives morality its worth andobligation. Nor, in general, has the school been dismayed by the magnitude or the obscurity of this problem. Possibly it has not fully realized that the question is nothing less than an inquiry into the highest good for man or the supreme end of human endeavor. Be that as it may, one cannot but be interested to find that, in spite of the distrust of reason generated by modern theories of knowledge, our evolutionary thinkers dare to face the problem which, in undisturbed consciousness of reason's might, ancient philosophers put in the foreground of their ethics. Even in an age of agnosticism thoughtful men come round to the sphinx-riddle, What am I here for? what is the end of life? The question may not, it is true, take precisely this form in the mouth of a modern evolutionary moralist, but that, after all, is substantially what he is bent on discovering and what he must discover — *must*, if his thesis is to be made good that morality is only a means to something else. And there is no logical reason why he should not appropriate the Aristotelian solution that man's highest good consists in the most perfect rational activity, that his supreme end or function is to inform life with reason and make his entire being the embodiment of reason. But, as a matter of fact, most typical evolutionary moralists have selected a very different ethical end — pleasure. They have maintained with Mr. Spencer that "the good is universally the pleasurable," and that conduct is made good or bad solely by its "pleasurable-giving and pain-giving effects."

Still the evolutionary moralist, even of the derivative school, is not necessarily committed to this solution of the problem. He may doubt that the supreme end of life is to get and to give the greatest amount of pleasure. And appropriating the language of the Rabelaisian decription of Carlyle's, on which Mr. Spencer has poured forth eloquent objurgation, our doubter may question whether the universe is merely "an immeansurable swine's trough," and whether "moral evil is unattainability of pig's-wash and moral good attainability of ditto." For certainly the hedonist cannot, in the absence of antecedent obligations which this theory excludes, but deem *his own* pleasure the highest good; and whether accepting or not the psychology of the school which teaches that nothing but one's own pleasure *can be* the object of desire, he will acquiesce in the ethical dictum of Benthan, that "to attain the greatest portion of happiness for himself is the object of every rational being." But as soon as this opposition between his own pleasures and the pleasures of other is brought distinctly into consciousness, and the former recognized as the end, the impossibility of constructing an ethic on this basis is manifest. There is no way across the chasm that yawns between "each for himself" and "each for others." And if man be merely a pleaure-seeking animal, you but mock him when you enjoin him to promote the happiness of others. Accordingly, a sincere and logical utilitarian who felt with Mill, that the spirit of his ethics was that of the golden rule of Jesus of Nazareth, would drop altogether the notion of pleasure, which has hitherto filled the system with inconsistencies, and allow the ethical principle, thus freed from the accidental setting of a psychological hedonism, to proclaim itself as the greatest *good* of the greatest number, or, better still, as the *well-being* of society. Whatever be the content of that well-being (and there is much in it besides pleasure), it, and not happiness either of self or others, is the end which utilitarianism pure and simple, the utilitarianism of Mill divorced from his more than dubious psychology, might set up as the ultimate end for every moral agent. And this, in fact, is the supreme principle of the ethics of Darwin, though he directs attention rather to the genesis of moral rules than to the reason for our obseving them. And though Mr. Spencer is too strongly influenced by the national ethics to forego the final reduction of morality to pleasure — and even the agent's own pleasure — he yet maintains that those acts are good which conduce to the welfare of self, of offspring, and of society. The same end is recognized by Mr. Leslie Stephen in his explanation of moral rules as means of social preservation; yet, Mr. Stephen has not been so unfaithful to what he calls his own "school" — Bentham, Mill, etc. — as to separate its psychology of self-seeking from its ethics of self-sacrifice.

When this divorce does take place, however — and already it is heralded in Darwin — there will be no longer in this respect a fundamental opposition between evolutionary ethics and common-sense morals. Attempts to patch up a truce, on the assumption that pleasures might through heredity be transformed into duties, have utterly failed. But the simple recognition of the welfare of society as an ultimate end is not to go outside of morality to find a reason for it, against which the intuitionist has always protested. It is to take one virtue, already recognized by the intuitionist, for the whole of virtue. And to that extent the two schools ate in essential agreement. A difference, however, appears when you inquire if there are not virtues which the general formula of promoting the well-being of others does not embrace. Common-sense seems to say there are other duties as original, as self-evident, and as obligatory, as benevolence. And it does look rather incredible that every man should be an end to others and not to himself. We do not easily rid ourselves of the conviction that goodness consists rather in the realization of a certain type of character in ourselves than in the performance of any external actions, though of course conduct promotive of the welfare of others would be one necessary outcome of the character thus indicated.

I come now to a third characteristic assumption of current evolutionary ethics — the fortuitous origin of morality through a process purely mechanical. This must, I think, be regarded as the fundamental tenet of the school; but in England, at least, it seems to have been taught with all the reserve of an esoteric mystery. The accredited expounders of the subject have in their exoteric writings enveloped this point in such a wrapping of extraneous discussions that even a master in ethics like Professor Sidgwick has hazarded the declaration that evolution, however conceived, can make no difference at all in our ethical theories. But, with all deference to do so eminent an authority, I hold that if this mechanical conception of moral evolution be conceded, the question of an ethical end — of what we ought to aim at — becomes unmeaning, since there cannot, in a literal sense, be any ends or aims for a being conceived as a mere mechanism, even though its random acts have through natural selection been solidified into habits, and habits, on the supervention of consciousness, been reflected as rules. And this interpretation of evolution would be as fatal to practice as to theory. An individual who really accepted it must regard moral responsibility as illusory, as nothing but an echo of the modes of conduct which enabled the human species to overcome what was untoward to its progress or what threatened its extinction. For him the entire preceptive part of morality must seem a baseless imposition. And in the courageous language of M. Guyau he could recognize nothing but *une morale sans obligation ni sanction.* No longer *avtonomes* man must perforce be *anomes.* Had this point been brought out as clearly by the English as by the French evolutionists, they would have seen that their own principles required them to dismiss the incongrnous problem of establishing the validity of moral rules, even if they still persisted in speculating on the origin of them. It is worse than idle for mechanical evolutionists to talk of the reason or end or ground of morality.

That morality has had a mechanical origin is, I have said, the fundamental assumption of current evloutionary ethics. The ancestors of man had no moral fibre in their constitution, but through long-inherited experiences of the consequences of conduct man has been rendered "organically moral." Just as intelligence, in general, according to the same theory, has been generated in unintelligent beings through the accumulation of modifications arising from intercourse between the organism and its environment, so the moral faculty, in particular, is the result of all those experiences whereby mutually repellent individual animals were fused together into society and enabled to perpetuate a victorious existence. The evolutionist conceives life as the continuous adjustment of inner relations to outer relations; so that, even before the rise of sentiency, the acts of living beings must have been adapted to their environment, and intelligence, when it did emerge, could be nothing but the consciousness of relations already blindly estahlished, and the function of conscience could only be to recognize the utility of what promoted life. The evolution of man — the self-conscious and moral person — from lower forms of life is referred to physical causation alone. As the human pedigree has been traced up to the simian branch of the animal tree, and no ground discovered for absolutely separating the latest from the earliest offshoots, our most eminent living biologist maintains that when Descartes declared all animals to be automata, his only error lay in excluding man from the same class. This conscious automaton is but the highest term of an animal series whose law of development is already known, and everything in his constitution is explicable by that law. But the evolution of life has realized itself through a mechanical process; consequently those distinctive characteristics which mark off the human from the simian species must be the products of the same process. As natural selection has endowed all beings with the constitutions and habits and faculties which they actually possess — the eagle with his eye, the bee with her sting, the lion with his rage and strength — so must natural selection have endowed man, not only with an erect attitude, but also with a reason that looks before and after and a conscience that responds to right and wrong. The mental and moral faculties are both reduced to the rank of natural phenomena. Indeed, to express their essentially derivative and, as it were accidental character, a new word has been coined, and intelligence is described as an "epiphenomenon." By this term is meant that consciousness is a merely accessory aspect of the human automation, a psychological index of corporeal movements which are the prime reality, a reflex of mechanism which would go on all the same without any reflex, just as an engine would move along the rails if it did not whistle, or a bird fly if it cast no shadow. But if the school interprets consciousness as an accident of the human automaton, it makes conscience an accident of this accident. First mechanism realizing itself in certain relations (by means of natural selection), then consciousness of these relations, then approval of their life-conserving tendencies, or conscience. The moral faculty is the recognition of social relations; it is the social instinct of the animals come to a consciousness of itself in man; and this social instinct is but the consolidation of habit, and habit is the product, through natural selection, of random actions struct out in the struggle foir life. Thus the moral nature of man is merged in the mechanism of nature. The logical, as the chronological, *prius* is, therefore, not intelligence, but mechanical action. The exegesis of Faust receives a startling illustration: *In Anfang war die That.*

This moral theory, therefore, implies and rests upon a system of metaphysics. I do not think we can too often reiterate that current evolutionary ethics is the outcome of a very dubious physico-physhical speculation. From overlooking this connection the issue between moralists of this scghool and of other schools has not been clearly discerned, and the very heart of the question has been generally left untouched. I do not, of course, mean to call in question the results of the astronomical, pghysical, chemical, and biological sciences. What one teaches about the gradual formation of the universe, and another about the gradual development of organisms on our globe, I accept implicityly. But because minerals and plants and the lower animals appeared before man, I will not, therefore, hold that they were adequate conditions to his production, or that there is nothing in him that was not generated through actions and reactions between an animal system and its physical or social environment. Such a doctrine used to be called materialism, but in deference to the feelings of speculative evolutionists the word has nowadays been dropped. All the objections, however, which were formerly urged against the derivation of mental and moral functions from material combinations, however finely organized, are still valid against the evolutionary identification of intelligence with the modifications produced in the nervous and muscular systems from action and reaction between the organism and its environment. Man is later on the scene than the unintelligent organisms; but whence his intelligence we know not, unless it be the emergence of something new from the fountain of being, from the underlying ground and sustaining cause of the whole evolutionary movement. Certainly it was not evolved by mere repetition of mechanical actions. Were intelligence not at the heart of the cosmos, it could not have turned up as the crowning glory of the development of life.

The same position may be taken up in opposition to the current evolutionary ethics. Biology warrants the belief that non-moral beings existed on our globe long before the appearance of the only moral being we know — man; and natural selection explains the process by which the latter may have been descended from the former. But natural selection, as we have already shown, creates no new material; it merely sits in judgment upon what has already appeared. Given acts, or habits, or moral practices, natural selection is the name for the survivl of the fittest of them, not the talismanic cause which origimates any of them. However they originate, they must have a definite relation to the constitution of the being that manifests them; and to suppose that moral sentiments, moral notions, moral practices, could be gracfted upon a primitively non-moral being is, in the first place, to take a grossly mechanical view of human nature and, in the second place, to trangress the limits alike of natural selection and of evolutionary science. Yet this is what id done by our evolutionary moralists. A moral law, they tell you, is the formulation by intelligence of the social practices instinctively followed by the more or less intelligent ancestors of man, these practices themselves having crystallized into habits from an inchoate chaos of random acts. We have in the preceding chapter considered Darwin's derivation of instincts from casual actions, and we have here only to inquire whether conscience is nothing but the social instinct illuminated by intelligence. Were it so, we could not fail to admire the manner in which morality was forced upon unwilling beings until at last appeared an intelligence capable of freely accepting it and heartily setting about its realization. As in the education of the human race, according to Lessing, religion is at first revealed only that it may ultimately become rational, why should not the practice of marality at first have been compulsory that it might in due time become free and gracious? But, after all, I believe an analysis of the facts will not suffer us to take this view of the providential government of the world. In the contents of the moral consicousness I find unique elements, unlike anything that went along with the earlier stages of the development of life, and absolutely incapable of resolution into practices useful for social survival blindly followed by the non-moral precursors of humanity. If the social instinct is, as the theory supposes, only a means of preserving society, how could intelligence ever take it for more than that? But in the moral consciousness of mankind there is clear recognition of an absolutely worthful. And, in the next place, if this be denied, there remains one element in the moral consciousness that forever distinguishes it from a mere intelligence-illuminated social instinct, namely, the sense of duty. Even if moral law be supposed nothing more than the expression of devices wrought out unconsciously in the course of aeons, for securing the vitality and well-being of society, why do I recognize myself under obligation to observe the law? This consciousness of duty, the most certain and most imperious fact in our experience, whence does it come if man have no moral fibre in his primitive constitution? On this rock the ethics of **Kant, giving scientific shape to human morality, is firmly intrenched. And no** better testimony to its security could be found than the shifts to which evolutionists are put when they attempt to resolve this element of the moral consciousness into race-accumulated experiences of utility. Mr. Spencer, indeed, supposes men to have been scared into moral obligation by the baton of the primitive policeman, the ostracism of primitive society, and the hell of the primitive priest. How a society could exist to deal out these political, social, and religious sanctions, *unless it rested on a moral basis*, the evolutionist does not explain. And one may, therefore, be pardoned for seeing here only another of the countless attempt to derive morality from ideas and institutions which already presuppose it. The *vsteron proteron* is the bane of evolutionary ethics. Naturally enogh, the sentiment produced by the terrors of ancient law, politics, and religion, will decay with the cessation of its causes; and as Mr. Spencer identifies this sentiment with moral obligation, one can understand how he reaches the paradox that the "sense of duty, ormoral obligation, is transitory." In another way the same conclusion is reached by M. Guyau, who follows Darwin. Conscience is the social instinct, he says, and the scientific spirit is the great enemy of blind instincts; it illuminates them, and in the flood-tide of light dissolves them; what habit has made, reflection unmakes; and nothing can save morality when conscience has met the doom of every instinct — dissolution under scientific reflection. "Pan, the nature-god is dead; Jesus, the man-god is dead; there remains the ideal god within us, duty, which is also, perhaps, destined one day to die." But the irrefragable reply to these oracular prophecies is that they rest upon a misreading of the actual record. *If* moral obligation be the effect of certain historical causes, it may decline with the decadence of those causes, and *if* conscience be a blind instinct, it may follow the supposed law of dissolution of instincts; but the conditional ground of the consequence is in neither case established, in neither case does it rest upon evolutionary science, in neither case has it any antecedent probability apart from the *a priori* prejudice of the utilitarian in favor of the derivative character of morality and the moral faculties. Instead of so accounting for the rise of a moral sense and moral obligation, as a kind of accident in our constitution, mankind (a few metaphysicians apart) persists in regarding them as of the very essence of human nature. The absolute "ought" cannot be the the product of any experience with the primitive policeman or priest, since (apart from the fact that there would be neither without it) experience only records what is advantageous for certain ends and cannot, therefore enjoin anything categorically. Hence the pretence of the evolutionists to have reconciled the experiential and intuitive schools of ethics cannot be sustained. Those predicates of the moral law which, in the earlier part of this chapter, we found the evolutionary theory claiming to account for — its simplicity, universality, etc. — are not its essential attributes; so that, even if the evolutionists contention be granted, he leaves untouched the fundamental constitnents of the moral consciousness — our sense of an absolutely worthful, the right, not merely the useful, and our recognition of its authority over us as expressed in the word "ought." For these ideas no experience can account, and every experiential theory virtually explains them away as the indispensable condition to its own plausibility. However long the process, whether extending through one generation, as the older utilitarians imagined, or through countless generations, as the evolutiono-utilitarians assume, there never will be success, as Lotze justly observed, in fetching into an empty soul, by means of the impressions of experience, a consciousness of moral obligation.

Nor, in fact, does evolutionary science, relieved of the metaphysical baggage with which it has hitherto been grievously freighted, require us to beleve in the possibility of this desperate feat. It assumes that morality has been developed through natural selection. And because natural selection presupposes a utility — a fittest that survives — the evolutionists have fallen into the fallacy of supposing that morality was *nothing but* a utility. That is the explanation of the plausibility of their ethical theory as expounded in the earlier part of the present chapter. And no other refutation, after all that has been said, need now be added except the reminder that natural selection, though wide-awake to the uses of things, is blind to their nature and essence. It takes advantage of the utility of morality, but no more determines its content and meaning than a positivist who passes over the question of the essence of things. It acts upon germs of all kinds, once they have been produced and are moving through phases of development; but it knows not what the germs are, whence they come, or what develops them. The whole question, so far as ethics is concerned, turns on the nature of those primitive modifications out of which morality has been evolved. But on that point evolutionary science has no answer of its own to give, and the blank has been filled by the preconceptions of evolutionary speculators. Subordinating, as the school has hitherto done, intelligence to mechanism, it has invarialy sough the first germ of conscience in a random action that proved useful to the species in which it was struck out. We have, on the contrary, maintained that this hypothetical derivation passes over the very essence of moral consciousness; nor can we imagine any other way of deriving it which does not already presuppose it. In opposition to this mechanical theory of conscience, we hold that it is an ultimate function of the mind, and that in germ as in full fruition it must be regarded, not as an action, but as *an ideal of action*. The consciousness of right and wrong is underived, and, like intelligence in general, witnesses to a supra-sensible principle in man — a principle which the wheels of mechanism, grinding through eternity, could never of themselves produce. This view of the subject may be affiliated to Darwinism as readily as the other. For an abiding ideal of action is, to say the least, quite as beneficial as a chance action; and wherever there is an advantage, there natural selection may operate. But natural selection does not determine the material upon which it works. Given the forms of primitive morality, whatever they be, natural selection only settles which shall perish and which survive. Its function is the negative one of sifting whatever has attained to positive existence. In the book of Job, Satan represents, according to Professor Davidson, the testing sifting providence of God: natural selection is the Satan of the evolutionary powers. Strange, indeed, that it should ever have been mistaken for the powers themselves!

The ethical conclusions here reached and co-ordinated with the doctrine of evolution and Darwinism (which I everywhere take for granted) are so opposed to those of most evolutionists that some fallacy may ber supposed to infect all our reasonings. After the evolutionary teachings of the last twenty years, it seems either blindness or disingenousness to maintain thast evolution leaves our ethical problems precisely where it found them. And so, in spite of all the preceding analyses and criticisms, the old objections are sure to recur. Does not the evolutionary doctrine of heredity imply that man is what his ancestry has made him, and so abrogate our belief in the freedom of the human will? And does not goodness cease to be divine when you have explained moral laws as a statement of the habits blindly struck ou and blindly followed by simian or semi-human groups in the struggle for existence? If morality is merely a formulation of the practices which, accidentally hit upon by some group of animals, made the group coherent and thus enabled it to vanquish rival groups with different practices, would it not seem merely accidental that justice and truthfulness are virtues, and not injustice and lying? For if these vices, or others, had enabled those primitive semi-human societies to survive, they would not have been vices, but virtues; for virtue is nothing but a useful means of social survival. Will not evolution, then, as thus interpreted, work revolution in our views of the moral nature of man, since it implies that morality is not grounded in the naure of things, but something purely relative to man's circumstances — a happy device whereby man's ancestors managed to cohere in a united society and so kill out rival and disunited groups.

Now, it is not necessary to deny either the social utility of morals or the influence of heredity in order to show that, whatever the first appearance, evolution is not in reality revolution in the sphere of man's moral nature. It is no doubt true that heredity supplies us with much of the material out of which we make our characters. But it is only by an oversight that we identify our character with the inherited elements out of which we form it. As Aristotle profoundly observed, nature does not make us good or bad, she only gives us the capacity of becoming good or bad — that is, of moulding our own characters. Emphasize as you will, then, the bulk of the inheritance I have received from my ancestors, it still remains true that in moral character I am what I make myself. On stepping stones of their dead selves men rise to higher things; and neither our ability to do this, nor the consciouness of that ability implied in the freedom of the will, is affected in any way by evolution.

But surely, it will be objected, evolution does mean revolution in our views of human nature, if it makes moral rules a mere social utility. I admit the conclusion, but reject its premises. For, as I have already urged, the facts of human life will not allow us to interpret morality as a mere accidental arrangement whereby our animal ancestors came out victorious in the struggle for life. I do not deny that morality would, as a matter of fact, be useful to any society practising it in the war of all against all in the struggle for life. That it is useful is clear from the readiness with which people follow Hamlet's advice to his mother and assume a virtue when they have it not. But if morality be nothing more than mere social utility, a mere device which enabled man's ancestors to kill out rival groups, I fail to understand how there has arisen in man a conscience which makes cowards of us all; a remorse which drives a Lady Macbeth to madness, and a Judas to suicide; a sense of eternal right so strong that no theory can make us believe we are hoodwinked into righteousness, truth, and justice, by the mere accident that lying, injustice, and unrighteousness were less useful in holding primitive societies together and enabling them to kill out their rivals. And all this might be conceded by the evolutionist, had he not fallen into the fallacy of holding that, becuae virtue is socially useful, therefore it is nothing but a social utility. There are other things besides morality which favor the survival of primitive societies. We have already spoken of the advantages of an erect attitude and of a sound intelligence. Yet the evolutionist does not call these characters *mere* social utilities. The eye, for example, has no exisence among the lowest animals; yet when it does appear, its own new story is accepted as a feesh revelation of fact. Instead of describing it as an advantage in the struggle for life, the evolutionist sees in the new organ the possibility of a deeper communion with reality; and the more developed the organ the more valuable its evidence. The earliest eye was probably nothing more than a tingling sensitiveness to light and darkness. The most developed eye discerns a spectrum of seven colors; and along with this advance it has also acquired the capacity of measuring distances, magnitudes, and situations. Both these functions of the eye were eminently useful in the struggle for life: they enabled their animal possessor to get food more easily and escape foes more deftly. Yet the evolutionist does not hold the eye is merely a utility. Bringing the surprise of something new and unexpected, the eye, he will recognize, is useful only because it makes us aware of fact. But if you accept the evidence of the eye when it testifies to the colors or sizes of objects, you cannot reject the depositions of conscience to the moral character of conduct and motives. This is a new mental function, and has the same claim upon you as the other. The validity of the intutition, "Injustice is wrong," is neither greater nor less than the validity of the perception, "Snow is white." The vision of both the outer and the inner eye is useful, but useful simply because each gives us new revelations of reality.

The same result is reached by comparing the deliverances of conscience with the discoveries of intelligence. The lowest animals have neither conscience nor reason. The infinite advantage of either we have already described. Even the germ of reason suffices to make man lord of creation. Think only of the significance of the discovery that twice two are four. An intelligence advanced to that point is on the way to geomety, trigonometry, and the calculus, to all those sciences whose application has chanted the face of the material world. As the highest mathematics is useful to us, so was the first germ useful to our ancestors. But it does not, therefore, follow that arithmetic is merely a social utility. On the contrary, it is useful for the reason that it brings man into deepening relation with fact; but its validity is wholly independent of its advantage to mankind, and only the satirist could suggest that twice two would be five if that product were more advantageous to us. Arithmetical facts cannot be determined by a plebiscite of utilitarians. And the same is true of the deliverance of conscience that injustice is wrong. Ultimate mathematical principles and ultimate moral principles have the same intuitive evidence; and it is not weakened hy the assumption that man owes his bodily organism to animals in which there was no trace either of a moral or a mathematical faculty. Fact is fact; and neither morality nor geometry ceases to be objectively grounded from the accident that our ancestors only gradually came to an apprehension of them.

From all points of view, then, we are led to the same result. Evolutionary science in general, natural selection in particualar, does not necessitate, or even indicate, a new system of ethics. It stands logically indifferent between intuitionism and utilitarianism, though from the accident that most expounders of evolution happened to be utilitarians there has arisen a belief that the two were in some way connected. In reality, evolutionary ethics, as hitherto expounded, is nothing but an arbitrary combination of utilitarianism in one or other of its forms wih a speculative metaphysics which discovers the ground of mind and conscience in an antecedent phyusical or nervous mechanism. And as such it not only has no support from evolutionary *science*, but is at the same time exposed to all the objections which the common-sense of mankind has always brought against every empirical theory of morals and every mechanical theory of intelligence.

Section Eight

GEORGE JOHN BLEWETT
(1873-1912)

8

Blewett's Vision of God

Morton MacCallum-Paterson

George John Blewett was an internationally respected Canadian philosopher-theologian over an eleven-year period at the turn of this century, yet his work is virtually unknown. He studied the new empirical psychology under four Wundtians: Kirchmann (Toronto), Kulpe and Marbe (Wurzburg) and Munsterberg (Harvard). He was at the centre of the philosophical idealist movement centred at Oxford at the turn of the century (studying under Caird of Balliol). During periods of tenure at two Canadian universities (Wesley, Winnipeg, from 1901-1906 and Victoria, Toronto, from 1906-1912) he wrote two major books[1] and in 1910 turned down energetic invitations from Boston University to fill the newly created Borden Parker Bowne Chair in Philosophy[2] He drowned at Go-Home Bay in Lake Huron in his thirty-eighth year while vacationing with his family.[3]

The fact that Blewett was trained and was comfortable in both mainstream philosophy and the new social sciences of psychology and sociology makes him a particularly fascinating Canadian intellectual. His career was short, and he faded from prominence within a decade of his death. Nonetheless, his place in the history of Canadian philosophy is secure. He was dealing with issues which were placed on the sidelines for several decades but which constitute a core tradition in the attempt to link science and religion. For Blewett, the "new psychology" of Wundt contained moves which provided insights into the nature and knowability of God.

Blewett interpreted the act of knowing as a natural event accessible to introspective analysis and experimentation. Under Kirschmann's guidance in the psychology laboratory at the University of Toronto, he was "trained" to introspect elements of consciousness, to map the structural connections between them, and, in the tradition of Kantian critical idealism, to determine the necessary conditions without which knowledge of the world, God and oneself are impossible. Indeed, as he argued in his doctoral dissertation, these three "realities" logically interpenetrate one another:

The source of that system of relations which is the eternal order of the world, is a single eternal self-conscious subject. It — or He —makes each member of the system what it is; makes the system itself what it is: and, in doing so, distinguishes himself from those members or elements and from any possible sums or sum of them. To him, the relations or laws, which are the order of the world are, as a single order, present in their completeness, i.e., eternally... each thing or fact, as it truly is, i.e., in the fullness or totality, and therefore in the eternity, of its relations, is constituted by and is present to, that self-consciousness.[4]

Blewett's argument is fastened at one end to a Wundtian introspective empiricism (the mind as a unified unifier) and at the other to a form of immanental theism in which God is understood as cosmic self-consciousness. In his Taylor lectures ten years later Blewett construed "connections in nature" (i.e., laws) as tantamount to unifications in self-consciousness. Hence his Spinozistic thesis that

...the laws of nature are, to their own extent, laws of experience; statements of the conditions under which certain elements or aspects of our experience are what they are; and in certain cases, *laws of nature are laws within human consciousness* —psychological laws, laws of the ongoing of the subjective process of experience.[5]

Connections between events in nature are inescapably epistemic, such that knowledge "of" them is internal to their very being. The wiring of the universe is psychic. And psychology a⅜ la Wundt becomes the basis for an idealistic theism in which God is the unified mind upon which a unified world (i.e., a *uni*verse) is grounded. God is not a datum, a thing, an element to be grasped, but the structural, relational, integrating consciousness which in being aware of the world actually *constitutes* the world.[6]

Blewett's account of the relation between human and divine mind contains hints of Martin Buber's later philosophy of meeting. Meeting between two minds — human or divine —consists of the merging of two fields of consciousness, each of which is understood as "will-plus-action." he avoids a Spinozistic pantheism by insisting that human and divine mind are each *separate* centres of consciousness, but the relation between them is internal; human mind is absorbed within divine mind. To meet God is to be within God. To apprehend God is to view both the laws of ones own mind — as well as what is known by means of those laws —as within the wider circle of a mind whose constitution is the complete set of laws of mind by which the complete world, a universe, is known. And what are the laws of the divine mind? The laws of nature, whose discovery is one of the chief ends of the human quest. Scientist and theologian are joining in a common quest, in which empirical method is the route both to self-discovery and to the "experience of God."

Blewett was preoccupied with mysticism throughout his career. In an essay on Erigena in *The Study of Nature and the Vision of God* he analysed his logic of participation in which each order of being "participates" in the next higher. God is the highest order, and participates in no other order.[7] But while his idealism flirted with the mystical way, he ultimately rejected it because it failed to deal with the reality of evil.[8]

In his Taylor lecture at Yale in 1910 (on the basis of which he was invited to Boston University), Blewett dealt with the problem of evil in terms of a kind of sociological theodicy. It is in the nature of the individual and of society to actualize need, but in cases where the first conflicts with the second, the first typically wins out. Individual self-interest is such that when the community frustrates it, the individual acts systematically and defiantly to destroy the community. Disorganization and the separation of social units and classes from one another are *characteristic* of human action — a remarkable accurate if dark portrait of a world which, two years after his death, would be plunged into international conflict. He speaks of the conflict between good and evil as seeming "decisively and absolutely to shiver the unity of the real world."[9] Laws of consciousness which underlie the world may make *possible* a unified cosmos, but sociologically and historically it is clear that that unification remains a yearning, not a reality.

It is at this point in Blewett's philosophy — a shiver rends the universe —that he turns toward a social soteriology in which human consciousness can be rendered safe within a reconstitutued society. To the extent to which an individual mind can be absorbed into divine mind in private consciousness, it is able also to incorporate into it the *tasks* of the divine mind. As in a home separate minds freely adapt themselves to a "family mind," so separate minds which are connected to the divine mind can, by an act of will, adapt their ends to those of God — who is the "home of persons." This metaphor (for which he was indebted to Wordsworth[10]) pervades Blewett's later writings, and was central to a christology in which Jesus is understood as articulating the fundamental insight about ethical interaction. It is familial. On the one hand, Jesus thoroughly participated in the sorrows of life (the dread shiver runs through the gospels). On the other hand, Jesus' familial identity with God as Father (in Whom he was "at home") made of him "the revealer and accomplisher of redemption" whose appearance on the earth was, for Blewett, the critical and determinative point in human history.

Clearly, being "at home in God" is for Blewett a category of action, not of security. In adapting oneself to divine tasks, there is a commitment to social change:

> ...no man's salvation, in this world or any other, is made perfect, until the social order in which he has his being is an order of righteousness; an order in which none is wronged, none is oppressed, none is made a mere means to another's ends, none has the ways of spiritual growth closed against him; but all men serve the good of all, so that any success to any man means an increase of life and of the goodness of life to all.[11]

For Blewett, epistemology merges into soteriology. To know oneself, one's world, and the divine mind, is a spring to action. The human will, in itself, is bent towards the destruction of community; when it is internally meshed into the mind of the "home of persons" it is fully itself, fully human. Integration into the larger mind, be it that of the wider community or of God, is for Blewett both an act of knowing and of personal recovery.

Blewett's brand of personal idealism rooted in empirical psychology begs for an analysis in the light of current tools of inquiry. His understanding of scientific method is dated. The dialogue between science and religion has become much more sophisticated. But there can be no denying Blewett's energetic commitment to relevance, and to the integration of philosophical and scientific knowledge. He died too young. But his ideas were centre-stage in what might be called the Edwardian era of Canadian intellectual history.

Notes

1. *The Study of Nature and the Vision of God* (Toronto: Methodist Book and Publishing House, 1907) and *The Christian View of the World*: Nathaniel William Taylor Lectures for 1910-11 (New Haven: Yale University Press, 1912).
2. See my "George John Blewett: A Forgotten Personalist," *Idealistic Studies*, VIII, no.2, May, 1978: 179-189 for an extended treatment of the Boston offer. My "Divine Encounter in Blewett," *Studies in Religion*, VI, no 4: 397-403 summarizes a number of main moves in his theocentric idealism. His place within the specific story of Canadian Methodist intellectual history is treated in my "The Mind of a Methodist: The Personalist Theology of George John Blewett," *The Bulletin of the Archives of the United Church of Canada* no.27, 1978: 5-41. Elizabeth Trott and Leslie Armour deal with Blewett's thought in their *The Faces of Reason* (Waterloo: Wilfred Laurier University Press, 1981): 321-353.
3. Blewett was born on December 9th, 1873 of Cornwall stock who had emigrated from England in the late 1840s and settled in North Yarmouth township in the Western corner of Canada West (near the present St.Thomas, Ontario). The family name had originally been Bluet, Britannic for what the English call the cornflower. His aunt, Jean (McKishnie) Blewett was to become a much beloved poetess and columnist; she named one of her three books *The Cornflower and Other Poems*(1906), and for many years she was editor of the "Home-Maker's Department" of the Toronto *Globe*. Blewett majored in political economy at the University of Toronto (1890-92), was a student teacher at the Methodist Indian School at Morley, Alberta under the Reverend John McDougall(1892-93), then served as a "saddleback" probationer-preacher on the Elbow River and Sturgeon River circuits of the Manitoba and Northwest Conference of the Methodist Church(1893-1895) under the superintendency of the Reverend James Woodsworth.

   He returned to University, this time to the honours Philosophy programme of Victoia College, from which he graduated in 1897 with three prizes, including a Governor-General's Gold Medal. He completed his theological training by correspondence in 1898, and enrolled in the Ph.D. programme in Psychology at the University of Toronto that fall. After two years he was encouraged by his professor, August Kirschmann, to conclude his studies at the University of Wurzburg (summer, 1899) and at Harvard University, from which he received his Ph.D. in 1900.

   Blewett won the prestigious Rogers Memorial Fellowship at Harvard, and decided upon post-doctoral studies at Oxford in the year 1900-01, no doubt on the advice of his friend, J.S.Woodsworth (son of James Woodsworth), who had himself studied there the year before. He concluded his overseas studies with a three month course in Sociology under George Simmel at the Royal University of Freidrich Wilhelm from May to August of 1901, before returning to Canada to the Chair of Church History and Historical Theology at Wesley College, Winnipeg in 1901. In 1906 he accepted the invitation of Victoria College, Toronto, to assume the Chair in Ethics and Apologetics.

George John Blewett married Clara Woodsworth (a first cousin of his friend, J.S.) on July 11th, 1906; in 1907 they joined the Madawaska Club, an association largely made up of Vic families at Go-Home Bay, just south of Midlan in Georgian Bay on Lake Huron. They purchased property with the intention of building a summer cottage. A son, John, was born in 1910, and a daughter, Constance, as born shortly after his death. He drowned while swimming alone in the early morning of August 15th, 1912.

4. "The Metaphysical Basis of Perceptive Ethics," (unpublished doctoral dissertation, Harvard University, 1900), 61.

5. *The Christian View of the World*, 179 (emphasis mine). During his graduate study at Harvard Blewett became intrigued with Spinoza's monism, and under the pseudonym of Basset Trewerdale Lanke, he submitted an essay entitled "The Philosophy of Spinoza with Special Reference to its Historical Position" in competition for the Graduate Bowdoin Prize. He won the prize ($300), beating out a fellow-Canadian, W.B.Munro, who was later to become an important theorist of government in the United States.

6. In this move Blewett was influenced by Josiah Royce, who was lecturing in England during his year at Harvard, but was one of his dissertation readers. Blewett expressed particular admiration for Royce's *The World and the Individual* (2 Vols., New York: MacMillan, 1899, 1901), in *The Christian View of the World*, 301.

7. See pp.289ff. in the same volume he examined the mystical strains in Hinduism, Parmenides, Plato, Plotinus and Spinoza as well, showing that pantheism denies what mysticism requires —the separate *individuality* of human and divine mind. See p.287n.

8. See *The Christian View of the World*, p.259. He accused the mystical tradition of avoiding the challenge of theodicy.

9. *The Christian View of the World*, p,257.

10. Stanza V of "Ode: An Intimation of Immortality from Recollections of Early Childhood," written 1802-04, in J.Butts, ed., *Wordsworth — Selected Poetry and Prose*(Oxford: Oxford University Press, 1964).

11. *The Christian View of the World*, p.299. This is a striking statement of the kind of social consciousness which marked much theological thought in Canada in the early decades of this century. Blewett and J.S.Woodsworth (later the founder of the socialist party, the Cooperative Commonwealth Federation) were, as I have indicated, close friends and related by marriage. They both studied under A.M. Fairbairn at Oxford, who exemplified the "social gospel" movement of the day. the Reverend Salem Bland, a controversial colleague of Blewett's at Wesley College, was later fired for his views, and ended his career as a columnist for the Toronto *Star*.

Plato and the Founding of Idealism

George John Blewett

In the pathetic and winning history of Mysticism one of the most marked features is a certain impersonality. Not that Mysticism has been without its special champions; in its history there are outstanding figures — the great and daring men of thought who clung to the hope of union with reality, even while they were formulating the world-shattering logic which puts reality beyond the reach of all the normal forms and energies of our experience. But these are not so much individual men of thought who by their own labour make their way to a new insight, and win a generation to it, and so become the founders of a school and a tradition. Rather they are voices for something wider than themselves; something that works dimly in the mind of an age, like a hidden ferment, and slowly gathers shape, and comes at last to the spoken word. When some great race finds life an unsatisfied hunger or a burden of pain; when some great civilisation, with all its skill and wealth and luxury, weighs itself in the balances and finds itself wanting; when some generation, possessed by the vision and the passion of religion, finds its established religion a thing external, ceremonial, priestly: — then, as by an original tendency of human nature, and with no need of historical support or derivation, the temper of Mysticism arises like a spirit moving upon the face of the deep; and, having arisen, finds its prophets. It is the business of the Idealist to persuade and convince men, as best he can, under all circumstances and in every spiritual climate; but the Mystic speaks usually to hearts made ready for his word; and, to them, speaks with overwhelming power. Indeed, the passage of mystic doctrine from land to land and age to age has seldom been more aptly described than by Professor Royce,[*The World and the individual,* p.85] when he calls to our minds the words of Coleridge's Ancient Mariner:

> I pass, like night, from land to land;
> I have strange power of speech;

---

*First published by William Briggs, Toronto, 1907, as part of *The Study of Nature and the Vision of God.*

That moment that his face I see,
I know the man that must hear me:
To him my tale I teach.

The history of Idealism has been very different. He who first formulated it, formulated it by the energies of the constructive reason in him; and formulated it well-nigh for ever. To its fundamental positions he worked his way slowly, sounding onward as through an unknown sea; availing himself of the diverse results of the earlier science of his race, but going far beyond anything of which it even had dreamed; and showing himself so pre-eminent in the power and insight of the labouring reason that since his day Idealism has never departed without profound loss from what is essential in his method and teaching, nor returned without receiving the touch and the inspiration of a new life.

In the first place, he fixed for ever the scientific point of departure of Idealism — the question how our knowledge is possible. Then, proceeding from that point of departure, he not only moved in the true direction in his attempt to comprehend the nature of reality and the meaning of our life, but moved so far in that true direction that the way was made easy to all who in later days could enter into his teaching as it really was. And another thing he did, in which his greatness as the founder of Idealism culminates. He stated his view of the world with a grace of temper, an elevation of soul, a prophetic and compelling passion, such as gave to his truth a double power and made it to the men of later ages an illumination and an austere allurement, a persuasion and a rebuke.

This Plato did; being one of those rare and most mighty spirits in whom the gifts and the insights that are given singly to other men, appear in combination, and in that combination take on a new and greater power, each contributing to the other, each enlightening the other, each deepening the other. First, there came to union in him the two great scientific currents in which the constructive thinking of the Greeks had hitherto run: the older metaphysic, Ionian or Italian, which sought to comprehend the universe as a universe; and the newer Socratic "way of ideas." In this combination each side found its true fulfillment in the other, so that, in the place of two brilliant but limited endeavours, there arose a single complete and solidly based and thoroughly luminous view of the world. Then, secondly, this synthesis itself was part of a still wider synthesis. On the one side, as the achievement just referred to indicates, he had in him the scientific mind. He had its intellectual disinterestedness, its passion after knowledge for its own sake, its instinct for looking straight upon facts and seeing them with clear eyes just as they are; he inherited, in a word, not simply the results of the previous scientific history of the Greeks, but also their scientific temper in the very perfection of those qualities which have made the Hellenic mind to all ages the pattern of the scientific mind. But he was possessed also, and to the very centre of his being, by the great practical passions: by the passion, moral and political, which seeks to shape life and the social organisation of life according to the good; and by the religious passion which apprehends, as the good, the ultimate principle of the universe, and thus sets the whole of man's life in the light of a heavenly vision, and directs all his energies to the works whose significance is eternal. And in him those things — that disinterested scientific temper, that passionate devotion to the realisation of the good, and that profound religiousness — were not warring tendencies; they were co-operating powers, each widening the scope and deepening the character of the others. And even this is not the limit of the union and co-operation in him of characters that ordinarily stand apart. Along with that scientific intellect, that moral and political and religious temper, there went the mind of the poet, and the capacities, both receptive and active, of the artist. And this side of his nature, once more, — in spite of the hostility that necessarily existed between him and **those artists of his race who either were artists and nothing more, or else** represented a reason earlier and and unpurified by criticism — really worked together with the others. He was half poet; but in him poetic intuition was a form of intelligence, rather than a rival of intelligence; and so the poet in him made him a greater, not a less, philosopher. He had the Ionian delight in beauty, and the Ionian command over the powers by which beauty is expressed; but he had also the earnestness of Lacedaemon — no Dorian saw more clearly than he the need in human life of simplicity, of austere discipline, of that gravity of mind which lifts a man above luxury, above levity, above the **habit of imitation. He had the unashamed Greek joy in the whole of existence;** yet he was haunted by a vision of eternity which condemned alike the world that now is, and the mythology of his race, and the political order of his state. He had the Greek delight in life, the Greek instinct for the exercise and development of all the faculties of the soul, the catholic Greek sense for completeness and integrity of life; yet he knew that life can reach its true wholeness and integrity, not by leaving all its elements and interests upon a level, but only by recognising the good, and putting it in its place of supremacy, and arranging the whole of life as the manifold system of its realisation.

Such was the many-sided reason that dwelt in Plato and helped to make him the greatest figure in the long history of philosophy. But there is still something else. A metaphysician is a man who seeks to ascertain the true meaning of our experience. And the man who would do that, must have more than scientific temper and scientific ability, more than a wide mind and large capacities of reason; personally and vitally he must himself possess, on all its greater and constitutive sides, the experience into whose meaning he would inquire. For himself, and with directness and integrity of devotion, he must have walked in the ways of life and have taken his part in the world's work. And this requisite, too, was fulfilled in Plato. It was not only that he was man of science, artist, poet; not only that he sustained the part of friend and of teacher; but his heart was linked to the greater causes in the life of his people; he was a citizen drawn to the welfare of the Greek states with an intensity of earnestness that had in it the possibility, and at last the actuality, of tragic pain. He not only had a vision of perfection, but felt the call to realise it; to realise it not abstractly nor in dream, but concretely in the life of his day — in the education which lasts from birth till death, and in the order of the state. He did not rest, as Windelband so finely points out, [at the close of his **monograph on Plato; a brief but most admirable account which ought to be** translated.] in his gaze upon the supersensuous world; he was not one of those saints of contemplation who "receive into themselves the great picture of existence and contemplate it in desireless peace." On the contrary, having brought from the eternal realm ideals for this, he took up "with passionate courage the struggle against the powers of the earth," and strove "with all the **energies of his soul 'to improve and to convert' the world"; he was — and is** —"the chief of all the spirits who exercise the energies of will." Such he was; and being such, there was no escape for him from the wrestle with the world, no standing apart from life, no remaining untouched by the storm of the times.

Thus, then, it was that, while Spartan armies were going to and fro upon the soil of Attica, there was given to the world in Plato its most perfect example, not of philosophy only, but of the philosophic mind. He was a great man of science; but he was more; he was a mighty spirit, taking part in the struggle of man upon the earth, and bringing to that struggle its illumination with eternal light. And so, too, it was with his view of the world and of life; it shows the intellect working at its very highest power; but it is more than a work of the intellect. It is the passionate vision and creation of the entire human soul; a vision and creation in which the working of the greater passions — the passion for the state, the passion for righteousness, the passion for eternity — goes hand in hand with the highest energy of the disinterested intellect.

In attempting to understand this philosophy of Plato's as a body of doctrine—which involves not merely apprehending Plato's conclusions, but apprehending also the forces and tendencies that operated in him to shape them — we have three things to remember at the outset. First, Plato was an Idealist from the beginning; from the beginning the root of the matter was in him — there were no Kantian wanderings. But secondly, his Idealism was not complete from the beginning. The Idealism of his early and middle years had in it an incompleteness which it was one of the great labours of his later years to remedy; and this later work gave to the whole structure of his philosophy at once greater depth, greater concreteness, and greater power. While thirdly, throughout Plato's whole life the forces that make, not for Idealism at all, but for Mysticism, acted upon him and found in his soul a great response.

These facts give us our plan of treatment. We are to consider an Idealist; but one whose Idealism (1) stands face to face with the great opponent of Idealism, (2) undergoes development from within. It will be wise to take the discussion in three steps: (1) To put down in summary form the conclusions which constitute the Idealism of his early and central years; and in doing this, to note what the internal incompleteness, just referred to is. (2) Then to turn to the other side, and consider the operation upon Plato, and in Plato, of the influences that lead toward Mysticism. (3) Finally, to consider the later stage of his philosophy, in order to see (*A*) how far he has made good the incompleteness of his earlier Idealism, (*B*) how far he has overcome, and how far yielded to, the influences leading him toward Mysticism. The two latter questions, it will be noted, do not stand apart; they are so closely **interconnected as really to form one question; for the more clearly and fully** Plato works out his Idealism, the more completely does he overcome the tendency toward Mysticism.

First, then, from the dialogues up to and including the *Republic*, we have to gather the ground-lines of the earlier Platonic Idealism, and to set these down in the form of a brief summary.

I

What Plato saw to begin with was that our experience, our actual present life, **in order to be what it is, must be a part in a system of reality greater than** anything that now appears to us. He saw — saw with a clearness which simply startles an English student turning back to him from Locke or Bentham or the Mills — that there is in our present experience something which this present world cannot give; that there operates in our experience something which that experience itself as it now stands cannot account for. For our experience involves — one might almost say, *is* — the operation of conceptions which, both in perfection and in universality, go beyond the particular things and facts and events to which we apply them, and which we comprehend by means of them. They, it must be repeated, are not merely present in our experience; they are active and formative in it. They are in our minds not merely as something possessed, but as something operative; operative in the whole process of our thinking and knowing and doing. The straight line, for instance, the perfect circle, the perfect square, the perfectly equiangular triangle — these conceptions and the many similar ones which might be named, are, in the first place, actual possessions of our minds; but not that only; they are absolutely essential to even the most elementary process of knowing the world, and in that process are continuously operative and continuously regulative. Yet this present world does not give them; there are no straight lines or perfect circles in nature. And again, as we know nature, so also we regulate our conduct, by conceptions which the present world cannot give because it has them not to give. We seek perfect truth, and justice absolute, and the courage that is complete in wisdom; but where are these to be found existing upon the earth? Here, then, in the elementary facts and the elementary form of our scientific and moral experience, is a great problem; and this problem is the point of departure for that great voyage of the intellect, to which Plato, by many interests, practical even more than speculative, was driven. As he advances from it, he works his way to a view of what a Greek would call the *form* — a modern, the *constitution* or eternal order — of the world; and to a corresponding view of the place, the development, the true function, of the soul as part of that eternal world. This view we have now to consider; though, as we go on to set it down in orderly outline, we must remember that Plato himself nowhere presents it in one systematically articulated account; for it was his habit to develop now one, now another, of the many insights which enter into it; and to develop these single insights, moreover, by the method which best corresponds to the process and struggle and gathering light of actual experience — the dialectic method.

(1) First, then, Plato finds the form or constitution of the world to be essentially rational; this is the keynote of his Idealism, and of all Idealism. And unless Platonic Idealism, and all Idealism, is to be radically misapprehended, it must be clearly understood what it means to say that the world is rational in its constitution. It means something more than that each of the various things of the world has independently in itself a rational nature. It means that all the things of the world form one rational *structure*; form a system or process in which reason is realised. A number of forms, each rational in the sense of being apprehensible by reason, but simply existing side by side, would not constitute a rational order. A rational order implies some common purpose, some supreme principle, which is realised in and through the total system or structure. That principle gives to each part or element in the system its place and function, and by giving to it its place and function gives it its meaning and reality. So that the principle itself is at once the immanent law and constitutive energy — is even, in a sense, the essential reality — of the whole system. This is true of any system, of any whole made up of parts, which is to be called *rational*. Most of all is it true of that greatest of all "ordered and organised" wholes which is the real world. If the real world is an "ordered and organised whole," it is the realisation of some one supreme principle, which is at once the source and the immanent law of the structure of the world, and as such gives to each of those individual forms that make up the system of the world, its place, its function, its character, its reality. This principle realised and fulfilled in the structure of the world, Plato, in accordance with Greek usage, calls the Good. To him, that is to say, the order or constitution of the world consists in an hierarchy of rational forms —as he called them, Ideas — with the Idea of Good at the head of the hierarchy. Or, to put it in one word, the Good, as the source and law of all individual determinations, of all individual capacities and functions, and thus of all individual being, is the principle of reality.[See *Philosophical lectures and remains of Richard Lewis Nettleship* pp 217-237].

The steps in Plato's dialectic advance to this insight were of course many. One of them we shall have to deal with later, in considering the forces that broke in upon Plato's Idealism, and made it all the greater by making its battle harder. Here, however, a brief hint at the general course of this part of the

Platonic argument will be sufficient. First, Plato saw that particular objects cannot stand alone. Their lack of an abiding form, their incessant change, their arising and their decay, show that they do not maintain their own being or exist in their own right. How, then, are they to be accounted for? At the very lowest — making your first concession to reason as small as you possibly can — you must go at least this far: that for each of the *kinds*, for each group of similar things, there must be some one abiding reality which fulfills itself through them and their changes. This abiding reality — to which Plato gave the name Idea — he, at the beginning of his work, tended to some extent to view as the common element that remained when the differences of the particulars were stripped away. But more and more he came to view it as an energetic principle, a creative power, which manifests itself in and through the things; so that instead of our being compelled to abstract from the differences to get it, it itself explains those differences. An Idea might perhaps be best defined for the modern mind by saying that each Idea, together with the things of which it is the principle, would form the object of a special science or special department of science.[E.Caird *Evolution of Theology in the Greek Philosophers* p.119]. But with this "lowest possible concession" we cannot stop. For these constitutive principles of the various classes of existence cannot themselves stand apart or maintain their own being. They are not independent existences, standing side by side for ever; they must be conceived as forming one order, one universe. And what that means we have already seen; they are the media or organs through which one highest principle, one supreme creative energy, the Good, fulfills itself.

(2) The nature and operative principles of our minds correspond to the nature and operative principles of the world; thus it is that knowledge and intelligent conduct are possible to us. The soul which is man, is in organic union with those constitutive principles of the world (the Ideas) — or, if you will, is in organic possession of them. It brings them, or the potentiality of them, with it as its equipment for the business of life, as its principles of knowledge and its standards of conduct. This insight Plato delighted to set forth in myths of unexampled splendour. But the meaning of the myths is plain: the real world is rational; the soul is reason; therefore, science and intelligent conduct are alike possible.

(3) But that nature of the soul, and those its operative principles, are developed only gradually, in and by that process in which we at once apprehend reality and come to be ourselves. In knowing the world, the reason which is man, recognising the presence and operation of those eternal principles in the world, comes more and more into possession of them, and so comes more and more truly to be itself. This apprehension of the world, in its gradual development, passes from stage to stage of clearness; passes, as Plato at one point says, through three lower stages to find rest in a fourth. [*Republic* 509]. The first two of these ("conjecture" and "belief"), which represent the working of the intellect below the "scientific" level, we need not dwell upon here. But we must notice carefully the third, and the transition from it to the

fourth. The third is what nowadays we should call the stage of the special sciences. Its defect is that each of its special divisions has its own point of view and its own point of departure; so that instead of seeing one universe in the light of one supreme principle, it almost has several universes. Or, as one may put it, it begins too far down the stream, and so, instead of seeing one stream, flowing from one fountainhead, it sees only several different currents. At this stage, then, knowledge is inaccurate in the sense of being abstract, "unfinished," incomplete. But in the fourth stage, knowledge becomes adequate in form to its object. For here knowledge directs itself to that supreme principle, only in the light of which can any particular thing whatever be truly understood; **namely, to the Good, which the whole system and structure of the universe is** intended to realise, and which, therefore, determines the place and function — that is to say, determines the reality — of each individual thing in the total system. So that the Good, just as it is the principle of being, is also the principle of knowledge. With regard both to the world and to our minds it is the principle of intelligence; for it is its activity, as giving to the things of the world definite determinations, definite places in the system, definite functions, that makes the things of the world intelligible; and it is only through an apprehension of it that our minds can enter fully and finally into a true apprehension of things, and so become truly and fully intelligent. Hence, too, knowledge of it (and conformity of character to it) is the ultimate object of education; and it is in the science which seeks to apprehend it, that education — for those who are able to go so far — culminates.

(4)To live in accordance with that true nature of the world is the true way of life for men. The world, as a system in which a supreme principle, the Good, realises itself (in measure and beauty and truth, as Plato said later [*Philebus*, especially 64-67]), furnishes the pattern according to which man should organise his life. Indeed that statement is too weak; for the world is the whole in which man lives; so that the Good which is the organising principle of *its* structure and order, should be the organising principle for *his* life. That is to say, the Good (that which the world exists to realise) is more than a *pattern* for man; it is that to which men should directly devote themselves and seek to realise. So that the Good, as it is the principle of **being,** and the principle of intelligence, is also the moral end for man. Morality means to know the Good which is the eternal law of the world, and to make it the supreme principle of one's own life. But further: men cannot realise the Good as solitary individuals. They must become what the world is — a *kosmos*, an "ordered and organised" society, a state. The state, then, is a human institute for the realisation of the Good. In accordance with that purpose and no other, the state is to frame its constitution, to train its citizens, to educate its legislators and statesmen; — is even to limit its own size, so that the individual citizen shall not be prevented from participating in the whole of its life. And if a man is compelled to live in a state whose constitution is evil or imperfect, let him organise his life so far as he can in accordance with the **order of the city whose "pattern is laid up in heaven";** [*Republic* 592] it is the model for all cities, and the only model for the man whose earthly city has an evil constitution; and, after death, it will receive those who have been faithful to its laws. [It is interesting to note how men's thoughts answer each other across the ages. Plato saw that our experience, in order to be what it now is, must be part of a reality.]

The foregoing statement is un-Platonic in form, but represents fairly, in terms of modern thought, the essential principles that had shaped themselves in Plato's mind by the time he reached middle life. If it were permissible to select any one Platonic statement as the most pointed expression of those principles, and of the view of the world which they constitute, it would be the comparison, in the *Republic*, of the Idea of Good to the sun. The sun is to visible things the source both of their being and of their visibility. Of their being, for he makes them what they are; he is "the author of generation and nourishment and growth, though he himself is not generation." And of their visibility, for he gives to them their capacity of being seen and to the eye its capacity of seeing them. In the same way the Idea of Good gives to all things their real and essential existence; and, by precisely the same creative or constitutive activity, it gives to them that rational character — that place in a rational system fulfilling a rational end — which is their knowable[507*seq.*] The Idea of Good, in one word, is the principle of being, the principle of knowledge, and, as is added a little later,[517C]. the principle of conduct.

II

Such a view concerning the form or constitution of the world, and concerning the place and development and function of the soul in the world, is Idealism. And yet, in anything that can be called a study of Plato, this view must stand as the beginning rather than as the end. In philosophy, battles easily won are usually either not worth the winning, or are won so easily because of the hard labour of earlier men. And Plato's battle was far from easily won. He fought over nearly the whole ground of philosophy; that it is, in fact, which makes him at once so deeply instructive and so infinitely suggestive.

First, as was pointed out above, in the Idealism whose main positions have just been set down, there is a certain incompleteness. It is incomplete in the conception of its highest principle. For it viewed the Idea of Good as a constitutive and organising principle. The Good exercises a creative energy; it is the source and home, the ordering power, the principle of unity, of the world. But that at once raises the question: In order to be such a principle, must not the Good be conceived as something more than simply the Good? If it is truly to be regarded as performing the supreme function of constituting and ordering the world, must it not be taken up into some still higher principle? Must it not, that is to say, be regarded as living and active spirit; so that the world would be viewed as constituted by an eternal spirit who is the subject of the world, whose Ideas are the regulative forms of the world, and the supreme law of whose activity is the Good?

To this problem Plato came in his later work. In that work he made, indeed, what looks like a fresh start; for he came at the problem from a somewhat different angle of approach, and used a different terminology. But really it is the same problem; and really, therefore, the advance is continuous [One of the reasons for believing—what here is taken for granted—that the *Parmenides*...is a genuine Platonic writing]. But before we go on to consider that advance, there is another matter to be dealt with. For, as also was noted above, throughout the whole of Plato's life, the forces that lead men, not to Idealism at all, but to Mysticism, worked upon him; and upon that many-sided mind, sensitive as it was to all spiritual influences, they could not be without effect. To these we must now turn; and in dealing with them we have to consider (A) in what form they acted upon Plato; (B) what influence they had, whether in breaking the unity and preventing the completeness of his Idealism, or in setting another view alongside of it. Then, finally, we can come to that thinking of his later years in which, so far as was possible to him, he dealt with both the great problems that beset him; and, by a certain development of his thought, at once put the keystone into the arch of his Idealism, and overcame — though to the end only in part — the mystic tendency.

(A) First, then, the influences that make for Mysticism fall into two great classes. For Mysticism has a twofold aspect. It is a type of speculative thought; but it is also a movement of the practical spirit. It is an intellectual conclusion; but usually it is also a conception of religion and a way of life.

(1) So that we have to distinguish, first, the more purely intellectual ways along which men are led to Mysticism. The general tendency manifest in these may be seen by considering the situation in which the philosophic intellect stands at the beginning of its work. For what sets it upon its work is the insight that experience can be what it now is only upon the supposition that reality goes far beyond the appearances which from moment to moment make up the fleeting content of experience. And the work to which this insight calls philosophy is, of course, the attempt to reach a form of consciousness more adequate than the everyday consciousness to the apprehension of that reality. But precisely in this beginning and in this point of departure there lies for the intellect a great danger. It should remember that the reality to which it is attempting to make its way, is sought as the explanation and the illumination of the experience from which it first set out. Or, in technical terms, it should remember that the desired universal and the present particulars are in organic connexion; that the noumenal order does not stand separate from time and from phenomena, but rather is the phenomenal order truly understood; else the one is no explanation of the other. But this very thing the intellect is tempted, not to say driven, to forget; and that by the nature of the situation itself. For what the mind is seeking to do is to pass from an experience of appearances to a consciousness of reality; and what stands out in the foreground, and is acutely felt, is, of course, not the likeness of the two, but

their difference. The reality — in its character surely it is that which the appearances are not. They come and go, arise and decay; it abides for ever, and is always itself. They are chained to eye and ear; it, for its existence and perfection, depends upon no perishing organs of flesh. Thus the tendency arises to separate the two: what they are, it is not; what it is, they are not. And the two being separated, the way of the soul is plain; in the vision of the perfect and eternal reality, it must forget, or resist, or despise, the present world.

This tendency takes many forms and operates in many degrees of power. ... It did its work almost completely, for instance, when, through generations of forgotten men, the Hindu mind, moving under a burden of sad experience, sought to reach the one fundamental reality by saying *Neti, Neti — It is not so, it is not so* — to every particular form of god or goddess and to every particular natural determination; and thus accomplished the vast march of thought from Veda to Vedanta. Or again, it swept in perfect intellectual clearness, and with one arrow-like flight, to its goal, when Parmenides sharply and abruptly set over against the world of the senses, a reality which purely and absolutely *is*, and is not flawed or limited or contaminated by any "is not." These thoroughgoing cases, as a rule, occur either at the beginning of a great civilisation, or in its decline: at the beginning, when the pioneers of thought, by sheer force of speculative daring, carry one-sided methods through to their conclusion; in the decline, when men turn away from the evil world, and the religious influences which we are to consider in a moment work victoriously upon them. But the logic of Mysticism is also able to secure a footing in the middle periods, when the great constructive and comprehensive minds are at work. In a different way, however; usually as a tendency concealed in some method which is accepted without question but, whose final significance is not perceived. In such a method Mysticism often lies implicit, until at last some intellect, fearless in its logic, but working in the service of the religious instinct, carries the method relentlessly to its conclusion, and shows reality to men as that with which they can enter into union only by renouncing the world and all the normal forms of experience.

For our present purpose, one such method is specially important. It is, indeed, simply a particular case of the general situation described a moment ago. The facts and events of the world, as they are given to us in our everyday consciousness, cannot stand alone. If we would really understand them, we must go to something wider than themselves; to the laws or principles which govern them, which hold them together and make them and their changes one connected and systematic world. In the language of philosophy, we must go to their universals. But how are we to conceive those universals? If we remembered that we seek the universal as an explanation of the particular, we should see that the universals must be active principles of synthesis — active and concrete principles which hold things together into one world, and by giving to each particular its place in the world give it its reality. The universals, that is to say, would be conceived as at once explaining and containing both the particulars and their differences and their relations; would be conceived as at once the source and the home alike of the particulars, and of the relations which link them together into one system, and of the differences which mark their individuality. And the highest universal would be the most concrete of all, being the source and home of the whole order of the world, of all the individuals in it, and of all the relations and differences which make them individuals and yet link them together by eternal laws in the one system of the world. But at the very beginning of the search for universals there is something which frequently leads us to forget all this. For the universal is something which is *common* to all the members of a class; they all share in it, and their sharing in it is the source of their reality. But how are we to get at something which is common to all the diverse members of a class? Surely nothing can be easier — simply strip away the differences and retain what is left. It is very natural thus to take for granted that since the universal is a form common to all the members of a class, the way to reach it must be by abstracting from the differences of those members. But natural as it is to drift into such a method, it puts you, as soon as you adopt it, into the grip of the logic of denial. For as you ascend from stage to stage, stripping away the differences from particular things and specific conceptions, your universals become more and more abstract, until at last you reach the end with an ineffable One which is beyond all natural determinations and all forms of reason; and union with which, whether speculative or practical, is therefore to be attained only in some experience which transcends all forms of reason and all ordinary activities of the rational spirit which is man. Thus it was, for instance, that mediaeval Realism with its strong tendency to ascend to the universal by the method of abstraction, led the way to Mysticism. When its method was taken up by men of deep inward religion and of an unflinching logic which not even canons and decretals could bind, that which was left to them at the end, after they had abstracted from the last differences — from the distinction between God the omniscient knower, and the world, ideal or temporal, which He constitutes and knows; and from the distinction between the persons of the Trinity — was that ultimate Godhead, that "still wilderness" which "never did look upon deed" and "where never was seen difference, neither Father, nor Son, nor Holy Ghost."[see the paper on Meister Eckhart in Professor Royce's *Studies of God and Evil*; especially pp. 276-282, and the words of Schewester Katrei as given on p.297.]. The same tendency, again, was manifest when Spinoza, on one side of his thinking, carried to the last conclusion a method and a principle which, coming from Descartes, seemed new, but in truth were as old as mediaeval Realism, and in the hands of a rigorous logician had in them the same potentiality of Mysticism. Or, to take an instance which lies at our very doors, the abstract tendency is present in the later thinking of Kant, and is in constant strife with that concrete or synthetic method which is Kant's proper contribution to modern philosophy; a strife so continuous that without reference to it, as the Master of Balliol in almost every chapter of his great exposition has to remind us, scarcely any leading point in Kant's critical philosophy can be understood [Indeed it might almost be said that in man's effort to come to realty, mysticism may arise from *any* important error, from *any* important misuse of catagories.]

In Plato both that general and this special form of the intellectual movement toward Mysticism are found. The explanation of our present world and of our experience in it, lies for him in a world of perfect and eternal realities, the Ideas, which are at once rational forms and rational energies. And, of course, he knew that the explanation and the thing explained must be in organic union: that world, he knew, must be the truth of this world; this world, truly known, must be a factor or element in the life of that, and a manifestation of its nature. But, like all high and clear spirits who are acutely sensitive to the evil and the imperfection of this world, Plato is tempted to let his soul dwell in that world, forgetting this, or despising it, or renouncing it, as a thing only of some secondary reality which in the presence of true reality stands condemned for ever. And to this temptation to set the two worlds apart, the one as shadow, the other as reality, he continually yields. Perhaps his keenest feeling is the feeling of the difference between the real world and this present world of the senses — this, inconstant, fleeting, full of change and decay; that, with its unchanging perfections of reason. And this feeling, as we are to see in a moment, was intensified by the form which the religious passion often took in him; and by the way in which he suffered from the resistance of his Greek world to that ideal which represents the demand of the real world upon present society. So that, in his central period, Plato, like Erigena, like Aquinas, like Spinoza, like Kant — like his own pupil, Aristotle — is torn between the synthetic and the abstract movements of thought, between *theologia affirmativa* and *theologia negativa*. It is true that the conflict of these tendencies assumed a very different form in him from that which it assumed in Erigena or Aquinas, in Spinoza or Kant. It is true also that the yielding to the negative tendency is less in him than in any of the others just named; true that the promise and the power of that thoroughgoing Idealism to which he was later to come is already in the dialogues of the central period. But none the less the strife is there. And in the special form mentioned an instant ago — *i.e.,* in advancing from particulars to class-conceptions — the strife is also there. In the earlier thinking of Plato there is a wavering between two views of the relation of a universal to the particulars grouped under it; the two views, as one may say, are present in solution. The one, regarding the universal as the common element in different individuals, tends to seek it by abstraction, by leaving aside the differences of those individuals, and to give it an existence independent and separate; making it, to use an expression of the later Plato, like a sail drawn over the individual members of the class. The other regards it as a synthetic principle, manifesting itself through differences, and therefore both explaining and containing those differences. And, as far as the former prevails, it makes possible, in the way already indicated, the logic of Mysticism.

(2) But, as we have seen, there is another order of influences making for Mysticism — the practical or religious; and it is only when these co-operate with the first that Mysticism in the completeness of its type arises. The nature of these may be indicated in this way. — To the religious instinct and passion,

in its higher development, two directions of movement are possible; and thus in man's effort after God two tendencies have arisen. These are seldom found in purity of type, ordinary religious life usually containing both, though approximating sometimes to the one, sometimes to the other. Of these tendencies the one which commonly is the earlier to prevail, whether in the individual or in any deeply religious age, is dominated by the sense of the sharp contrast between the world and God; the world as evil, God as altogether good; or the world as nothingness and vanity, God as all in all. But the later and more thoughtful tendency sees that Manichaeism in *any* form shatters religion itself; that the religious life in its every step implies an organic connexion between God and the world; God being led by the goodness of His nature to impart Himself; the world being a process wherein, by that increasing impartation of Himself, He realises an eternal purpose which itself arises from His nature and is the expression of it. The religion of this latter type is the wider and the profounder; in a certain very important sense, it is really the more religious. But the religious of the former kind is usually the more intense and overmastering. It makes ascetics and warriors; and it has in it at least the beginning of Mysticism. For on the one hand it presupposes an eternal reality and the possibility that man can become at one with it; and it makes the quest after such union the supreme business of life. But on the other hand it is convinced that upon no such ways as those of the present world, through no such energies as those of man's natural soul, is that union to be attained.

Now, Plato was a man profoundly religious. And both his native character and the circumstances of his life made it inevitable that at least occasionally, under special stress of the world's evil or the world's tragedy, the religious temper in him should assume the first rather than the second of the two forms just distinguished. For in him was the grave Dorian austerity which can lift men with indignant scorn above the allurements of the world, and the hunger after eternity and after perfection, which in this world, or in any world made after the fashion of this, can find no rest; and that inborn purity of mind, observable in fine and high spirits, which turns instinctively away from evil and seeks its home with a reality in which evil and the trouble of evil have no place. And his outer life was fitted to develop the world-denying instincts within. Only too well he knew the saddening of the soul which comes to men who enter upon life with high devotion to the welfare of their society and to the great causes in which that welfare consists, and find the world to be a body of death, immovable by that passion, unresponsive to those purposes. It was not merely that the men of Athens, the best of them as well as the worst, had slain his master. But in him a high ethical and political passion, the passion of the reformer who has gazed upon heavenly perfection and seeks to bring it to the ways of earthly society, broke in vain against the life of his day; broke in vain against the pride of the elder Dionysius; in vain against the life of Athens, where the citizens were no longer men of Marathon, but loved comfort and cleverness and unstable change more than righteousness; in vain against the general political condition of the Greek world in the period that runs from the day of the Thirty to the coming of the Macedonian. And so it came to pass that through the whole course of Plato's life there ran that same tragedy of passion and of hope which filled the early years of Wordsworth. The passion of the prophet and of the reformer shattered itself into despair against the circumstances of the age, and against the brute power with which political inefficiency and political corruption can maintain themselves against high ideals and high character.

(B) Thus, then, the influences that lead toward the doctrine and life of the Mystics, acted upon the founder himself of Idealism. What response, we must next ask, did they call forth? what result had they in Plato's view of reality and of the way of life? One thing is clear to begin with. They have influenced very deeply the tone and expression of the Platonic philosophy. It presents itself to its students as a many-coloured web shot through and through with mystic motives. Not only toward what we commonly call the things of the world, but also toward many even of the virtues in their ordinary exercise, and toward the opinion which is at least a potentiality of knowledge, and toward many even of the greater literary and artistic forms, Plato takes up frequently the true Mystic's attitude of pity and renunciation and rebuke. And he has the Mystic's strange and compelling glory of speech, the power mingled of **prophecy and poetry, which, logically or illogically, has fallen so often to the** lot of those who use speech only for winning men to the silent life. In calling men to the renunciation to the world, to the practice of death, his words take on the tint of Mysticism, just as sometimes, on evenings late in autumn, the sky that bent over the work of the day ceases to be a thing of this world, and with stern magnificence and yet with beauty unutterable testifies against the weariness and the ambitions of the earth, and against the men who in these things lose themselves.

Nevertheless, the outcome in Plato was not Mysticism. It was not to be that among men of Greek speech the great argument which Parmenides had left a thing purely intellectual should advance to "do the full work of a philosophy" as an ethic and a religion. Though Plato revered Parmenides, and though of all the Hellenes he was the most fitted in character and experience to respond to the appeal of Mysticism, yet the very fact that he *was* a Hellene made it impossible that it should be his vocation to lift the Parmenidean view of reality into a wisdom for the guidance of life, and to give to that wisdom its language of irresistible persuasion. The Greek loyalty to reason and the energies of reason; the Greek love of definite and specific form; the Greek belief that such form is truly and essentially characteristic of reality: — these held the field. He was not won away from his view that the forms and energies which constitute reality are forms and energies of reason; and that this rationality of the real means that it has one supreme and organising principle, the Good, without devotion to which reason is not reason. And holding to this, he is not a Mystic. For though he may sometimes speak of the present world with the voice of a Mystic, yet there remains a difference which is essential. The relation between Plato when he goes farthest toward Mysticism, and that the thoroughgoing Mystic, might be stated in this way. — Both believe that there is a reality untroubled by change or evil or decay. Both believe that in union with that reality lies the welfare and blessedness of the soul Both believe that it is beyond all reach of sense-perception. But the Mystic goes on to add that it lies just as much beyond all forms of reason as it does beyond sense-perception, so that if you would apprehend it, and make it your own, and become at one with it, it must be in an immediacy of experience which transcends reason, transcends all ordinary forms of cognitive and moral experience. While Plato urges, on the contrary, that the truly real is the very perfection of reason the very perfection of all rational form and rational energy, and that it is by perfecting the reason within you — reason in the greater sense of the word, not the mere logical intellect — that you draw near to it. With the Mystic, to put it in a word, the negatives directed against the present world, and against the life that men live if they walk in its ways, are uttered in the name of a reality above reason; with Plato those same negatives are uttered in the name of a reality which is the completeness of reason.

So that Plato, even though you can learn a great deal of practical Mysticism from him if you have the right kind of soul, remains an Idealist. Yet the influences which we have been considering were by no means without their effect. They were not able to make the earlier Plato a Mystic. But they *were* able to do something: they were able to determine the type of his Idealism. They caused it to be of that modified type, . . . Abstract Idealism: that which regards the genuine reality and the true home of the soul as a world of pure reason (in that larger sense of the word already indicated), from which this present world of the senses is separated as a realm of merely secondary reality; so that the union of the soul with the genuine reality is to be won, its citizenship in that world accomplished, only by a life in which sense-experience is not an integral element subserving the interests of the spirit, but is regarded rather as an alien atmosphere to be escaped from.

In setting down the broad outlines of the earlier Platonic Idealism we noted as a matter of fact, and without considering the explanation, that there was an incompleteness in its conception of its highest principle. What we have now seen might almost be put in this way: that corresponding to that incompleteness at the top, there is an incompleteness at the bottom; the world given to the senses is not clearly and unwavering viewed as a manifestation of the highest principle, and as a factor in its realisation of its purpose.

This, however, we must understand somewhat more fully. And that can best be done by returning to that summary outline, and considering in what way the negative tendency, when it comes to the front, is able to modify each of the four positions there indicated.

(1) First, then, Plato often speaks as if the system of Ideas were not so much the form, or order, or constitution, of the one universe which we know and of which our present experience is an integral part; but were rather a universe existing by itself and complete in itself — the *real* universe; and this

sensible and temporal process in which we now live, a system having only a secondary reality. So that, in this aspect of Plato's thought, we approach to a theory of two worlds: one of absolutely pure reason and complete righteousness, where without hindrance the Good perfectly realises itself; the other an imperfect realm of sense and time. And of this lower world Plato speaks in varying tones. Sometimes he makes it a shadow, or a hindrance, or a prison. From it the good man seeks to escape, philosophy as a "practice of death" being his way of deliverance. At other times he views it as in some sense organically connected with the world of Ideas. The things of this world have some share, by participation or imitation or however it be, in the nature of the Ideas; so that in this world, even in the forms and activities of the "unexamined life,"[*Apology*, 38A] some fulfillment is possible of that Idea which is the life-giving sun of the real world — the Good.

(2) But when Plato has to deal explicitly with the question of the possibility of knowledge, what will he do with his tendency toward a two-world theory? For in knowledge the two worlds are together; particular and universal are in organic connexion. Knowledge is really an interpreting of particulars in the light of their universals. Or, if you have failed to see that, and regard knowledge as having to do only with universals — so that the process of gaining knowledge is a passing *out of* particulars to universals — still the very fact that you *can* pass from the one to the other shows that the two are in connexion. What Plato does is very remarkable. He maintains — to explain the possibility of knowledge he *must* maintain — his belief in the correspondence of the nature and principles of our minds to the nature and principles of reality, and in the consequent capacity of our minds to form class-conceptions which represent to us the Ideas. But when his sense of the gulf between the two worlds is strong upon him, he expresses that belief not scientifically, but prophetically, in myths and parables that for blended charm and majesty stand unequalled in literature. The souls of men — so in these he teaches — pre-existed, and in their pre-existence gained some glimpse, fuller or narrower, of the Ideas. That vision, when they fell to the earth, they retained in a sort of latent memory; and so bring with them to their present life the potentiality of true knowledge. Under the stimulus of the things of this world, which imitate the Ideas or share somehow in their nature, that potentiality is realised, or may be realised; the ancient vision, called from its latency into clear consciousness, becomes what we call knowledge or science, but what truly is Reminiscence. It will be observed what this really means. It means that, even when Plato is using the speech of Abstract Idealism, the root of Concrete Idealism is in him. For while the form of language used in such a myth as that of the *Phaedrus* sets the two worlds apart, its essential meaning joins them together.

(3) Under the influence of the separation of universal and particular, of Idea and phenomenon, the "stages of knowledge" come to be represented, not so much as stages in a development in which we pass from the vague and inadequate to the clearer and more adequate, from the abstract to the con-

crete, in one word, from the particulars in isolation to the particulars seen in the light of the Idea of Good as elements or factors in its realisation; but rather as different *kinds* of insight relating to different orders of objects. Knowledge and opinion are different faculties and have to do with different kinds of subject-matter. The sphere of knowledge is being; but the sphere of opinion is that mixture of being with non-being (*i.e.*, of the Idea with empty space) which is the present world. The one is absolute and infallible, as having grasped the supreme principle of the real world and seeing everything in its light. But the other is relative and erring, tossing about in a region which is half-way between pure being and pure non-being.[*Republic* 476-480) He who has failed to grasp the Idea of Good which is the supreme principle of all reality and therefore the master — light of all vision of reality — can we allow his "opinion" to be a genuine stage on the way to knowledge? Rather we must say of him "that he knows neither the essence of good, nor any other good thing; and that any phantom of it, which he may chance to apprehend, is the fruit of opinion and not of science; and that he dreams and sleeps away his present life, and never wakes on this side of that future world, in which he is doomed to sleep for ever."[*Republic* 534C...]

(4) So far as the two-world theory prevails, the rule of conduct, "live in accordance with the true nature of the world," comes to mean: Rise to citizenship in the real world, and in order to do so separate yourself from the life and the ways of this present world. Positively, that is to say, the good man is called to a life not of this world. While, negatively, it is held that the Good cannot be realised under the ordinary forms of our present experience, so far as that experience is one of time and sense; so that "demotic virtue," instead of being viewed as a genuine though inadequate stage in the realisation of the Good, is regarded as a phantom of virtue calling for down-right condemnation. Both these sides of the abstract tendency come frequently to expression in Plato; but the place where they secure their most continuous and impressive statement is — with singular appropriateness — in the *Phaedo*. The man of philosophic mind "is always pursuing death and dying," and "has had the desire of death all his life long." But what is "the nature of that death"? It is that "release of the soul from the body" which enables the soul "to exist in herself."[64ABC] For the body is a hinderer in the acquirement of knowledge. The senses which it brings to the soul are "inaccurate witnessess."[65A] So that the soul, if she attempt "to consider anything in company with the body" is "obviously deceived"; and if she is to gain a revelation of true existence, must gain it in that thought in which "the mind is gathered into herself, and none of these things trouble her, — neither sights nor sounds nor pain nor any pleasure," in which "she takes leave of the body and has as little as possible to do with it," in which "she has no bodily sense or desire, but is aspiring after true," in which she is free from all the troubles and evils of the bodily life, hunger and disease, "loves, and lusts, and fears, and fancies of all kinds, and endless foolery," "wars and fightings and factions."[65,66] So long as the soul uses the body as an instrument of perception (*i.e.,* uses the

senses), she is "dragged by the body into the region of the changeable, and wanders and is confused; the world spins round her, and she is like a drunkard, when she touches change. . . . But when returning into herself she reflects, then she passes into the other world, the region of purity, and eternity, and immortality, and unchangeableness, which are her kindred, and with them she ever lives, when she is by herself and is not let or hindered; then she ceases from her erring ways, and being in communion with the unchanging, is unchanging."[79ED] It is at this existence of the soul in herself alone, in which "the soul in herself" beholds "the realities of things," that philosophy (in Plato's sense of the word) aims while the soul is still cumbered with the body. "The lovers of knowledge," says Socrates, "are conscious that the soul was simply fastened and glued to the body — until philosophy received her, she could only view real existence through the bars of a prison, not in and through herself; she was wallowing in the mire of every sort of ignorance, and by reason of lust had become the principle accomplice in her own captivity. This was her original state; and then, as I was saying, and as the lovers of knowledge are well aware, philosophy, seeing how terrible was her confinement, of which she was to herself the cause, received and gently comforted her and sought to release her, pointing out that the eye and the ear and the other senses are full of deception, and persuading her to retire from them, and abstain from all but the necessary use of them, and be gathered up and collected into herself, bidding her trust in herself and her own pure apprehension of pure existence, and to mistrust whatever comes to her through other channels and is subject to variation; for such things are visible and tangible, but what she sees in her own nature is intelligible and invisible. And the soul of the true philosopher thinks that she ought not to resist this deliverance, and therefore abstains from pleasures and desires and pains and fears, as far as she is able;" — delivering herself thus from the dominion of pleasure and pain, because "each pleasure and pain is a sort of nail which nails and rivets the soul to the body, until she becomes like the body, and believes that to be true which the body affirms to be true; and from agreeing with the body and having the same delights she is obliged to have the same habits and haunts, and is not likely ever to be pure at her departure to the world below, but is always infected by the body; and so she sinks into another body, and there germinates and grows, and has, therefore, no part in the communion of the divine and pure and simple."[82E,83] So that philosophy, while we remain upon the earth, is a study and practice of death. But that the long purification and deliverance may be consummated, the body must be more than subdued; it must die, so that the soul may take up her dwelling altogether "in her own place alone." And hence, when the day of death comes, the true lover of wisdom will depart with joy, having "a firm conviction that there, and there only, he can find wisdom in her purity."[68B] The soul "which is pure at departing, and draws after her no bodily taint, having never voluntarily during life had connexion with the body, which she is ever avoiding, herself gathered into herself;" — such a soul cannot "at her departure from the body be scattered and blown away by the winds and be nowhere and nothing," but "herself invisible, departs to the invisible world —to the divine and immortal and rational: thither arriving, she is secure of bliss and is released from the error and folly of men, their fears and wild passions and all other human ills, and for ever dwells, as they say of the initiated, in company with the gods."[80E,84B,81A] While, on the other hand, the virtues which do not measure up to this level — the "demotic" virtues, the virtues of men who live in the sphere of sense and time, and are busy with the matters of this phantom world, and are unguided by the vision of that Good which is the source and form of all virtue: — these cannot properly be called virtues at all. The courage of such men is but another form of fear. They face one evil because they fear a greater; they are courageous because they are cowards. Similarly their utilitarian temperance is intemperance; they abstain from one pleasure because they desire another, overcoming pleasure in one form because they themselves are overcome by it in some other form.[68DE] They do not know that "the exchange of one fear or pleasure or pain for another fear or pleasure or pain, and of the greater for the less, as if they were coins, is not the exchange of virtue."[69A] Wisdom — *i.e.,*, the apprehension of the Idea of Good and the viewing of things in its light — is the "one true coin for which all things ought to be exchanged"; and the virtue which is made up of the goods of the earth, severed from wisdom and exchanged with one another, "is a shadow of virtue only, nor is there any freedom or health or truth in her."[69B]

To sum up, then, what we have so far seen, we must say that the two tendencies which have been the main currents in the greater history of philosophy and of religion, are both present in Plato: the synthetic, which in philosophy gives rise to what we have called Concrete Idealism; and the abstract or negative, whose partial triumph gives rise to Abstract Idealism, but whose complete domination in a profoundly religious mind is the source of Mysticism. But we must also note the relation in Plato of these two tendencies. The tragedy of the world lay close at his heart; and the most impressive thing in all his writing is his prophesying against the world. But in spite of that, we must make no mistake about the fact that even in his earlier and middle years his deepest loyalty is with the synthetic tendency. True, its victory is in this period never complete. Again and again Plato draws the line sharp and hard between science and opinion, between demotic morality and true virtue, between the soul in the body and the soul freed from the body, between the real world and the cavern of our sense-experience; again and again with sad earnestness he exhorts men to practise death that they may truly live, and to fly from the world to God. But with all this, the deepest impulse of his philosophy is toward an organic connexion of our present life, and of the system of things in which it is lived, with the ultimate principle of reality. This, of course, is a question of the final impression which the whole body of his writings in the periods in question makes upon the reader. But special reference may be made to two subjects which already have taken pre-eminent place in his thought: the state as the greatest of human institutions for the concrete realisation of the Good, by the bringing of men's lives out of confusion, out of self-willed individualism, into an order which reflects the order of eternal reality; and still more, . . . education as that in which men, not by suppression of the normal energies and capacities of their nature, but by the development and discipline of these, are led throughout the whole of life in knowledge and in character toward the Good.

But Plato, lover of truth for its own sake, and master of that dialectic method which criticises its own conclusion and brings to light the further problems implicit in it, and corrects or enlarges it until those problems are adequately solved would have been something less than himself if he had left his philosophy in this strife of tendencies. Plato was a man to look his own problems in the face; and therefore the passage of years brought to his Idealism a steady growth in thoroughness, in self-consistency, in mastery of its materials. He felt that in some genuine sense everything which you cannot decisively reject as mere unreality, mere void nothingness, must be organically connected with the supreme principle of reality; indeed, that is the cardinal instinct of all philosophy, and its presence in Plato compelled him to face the problems that arose from his tendency to separate the world of pure reason and perfect goodness from the world of sensible and temporal experience. With these problems he dealt in his later period, which might almost be described by saying that in it the conflict between the two types of Idealism comes explicitly forward and is settled, so far as was possible to him, in favour of the Concrete.

III

But this brings us to the third step of our work. We have to consider that later thought of Plato in which he apparently makes a new start, but really carries directly forward the development of his Idealism. In approaching this it is necessary to have in mind the exact situation in which at the beginning of that later thought he finds himself. Hence it is advisable to note again, first, the problems which remain for him from his earlier thinking; secondly, the positive insight which he carries forward with him and upon which any advance in solving those problems must be based. The problems, as already we have seen, are two. (1) There is a problem connected with the conception of the highest principle. If the Good is to be regarded as the creative energy and organising principle of the universe, must it not be conceived as something more than simply the Good; namely, as self-conscious and self-determining spirit, which constitutes the world in a view of an end — the Good — and shapes its structure and process according to definite types and fixed laws — the Ideas? (2) There is the problem raised for him by that negative aspect of his system which we have just been considering — his tendency to exclude from genuine reality the sense-world and the human experiences and activities connected positively with it. Or, putting these two problems together, we may say, as was noted above, that what Plato has to face is a double incompleteness in his Idealism: an incompleteness at the top — *i.e.,* in its conception of the highest principle; and a corresponding incompleteness at the bottom — the inability to comprehend the sense-world as an organ and manifestation of the highest reality. Secondly, with regard to the positive insight which Plato carries forward from his earlier Idealism to his later, what we have to remember is this. — If you have been led to draw a line through the universe, and to say that what is above this line is truly real, while what is below it is unreal, or only partly real, that mistake is not necessarily a fatal one. For if, with regard to what you *do* consider as real, your method is the true one, the synthetic one, it is likely sooner or later to break the barrier which you have erected around the field of its operation, and to go forth to reclaim the banished parts of the universe. And this is very nearly Plato's case. For, however prone he occasionally may be to look upon . . . the things of the sense-world with the eyes of a Mystic, yet, as we have already seen, when he comes to describe what to him is the genuine, the undoubtedly real, world, his method is the thoroughly synthetic method of Concrete Idealism. The real world, precisely in the name of which he sometimes denies and denounces this present world, is to him no ineffable One. It is a world rational and rationally organised. Rational, for it is made up of rational forms or energies (the Ideas) and rational distinctions are of its very essence. And rationally organised; for it has one supreme principle, the Good, which is a true universal of universals — no mere abstracted common element, but an eternally creative energy, a truly active and organising principle, the source and home and explanation of all the other Ideas, of all their differences, of all their determinations, and therefore of their whole reality and their whole knowableness. Thus we may say fairly that the central battle of Idealism is already won in the thinking of Plato's middle period. In fact, we have seen reason for saying more than that. As a special evidence of how that central victory extends itself along the whole line, we have had to mark the way in which Plato causes the interest of the ideal world to come over and prevail concretely in this, in two great realms, education and the state: education as advancing through orderly stages toward the apprehension of the Idea of Good; the state as the human institute for its concrete realisation.

We have to turn, then, to the last stage of Plato's thought. In it, as was noted above, we seem to come upon something new. The Ideal Theory seems to have fallen into the background, and a new inquiry to have been made into the constitution of the world, which leads directly to the conclusion that the world is a work of active intelligence. Really, however, the advance is continuous, as we shall see if we follow its own line of movement. Let us consider, then, somewhat more fully just what the problem is, which arises for Plato out of the dualism, the two-world theory, toward which the facts of life had in earlier years driven him. The problem raised by the separation of the two worlds — whether the antithesis be left sharp and hard, or modified into something not far from organic connexion — is twofold. [A twofold problem which, it may be observed in passing, has haunted theology even more than philosophy.] First, how came this present world into existence at all? Reality is with the other world. Then this world, if it has any reality at all, must have its source in that world. But why does that world, complete in its eternal perfection, go beyond itself, to constitute another world, its counterpart or its shadow? What is there in its nature which impels it thus beyond itself, and leads it to communicate itself, and drives it to the energies of creation? Secondly, if that world is the source of this, how is it that this world depart so far from the nature of that? how is it that that world has given rise to something so much unlike itself — nay, so contradictory to itself? How from that world of reason and purity, of blessedness and perfection, has this scene of imperfection and pain, of sorrow and an imprisoning body, of folly and madness, arisen? It is with problems of which the foregoing is a statement in modern dress, that Plato deals in the great group of dialogues — *Parmenides, Sophist, Statesman*, and especially *Philebus* and *Timaeus* — in which his philosophy, laying aside at times its charm of expression and showing itself grey with the labour of thought, reaches its height of metaphysical comprehension.

First, then, how came this present world into being at all? How came the world of Ideas to go outside of itself, to go beyond its own completeness and perfection and become the source of another world? Here it may be advisable to pass at once to Plato's final answer, then to come back and follow the argument by which he leads up to it. That final answer is given by an interpretation (seen in preparation in earlier writings) of the character of that supreme principle of the real world, which formerly Plato had called the Idea of Good. It — or following Plato's example in the *Timaeus* let us say, he —"was good, and the good can never have any jealousy of anything. And being free from jealousy, he desired that all things should be as like himself as they could be."[*Timaeus*, 29E] That is to say, it is of the very nature of the supreme principle to communicate itself, to impart to others its own being and character and blessedness; so that the nature itself of the supreme principle is the ground of the existence of beings, other than the supreme principle, and yet sharing in its nature and, therefore, in its reality.

So far as this conclusion prevails — we shall see presently that Plato was not able to carry it out into all its consequences — it is Concrete Idealism. The advance to it which we have now to consider, was a long one. Its central conception, that the supreme reality does not stand apart, but is the fundamental energy of the whole process of the world, and that it is so because by its very nature as goodness it is essentially self-communicative — a conception with which Plato, myths or no myths, is thoroughly in earnest — is already present in the comparison of the Idea of Good to the sun [Republic,506-509] in the latest-written section of the *Republic*; and also in the criticism of Anaxagoras in the *Phaedo*.[97-99, especially 99] But the dialectical conquest of it was no quick or easy process. It is worked out in that group of dialogues which, logically and perhaps chronologically, opens with the *Parmenides* and closes with the *Philebus*. This great piece of dialectic has two sides; a side polemic, a side constructive.

The polemic side — with an occasional pause to crush the head of materialism or sensationalism, when these happen to cross the path — is directed in the main against that great argument of Parmenides which shuts reality up into motionlessness for ever. The spirit of Parmenides was very congenial to Plato, and wrote itself deeply upon certain aspects of his earlier Idealism; "my father Parmenides," Plato might have said as appropriately as the Eleatic Stranger of the *Sophist*.[241E] Yet the two systems are at bottom completely irreconcilable. If the argument of Parmenides could have secured full right of way in Plato's mind, it must have shattered any form whatever of Idealism; must (considering the religiousness of Plato) have led him at last to a complete Mysticism. So that even the earlier form of Plato's Idealism was built up in the face of Parmenides. And if there was to be any development of that earlier Idealism, it must make its way, so to speak, over the dead body of the Parmenidean argument. The argument of Parmenides, then, Plato shatters in the one way possible; namely, by attacking it at its source and taking away that radical disjunction of being and non-being, of *is* and *is not*, upon which it is based. This is done by showing that non-being exists and is a kind of being; the meaning of which, in modern speech, is, that reality is not an indivisible one, but that there are differences and distinctions within it; that reality, so far from being an undifferentiated and ineffable unity, is a rational system.[*Sophist*, 241 E-260. It is interesting to compare Hegel's *Logic*].

This having been done, the way is open for the constructive advance. By a very keen argument (which, it is worthy of note, proceeds explicitly from the question of the possibility of knowledge) it is shown that in true being there is is motion— "motion and life and soul and mind." True being is not "devoid of life and mind." It does not "exist in awful meaninglessness, an everlasting fixture." And having mind and life, it must "have a soul which contains them." And, furthermore, having life and mind and soul, it cannot "remain absolutely unmoved."[*Sophist*, 246-249]. In the *Philebus*, the view thus prepaired for comes to pointed expression. Mind is "king of heaven and earth." It "orders all things"; for "all this which they call the universe" is not "left to the guidance of unreason and chance medley," but is "as our fathers have declared, ordered and governed by marvellous intelligence and wisdom." [*Philebus*,28]

Thus, then, the real world comes explicitly to be conceived as a world of rational activity, and its highest principle as at once the supreme intelligence and supreme energy of the universe, acting in "creation" and "providence"[*Timaeus,* 30] according to its nature as reason and goodness. And with this the view of the *Timaeus*, started above—the view that the perfect god , being good, is led by His nature to communicate Himself and so becomes the author and father of the universe—-is made possible , not merely as a prophetic insight, but as the culmination of a reasoned idealism.

So far, we have been following Plato's own line of advance.But at this point let us stop to consider how far the problems left over from the earlier idealism have been met in the argument just outlined. Those problems, it will be remembered, were two: one, so to speak, at the top, the other at the bottom, of the Platonic Idealism; one connected with the conception of the highest principle, the other with the interpetation of the sense-world. And the latter breaks again into two: (1) Upon the two—world theory, how do you account for this present world at all—why, when the real world is eternally perfect and complete, did it go out of itself to give rise to another world? (2) When the real world became the source of this, why did it apparently contradict its own nature, giving rise to a world so different from itself, so imperfect and so evil? It will be seen that the argument that we have just been following, brings forward—though it does not with any fulness articulate—**the conceptions necessary for solving the first of these problems and the first** part of the second. And it furnishes a basis for dealing with the remaining part of the second. For such a view makes it possible to regard this present world as in organic connexion with the highest principle of reality. When that principle is viewed as active and self-determining reason, and as a goodness which cannot remain in itself, but is led by its very nature to go out of itself and communicate itself, it is scarcely possible to regard this present world, and all worlds, — "all time and all existence" — as anything other than as the field of its activity, the process in which it fulfils its own nature by communicating itself and so realizing the Good. And such a view, if he could have clearly entered into it, it would have enabled Plato to look with eyes of faith upon those aspects of the present world which so grieved him. Its imperfection, its struggle and unrest, its tragedies of unrewarded toil, of baffled devotion, of defeated righteousness, would have been accepted by him as elements in a process in which a wisdom, too vast for us to understand its separate steps, is fulfilling itself.

Does Plato, then, take this last step, which would have made his Idealism as thoroughly concrete as possible to human insight? The answer falls into two parts.

First, he took up positions which look toward it, which, one might almost say, contain it implicitly. In the *Philebus*, for instance, he puts the capstone upon the argument which was outlined a moment ago by applying it directly to man's life. The characters of the divinely organized universe — Beauty, Symmetry, Truth[*Philebus*, 65A] — are to be adopted by man as the characters to be realized in his own nature and life. But the most striking instance of all is furnished by a work of Plato's which is described sometimes as a falling from faith, as a forsaking of the height for the lowland, or even as an example of the hollowness of philosophy which fails its desciples at the last; but which in truth is one of the most nobly pathetic chapters in the spiritual history of man. For that is what we must say of the *Laws* when we consider the position it holds in Plato's life. Much earlier, as was pointed out above, the essential concreteness in the temper of his Idealism manifested itself in his devotion to the state. It had been the greatest work of his middle life to set before his disciples a picture of the state as it should be. Then, in later years, endeavoring to make his presentation of the true polity more concrete, he entered upon that magnificently conceived design which would have given an almost epic completeness to the *Republic*, but of which the *Timaeus* is the only finished part. The ideal state he had described. Now he would show it taking its place and discharging its function in the world, holding its own in struggle, and showing "by the greatness of its actions and the magnanimity of its words in dealing with other cities a result worthy of its training and education."[*Timaeus*, 19C]. To this end, Timaeus was to begin with the generation of the world and carry its story down to the creation of man; and then Critias was to receive the men thus created, and show the place and life and work of the ideal state by describing how an Athens, which once was, maintained the freedom of the whole of Europe and Asia, when a mighty power from the Atlantic made an expedition against them.[*Timaeus*, 27E] But even this was not enough. The desire to bring the ideal into some more feasible connexion with the life and ordinary nature of man, led to another step; and that step was the *Laws*. At the end of his life, when we should have expected his connexion with the world to be growing fainter, his aloofness from it to be increasing-precisely then it was that Plato, seeking at least some measure of the effective operation of the heavenly ideal in the affairs of the earth, bent his sublime head, and turned to the daily life and unaspiring minds of men, and outlined — in a collection of sketches and fragments edited by some later hand — a "second-best" constitution, more applicable, as he thought, to the life of this present world than that polity which in earlier days he had sketched in strict following of the pattern laid up in heaven. The endeavour of the *Laws* is no apostasy from Idealism; it represents no loss of belief in the heavenly pattern. But it *is* a recognition that there is a difference between heaven and earth, between the eternal ideal and the present state of human affairs; that, therefore, it is vain to expect in one step and by one single stroke to realise the order of heaven in the life of the earth; for the ideal realises itself through many intermediate stages, and the only way to the heavenly glory is by making the best of this present twilight. Indeed, Plato almost reverses what we commonly take to be the normal relation of the abstract and the concrete theology in a man's life. We usually expect that a man will begin life with delight in this world, with thoughtless participation in its interests and enjoyments; and then, when he grows old and the graver and longer interests of the soul enforce their claim, that he will look away from this world toward heaven. But Plato belongs to another order of men. These, by native purity and loftiness of mind, aided, it may be by some hopeless sorrow, are brought early in life to feel that "whatsoever is not God, is nothing, and ought to be accounted as nothing."[*De Imitatione Christi*, III.31.2]. And from this they draw the great practical lessons, *de neglectu omnis creaturae, ut Creator possit inveniri*, and *de se tenendo tamquam exule et peregrine super terram*.[*Ibid*. III.31, and I.17.1] But as life goes on, and reflexion deepens, and religion joins hands with reason, and the world's great need forces itself upon the mature soul, more and more they turn, with a certain grave and wistful devotion, to take their places in the world and to give their hearts to its labours, its interests its causes. And Plato, though there was no statesman's post for him at

Syracuse or Athens, found at last his place. It has already been noted how his defeated passion for the state answers to the defeated political hope of Wordsworth. The parallelism holds to the end. Each found, for the problem of his practical life and personal activity, the same solution; of each, one can say in Windelband's fine expression,[*Platon*, S.29] *seine That ist seine Lehre.* For each, the defeated passion in him, and the mighty thoughts that had grown in the soil of that defeat, found expression by voice and pen; and, finding expression, entered upon a field of influence greater than ever was given to statesman entrusted with the framing of constitutions, or the administering of affairs, in Sicily or Athens or Paris; going forth to be a guide and an inspiration, while the world of men continues, to the highest hearts in every land.

There are, then, in Plato's later thought — especially in his practical interest, his interest in education and the state — positions which imply the organic connexion of this present world, marred though it is by evil and unrest, with the final principle of reality. But, as was indicated above, this is only part of the answer to the question now before us. The other part is that with regard to the world of sensible experience, this implicit view is never brought to clear articulation; on the contrary, in Plato's express doctrine the opposite view, prevails to the end.

In the last analysis, the cause of this failure clearly and unwaveringly to view the world of sensible experience as a manifestation of the supreme principle of reality lies in the fact that Plato's latest conception of that supreme principle never quite comes to its rights. If he had been able clearly to articulate his conception of that principle as active intelligence and self-imparting goodness — in one word, as self-determining and self-communicating spirit — he would have been compelled to view the sense-world, and our experience in it, as a stage of the process in which that principle is fulfilling its nature and realising its purpose. But only in many ages, only in many leaders of the thought of the ages, could so great a work be done. To no one man was so great an intellectual achievement possible. Plato, we may say, hit the core of the solution; but it was scarcely given to him to go back over all his system, and in the light of that central truth to work it into a thoroughly articulated view of the world.

For one thing, ancient thought had not clearly apprehended the nature of self-consciousness or spirit as it is in man himself. When you have seen that the self-consciousness, which is man, in a sense constitutes its own objects and so "makes nature"; and that in doing this it exercises a synthetic power — is an active principle of unity in diversity, linking many facts into one experience and thus constituting both the facts which make up the experience and the experience which is made up of the facts: — then you can advance with secure footing to the view that the principle of union implied in the existence of the universe is a self-conscious and self-determining spirit which constitutes and links into one system the apparently conflicting facts of the world, and through many stages wherein men suffer, and are blessed, and at last become truly themselves, realizes its purpose. But an insight into the synthetic or creative energy of self-consciousness as it is in man never became the explicit point of departure for Hellenic thought.[Windleband,*op. cit.* S.74.]. Hence, while it was possible for Plato to come to the belief that mind is "king of heaven and earth" and "orders all things," it was scarcely possible for him to articulate that belief into a thoroughly organic view of the world.

We shall best see this, however, by turning to Plato's own treatment of the problem now before us. Granted — so that problem stands — that the supreme principle of the real world, being good, must go beyond itself to communicate its nature and impart its blessedness, why must the created world be one of imperfection? Why is it not like its source in perfection and blessedness? Has not the supreme principle, in going out into such a world, contradicted rather than obeyed its own nature?

The part of Plato's theory which corresponds to this question may be put in this way. — When the supreme principle goes out of itself upon that creative activity, into what region does it go forth? Manifestly into the region of non-being. So that the created world is a mixture of being and non-being. That is to say, it is a world of becoming, and therefore of imperfection, and of all the evils of imperfection.

But such an answer has two possible meanings. Upon the first meaning, the total explanation of this going out into the region of non-being and creating there a world which is a mixture of being and non-being and is, therefore, subject to imperfection and evil, lies in the divine nature itself which thus goes forth. In other words, it is affirmed that the supreme principle must begin its creative work with something less than perfection—something less than completely realised "Being" — in order to achieve its purpose at all. If it is to fulfill its purpose, that communication of itself to other beings to which it is impelled by its nature, must not be a creation of perfection by perfection. For in that case the perfection of the created beings would be, after all, a sort of sham battle; would be a sort of gaining the goal without running. To lay aside metaphor, it would be only an apparent perfection, being radically flawed by the fact that those who have it, were absolutely passive in the acquiring of it. If it is really to be *their* perfection, and not just a divine perfection laid upon them from the outside, they must themselves conquer it; they must themselves be active, must themselves labour and suffer, in the process of its attainment. They must, therefore, begin not at the top of the scale, but somewhere lower. In Plato's language they must begin out in the region of non-being. Beginning there, they must work their way toward true and pure being, by a process in which their own labour and struggle is answered by ever increasing impartations to them of the divine nature.

This, then, is one possible meaning of the view that creation is a process in which being goes out into the region of non-being; and that the world which arises is consequently a mixture of being and non-being, an order, that is to say, of becoming and imperfection. And such a view is Concrete Idealism. For it sees this world of time in organic connexion with the realities of eternity. It sees this present order of things, and our human struggle upward through its imperfection and evil, as a process in which, by no sham battle, but by most real achievement, the divine nature fulfils itself by imparting itself to other beings.

But upon the other meaning, the explanation of the fact that the created world is blended of being and non-being is made to lie, not in the essential nature and conditions of the divine activity in creation but in the nature of the region of non-being into which that activity goes forth. Non-being, that is to say, really is viewed as a second eternal principle of things. It is regarded as having a nature of its own, power of its own; as being able, by its stubbornness, its recalcitrancy, its unsuitability to the divine forms which are to be impressed upon it, to thwart or impede the creative energies of the divine nature, and so to diminish the perfection of the created world. And upon the whole it is to this view that Plato is driven. His general description of non-being — that it is a mere potentiality of taking on form, an incomprehensible something which receives all things[*Timaeus*, 51A]; his particular description of it is empty space:[*Timaeus*, 52] — these pass over into statements which imply that non-being is, somehow, more than a mere empty field in which being can work, more, that is to say, than the mere possibility of creation. It has a power of positive resistance in it; this is explicitly called Necessity[*Timaeus*, 48A, 56C], and is viewed as a co-eternal principle able to limit and hinder the purely rational creative energy, so that the resultant world is not purely rational, but is a mixture of sense and reason.[*Timaeus*, 44(cf. *Phaedo*, 66)].

So that to the end there is a measure of dualism in Plato. Indeed, for him there is no escape from it. For, on the one hand, he was acutely conscious of the imperfection of the world. And, on the other hand, in his day it was not possible for human thought to conceive the intelligent and self-communicating goodness, which is the supreme principle of reality, as fulfilling its purpose of self-communication by a process which begins with something lower than its own eternal perfection; by a process, that is to say, which, to the created beings standing in it, is one of evolution and of the struggle and suffering that evolution involves.

IV

Plato's philosophy, then, was one that laboured toward concreteness; laboured toward a conception of the highest reality as a mind perfect in reason and goodness, self-communicating, and therefore the author and father of a universe. But to the end that effort is in part defeated. Plato's acute sense of the evil in the present world makes him feel that it is deeply sundered from genuine reality; while, on the other hand, he has not entered sufficiently into possession of his highest conception to be enabled — or rather, to be compelled — to view the supreme mind as a synthetic principle realising itself through the total process of the world.

So that a measure of the negative theology is in him to the end. And it makes him grave and austere. We have already seen how in the very years when his hold upon life and his delight in its greater energies must have been at the height, a certain stern and sad and uncompromising aloofness marked even his devotion to the state. Scarcely can the true statesman bear rule in the city of his birth. The "city which is his own" has its pattern laid up in heaven. It he will seek to behold, and in accordance with it will organise his life. But "with any other city he will have nothing to do."[*Republic*, 592]. And something of this temper remained in him throughout life. Hardly can he reconcile himself to the world. To the last it stands at the bar of his thought as a product of perfect reason, but perfect reason working in an alien realm and upon alien material and prevented thereby from fulfilling itself; while the religious spirit in him feels instinctively that the reality with which it longs to be at one is something far other than this world, something far removed from the whole order of things, the whole system of life, which has its being in space and time. And so to the end he continues to speak in that characteristic note and tone which in all ages has drawn to him high and pure hearts to whom the penetrating insights of his science were a closed book — the note and tone of the man who, having lifted up his mind to the things that are eternal, prophesies against the world, and exhorts men to fly from the world to God.

Thus the Greek spirit was transformed in Plato. Its mastery over the resources of the present life, its habitual delight in the activities of the day that now is, its quick susceptibility to every interesting thing and every beautiful form that the world affords, its proneness to lose itself in these and make the most of them before the evil days come in which the pale shade has no more delight in life: — all this was in Plato, but in him as something that stands rebuked. Always he had disliked the volatility and fickleness of the Athenians of his day; always his sympathy had been with the grave strength of the men of Marathon or the austere discipline of Sparta. And upon all this there had supervened an infinitely profounder spiritual power, against which his science made gradual headway, but which it could never wholly overcome — the tendency of a pure and high mind and of a heart religious with the religion of eternity, toward the absolute condemnation of the things of the world in the light of a vision of the heavenly perfection.

When the genius of Greece still was young, and interpreted the life of nature in accordance with the life of its own soul, it shaped out in legend an unintentional prophecy of this transformation which it was itself to undergo when its doom was descending upon it, and in the soul of its greatest son, it turned itself toward the things of eternity. The daughter of the earth-goddess led the life of a happy child, playing among the flowers in the meadows of Enna, lost in momentary pleasures , absorbed in momentary griefs. Very direct and simple was the unity of her mind with the beauty that surrounded her, and with her home the kindly earth; and her heart was very close to her mother's heart — for there was no barrier of knowledge or of vision or of experience that could come between. But when Hades suddenly had taken her to him, and set her at his side on the inexorable throne from which the issues of all things mortal are seen; and when Demeter, making desolate the earth, had compelled the restitution of her child for the happier seasons of the year: — she who returned to Demeter's arms was not she who has gone. Persephone it was; but no longer the happy child of the Sicilian meadows. A stately queen she came, in her eyes the unfathomable wisdom of the kingdom of the dead, in her bearing the majesty of the dark king her mate, at her heart a grave astonishment as she looked upon the hapless creatures, her mother's friends, the men who till the earth, and struggle for things that pass away, and mourn as the objects of their foolish quests perish in their hands. Never while the system of the universe endured could Demeter have her child again. Henceforward she must walk through all her genial summers, companioning, not with a happy child, but with the majestic woman whose eyes, "imperial, disimpassioned," had gazed upon uttermost mysteries and ultimate doom. And yet it may be that Demeter, having thus undergone her fate, came at last to find it good; for it may be that the nature of the Immortal Gods, unchangeable at her heart, caused her at last to rejoice with a joy that had never been in her life before, when she found at her side no longer the child that played in Enna and by night lay close to her mother's heart, but a companion god, thinking godlike, thoughts achieving godlike things, queen of the world of the dead.

The genius of Greece might in this almost have been speaking of itself. The philosophy of Plato is the Persephone's journey of the Greek spirit. In him it looked upon ultimate things, and so was led to regard with other eyes the life of the earth. And undoubtedly the "hidden wisdom of the world" was in this. For while it is true that the beginnings of human life, and its divinely appointed end, are in organic connexion, it is also true that the end is far from the beginning; a great journey, a mighty discipline, lie between. Earth and heaven are parts of one universe; but earth is very different from heaven, and the ascent is steep and long. The nature of the world, and the meaning of life, can be known only in the light of the divinely intended synthesis toward which the whole creation moves; but the very vision of that synthesis is false vision unless it makes clear how far apart the antithetic members of the system now stand, and how vast must be the process that reconciles them in the life of the ultimate city of God. Hence the men of the negative theology, though they have overstated their truth and made the difference between eternal reality and our present life absolute and hopeless, yet by their very insistence upon the difference itself, have done profound service to humanity. We all need their lesson; and need it the more that our age is altogether disinclined to learn it. A few can learn it in the school of the Mystics. But most of us, touched, if not controlled, by the scientific mind of our day, and devoted practically to mastering the things of the world, can learn it only as it takes on humane forms and goes hand in hand with the synthetic spirit of science. And precisely thus it is that it appears in the urbane but solemn teaching of the great son of Ariston.

Section Nine

HERBERT LESLIE STEWART
(1882-1953)

9

Stewart, Carlyle and Canadian Idealism

J. Douglas Rabb

In the introduction to his book *Modernism, Past and Present*, Herbert Leslie Stewart declares "To deny the evolution of man is not more groundless than to affirm that in evolution lies the key to man's whole significance.[1] He goes on to argue that

> He who would explain the variety of species by separate creations has missed the lesson of the laboratory and the museum. But he who would reduce our discernment of 'the absolute values' to a mere physiological or chemical process is like him who can see in music a mere vibration of strings, or in painting no more than the movements of a brush.[2]

Stewart is responding to the challenge of evolution in a way which is typical of the early Canadian idealists. He defines "Protestant Methodism," for example, as "the bold facing of this challenge, to reshape the Protestant Creeds in such a fashion as will reconcile them with scientific and historical knowledge, and yet retain what is distinctive in the Christian message to mankind."[3] Leslie Armour and Elizabeth Trott have described this kind of "accommodationist" tendency in Canadian thought in terms of what they call "philosophical federalism," a willingness to attempt to understand and accommodate philosophical positions opposed to one's own. As they put it:

> In English Canadian philosophy reason is used as a device to explore alternatives, to suggest ways of combining apparently contradictory ideas, to discover new ways of passing from one idea to another.[4]

Like many of his earlier Canadian counterparts Stewart supports his accommodationist views with a form of idealistic metaphysics. He did not, however, become an idealist until after he moved to Canada in 1913 to accept a position at Dalhousie University. Upon graduation from Oxford he became lecturer in Moral Philosophy and History of Philosophy in the Queen's University of Belfast where he delivered a series of lectures which he published in 1912 under the title *Questions of the Day in Philosophy and Psychology*. In this work he is, as Armour and Trott confirm, "a convinced realist of the turn-of-the-century sort — one of those who reacted against the central idealist claim that there is a unity of man and the world, of consciousness and object, of reason and its subject-matter.[5] Armour and Trott go on to suggest that his conversion to idealism was due at least in part to his attempt to understand why the world was at war in his study *Nietzsche and the Ideals of Modern Germany* published in 1915.[6] "The . . . book probably brought the beginnings of a change in Stewart's larger philosophical outlook if only because in that writing it forced him to reassess the power of ideas and the nature of competing claims about the nature of reality."[7] Further evidence of his "conversion" to idealism, and a clear statement of that idealism can be found in three papers he published on the thought of Thomas Carlyle. The three papers in question are "Carlyle's Conception of Religion," *The American Journal of Theology*, 1917, "Carlyle's Place in Philosophy," *The Monist* 1919, and "Carlyle and Canada," *The Canadian Magazine of Politics, Science, Art and Literature* 1921. In these three papers Stewart makes it quite clear both that he is in sympathy with Carlyle and that he regards Carlyle as an idealist. What is of most importance, however, is Stewart's sympathy with, and restatement of , Carlyle's criticism of scientific realism:

> The methods of the sciences, and that of metaphysics which is no more than a unification of the sciences, can tell us nothing on the problems which matter most of all, problems of the ground of all being, of freedom and necessity, of good and evil, of the nature and prospects of the soul. For that with which the sciences deal is always something which I call *mine* but which I cannot call *me*. every attempt to resolve the latter into the former may be convicted of a contradiction, for it takes as independently real those objects which can exist and contain meaning only in reference to a subject. Science is thus always a study of some aspect of *clothes* and to know the limitations of science we require above all a *clothes-philosophy*.[8]

Not only did Carlyle criticise scientific empiricism, in the sense of drawing our attention to its limitations, but Stewart obviously agreed with this line of criticism. He states explicitly in his *Monist* article:

> It is to the glory of Carlyle that he maintained throughout the frenzy of English empiricism a firm hold upon the larger issues, and that he did so from no mere prejudice, social or theological, but from a clear sighted recognition that empirical methods must quickly spend themselves, leaving the old problems just where they were.[9]

It is not difficult to read this passage as a piece of self criticism which Stewart levies against his own former realist position. Stewart can thus be seen as part of the tradition of Canadian idealism. The idealism which Stewart found in Carlyle attempts to do justice to both the moral nature of Man and the mechanical laws of nature. It can thus aptly be described using Armour and Trott's concept of "philosophical federalism." As Stewart puts it:

> The starting point for Carlyle's own cosmic scheme is just the contradiction between man as moral personality and the world as fixed under mechanical law within which this personality must unfold itself. It was necessary that these two aspects of the universe should somehow be thought together.[10]

Stewart was not simply reading this form of idealism into Carlyle. It was there in Carlyle to be found; and, in all likelihood, it was what first attracted Stewart to Carlyle. In his article on "Carlyle's Conception of Religion" Stewart states:

> It is a cardinal sin of present day critics to attribute to a writer, not the opinions which he avows, but the opinions which in their judgement are legitimate inferences from something he has said, even though these inferences may be expressly contradicted by what he says elsewhere.[11]

The fact that Carlyle's idealism seems to satisfy one of Armour and Trott's criteria for Canadian idealism, i.e., philosophical federalism, raises some interesting questions about the whole notion of a distinctive form of Canadian philosophy. Carlyle, for obvious reasons, cannot be a Canadian philosopher. On the other hand, Carlyle's idealism is neither typically German nor typically British. Carlyle's idealism is, if anything, typically Carlyle. Further, the concept of philosophical federalism is really intended only as a general description of some of the common features of Canadian philosophy and should not be taken as a criterion, much less the criterion, for class inclusion.

Returning to Stewart, the concept of philosophical federalism manifests itself in other aspects of his work as well. As an Irish Canadian Stewart served as both president and official historian of The Charitable Irish Society of Halifax. He compiled and published the Annals of the C.I.S. (1786-1836) under the title *The Irish in Nova Scotia*. In this book he makes clear his admiration for the religious and political tolerance of the C.I.S.. Indeed, he suggests that Ireland itself could learn from such tolerance. He has no doubt that the Irish in Nova Scotia are far more tolerant than those in Ireland:

> A clause in the Constitution of the Charitable Irish Society requires that at its meetings there shall be no political or religious controversies, and all present members will agree that the limit thus imposed is never transgressed even at a time of crisis for religious or political values. It would surely be well if there were some such institution in Ireland itself, with a like self-denying ordinance for zealots to observe at five meetings each year. Thus to suspend dispute must at times have been difficult in the Halifax of the closing years of the eighteenth century and the opening years of the nineteenth. But certain temperamental qualities seem to have

> favoured the Irish here: the same which led to Nova Scotia's establishment
> of political equality among men of all Churches half a dozen years before
> it was established in Britain.[12]

Although Stewart uses the expression "we Irish" throughout his book *The Irish in Nova Scotia*, nevertheless there can be no doubt that he regarded himself first and foremost as a Canadian. this comes out very clearly in his paper "Carlyle and Canada." In this paper he praises Carlyle for being one of the few voices in the Britain of the 1850s raised in support of continued ties with Canada in spite of the claims of Downing Street that "we are losing money on the business."

> It was the current doctrine that these dominions of the Crown had a sort
> of sentimental charm... but that, like the proverbial white elephant, they
> cost far more than they are worth, that in the end Canada, for instance,
> was sure to break away, and that whether the change took the form of
> subjection to the United States or that of setting up an independent
> government the mother country would gain far more than she would
> lose.[13]

Stewart writes as a Canadian, admittedly a Canadian who wishes to retain some ties with Britain, when he declares ". . . there is not now a true Canadian whose pulse is not quickened and whose blood is not stirred as he turns back to Carlyle's passages of withering scorn towards those who would have acquiesced in a breach with the British Commonwealth across the seas."[14] Stewart did reject Carlyle's proposed solution. "He would send out a 'real Governor of Men,' one of his heaven-inspired heroes, to hold office for a prolonged period, to treat rebellion with salutory rigour. . ."[15] Stewart prefers self-government:

> We all know, as Liberals knew even then, that such a plan would have
> defeated the purpose it was meant to serve. . .. We know among the chief
> roots of the Canadian loyalty in which we now exult is that system of free
> self-governing institutions which were once branded as the parent of
> revolt.[16]

Although Stewart admired Carlyle, he was not uncritical. In a review essay on Hitler's *Mein Kampf*, for example, he draws some interesting parallels with Carlyle's *Latter Day Pamphlets*[17]. This review essay, first published in *The University of Toronto Quarterly*, July 1939, was republished in a collection of articles and radio broadcasts entitled *From a Library Window: Reflections of a Radio Commentator*. This book is an excellent source for Stewart's later views which he states quite candidly. It contains, for example, his address to the 1934 Convocation of Pine Hill Divinity Hall, Halifax, in which he argues that "if it was the mediaeval fault for philosophy to be over deferential to theologians I think it is often the fault of our age for theologians to be over deferential to philosophy."[18]

In the following essay, Stewart presents a sympathic account of Carlyle's idealism. Stewart's accommodationist use of reason can be seen in his acceptance of both scientific law and the freedom required by morality. In order to see how he accommodates both religion and science it isimportant to note that Carlyle's idealism, his "clothes philosophy" as he calls it in *Sartor Resartus* (the tailor retailored) embodies a religious attitude in which the empirical world is seen as a manifestation of the Divine, as "the garments of God."

Notes

1. Herbert Leslie Stewart, *Modernism, Past and Present* (London, 1932) p.xxix.
2. *Ibid.*, *Modernism, Past and Present*, p.xxix.
3. *Ibid.*, *Modernism, Past and Present*, p.7.
4. Leslie Armour and Elizabeth Trott, *The Faces of Reason* (Wilfred Laurier U.P., Waterloo, 1981) p.4.
5. *Ibid.*, p.402.
6. He does warn in his preface that "this is neither a book on the war nor a book on Nietzsche's philosophy; it is an effort to assist those who wish to correlate the moral outlook of Germany with one personal influence by which, beyond doubt, it has been in part directed." Herbert Leslie Stewart, *Nietzsche and the Ideals of Modern Germany* (London, Edward Arnold, 1915) p.vi.
7. *The Faces of Reason*, p.403.
8. H.L.Stewart, "Carlyle's Place in Philosophy," *The Monist* vol.XXIX, 1919, p.170.
9. *Ibid.*, p.180.
10. *Op. cit.*, *The Monist*, vol.XXIX, 1919, p.171.
11. H.L.Stewart, "Carlyle's Conception of Religion," *The American Journal of Theology*, 1917, p.56.
12. H.L.Stewart, *The Irish in Nova Scotia* (Kentville, N.S., Kentville Publishing, 1949), p.191.
13. H.L.Stewart, "Carlyle and Canada," *The Canadian Magazine of Politics, Science, Art and Literature* vol.LVI, no.4, February 1921, p.320.
14. *Ibid.*, p.321.
15. *Ibid.*, p.322.
16. *Ibid*, p.322.
17. H.L.Stewart, *From a Library Window: Reflections of a Radio Commentator* (Toronto, 1940), pp.111-113.
18. *Ibid.*, p.244.

CARLYLE'S PLACE IN PHILOSOPHY

Herbert L. Stewart

Carlyle was not, in the technical sense, a philosopher. According to one eminent critic [Herbert Spencer; see *Autobiog.*, I, 380ff] it is a monstrous thing to have applied such a name in any sense to the man who never set out from premises and reasoned his way to conclusions, and who never thought calmly but always in a passion. Indeed the objurgatory tone in which Carlyle alludes to the current systems and controversies may well suggest a complete detachment from any "philosophic" interest whatever. Such speculation betokened for him a sceptical, and hence a paralytic, period of the world. He looked back with wistfulness to the time when all men could still avow the same unhesitating *Credo*, when Mother church still supplied to each a competent theory of the universe.["Characteristics," *Crit. Misc.*,III,29] What William James has called the "divided soul" was to Carlyle an object of constant pity, and we can imagine the rapture with which he would have welcomed the conception of the "once-born." It was he who coined the phrase "disease of metaphysics."[*Ibid.*, p25] It was he who said that religion had degenerated into theories of religion, into mere apologetics "endeavoring with smallest result to make it probable that such a thing as religion exists." [*Ibid.*, p.23] It was he who dismissed political science with the scornful comment that this sort of inquiry makes ever a renewed appearance in ages of decadence.[*F.R.,* II,7 Cf. "Charateristics," *Crit. Mics*, III,13] It was he who instituted that pungent contrast between Bacon, "discovering a new method of discovering truth" — a *novum organum* which was to "make men of us all" — and Kepler, "making by natural *vetus* organum, by the light of his own flaming soul . . . the greatest discovery yet made by man."[*Histotical Sketches*, p. 132] And it was he who stigmatized as an ultimate unsurpassable folly in modern thought the enterprise of "accounting for the moral sense."["Shooting Niagara," *Crit. Misc.*, V, 28]   One must, indeed, remember his concession that the mental sciences, although an evil, are a

*First published in *The Monist*, Vol. XXIX, No.2, April 1919, pp. 161-189.

necessary evil. He held that they could reach no positive result, but that they must be pursued to their end, that they must be judged, as our Hegelians would say, by themselves at a further stage. It was something that reflection should thus be brought to a wholesome crisis, that it should be made to demonstrate its own futility, and the fire of scepticism thus burn itself out.["Characteristics" *Crit. Misc.*,III,40] the way would then be clear for a reassertion of the healthy instincts and intuitions of mankind. Yet surely, if we bring together the relevant passages in Carlyle's works, we find that his own method of thinking yielded something far beyond this merely negative outcome. Like every one else who has set out to overthrow systematic reason he has ended by giving us a system, more or less coherent, of his own. The present article will limit itself to the field of ethics and metaphysics, endeavoring to show that Carlyle's genius there anticipated some results to which a later generation had to attain step by step. It is true that he expressed himself in a language very different from that of the schools. Much of his energy was devoted to denouncing the utilitarian ethics, but a Mill or a Bain could see little in what he said which even called for a reply, little more in short than a windy rhetoric which invariably missed the point. And even philosophers far removed from Mill or Bain have not, as a rule, thought of Carlyle as among the effective critics of empiricism. They have felt that the true answer is not his, but that of a calm, scientific analyst. I shall contend on the other hand that, so far from being in this province only a heated and irrelevant rhetorician, he laid his finger with astonishing accuracy upon just those weaknesses in the empirical school which later examination has forced all men to acknowledge. He avoided the technical jargon, and made his points in his own way. If those points are now among the common-places of text-book criticism, we must remember that fifty years ago to the dominant English philosophy they were rather obscurantist paradox. It is time for us to give due credit to one whose sensibility, like that of the artist in *Daniel Deronda*,[*Daniel Deronda*, Chap. XLI] seized combinations which science now explains and justifies.

I

a It is usual to quote *Characteristics* as containing the principle that philosophy is a useless and an impossible pursuit. But this was not Carlyle's earliest, and it is not his most constant, attitude. His complaint in *Signs of the Times* is rather that the subject is dead, gone with Dugald Stewart, "its last amiable cultivator." And he found the cause of its death in the fact that it had become completely mechanized. The *Zeitgeist* was wholly mechanical. Power looms, steamships, school "methods" in education, institutional churches, "Royal and Imperial Institutes" for the advancement of literature, — these were all products of a common spirit, all tokens of the prevailing trust in machinery. Did not the new-fangled incubator threaten to supersede the activities of the brood-hen?["Signs of the Times," *Crit. Misc.*, II,60] This faith in external apparatus seemed to Carlyle to have gone much too far, for it had obscured the one thing needful. Creative work had its ultimate source in a native insight, which could never be analyzed into a combination of forces artificially put together. It was the silent thought of a Newton, with little equipment beyond paper and pencil, which had given us the system of the planetary paths. What one saw in the later, mechanical days was a museum with retorts, digesters, and galvanic piles, where Nature was being interrogated by "some quite other than Newton," and Nature in turn showed no haste to respond.[*Ibid.*, p.62]

The same spirit had given us mere physiological psychology as an account of man's intellectual life. Carlyle saw with horror that the school of Locke still reigned, with its laws of association, its resolving of the mental enigma into a problem in coexistences and sequences as these reveal themselves to a superficial introspection. Thinking was "explained" by having its physical concomitants pointed out. The hope seemed to be cherished that higher power microscopes might yet enable mind itself to be *seen*! Had not Cabanis lately announced that thought is a "secretion" and that the spiritual product which we call poetry is the special province of the smaller intestines? This to Carlyle was not so much a falsifying as a simple ignoring of the true philosophic problem. Where mechanical causation was thus assumed as the key to all phenomena, no one would raise the previous issue as to the very notion of cause. The grand secrets of the soul's relation to time, to space, to the universe of matter, and to God, had quietly dropped out of sight.[*Ibid.*, p.64]

The futility of this mechanical method is illustrated by a profusion of examples from the moral and social sphere. Bentham had envisaged mankind after the manner of physics, as a collection of spiritual atoms, each acted on by motives, which turn out in the end to be varied combinations of a single motive — the desire for pleasure.[Cf., e.g., *Heroes*, Lect. II] Yet who ever saw a human being thus dragged hither and thither by impulses external to himself? How could such a formula explain the heroisms and the chivalries of history?[*Sartor*, III,3] Was it not plain that a nice balancing of this motive against that, with a determination at all costs to procure for oneself a surplus for enjoyment, was just the account which should *not* be given of Crusaders, of Puritans, of Christian martyrs, of French Revolutionists, of any one in short who acted under a flaming passion? So far from its being true that mankind could follow only the line of greatest ease and of least resistance, we should rather say that enterprises of hardship and of difficulty are the real allurements for the human heart.[*Heroes*, II] Witness of the poor swearing recruit who does not think primarily of the shilling a day but of "the honor of a soldier," and even the most frivolous class in our society who, if they can remember nothing else, still make much of what they call "a point of honor."[*Ibid.*] For the principle of greatest happiness thank God there were always some who would substitute the principle of greatest nobleness.

Moreover, argues Carlyle, if we grant for a moment his atomistic psychology of motive, we shall be left with the idea of obligation not only unvindicated but even unexplained. For the criterion of mere pleasingness could give no priority to one pleasure over another. Nor was there any principle by which such random impulses in a multitude of men could be united into a social whole. If every man's selfishness, infinitely expansive, were to be hemmed in only by the infinitely expansive selfishness of every other man, upon what centripetal force could we reply to prevent a return to chaos?["Voltaire," *Crit. Misc.*] Conscience surely was something more than a suborned auxiliary, useful for social proposes to the constable and the hangman. The checks and balances and all the cunning mechanism of self-interest which utilitarian philosophers valued so highly were nothing but so many efforts to solve this problem: "Given a world of rogues, how to produce an honesty from their combined action?"[Cf. Bentham's own description of Panopticon as "a mill for grinding rogues honest and idle men industrious." (*Works*, X, 226)] Terrors of conscience to such men would be of little worth, not to be compared, for example, with diseases of the liver. If obligation meant no more than this, then "not on morality but on cookery let us build our stronghold; there, brandishing our frying-pan as censer, let us offer sweet incense to the Devil, and live at ease on the fat things he has provided for his elect."[*Sartor*, II,7]

The last unavailing protest against this spirit of mechanizing had, in Carlyle's view, been raised by the Scottish school, which was clear-sighted enough to recognize whither things were tending, but was itself too deeply sunk in the same error to find any solution. Reid had a dim notion that something was wrong, but knew not how to right it. So, instead of boldly denying the premises. He "let loose instinct, as an undiscriminating bandog to guard him against the conclusions!"["Signs of the Times," *Crit. Misc.*, II,64]

b. But our author has a more serious criticism upon philosophers than any which confines itself to the method or the results of a particular group of them. In *Characteristics* he appears at all events to contend that the whole enterprise of philosophy involves a mistake.

He likens the questioning mind to the disordered body. In each case an acute consciousness of self is a symptom that something has gone astray. The normal organ does not need to be watched, or constantly readjusted, and the normal spirit would never be distracted by "problems" or arrest its harmonious functioning in order to introspect. This analogy is driven home by vivid examples; — the rude countryman, in perfect health just because, so far as he knew, he had no "system"; the skilled boxer, innocent of anatomy, who would not hit better for having studied the *flexor longus* and *flexor brevis*; Walter Shandy whose reasoning was not perceptibly improved by a course in Aristotle. Anatomists and metaphysicians were to be reckoned among the melancholy products of the fall of man. The beam of white light renders all things visible, but, because of its very whiteness, is itself unseen, and some irregular obstruction is required to break it up into colors. In the same sense discussions, about virtue for example, are a sign that virtue is on the wane. Patriotism is losing its grip when men write treatises to give it a basis. Social cohesion is in a bad way when a *Contrat Social* is needed to solder men together. The publication of Paley's *Evidences* was an ominous portent for religion. For everywhere the token of health is unconsciousness, and the token of disease is an anxious listening to oneself.

Applying this to metaphysics, our author points out that the quest for a theorem of the universe proceeds from a break-up of the true spiritual unity. And at bottom what it asks is impossible. The universe cannot be put into a theorem by any finite mind. If he had to choose between them Carlyle would prefer dogmatic to sceptical speculation; not that either can heal the disorder of the soul, but that one is, relatively speaking, a stage of convalescence, the other a stage of relapse. The whole spurious problem means an attempt of the mind to pass beyond itself, to reach a point of view from which it can judge not only other things but itself also *ab extra*. The act of knowing is everywhere conditioned by the subject-object contrast; yet the metaphysician would fain compel this very machinery to account for the conditions of its own action. He would know absolutely that which, *ex hypothesi*, he can know only as related. Carlyle illustrates this procedure by two similitudes which are at least as striking as any which the critics of absolutism have since devised, that of the athlete who would so develop his sinews that he may be able to lift up his own body, and that of the Irish saint who swam the Channel, carrying his head in his teeth.["Characteristics," *Crit. Misc.*, III,27]

Such being the metaphysical purpose, it was easy to see why the labor of thousands of years had been so inexpressibly unproductive. For instance, how pathetic, yet how fatuous, had been the attempts to demonstrate a God! As if a God who could be *proved*, or — more ludicrous still—rendered *probable*, would not thereby take his place as just one object among other objects, rather than as that in which all alike live and move and have their being! What, asks, Carlyle, was this problem which the poor deists set themselves, but to ground the beginning of all belief in some belief earlier than the beginning?["Diderot," *Crit. Misc.*, 237] And was it not high time to confess that if intellect, or the power of knowing and believing, is synonymous with logic, or the mere power of arranging and communicating, no proof of a Deity is to be had? At the utmost one might reach that *Etre supreme*, the subject of Robespierre's "scraggiest of prophetic discourses."["Mirabeau," *Crit. Misc.*, 407; cf. *F.R.*, VI,4] Metaphysical theology had been but the multiplication of words, until the earth groaned under accumulated phrases, but the enterprise was fore-doomed from the start. "*Cogito, ergo sum*: Alas, poor Cogitator, this takes us but a little way . . . The secret of man's being is still like the Sphinx's secret, a riddle that he cannot rede."[*Sartor*, I,8] For Carlyle's own part, the utmost he had got from metaphysics —and it was no small gain in a sense — was the bliss of becoming delivered from them altogether.[*Lectures on Literature*] Hume and Diderot on the one side, Kant on the other, served but to refute the alternative conclusions, and to confirm by trial what might have been fore-told from the very terms of the problem, that the metaphysical road leads nowhere.

II

It has often been said that a thoroughly consistent scepticism ought to be silent, and one might conclude from the foregoing argument that its author would advance no positive doctrine of his own upon subjects which he had thus declared inscrutable. Moreover, his repeated insistence on the vanity of all "speech about the unspeakable things" has given rise to the well-worn jest that Carlyle preached the gospel of silence in thirty volumes. But we have seen that the discussion which on these high altitudes he condemned as useless was that of the logical or demonstrating type, where the basis of all thought is forced under thought-categories, and the arguer affects to prove that which is already assumed in every process of proof. If the sphere of science may be compared to territory which we can look at from outside, what is the analogue to that ground which we cannot see, just because we have to stand upon it in order to see all the rest? If it should turn out that logical demonstration is not man's only organon of truth, one may without incoherence set forth in words that other spiritual functioning, so far as words will serve to give it expression. The route by which Carlyle thus went forward to his cosmic scheme seems to have been as follows.

Destructive criticism has so far simply cleared the ground. If it has been correct it has shown that the methods of the sciences, and of that metaphysic which is no more than a unification of the sciences, can tell us nothing on the problems which matter most of all, problems of the ground of all being, of freedom and necessity, of good and evil, of the nature and prospects of the soul. For that with which the sciences deal is always something which I may call *mine* but which I cannot call *me*. Every attempt to resolve the latter into a combination of the former may be convicted of contradiction, for it takes as independently real those objects which can exist and contain meaning only in reference to a subject. Science is thus always a study of some species of *clothes*, and to know the limitations of science we require above all a *clothes-philosophy*. "Let any cause-and-effect philosopher explain, not why I wear such and such a garment, obey such and such a law, but even why I am here, to wear and obey anything."[*Sartor*, 1,5] The real question thus becomes one which is scarcely possible to formulate, and wholly impossible to answer, within the categories of cause-and-effect reasoning. For the thing we seek to know is not what particular effect was produced by a particular cause, but what is the total significance of a universe in which such a nexus of causality has been established, and whether that nexus is itself an instrument in a deeper plan. Our very capacity of putting this problem is itself a token that we are not mere items in the series whose meaning we thus challenge. We are able somehow to get outside of it, to become its critics. And although the intellectualist metaphysicians have so far attempted the absurd task of construing it as a whole through principles which are valid only from part to part, the very persistence of their effort proves how fundamental is that impulse which they have so blunderingly followed.

Thus for Carlyle as for Wordsworth the unique position of man in the universe was evidenced above all by his

> obstinate qustioning of sense and outward things.

Man's unhappiness came of his greatness. The happiness of one shoeblack could not be assured by all the finance ministers and upholsters and confectioners of modern Europe, for the shoeblack had a soul quite other than his stomach.[*Ibid.*, II,9] The starting-point for Carlyle's own cosmic scheme is just the contradiction between man as moral personality and the world as fixed under mechanical law within which this personality must unfold itself. It was necessary that these two aspects of the universe should somehow be thought together. Their unification through a mechanizing of the moral life, or through a subjection of mind to one of its own categories, had already proved impossible. What other alternative remained? Carlyle turned for a reply to that way of thinking which under the title. "German philosophy" had just begun, chiefly through the influence of Coleridge, to make its voice heard in England.[Cf. Mark Pattison's statement that even the Oriel "Noetics" know nothing of Continental philosophy. (*Memoirs*)] It is Carlyle's high distinction that he was one of the two men in the English-speaking world who, as early as 1829, pierced beyond the din about "laws of association" to the deeper issues which Kant had raised for European thought. It is doubtful how far Kant's work was known to him at first hand. He seems to have come onto contract with it mainly through such writers as Fichte and Novalis, and, by a singular latitude of interpretation, to have read similar ideas into *Wilhelm Meister* and *Faust*. Nor did he ever take up definite discipleship in the Kantian school. He uniformly speaks of the *Kritiken* as Plato spoke of the conversations of Parmenides; they had suggested to him ideas of far-reaching fascination, upon whose truth he did not presume to pronounce, but whose enormous significance the shallow talkers around him would do well to appreciate if they could.[Cf., e.g., paper on Novalis] One can easily see, however, that Kant is the true source, direct or indirect, of his whole further development.

Exactly in the spirit of the *Critique of Practical Reason* he lays it down that the approach to a constructive philosophy must lie through the moral consciousness. "The true Shekinah is man."[*Sartor*, I, 10; cf. *Heroes*, I,10] And it is man not on the side of his discordant impulses, or his mushroom speculations. It is man as conscious of duty, as recognizing within him a categorical imperative. Carlyle is very insistent that on the rational and objective, as contrasted with the emotional and subjective, doctrine of conscience the whole fabric of one's world-view must depend. He notes it as a token of the sceptical eighteenth century that men ceased to take moral obligation as intuitive and began "accounting for" it, moreover that they spoke of the antithesis between right and wrong as appreciated by a "sense," as if we had a relish for certain actions, "a sort of palate by the taste of which the nature of anything might be determined."[*Lectures on Literature*] He pities poor Burns as one in whom even at his best morality was "as instinct only," not a rational conviction.["Burns," *Crit. Misc.*] He pours scorn upon the attempt to conjure moral objectivity out of sentiments of honor, upon Diderot's "perpetual clatter about *vertu, honnetete, grandeur, sensibilite, ames nobles*, and "that interminable ravelment of reward and approval virtue being its own reward."["Diderot," *Crit. Misc.*, III,239] He sets in glowing contrast the Mohammedan heaven and hell. Gross and material though they were, we have here a testimony to "that grand spiritual fact and beginning of facts" that "good and evil are no matters of degree, but that they are eternally incommensurable the difference not one of finite but one of infinite moment."[*Heroes*, II] And he returns again and again to Kant's similitude between the starry heavens and the law of duty as a depth of vision beyond which no man has ever seen or can see.

Although in the paper on Novalis he speaks of the contrast between reason and understanding as one whose subtlety baffled him, while he suspected that it was somehow profoundly true, it is clear that Carlyle had worked his own way to a very similar distinction. Kant's insistence that the moral judgment proceeds from a faculty higher in kind than that which cognizes the relation of object to subject in a mechanically ordered world, is consonant with the whole thought of *Sartor*. Indeed this was but the technical statement of what has been fitly called Carlyle's "mysticism" — a word which amid all its vagueness stands at least for this, that the deepest of all truths are known otherwise than by resoning. Whether he got this principle from Fichte, or from Bohme, or from Jacobi, is a matter for the Carlyle antiquaries to decide. One may perhaps recall in this connection the protest of Coleridge against those who "have no notion that there are such things as fountains in the world . . . and who would therefore charitably derive every rill which they behold flowing from a perforation made in some other man's tank."[Preface to *Christabel*] Carlyle's mysticism was at least worked out in an individual way. We get it, for example, in his scorn of those who dwell only "in the thin rind of the conscious,"["Diderot," *Crit. Misc.*,III,234] who recognize like the Encyclopaedists no truth except that which can be debated of, and to whom in consequence the sanctuary of man's soul stands perennially shut." We get it again, in his famous theory of genius as ever a secret to itself,["Characteristics," *Crit. Misc.*, III,5] of the discoverer as imcomparably beyond the reasoner,[*Ibid*, 6.] of the truly original mind as unaware of all but a mere fraction of its own active forces.["Sir Walter Scott," *Crit. Misc.*, IV,49] Carlyle would not readily have accepted an idea on this subject from Mill, but he does seem to have had in view just what Mill defined as the purpose of metaphysics, the study — not as in logic of those truths which are admitted on evidence but — of those other truths which may reasonably be admitted without evidence. That there are such truths he was firmly convinced. Where are they to be found?

If the human soul is the true Shekinah it seems to follow that we must look in man for a light upon the universe, not *vice versa*. If his being cannot be dissolved into uniformities of coexistence and sequence borrowed from the physical sphere, perhaps the outer world may unlock its secret to the key which is furnished by the moral consciousness? Unity may be reached, if not through the mechanizing of man, then through the spiritualizing of nature. By this, however, Carlyle understood no deistic doctrine of a divinely contrived machine, nor yet a world conceived as subject to recurring interference by its Maker. There were no miracles, except in that deep sense in which all is miraculous, the sense that nothing occurs as the result of blind forces, and that behind every scientific "explanation" there remains a mystery which no science can probe. For the cosmic outlook which he thus commends Carlyle has chosen the suggestive name "natural supernaturalism."

He defends it in the first instance by the familiar arguments of the idealist. These come oddly enough from one who professes to have abjured metaphysic, but the paper on Novalis in which they occur belongs to that early period in which Carlyle was still highly speculative. Moreover, if he talks Berkeleianism, he does so not as one who is assured of that system's truth, but rather as one who sees in it enough to stagger the confident apostles of matter and motion. Common sense is convicted of resting upon a spiritual postulate, the postulate that the world is interpretable, that the senses reveal things as they really are, hence that the Power which made and the mind which studies nature are harmonious. "So true is it that for these men also all knowledge of the visible rests on belief of the invisible, and derives its first meaning and certainty therefrom."["Novalis," *Crit. Misc.*, II,25] We are reminded of the relativity of every sense-datum to the organ that receives it, and of the consequent doubt as to what the *absolute* existence of any object can be. Fichte's principle of all phenomena as due to a non-ego, regarding which the last scientific analysis leaves a residuum that is unknowable, is combined with Kant's subjectivity of space and time to lead us into a reverent agnosticism. The reign of wonder is declared to be native to man, for it belongs to him both at his lowest and at his highest. But it is an intermittent reign. In seasons of superficial *Aufklarung* it is sort of "reign *in partibus infidelium*."[*Sartor*, I,10]

The use of this last phrase is typically Carlylean, one of those reveling comparisons by which, as with a flash, the whole tenor of an abstract argument is lit up. The ubiquitous sway of wonder, against which Diderot and the rest of the cocksure Encyclopaedists had effected a local revolt, would reassert itself, even as the Church looked forward to winning back her temporary apostates. Carlyle exhausts himself in depicting how deep is that mystery which real thinkers must acknowledge. Only the surface of things had been or could be penetrated by reflection. What availed it to know that nature was a system, while the laws of the system were known to only an infinitesimal extent? Who could say, for example, what is and what is not miraculous? To the Dutch King of Siam any one with an air-pump and vial of vitriolic ether might work miracles at will. Our most learned physicist was, relatively speaking, like the minnow that is familiar with the pebbles and crannies of its native creek, but ignorant of trade-winds, eclipses, and monsoons by which the condition of the creek is determined.[*Ibid.*, III,8] Man had become so completely the dupe of system that whatever happened frequently was *eo ipso* taken as understood, and only the exceptional was admitted to be mysterious! Nay, it was often sufficient that an event should have received a recognized *name* in order to take it out of the realm of wonder, and place it, neatly 'icketed and labeled, among our mental conquests. Yet was it not so that the ǫry commonest facts were among the most inexplicable? "Thou wilt laugh at ıll the believe in a mystery? . . . *Armer Teufel*! Doth not thy cow calve? Doth not thy bull gender? Nay, peradventure, dost not thou thyself gender? Explain me that, or do one of two things: retire into private places with thy foolish cackle; or, what were better, give it up and weep, not that the world is mean, and disenchanted, and prosaic, but that thou art vain and blind!"[Cf. *ibid.*, I,11]

Our scientific categories were thus, for Carlyle, mere modes of human classification, which had been found useful within that relatively microscopic area which man has reduced to order. It is against the mistake of accepting them as explanatory of the universe as a whole that Teufelsdrockh does not cease to protest. He is thinking of a metaphysic which employs as ultimately valid such notions as matter and force, forgetful that these are relative to the point of view of the sentient observer, that they are anthropomorphic in the sense of having been borrowed from the inner experience of volition, and that they are thus rather imposed upon than contained within the immediacy of consciousness. He aptly compares this confusion to that of one who should take the clothes in which a figure was dressed for the figure itself. In particular Carlyle welcomes the demonstration by Kant that space and time, the essential forms in which all scientific knowledge has come to us, are products from within, not data from without. He sees here an intelligible construing of the religious doctrine that God is omnipresent and eternal.[*Ibid.*, I,8] For its difficulty vanishes once we realize that God exists neither in time nor in space.

Thus the Ultimate Reality is conceived almost as Spinoza conceived his Absolute, revealed under attributes to the human understanding, but in no way bound under such attributes in its essential nature. Carlyle, whose acquaintance with Spinoza seems to have been through the medium of Goethe, could find no more adequate expression for this than in the memorable words of the Earth-Spirit in *Faust*:

In Lebensfluthen, im Thatensturm
Wall'ich auf und ab,
Wehe hin und her!

Geburt und Grab,
Elin ewiges Meer,
Ein wechselnd Weben,
Ein gluhend Leben,
So schaff' ich am sausenden Webstuhl der Zeit,
Und wirke der Gottheit lebendiges Kleid."

But that subjectivity under which he condemns our scientific concepts he will not extend to our moral convictions. There is nothing Spinozistic about his treatment of the antithesis between right and wrong. It is never alluded to, in the fashion which we should expect from such a beginning, as a "mode of finitude," or, as Mr. Bradley would say, as a stage in the progress to a point of view at which morality will be seen to be appearance. On the contrary, it is made the root from which objective knowledge, otherwise impossible, is made to spring. Man's intuition of duty is not only sure, it is the ground of his surety that the Absolute too is moral. Carlyle almost coincides with the attitude of Hermann Lotze, that metaphysic, otherwise a confusion in which any judgment is as demonstrable as any other, becomes an intelligible whole when we take the distinctions of conscience as not only *a* truth, but the beginning of *all* truths.

Finally, although such knowledge of the universe as spiritual is not to be attained by reasoning but through moral insight, Carlyle is ready to grant and even to insist that observation and experience may confirm or illustrate a belief which they are powerless to originate. The design argument was useless to create faith, for its strongest evidence lay in the phenomenon that man *searches for* design, and this evidence the poor doubter, by the very fact of his doubting, was unable to appreciate.[Cf. "Diderot," *Crit. Misc.*, III] Yet the contemplation of natural adjustments in all the wonder of their detail might well strengthen a belief in divine order that was already held on higher grounds. The course of history was redeemed from chaos when history was looked upon as the working of the finger of God. But that man's life should be a moral cosmos rather than a moral chaos would appeal only to those by whom the judgments of conscience were already revered. Carlyle rejoiced, however, that man's spiritual nature has a better source from which to sustain itself than by hunting high and low for empirical corroborations that the world is other than a dead machine. He was not dependent on considerations which a Voltaire might "dispute into, or dispute out of" him. Even as consciousness of duty was the mainspring of faith, so it was by the performance of duty that faith became assured. If the universe is the expression of a moral purpose, then those who live nearest to that purpose will be best certified of its reality. The remedy for doubt lay in work, and the work to begin with was the work closest to one's hand. Searching for God by argument was like searching with a rushlight for the noonday sun. If any man will do His will, he shall know of the doctrine.

There is much in natural supernaturalism which is closely analogous to the once famed "transfigured realism" of Herbert Spencer, just as there is much in Carlyle's apparently pantheistic passages of reverence for "the All" which reminds us of the cult of the Unknowable. It is when moral enthusiasm bursts the barrier of abstract thought that he forbids most definitely this tempting comparison. We shall probably find the most perfect embodiment of his world-view not in any articulated system that could be named, but in two stanzas by the poet Clough:

> And as of old from Sinai's top
> God said that God is One,
> By Science strict so speaks He now
> To tell us There is None!
> Earth goes by chemic forces; Heaven's
> A Mechanique Celeste!
> And heart and mind of human kind
> A watch-work as the rest
>
> Is this a Voice, as was the Voice,
> Whose speaking told abroad,
> When thunder pealed and mountain reeled
> The ancient truth of God?
> Ah, not the Voice; 'tis but the cloud,
> The outer darkness dense,
> Where image none, nor e'er was seen
> Similitude of sense.
> 'Tis but the cloudy darkness dense
> That wraps the Mount around;
> While in amaze the people stays,
> To hear the Coming Sound.[*The New Sinai*]

III

What value are we to set upon these varied suggestions, both critical and constructive? The late Professor Windelband has very justly remarked that the philosophic movement of the nineteenth century turned upon "the question as to the degree of importance which the natural-science conception of phenomena may claim for our view of the world and life as a whole."[*History of Philosophy*, tranl. by J.H. Tufts, p. 624] He attributes the immense progress of that conception during the earlier years of the century to two causes, the definiteness of scientific results and their utility of application to practical needs. Side by side with this progress one recognizes a decay of the interest generically spoken of as "metaphysical." Its position could not be re-established until men saw again that science, however definite and certain, moves in a limited sphere, and that the needs of the human spirit go far beyond anything that can be described as "practical."

It is the glory of Carlyle that he maintained throughout the frenzy of English empiricism a firm hold upon the larger issues, and that he did so from no mere prejudice, social or theological, but from a clear-sighted recognition that empirical methods must quickly spend themselves, leaving the old problems just where they were. He once remarked of the eighteenth century that there was illumination indeed, of a kind, "but except the illuminated windows almost nothing to be *seen* thereby."["Voltaire," *Crit. Misc*] He would have said the same of that "psychogonical method" by which Mill was once thought to have made metaphysics an obsolete pursuit. Psychology is a natural science; as such it rests upon the common axioms and postulates of scientific procedure; and if we have no criterion beyond itself by which the limit of this procedure can be determined, the inference is not that metaphysic must become psychological but rather that it must be abandoned. Carlyle laid down this principle as clearly as Edward Caird himself. And he laid it down at that most opportune moment when psycho-physics threatened to run riot, when phrenology was becoming all the rage, when even Emerson allowed himself to name Spurzheim, in the same intellectual class with Lavoisier and Bentham,[Essay on Self-Reliance] when even George Sand was poring over the new mapped areas of the phrenological skull.[Cf. Doumic's *George Sand*, p.143] One need not quarrel with him about his rhetoric. If he spoke at times of philosophy in language fit only for the lips of G.H. Lewes, the idea he had in mind was one to which no one like Lewes ever rose. Against phenomenalism of every type he waged the war of a genuine philosopher. Perhaps no admonition could have been more in place to the circle he addressed than his memorable call to close their Voltaire and open their Goethe.

The side of phenomenalism upon which he first seized as surest to reveal its break-down was the mechanizing of the moral life. One must feel no slight amazement at the completeness with which Carlyle anticipated almost every criticism which has since been passed upon the utilitarian moralist, and upon that atomic psychology which their system as then announced took for its starting-point. For, excepting his short and very unfruitful apprenticeship in the lecture-room of Thomas Brown, he was no technically trained philosopher. He belonged to the class now so nearly extinct of the general "man of letters" — like Macaulay, for example; and if we would appreciate his insight we cannot do better than compare Carlyle's assaults upon Bentham and James Mill with the vacuous cleverness of Macaulay's attempts in the same direction in the *Edinburgh Review*.

What are the main objections which have since been urged against utilitarianism — objections under the stress of which that system has been rendered obsolete for most of us, and transformed beyond identification by those who still give it a sort of adherence? That a motive is no independent force acting upon the will from outside, and that thus the analogy of a physical system which was once so freely invoked is lacking in its essential; that the picture of man forecasting more or less pleasurable states of himself and deciding either consciously or unconsciously in view of the algebraic surplus is an intellectualist caricature of real life; that even if "character" were simply the name for a mechanical aggregate of impulses not all of these can be called "desire for pleasure" as shown by the crucial instances of a soldier who dies for his country, a martyr who sacrifices himself for a principle, and in short every one who forgets calculation in an overmastering enthusiasm; that society cannot be resolved into a collection of units where one man's gain must be another man's loss and the happiness of the greatest number is thus merely the least of many evils, but that the unity is organic, and gain anywhere must, rightly considered, be gain for the whole; that, assuming as primitive a universal selfishness, no alchemy of logic can educe a universal benevolence — "From 'each for himself' to 'each for all' no road!"[Martineau, *Types of Ethical Theory*]; that distinction in kind between pleasures cannot be reconciled with Mill's initial basis, but involves a criterion other than pleasingness, introduced simply because obligation could not without it be preserved. These are the commonplaces of later criticism, embodied in almost every modern ethical text-book, and, whatever their cogency, each of them was advanced in *Sartor*, in *Heroes*, in *Past and Present*. If they are there clothed in flowing eloquence, this fact, although it is apt to make the school philosopher distrustful, should not give their author a lower place than we assign to those who after a generation's reflection have reached precisely the same results, but have stated them with the canonical formality and the canonical dulness.

Again, Carlyle saw what was hidden from most in his time, that the real weakness of the empiricist, school lay in its picture of the mind as wholly passive, and in its ignoring of the mental *spontaneities*. The stock in trade of Bentham's critics lay very generally in appeals to "the testimony of consciousness" as guaranteeing this or that principle which they valued but could not satisfactorily prove, and again in threats of unpleasant consequences for religion or morality if the basis in intuitions were given up. The obvious reply was that of Mill, that the alleged voice of consciousness had been arbitrarily reported, that if scientific laws had their root in experience religion and morality might be grounded in the same way, and that in any case the practical consequence of accepting a belief had no legitimate place in the discussion of its truth or falsity. Carlyle in not a few passages has suggested the far more telling attack with which we are now so familiar. He challenged the empirical psychology. He arraigned Bacon as having forgotten in his account of the procedure of science just that element which is most essential to its success, and of offering us only "better methods of labeling, of mixing, compounding and separating." The *novum organum* had affected so to mechanize the process that every man should become by the use of this improved instrument as good a reasoner as any other, just as a dwarf and a giant are equalized by the possession of fire-arms. Why not, if the machinery of the mind was just a passive sifter by *tabula praesentiae, tabula absentiae*, and *tabula graduum*, once the material is presented in experience? Who does not see here precisely the criticism to which Bacon's logical method has since been subjected, that it neglects the active element in mind, the sagacious bethinking oneself of an hypothesis? Still more impressive is Carlyle's insistence that a moral judgment is psychologically falsified if it is thought of as produced from without rather than from within. A striking passage in *The French Revolution* suggests that whole doctrine of values and valuing which is perhaps the most signal advance in the ethical thought of our own time:

> For ours is a most fictile-world; and man is the most fingent, plastic of creatures. A world not fixable; not fathomable! An unfathomable Somewhat, which is *not we*; which we can work with and live amidst — and mould miraculously in our miraculous being, and name World. But if the very rocks and rivers (as metaphysic teaches) are, in strict language, *made*, by those outward senses of ours, how much more by the inward sense are all phenomena of the spiritual kind; dignities, authorities, holies, unholies! Which inward sense, moreover, is not permanent like the outward ones, but forever growing and changing.[*F.R.*, I,2].

Again, Carlyle's constant polemic against the reduction of morality to a mode of individual feeling — a polemic which to the present writer seems still imperative — has to be understood with special reference to a certain moral degeneracy in the period that was immediately behind him. Diderot's *sensibilite* and *ames nobles*, were not peculiarly French. The moral-sense theorists of England stood in far closer relation than is generally observed — a relation pointed out with great acuteness by Coleridge[In *Aids to Reflection*] — to the moral spirit of their age. It was eighteenth-century sentimentalism that roused Carlyle's abhorrence. There was more than one side to that "enfranchisement of the passions" as Professor Dowden called it. It appeared in the emotionalism of the Wesleyan revival and in the philanthropy of Howard and Wilberforce. But it also appeared in *Tom Jones*, in *Tristrom Shandy*, in *Humphrey Clinker*, in Schiller's *Robbers*. The reaction against Puritanic rigor had produced an apotheosis of impulse. Everything became forgivable to those who "could be touched by a delicate distress." Carlyle saw clearly the ethical upshot of this tone of thinking. He saw that it was of quite subordinate importance whether we believe in Shaftesbury's "taste" or in More's "boniform faculty" or in the utilitarian "maximization of pleasures" or in any other doctrine which interprets the moral contrast as a struggle among various emotions for the dominance of the will. No striking of an average among such data of personal preference could escape the inherent subjectivity. Moreover, he discerned that in the grounding of morals upon objective reason lay the basis for a real metaphysic. Anti-metaphysician as at times he seemed to be, he was teaching metaphysians much of their own business. Into how wretched a state that study had passed in Scotland at the date when *Signs of the Times* appeared, may be judged from the fact that the versatile and vivacious "Christopher North" was judged duly fitted to represent the subject in a chair at Edinburgh. Jeffrey was rejoicing that Dugald Stewart had proved the plain man to be in the right after all, so that metaphysics, now shown to be absurd, might henceforth be neglected. Stewart himself, having tried to read Kant in a Latin version, had given it up in despair, declaring his "utter inability to comprehend the author's meaning." At such a moment it was Carlyle who proclaimed that new era in speculation which every one has now come to acknowledge, who declared that though the old level of ontological discussion had disappeared a new level had revealed itself, and who kept imploring the official representatives of philosophy to acquaint themselves with that vital literature which was coming to them from the Continent. And though his own knwoledge of German thought was somewhat amateurish, it was that of a brilliant amateur, from whom the professionals, by no means brilliant, had much to learn. The critique upon absolutism in *Characteristics* reads like a passage from William James. And *Sartor* is our evidence that for Carlyle the problem of personality had assumed that crucial character upon which no "personal idealist" could desire to improve.

But if Carlyle's strength lay in flashes of intuitive genius rather than in sustained and disciplined thought, a corresponding account must be given of his weakness. Much that he said of the futility of science must be allowed to have been mere wild and whirling words. Spencer hit the nail on the head when he complained that Carlyle spoke incessantly of the "laws of this universe" and our need to reverence them, but at the same time poured contempt on those who were patiently discovering what these laws are.[*Autobiography*] His contempt for logic was its own nemesis, when he laboriously built up a system to prove that systems are impossible. The idea underlying his famous description of metaphysics as disease was, of course, far from new, and in the enforcement of it he seems to have been the dupe of his own vivid rhetoric torturing a very partial analogy. That speculative restlessness is apt to beset an enfeebled will is one of the many morals which have, rightly or wrongly, been discerned in *Hamlet.* Hegel in a paragraph which every one knows by heart had spoken of the owl of Minerva as taking her flight when the shades of night begin to gather. And since Carlyle's time the same point, possibly borrowed from him, has been exuberantly worked by Nietzsche,[In *What I Owe to the Ancients*] when he tells us that only a decadent age will evolve "problems," and that in estimating our debt to the Greek world we should place the virile self-confident Thucydides far higher than the brooding, hair-splitting Plato. The comment which at once suggests itself is that if an age has in one sense lost, it has in another and a better sense immensely gained by becoming aware of its own spiritual incoherence. And when Platio declared *ho anexetastos ou biotos anthripo,* he said what all men like Carlyle would have done well to ponder. It is no doubt tempting to cherish a wistful regret for the perfection of the medieval synthesis between thought and life, although a too romantic spirit is apt to represent this harmony as far deeper than it was. It has been well pointed out that the best English thinkers in each period of the Middle Age itself looked back to some point still earlier as an uncorrupted past, and one may guess that at every such point the retrospect was delusive.[Cf., e.g. G.G. Coulton, *Chaucer and his England*, Chap. I] As George Meredith has remarked about the poetic idealizing of the circle of chivalry, this attitude may perhaps be encouraged for the pleasure of the imagination.58 But even granting that the so-called times of faith were free from our modern restlessness, the inference is not that inquiry is at best an inevitable evil. Many of the things by which it is awakened may be evil, but in itself inquiry is an intrinsic good, and the evils which provoke it would not be less but greater if it were absent. Peace of mind comes either from rising above or from sinking below the problems that would disturb it, and surely Carlyle of all men should have been the last to suggest that the mere happiness of intellectual immaturity or intellectual stupor is not dearly bought. Nor does it seem to be really needful that growing reflection should bring with it an impairment of moral nerve. To take our author's own parallel from medicine, it may be that we should never have evolved physiology if we had not known a break-down in health. But does it follow that the better physiologists we are the more unhealthy we must become?

Again we may regret that the reaction against "profit-and-loss" morality should have made Carlyle so *uncritical* an intuitionist,should have blinded him to the need for forecasting results of action, should have led him into his absurd tirade against the reformatory and deterrent view of penal justice,[In *Latter-Day Phamphlets* ("Model Prisons")] should have prevented him from distinguishing between casuistry that is honest and casuistry that is dishonest. And Julia Wedgwood has well complained that in him the immense portent of Darwinism — the whole transforming movement of thought that had gone so far even while he yet lived — aroused neither enthusiasm nor hostility. For Carlyle evolution was simply as if it had never been. But perhaps his strangest feature of all, one by which some of his other inconsistencies are to be explained, was his lifelong acknowledgment of discipleship to a writer whose creed fundamentally contradicted his own. Few pictures from literary history are more impressive than that of the raw Scottish lad wandering over the moors of Dumfriesshire with his precious copy of *Faust*, and declaring to himself that this poet, almost unknown to Englishmen, had a far wider range and a far fuller note than all the Byrons and Scotts over whom London *salons* had gone mad. It was a case of deep calling unto deep. But once he had taken it upon himself to introduce Goethe to the English-speaking world, Carlyle seems to have forgotten all the obligations of a critic in the zeal of a devotee. A very little of that healthy questioning which he applied, for example, to every work of Diderot or Voltaire would have shown him what a difference there was between the spirit of *Faust* and the spirit of *Sartor*.

Whatever else Goethe may be called, we can in no sense call him a Puritan, yet Puritan was the one single name that fitted Carlyle. That the irreducible contrast of right and wrong should be the basis for a cosmic reconstruction was as far as anything could be from the genteel doctrine of *nil admirari*, the superiority to all enthusiasms, art for art's sake, and impartial hospitality to all experiences in a completely rounded life. Cromwell and Knox should assuredly have felt that they had a strange colleague in Carlyle's gallery of heroes. They would have asked what they had in common with one whose interest was to show that the things they loved and the things they hated were alike essential to the harmony of the Whole, and they would have thought it doubly strange that they should have been placed together by a critic who held that not only truth but the beginning of all truths lay in holy intolerance of the evil by the good. Voltaire's noble stand for Calas was a far better proof of kinship with such company. Yet to Carlyle Voltaire was the prince of *persiflage*! Hero worship surely never misled one's judgment further than when a worshiper could see in Newman and Keble only the hollow phrases of formalism, but thought he heard organ notes of moral regeneration pealing from Weimar.

Section Ten

DARWINISM IN CANADA
W.D. LIGHTHALL
(1857-1954)

10

Darwin Among the Canadian Poets

S.R. MacGillivray

Canadian poets writing in English in the nineteenth century seem never to have felt the need to explore fully in their poetry the effect of the findings of geologists and biologists on traditional religious belief. There is no sign of that exacerbation of spirit turned to poetic account such as one finds in Tennyson's *In Memoriam*, in Browning's *Paracelsus* and in the works of many of the minor figures of British Victorianism. Only rarely is the impact of science even addressed directly. A.D. MacNeill's *Genesis and Evolution,* a thirty-eight stanza poem supportive of Darwin's position, is the exception that proves the rule.[1]

Instead, the Canadian poets seem to have found it possible either to ignore completely the entire issue or to reformulate Darwin's findings in such a way that they could reassert God's providence and design acting behind and through whatever face it had been discovered that nature was wearing. The poetry of Agnes Maule Machar encompasses both positions. "Beyond the Darkness" is entirely typical of the poetry that is seemingly oblivious to the scientific discoveries of the day:

> Earth's Fairest scene — the farewell of the day
> Our eyes still follow sadly — though so soft —
> The Rose and purple hues, commingling soft, —
> So rich — so bright — so swift to pass away!
> But yet we know the darkness will not stay,
> And so, with hopeful hearts we sink to rest,
> And sleep comes gently to the wearied breast,
> Till darkness pass to dawn, and morning gray
> And then to full clear daylight, — so we pray
> To Him who made the darkness and the light, —
> Whom Nature's myriad forces all obey; —
> Grant us the faith to look beyond death's night,
> Teach us *that* darkness, too, shall pass away,
> Help us to look with faith's unerring sight,
> To where, beyond the darkness, there is day!"[2]

It is not that Miss Machar was unaware of what science was pointing to; but even in the poems where she shows her awareness, such as in her three sonnet sequence, "Present Day Sonnets," she proclaims in response to a scientific frame of mind that says "Fact.../ Must be our guide of life from day to day" and "Where science guides us not we may not pass" that "We venture not to sound the depths that hold/A fuller knowledge from the straining eye/Enough that to our hearts *He* makes reply/Who is our faith...."[3] It is possible to hear in the italicized words the determined note that retains in nature and nature's doings the guiding hand of God.

Such poetic sentiments are typical not only of the work of Miss Machar but also of the work of many other writers of the day such as Seranus' (Mrs. J.W.F. Harrison), "Arcturus" (Catherine Stratton Ladd) and a host of others. Their poems found a ready place in the pages of the *Canadian Magazine*, *The Week* and other journals of the day.

Still it is interesting to note that for the most part Canadian poets did acknowledge the impact of science, even if they found it necessary to re-mould scientific discovery according to their own perceptions. Charles Sangster, without doubt the pre-eminent poet prior to Confederation, notes in one of his sonnets, clearly indebted to Tennyson's *In Memoriam*, that:

> - Above where I am sitting, o'er these stones,
> The ocean waves once heaved their mighty forms.[4]

and Mrs. Harrison in "November" notes that:

> These are the days that try us; these the hours
> That find, or leave us cowards — doubters of Heaven,
> Sceptics of self, and riddled through with vain
> Blind questionings as to Deity. Mute, we scan
> The sky, the barren, wan, the drab, dull sky,
> And mark it utterly blank.[5]

Such acknowledgment continued throughout the century.

It may have been easier for Canadian poets to deal with the changed perceptions of nature that were encouraged by contemporary geology and biology than for their British counterparts. From the beginning it was much more difficult for a Canadian poet to be entirely comfortable with nature in the same way as, say, Wordsworth. For him, Nature could be unreservedly "the guide, the guardian of my heart, and soul/Of all my moral being"[6], but for the Canadian poet the experience of the raw primeval forest of the new world provoked Goldsmith's sense of "a wilderness of trees"[7], Burwell's "sylvan gloom" and "dubious maze"[8], and Crawford's "pulseless forest, lock'd and interlock'd/ So closely bough with bough, and leaf with leaf" which "felt no throb/To such soft wooing answer . . ."[9] In the context of a nature which was untamed and seemingly untameable, either in technique or imaginative terms, well might the Canadian poet "pray/For such an eye as Wordsworth's, he who saw/System in Anarchy, progress in ruin, peace/In devastation."[10]

And it was with just such an eye that the best-known figures of the Confederation period did attempt to see their world. Their seeming acceptance of the Darwinian hypothesis was made easier by the formal training that three of the four had received at university. Charles G.D. Roberts, Bliss Carman and Archibald Lampman — the first two at University of New Brunswick and Lampman at Trinity College, Toronto — were all well-trained in the classics, and their poetry is redolent of that "earth-loving Greekish flavour"[11] that so attracted Lampman to Roberts' early work. The problem for these poets was to reconcile their love of the idea of a landscape humanized in imaginative terms, and which may be an expression of the divine, with their personal experience of that same landscape which is not at all humanized and which in response to the piper-poet's lays was very apt to assume the frighteningly indifferent aspect of that nature that responds to the desperate prayer of Charles Heavysege's Jephthah with only:

> . . . the hoarse, bough-bending wind,
> The hill-wolf howling on the neighbouring height,
> And bittern booming in the pool below.[12]

The idea of evolutionary process provided the integrating factor which satisfied both perceptions. On the one hand, evolution from lower to higher forms suggested an on-going process that was under the direction of some mysterious power, providing a sense of purposefulness in and unity to life. On the other hand, the process in its particular manifestations necessarily involved the pain, separation, death and seeming indifference that were part of the poet's perceptions and experiences of natural phenomena. In the idea of evolutionary process integrating the idealism of significance and purpose and the experiential actuality of isolation and death, the Canadian poet found a ready-made structural device for the poetry. There was therefore no need to debate or otherwise discuss the idea of evolution. Instead, the poet could immediately address the questions of spiritual significance and meaning, making the evolutionary idea an implicit part of the work.

Evolution's insistence on the physical relationship between lower and higher orders allowed the poet to recognize himself as a kind of latter day Antaeus, drawing strength and sustenance from mother earth. Many of the poems of Charles G.D. Roberts emphasize the restorative effect of mother earth on a human race that has somehow lost, become separated or even alienated from, the primary values of simplicity, truth and meaningful relationship:

> O Land wherein my memories abide,
> I have come back that you might make me tranquil,
> Resting a little at your heart of peace,
> Remembering much amid your serious leisure,
> Forgetting more amid your large release.[13]

The poet knows that he can turn to the earth mother because:

> ... through the common grass
> Our atoms mix and pass.
> We feel the sap go free.
> When spring comes to the tree,
> And in our blood is stirred
> What warms the brooding bird.
> The vital fire we breathe
> That bud and blade bequeathe,
> And strength of native clay
> In our full veins hath sway.[14]

and:

> Rocks, I am one with you;
> Sea, I am yours.
> Your rages come and go,
> Your strength endures.
>
> Fir-tree, beaten by the wind,
> Sombre, austere,
> Your sap is in my veins,
> O kinsman dear.
>
> Your fibres rude and true
> My sinews feed —
> Sprung of the same bleak earth
> The same rough seed.
>
> O rocks, O fir-tree brave,
> O grass and sea!
> Your strength is mine, and you
> Endure with me.[15]

The whole of the evolutionary process and Roberts' part in it expressed in the confident rhythms of "As Down the Woodland Ways," of which the following stanzas may be taken as typical:

> As down the woodland ways I went
> With every wind asleep
> I felt the surge of endless life
> About my footsteps creep.
>
> I felt the surge of quickening mould
> That once had been a flower
> Mount with the sap to bloom again
> At its appointed hour.
>
> Through weed and world, through worm and star,
> The sequence ran the same —
> Death but the travail-pang of life,
> Destruction but a name[16]

It is difficult to discover from Roberts' poetry any consistently developed idea of the means by which man arises from the same creative life force that links him to natural phenomena on the one hand and yet has him aspiring to a place beyond the stars on the other. But it is clear that his perception of man is that of a creature who must acknowledge the claims of physical relationship with the world he inhabits and through this acknowledgment reach towards his spiritual self. In an essay for the *Manitoba Free Press* Roberts, in discussing his religious convictions, declares his belief in the immanence of the divine and dismisses any religion that "cannot face, accept and assimilate all material facts which science has revealed, or may conceivably reveal." He goes on to declare that "the spirit of man is a spark, an emanation of the Deity" and writes of what he considers to be a fact of human existence, "spiritual evolution." For Roberts, it is almost a given that man's evolution is both physical and spiritual, so that what begins physically is continued spiritually through what he calls "planes of perfection." Such a view of life is clearly predicated on "happiness in aspiration, in growth rather than in the ripeness of completion, and would fain mount, and that hardly, to eternal life." "[T]his theory of spiritual evolution," he suggests, "seems to me to afford a most stimulating outlook."[17]

Bliss Carman, Roberts' cousin, is also responsible for a number of poems that emphasize the restorative powers of a renewed and renewing relationship with nature. The best known of such poems is "Spring Song" ("Make me over, Mother April"). But Carman is also the poet from this period whose interest in evolutionary thought can be most fully identified.[18] "Pulvis et Umbra" is just the most frequently cited poem from the number that Carman wrote in the late eighties and early nineties testifying to his interest in the evolutionary idea. In the earthly life man may live a life characterized by pain, separation and shadow, but it is still possible to "crush the clearer honey/In the harvest of the years" and eventually to emerge into the light of a greater truth:

> For man walks the world in twilight,
> But the morn shall wipe all trace
> Of the dust from off his forehead,
> And the shadow from his face.[19]

Like Roberts, Carman recognized the divine in nature and man. For him, too, spiritual nature is part of a World-Soul itself evolving toward perfection. Writing of man, Carman notes that:

> He shall be born a spirit,
> Part of the soul that yearns,
> The core of vital gladness
> That suffers and discerns,
> The stir that breaks the budding sheath
> When the green spring returns, —

> He shall be born to reason,
> And have the primal need
> To understand and follow
> Wherever truth may lead, —
> To grow in wisdom like a tree
> Unfolding from a seed.
>
> For he must prove all being
> Sane, beauteous, benign,
> And at the heart of nature
> Discover the divine, —
> Himself the type and symbol
> Of the eternal trine.
>
> An out of primal instinct,
> The lore of lair and den,
> He shall emerge to question
> Who, wherefore, whence and when,
> Till the last frontier of truth
> Shall lie within his ken.

Eventually man shall be:

> A creature fit to carry
> The pure creative fire,
> Whatever truth inform him,
> Whatever good inspire,
> He shall make lovely in all things
> To the end of his desire.[20]

Archibald Lampman in a number of his poems shares Roberts' essentially Meredithean view of nature and of the need to align blood, brain and spirit with nature's ways. For it is only in this primal relationship that man most truly becomes himself and able to see, in the Wordsworthian phrase, "into the life of things." In the final stanza of "comfort of the Fields" the poet comments:

> Far violet hills, horizons filled with showers,
>   The murmur of cool streams, the forest's gloom.
>   The voices of the breathing grass, the hum
> Of ancient gardens overbanked with flowers:
> Thus, with a smile as golden as the dawn,
>   And fair cool fingers radiantly divine,
>   The mighty mother brings us in her hand,
> For all tired eyes and foreheads pinched and wan,
> Her restful cup, her beaker of bright wine:
>   Drink, and be filled, and ye shall understand![21]

Eventually, what begins in a symbiotic relationship with earth becomes a transcendent vision of reality which informs all of life with meaning because as the final few lines of "Outlook" suggest:

> . . . there shall come
> Many great voices from life's outer sea,
> Hours of strange triumph, and, when few men heed,
> Murmurs and glimpses of eternity.[22]

This higher consciousness of the essential unity of life is also seen in such well-known poems as "In November" and "Heat."

In his vision of an evolutionary principle which involves the gradual realization of a higher consciousness in this life, Duncan Campbell Scott is closest to Lampman. Yet in his recognition of the possible continued evolution of the soul in the afterlife Scott is much closer to Roberts. Poems such as "Improvisation on an Old Song," *The Height of Land* and *Lines in Memory of Edmund Morris* suggest not only the "*Going, going, all the glory growing*" ("Improvisation") but also the emergence into a new consciousness of being. The possibility of such a new consciousness is developed as a series of rhetorical questions in *The Height of Land*:

> How often in the autumn of the world
> Shall the crystal shrine of dawning be rebuilt
> With deeper meaning! Shall the poet then,
> Wrapped in his mantle on the height of land,
> Brood on the welter of the lives of men
> And dream on his ideal hope and promise
> In the blush sunrise? Shall he base his flight
> Upon a more compelling law than Love
> As Life's atonement; shall the vision
> Of noble deed and noble thought immingled
> Seem as uncouth to him as the pictograph
> Scratched on the caveside by the cave-dweller
> To us of the Christ-time? Shall he stand
> With deeper joy, with more complex emotion,
> In closer commune with divinity,
> With the deep fathomed, with the firmament charted,
> With life as simple as a sheep-boy's song,
> What lies beyond a romaunt that was read
> Once on a morn of storm and laid aside
> Memorious with strange immortal memories?[23]

In a lyrical commentary in *Lines In Memory of Edmund Morris*, the rhetorical questions posed in *The Height of Land* are answered. Man stands at the threshold of a new beginning, a beginning which in turn will lead to other new beginnings, an endless succession ever onward, ever upward.

> We of the sunrise
> Joined in the breast of God, feel deeper the power
> That urges all things onward, not to an end,
> But in an endless flow, mounting and mounting,
> Claiming not overmuch for human life,
> Sharing with our brothers of nerve and leaf
> The urgence of the one creative breath, —

All in the dim twilight—say of morning,
Where the florescence of the light and dew
Haloes and hallows with a crown adorning
The brows of life with love; herein the clue,
The love of life—yea, and the peerless love
Of things not seen, that leads the least of things
To cherish the green sprout, the hardening seed;
Here leans all nature with vast Mother-love,
Above all the cradled future with a smile.
Why are there tears for failure, or sighs for weakness,
While life's rhythm beats on? Where is the rule
To measure the distance we have circled and clomb?
Catch up the sands of the sea and count and count
The failures hidden in our sea of conquest.
Persistence is the master of this life;
The master of these little lives of ours;
To the end—effort—even beyond the end.[24]

It is clear that the major figures have in their poetry attempted to re-cast their perceptions of the significance of human life in the light of the advances in science. More particularly, they have accepted what they saw as the Darwinian thesis about the evolution of physical being, and to that they extended the notion to include the evolutionary principle as the operative mode in the development of the soul. In some cases (notably Carman and Scott's) man's development is toward the governing spiritual principle of the universe; in others (notably Roberts and in some of Lampman's poems), the development is toward identification with the Godhead itself. In his sonnet "In the Wide Awe and Wisdom of the Night" Roberts concludes his search for ultimate reality and discovers:

At last I came before him face-to-face —
And knew the Universe of no such span
As the august infinitude of Man.[25]

And in the third sonnet of the three bearing the title "The largest Life," Lampman, in identifying a growing beauty "at the goal of life," suggests that we must:

. . . address our spirits to the height,
And so attune them to the valiant whole,
That the great light be greater for our light,
And the great soul the stronger for our soul:
To have done this is to have lived . . .[26]

A number of the minor poets of the day also dealt with the implications of the advance of science. Among those who might be noted are Robert Norwood ("After the Order of Melchisedec," "A Song of Evolution")[27], Frederick George Scott ("A Dream of the Prehistoric," "A Song of Triumph," "Natura Victrix")[28] and A.M. Stephen, whose poem "Superman" traces the evolution of man "Up through these forms of clay" by means of beauty and love until such time as "The World is flesh and all of heaven glows/ Within the crucible of earthly form" and "We are as gods!"[29]

Whatever the nature of the relationship between man and the ultimate reality, it is clear that the poets of the day used the Darwinian hypothesis for their own poetic purposes. And, as Lionel Stevenson points out, there are two principal issues: first, there is the clear perception that evolution is a process that, however seemingly erratic, is directed by some power—God, World-Soul— and in this context the acts of human life and the phases through which life proceeds have significance and meaning; second, the evolutionary process is an on-going one which is not complete and which may continue after physical death.[30] What emerges from this for the Canadian poet is the placing of man in the context of a continuing spiritual importance which, at the same time, acknowledges the contributions of modern science. More specifically, the Canadian poet could continue to celebrate the spiritual significance of nature as an expression of the divine while he could also acknowledge the experiential reality of nature's seeming indifference or even cruelty.

It would be misleading, however, to suggest that the various poets, some of whose works have been cited here, had a fully articulated system of beliefs. They all, in varying degrees, certainly used the Darwinian hypothesis as a structural principle in their poems, but this is far from suggesting on the part of any one poet a philosophical system or even a set of consistent beliefs contained in the poetry. W.J. Keith has pointed out the problems in dealing with Roberts in this regard[31], and examples might well be multiplited from the list of the others. There was a literary figure, however, who did attempt a synthesis of the ideas of the day and that was W.D. Lighthall.

William Douw Lighthall was born in Hamilton, Canada West, in 1857, but he was educated in Montreal at the montreal hight School and McGill University (B.A. 1879; B.C.L. 1881; M.A. 1885), and is most fully identified as a prominent member of various circles social, literary and legal of that city. He was a mayor of Westmount (1900-03), a member of the Royal Society of Canada from 1905 (he served as its president, 1918), served on various other municipal bodies, and was a practising lawyer. His claim to the attention of Canadian *litterateurs* rest principally on his anthology of Canadian poetry, *Songs of the Great Dominion*, published in 1889. But Lighthall was also responsible for three novels (*The Young Seigneur; or, Nation Making* 1888; *The False Chevalier; or, the Lifeguard of Marie Antoinette*, 1898; *The Master of Life: A Romance of the Five Nations and Prehistoric Montreal*, 1908), two historical sketches of Montreal (*Montreal After 250 Years*, 1892; *A New Hochelaga Burying-Ground Discovered at Westmount Spur of Mount Royal, Montreal, July-September 1898*, 1898), a guide book (*Sights and Shrines of Montreal: A Guide Book For Stranger and A Handbook for all Lovers of Historic Spots and Incidents*, 1907), a book of poetry (*Old Measures: Collected Verse*, 1922) and a number of literary essays such as that which introduces his anthology of Canadian poetry.[32] Lighthall was also deeply interested in tring to reconcile new ideas and a new outlook with more conventional systems of thought. To this end, he wrote a series of essays, principally for *The Philosophic Review*, beginning in 1884. The end result of his efforts was *The Person of Evolution,* the definitive edition of which was published in 1933.[3]

In *The Person of Evolution* Lighthall outlines his beliefs about the existence of a superpersonality which is transcendent and which provides the only reasonable explanation for the innate recognition of humans about which is moral and what is not. In effect, for Lighthall:

> Morality consists in the trancendence of the individual viewpoint and in the acceptance of the proposition that the only acceptable motive for such a transcendence would be provided by knowledge of the fact that our surface individuality is only a feature of a larger personality.[34]

All aspects of the phenomenal world, including human consciousness, are self-expressive actions of the "superperson". But the superperson has to proceed by means of trial and error in an evolutionary way. This necessarily means that while there will be aspects of being that are beautiful and good, there will be other aspects that are necessarily ugly, painful and bad. In the over-view of human existence that is afforded by Lighthall's beliefs, the world is essentially good and is getting better. Lighthall's idealism is in his view supported by the discoveries of 19th century science, and there is little doubt that he would have agreed with the position taken by Roberts that whatever the thrust of human belief, science and science's truths have to be accommodated.

Whatever the merits of Lighthall's views as philosophic construct, his attempt to use the findings of science and reconcile these with his own idealism is not only consistent with his own poetic practice: it also might well serve as a rationale for what is present, in varying degrees, in the poetry of his contemporaries. They, too, show the attempt to reconcile intuitive feeling and scientific fact in the crucible of personal experience. They, too, seem to accept a sense of evolutionary progress. They, too, are demonstrably heterdox in their nominal Christian belief.[35] It is not too much, then, too suggest that Lighthall is a quite typical literary figure of his period in trying to reconcile the old and the new modes of perception. As a spokesman for his generation, he has the advantage for the reader in that he has more clearly than most tried to set forth his beliefs for our consideration.

Notes

1. *Literary History of Canada,* 3 vols., ed., Carl F. Klinck (Toronto: University of Toronto Press, 1976), 1, p. 122.

2. Agnes Maule Machar, *Lays of the True North* (Toronto: Copp, Clark, 1902), p. 203.

3. IBID., p. 196.

4. Charles Sangster, *The St. Lawrence and the Saguenay and Other Poems; Hesperus and Other Poems* (Toronto: University of Toronto Press, 1972), p. 169

5. S. Frances Harrison (Seranus), *Pine, Rose and Fleur de Lis* (Toronto: Hart and Company, 1891), p. 137.

6. *Lines Composed a Few Miles Above Tintern Abbey*

7. Oliver Goldsmith, *The Rising Village in Canadian Anthology*, eds. Carl Klinck and R.E. Watters (Toronto: Gage Publishing, 1976), p. 24.

8. IBID., p. 16.

9. IBID., pp. 83-4.

10. Harrison, p. 138.

11. Archibald Lampman, "Two Canadian Poets," in *Masks of Poetry*, ed. A.J.M. Smith (Toronto: McClelland and Stewart, 1962), p. 30.

12. *Canadian Anthology*, p. 76.

13. "At Tide Water" in *Selected Poetry and Critical Prose of Charles G. D. Roberts*, ed. W.J. Keith (Toronto: University of Toronto Press, 1974), p. 152.

14. "Origins" in *Canadian Anthology*, pp. 105-6.

15. "The Native" in *Selected Poetry and Critical Prose of Charles G.D. Roberts*; pp. 176-77

16. *Canadian Anthology*, pp. 106-7

17. Charles G.D. Roberts, "My Religion," *Manitoba Free Press*, Saturday, June 5, 1926, p. 27.

18. John Robert Sorfleet, "Transcendentalist, Mystic, Evolutionary Idealist: Bliss Carman, 1886-1894," in *Colony and Confederation*, ed. George Woodcock (Vancouver: University of British Columbia Press, 1974), pp. 189-209.

19. "Pulvis et Umbra" in *The Poems of Bliss Carman*, ed. John Robert Sorfleet (Toronto: McClelland and Stewart, 1976), p. 150

20. "At the Making of Man" in *The Poemes of Bliss Carman*, pp. 110-113.

21. *The Poems of Archibald Lampman*, ed. Margaret C Whitridge (Toronto: University of Toronto Press, 1974), p. 150.

22. IBID., p. 108.

23. Duncan Campbell Scott, *Lundy's Lane and Other Poems* (Toronto: McClelland, Goodchild and Stewart, 1916), pp. 75-76.

24. IBID., pp. 189-90.

25. *Canadian Anthology*, p. 103.

26. *The Poems of Archibald Lampman*, p. 301.

27. Robert Norwood, *The Piper and the Reed* (New York: George H. Doran Company, 1917).

28. Frederick George Scott, *Poems: Old and New* (Toronto: William Briggs, 1900); *Frederick George Scott: Collected Poems* (Vancouver: Clarke and Stuart Co., Limited, 1934).

29. A.M. Stephen, *The Rosary of Pan* (Toronto: McClelland and Stewart, 1923), pp. 67-8.

30. Lionel Stevenson, *Appraisals of Canadian Literature* (Toronto: Macmillan, 1926; rpt. The Folcroft Press, 1970), p. 95.

31. W.J. Keith, "A Choice of Worlds: God, Man and Nature in Charles G.D. Roberts," in *Colony and Confederation*, pp. 87-102.

32. "Lighthall, William Douw (1857-1954)," *Oxford Companion to Canadian History and Literature*, ed. Norah Story (Toronto: Oxford Press, 1967); *Oxford Companion to Canadian Literature*, ed. William Toye (Toronto: Oxford Press, 1983).

33. Leslie Armour and Elizabeth Trott, *The Faces of Reason: An Essay on Philosophy and Culture in English Canada, 1850-1950* (Waterloo, Ontario: Wifrid Laurier University Press, 1981), pp. 380-81.

34. IBID., p. 381.

35. See for example Barrie Davies; "Lampman and Religion," in *Colony and Confederation*, pp. 103-123.

The Person of Evolution

William Douw Lighthall

[The following is taken from chapter III in which Lighthall discusses the nature of the superperson (God). Lighthall's book contains 249 numbered sections. His numbers are reproduced here.]

[45]Being therefore forced to dismiss all forms of the view that the evolution of human consciousness, with its affective character, is arrived at by simple gradual integration; and consequently having accepted the alternative theory of a conscious purposer adequate to the ends obtained, the next query is: What is the conduct of that purposer?

[46]We may now propose for this purpose still a further name — *the Person of Evolution.*

Let us sketch out its history since the appearance of life, as we know it, on this globe. Wherever, in the course of its development into the line of living forms, we recognize the presence of consciousness, its every action presents the characteristics of a movement towards some objective (such as food) which *follows the joy-and pain law.* This parallelism of objective movement with subjective feeling constitutes the universal type of living action and is the universal type of willing. All living action is willing, and all is by nature purposive. All other apparent purposed, however complicated and by whatever terms called, are in the final resort but forms of this typical act. Results show that the point of view of the Person of Evolution and not that of the individual, is that alone from which our *higher* purpose can be understood. For the living acts and purposes which the latter imply are acts of our larger life: and in them the impulses of many individuals outside of us, and of many individuals within us, are correlated. It is a special work of the Person of Evolution to correlate them and thus arouse in us "our best instincts" — those from the viewpoint of its wider sentiency.

*First published by Macmillian, Toronto, 1933. Selections by S.R. MacGillivray.

[47]In the lowest forms of protoplasm, the evolutionary Person, brillant and purposive, strove against difficulties of material. Its aim was to work out such a mechanism as would permit in the end the attainment of perfect joy. Bare structure, bare permanence, bare order, bare intellect, bare perception, had no value to it apart from affective feeling. According to our theory, it found in the ocean the components of that highly complex, unstable material, — protein, — which responded flexibly to its power of shaping the motions of matter, — a power that the internal nature of which transcends our cognition. In that material, while it was still unorganized, the Person of Evolution was able to find and shape forms accompanied by a diffused, imperfect pleasure. **Its method was trial and error. It tried all the various protoplasmic** combinations as they occurred, and elected to continuance those that proved the best instuments of joy. Progressively it ultimatelly attained structures fit for a certain permanence of joy. These were the *organisms*, those electromagnetic machines automatically repairing destructions and giving easy courses to the ertrant energy. Later, and doubtless long (but still calculable) ages after the deposit of our oceans and their oozes, the Person of Evolution acheived the amoeboid forms, "active lumps of jelly," in which the elementary consciousness and typical acts of willing are now recognized, and which, by devision, it sustained in that degree of permanent organization which we call *reproduction*, thus perpetuating and immensely increasing the desired forms. It acheived all these results slowly, not because blindly, but restricted by time and the intractability of matter. The nature of that intractability doubtless also transcends our cognition. So, in process of time, the Person indefatiguably achieved all the evolution of animate consciousness **— as well as all the vast variety and processions of form of matter with which its phenomena are associated. The history of its progress is written in** palaeontology and comparative biology. From the throwing out of the simplest and faintest forms of low consciousness and the gradual shaping of them through successive adaptations of nervous systems and brains up to the prsesently developed apparatus of man, they are all products of its one persistent series of purposed acts, modelled on the same principle as the typical act of willing, and correlated together by the living viewpoint of the Outer Consciousness.

In the scale of living beings known to us biologically, each includes in its mental makeup of all its ancestors, Those ancestors still actually alive within us, according to the principle of "biological immortality" whereby each of them has simply divided himself and passed on his divisions (except the sarcoplasm) alive to his decendants, with all the hidden memories and influences of the ancestral history. In that respect each of us is many hundreds of millions of years old. We never escape the influence of the primeval, the far distant, the universal, and of relation to everthing.

[48]To the Person of Evoultion the individual is an organ, a member of its community body, a kind of cell of its multicellular whole. It sees all and feels for and in each, but with wider vision. To it there is, in a sense, no such thing as a subordinate individual; all are one creature: the whole process of subdivison has never obliterated that unity nor dissolved the connection between each part. The disconnection of individuals is an illusion. *There is no such thing as a fully disconnected individual.* The visioned purpose of the Person of Evolution has been from the beginning a clear idea of perfect and continuing universal joy. As the Outer Will, it guides the amoeba in its attraction to food, and in its reproduction by self division, the ant and the bee in all their cooperative community behaviour, it beckons the eel from its mysterious birthplace in the darkest deep of the Sargasso Sea, leads it in infancy across to the rivers of Europe, and in after years back again, with the strange sacrifice of its males; it directs the bear, the deer and the wolf in the wisdom of the wilds and the love of their young; it calls the buffalo bull to die for the herd, teaches the beaver how to fell trees and build dams and family dwellings, constructs their bodies **as wonderfully as their minds, their communiyies as wonderfully as their** bodies, and, effecting these ends still more marvellously in men, urges them also to the complex endeavours of civilization and culture, to the pelfless call of the patriot, to the scientists' passion of truth, and to the apparent self-destruction of the martyr. None of these urges can be understood from the point of view of the individual: but they can be understood from that of one community being.

It was the Person of Evolution who invented the human eye, after devising and relegating to one side the various rudimentary and compound eyes and those of crabs, fishes, and birds. It was it also which purposed the human cerebrum, after building up the nervous system of the invertebrates, the spinal ganglia, the medulla oblongata, the cerebellum and the smaller cerebra of the dogs and Simians. It originated all communities, the matings amd passion of all pairs, the inter-working of all bodily cells, the complicated operations and instincts of insects, the customs of the herd, the pack and the family, the loyalties of the tribe, the nation, the empire and humanity. Reason itself proceeds from it, with all that Reason brings to us, and all it will bring. Reason is but the consciousness of wholes, and their implications, — the Outer Consciousness — human reason is that consciousness imperfectly present in us.

[49]Here we must again at the risk of too much repetition, emphasize the significance of the affective. The outstanding mark of the power of the Person of Evolution is not the ingenuity of its forms, but the successes which it has achieved through them in advancing the diffusion and permanence of joy. From time to time it abandons and obliterates the forms.

[50]Pessimistic criticism has constantly pointed to its failures and imperfections. These have been many and the Pessimists do well to cause

them to be discussed. But there are two great answers to pessimism. One is that the essence of the act of will is at least a power in some degree to escape evil and purse joy: it is not a complete helplessness. The other is that, through the continuing form of this power, progress is actually attained.

Pessimists cite new pains that arise at every stage of advancement towards apparent happiness. But they overlook, among other things, the achievements of the Person of Evolution in anaesthetic devices. Among these devices to combat pain are the low sensibility, and even insensibility, to pain of the lower animal forms.; their absence of imagination and prevision; their great automatism; animal fatalism; coma preceding death; collapse; the quickness of their death.

In both men and animals, death in itself is the great anaesthetic. And to the Outer consciousness death is but an incident, not an end. Sleep in its various forms, is, next to death, the most universal anaesthetic. In intellectual man, however, the supreme anaesthetics can be hope and faith. The joys of these, such as that of the mother in childbirth, coalescing in the common clearing-house of the feelings, are able to conquer and neutralize the severest pains. Even philosophy can do much; but not so much as the "consolations of religion," where the highest hopes of faith are the instinctive promises of the Person of Evolution.

[51]For pains ordinarily consist of two parts: — the original, and its representation, the latter of which is often the only suffering. Habit, reason, courage, fatalism, suggestion and autosuggestion, are anaesthetic. We can neutralize most of our ills if we but organize the anaethetics. Nor must we omit the arts and material of medicine and surgery.

[52]**In fine, judging by the advances continually made, we may legitimately** hope to entirely covercome pain in the due course of Progress, which is itself the law of Evolution. In the "economy of Nature," the Person has often followed courses which to us sometimes seem open to imputations of ignorance, blindness, or subhuman helplesness and are often made grounds for blame. Why did it not proceed directly and immediately to its aim? Why the lower and imperfect forms of living things? Why the vast losses and **extinctions of the less fit? Why the horrible carnages? Why, if it were so** conscious from the beginning, of the ends in view, did it not construct men and supermen at once, without passing through the experiments and the failures of so many ages? Is not the reason *because it could not*, because, like us, it was striving, exploring, pushing its way from step to step through the **maze of elusive and intractable matter, both protoplasmic and azoic? Finding** its way and assuring its footing from physical combination to combination. This at least terrestrially, was simply its nature, as we see it. Also did it not have at least this partial justification, that it left orders, genera, species and varieties suited to countless habitats to which beings like man could not be adapted, and which provided it with innumerable organs of consciousness in what to us are inaccessible places. The lives of these in their several regions are

all, like the gambolling water snake in "The Ancient Mariner." those of creatures of joy. **In themselves of small account as individuals, their** function is immense throug the Person of Life.

[53]As the mental outlook of the developed man is the chief key we have to the interpretation of its outlook let us try to imagine what would happen if the man's consciousness were widened to its sphere. In such a situation the man would experience a vast inclusive consciousness, highly organized and extended, while at the same time concentrated in a most brillant centre, mobile and sleepless. There is a problem, however, which shows that some imperfectior exists in the simultaneity either of its observations or of its ability to follow up. It is the problem why different minds differ so radically as they do both in instincts and in their application? Why should it inspire the prophets of Israel to denounce the offering of childern to Moloch, and *at the same time* the priests and devotees of Moloch to thrust the infants into the flames on the knees of the frightful idol of Tyre and Carthage, — the horror of the ancient world? Its process of behaviour is evidently not one of *simultaneity* at all points. Sometimes it even has backwaters of apparent degeneracy to be explained. Its flood of Progress is uneven. Has it not many centres of Attention? and how is it that these are so slowly coordinated? A least however the devotees of Moloch were misled. They thought they were following holy voices. Perhaps the general explanation may be that it is the connections from the lesser beings to the greater that are imperfect in such cases. Those who obey the urge to listen to the holy voices will ultimately hear them. Imperfection is an inevitable stage in progress.

[54]Under whatever conditions, nevertheless, of time and imperfection its consciousness appears to operate through a mighty system of mechanism, of which all living beings are organs. The past of all living beings would be present to it in memory more or less coordinated. The future would not be as clear to it as the past; but its progressing grasp of all the workings of the universe would bring before it an imaginative insight of the future beyond human power to picture. In each living being, such as man, it would see laid bare all the inner life, and would appreciate and judge the feelings, relations and rights of each, and arrange their harmony.

[55]We have not the means of perfectly understanding its field of knowledge and purpose in the universe beyond that of proto-plasmic beings. To attempt to do so is but speculation, though natural and having value. Not only would it possess the intimate knowledge and vision described, but the urge and power to act according to them. From this knowledge, do not some glimpses reach the individual man in such forms as flashes of genius and promptings of **the Inner Light? And at least from its will, come such messages to the man as** impulses to public service and patriotic and religious martyrdom, as well as all his instinctive promptings.

[56]To the Outer Consciousness, some of the problems of philosophy would appear in new lights. No longer would Freewill and Necessity seem to conflict, as they do from man's standpoint, for man's necessity would be his own deeper will. No longer would the principle of "instinct" require to be profoundly differentiated from "reason", nor real "faith" from either. "Practical reason," the "moral intuition" would be explicable as "instincts" from the point of view of the hyperpsyche, *i.e.* of the many not the individual. No longer would there exist any conflict between "moral sense" theories and those of altruistic joy-and-pain. Selfish and antisocial pleasures would be outweighed by the overwhelming co-ordinated joy of the larger mechanism. The poor attempts of the old Utilitarians to explain the action of the altruistic instinct by "attendant satisfactions," "sanctions," "the pleasures of sympathy," "admiration," and so forth, would have no raison d'etre. That great philosopher and tremendous saint, Jesus, who said, "he that saveth his life shall lose it," was also the profoundest psychologist.

Section Eleven

Canadian Responses to Darwinism
J.W. Dawson (1820-1894)
Daniel Wilson (1818-1892)
W.D. Le Sueur (1840-1917)

11

Canadian Responses to Darwinism

Thomas Mathien and J.T.Stevenson

It is now a commmonplace that a number of intellectual developments which occurred during the middle years of the nineteenth century had a major, even traumatic impact on the views of the educated English speaking public. One major event was the development of a revolutionary approach to the study of biblical texts utilizing comparative readings, historical linguistic studies and the search for archaeological evidence. This movement, larded with assumptions about history derived from German philosophy and scholarship, gained significant attention with the 1848 translation by George Eliot of David Friedrich Strauss' *Das Leben Jesu* (1st ed., Tubingen, 1835-6) and had spread even into respectable church and university circles with the publication of *Essays and Reviews* (1860).[1]

The impact of higher criticism on established religion and philosophy was paralleled and reinforced by a cluster of advances in the natural sciences. The extensive geological investigations of the first half of the century persuaded many investigators that the earth was of much greater antiquity than was consistent with standard interpretations of the Biblical account of creation.[2] An increasing emphasis on the uniformitarian hypothesis, the exceptionless application of natural law, which was sometimes used in the natural theology of the day as an evidence of God's capacity as a designer, led to skepticism about miracles and about the efficacy of prayer.[3] Together these ideas induced a skepticism about great ancient catastrophes that could be regarded as a sign of special divine intervention in the planet's history.

Even more disruptive to received views, however, was the proposal in 1859 by Darwin and Wallace of the theory of the origin of species by variation and natural selection. This theory was made current by the widely-circulated *On the Origin of the Species by Natural Selection* (1859) and incorporated both the uniformitarian hypothesis and the results of the geological work of the period. This work was extended by the *Descent of Man* (1870) to offer an account even of human moral and intellectual capacities that made no appeal to an act of special creation. The Darwinian principle of natural selection —with its suggestion of unplanned variation, of competition rather than harmony in environmental niches, of the absence of fixed boundaries between species — stimulated a great confrontation between common religious beliefs, the metaphysical doctrines associated with them and the theoretical claims of many scientists.

This confrontation had its polemical side but was by no means always a direct argument between religious doctrine and established science. Many scientists were believers, and Darwin's views were far from securely established. Some reviewers were content to point out genuine or supposed deficiencies in the evidential bases for the theory of natural selection without arguing about the religious implications of the theory.[4] Others, of course, were not.

The disputes about evidence may be divided into two types: substantive disputes about whether the theory was consistent with and could explain known facts, and methodological disputes about the theory of inductive evidence and the nature of the explanation.[5]

Let us cite two examples of the former. The theory implied, or seemed to imply, continuous development. The fossil record, on the other hand, displayed discontinuity: in many cases where intermediate forms were sought, none could be found.[6] Darwin and his immediate followers also could not connect variation and descent in such a way as to account for the preservation and accumulation of variations from generation to generation in the face of many well-known examples of reversion to type.[7]

On the methodological side, there were doubts about the use of indirect evidence without supporting direct evidence, about the appeal to unobservable events or occult properties, and about the use of statistical observation. These doubts were buttressed by standard doctrines of the day about scientific method. Since there was no direct evidence of the development of new species from old, only indirect — and it was thought insufficient — evidence could be adduced for Darwin's theory.[8] Yet other theories, including Darwin's own theory of the origin of coral reefs, that relied on their ability to account for a wide variety of phenomena but that lacked direct support for many of their features, escaped this sort of criticism. The claim that the Darwinian approach to natural history involved occult qualities and unobservable events could, with equal justice, be directed against accepted scientific disciplines such as Newtonian mechanics.[9] The principal explanatory advantage of Darwin's theory, its ability to present a unified explanation of a wide variety of phenomena without requiring supernatural intervention, was only occasionally noted and not much appreciated.[10] The statistical nature of the explanations offered by the theory was also seldom thoroughly understood.[11]

The initial response of many English-Canadian intellectuals to Darwin was very much like that of the conservative scientists and thinkers elsewhere.

Sir John William Dawson (b.Pictou, N.S., 1820; d.Montreal, 1899) is one good example of this reaction. A Scottish trained geologist, collaborator with Lyell, and Principal of McGill College after 1855, he accepted the extreme antiquity of the earth but attempted to reconcile it with Christian doctrine by treating Genesis references to "days" as references to epochs and by arguing for special creations and mass extinctions at the beginnings and ends of these geological epochs.[12]

His review of Darwin's *Origin* appeared in the *Canadian Naturalist*, a periodical closely associated with him and with the Natural History Society of Montreal, in 1860.

Some of its criticisms are substantive. Darwin, it is claimed, has not dealt sufficiently well with the geographical distribution of existing species, with the discontinuities of the historical record, and with the problem of reversion to original type of many of the offspring of many variants. He does not deal adequately with the differences in the tendencies of species to produce variants, and neglects the fact that whereas most domestic species of animals and plants show a great readiness to vary this is not so in the vast majority of wild species. He has also neglected the role which cropping predators play in the health and success of prey populations in many ecological niches. Dawson admits that extinctions occur in situations where variation is limited, but seems to think that Darwin is committed to a more or less constant rate of variation (and of adaptive variation) in all species. Dawson, on the other hand, suspects that the rate of variation within a species can change over time and in direct response to environment.

Other of Dawson's objections are more methodological. They include the standard one about leaping beyond what the evidence justifies (and hence "into an unknown and fathomless abyss"), and the claim that an improper analogy has been drawn between the origin of varieties within a species and the origin of new species. He takes a firm position that specific distinctions require differences in instinct, constitution, habits and the like; that generic distinctions require "structural" differences; and that specific differences imply the sterility of any cross-specific hybrids, while cross-varietal offspring are generally fertile. In addition — and this is connected by Dawson with the tendency of species to revert to type — it is claimed that there is a specific force in each species which tends to eliminate variations regarded as acquired and "unnatural." Perhaps because of his belief in such a force, Dawson makes no complaints about appeals to occult qualities.

The introductory and concluding sections of Dawson's review give some indication of underlying religious concerns. He is at some pains to underline the limitations in knowledge which the scientist must accept. Science must remain humble in the face of the mysteries that surround it. These mysteries stimulate investigation, but, as new knowledge removes some of them, others appear. The origin of species is one such mystery. By threatening what Dawson regards as fundamental principles of classification, Darwin's theory undermines its own evidential foundation.[13] Appeal to special creation of each species allows free investigation of them: their succession in time and distribution in space, their safeguards against extinction, and their limitations as regards variation. Dawson is proposing a science restricted by mysteries and dependent on awareness of divine intervention for the certainties that it does provide. For him, science is not only consistent with revealed truth, it depends on some of these truths for its success.

Sir Daniel Wilson (b. Edinburgh, 1816; d. Toronto, 1892), longtime professor of history and of English literature at the University of Toronto as well as an early student of pre-historic archaeology and ethnology, had occasion to react to the *Origin* in early 1860 in his capacity as president of the Canadian (later, Royal Canadian) Institute. This response appeared as part of the President's address in the March 1860 number of the *Canadian Journal of Industry, Art and Science*, the organ of the institute and the vehicle for many of the writings of Toronto academics. This journal published a much wider variety of articles than the *Canadian Naturalist*. Besides articles on natural history and biology, it produced articles on the physical sciences, geology and mineralogy, mathematics, philosophy and psychology, ethnography, linguistics and archaeology, Latin inscriptions and Ontario local history.[14] In fact, its contents reflected, on the one hand, the intellectual preoccupations of those involved in editing the journal and running the institute and, on the other, the desire of its readership to keep abreast of science. The second interest is most evident in the annual addresses of the president which survey the scientific and technological developments of the previous year. The first is apparent from the authorship of articles and reviews: George Paxton Young contributed in philosophy and mathematics, John McCaul wrote endlessly on Roman inscriptions in Britain and, during the 1870s, Henry Scadding wrote on early Canadian history and the local history of Toronto.

It is in the context of his presidential addresses that Wilson commented on Darwin's *Origin*.[15] His comments are more those of a humanist with an amateur's interest in science than of a technical scientist. His 1860 response is preceded by assertions of local pride in the material advances made in Canada West, in the operations of the Toronto Magnetic Observatory, and in the work of Canadian geologists. The general air of the piece is one of optimism about progress in science and technology. It closes with a series of memorial notices of recently deceased explorers (the Franklin expedition), engineers and scientists.

The discussion of Darwin occurs as part of a discussion of the more general issue: *What is species?*[16] Wilson recognizes that the answer had great import for palaeontology, zoology, ethnology, and the relation of science to theology. Extreme positions are described: that of those who regard species as a conventional way of dividing up a changing and complicated reality, and that of those who try to reconcile their belief in the fixity of species and a species-essence with the fossil record by assuming the occurrence of catastrophic extinctions and recreations on earth. In the evaluation of these answers Wilson recommends the avoidance of foregone conclusions and the honest examination of evidence. He seems to regard the issue as an empirical rather than a conceptual matter.

He does offer a definite opinion on one point. The implications of the theory of natural selection — and of other theories about transmutation of species — do not seem to be supported by the facts **available** to him. If human beings are the product of such selection, then the fossil record should contain remains intermediate in form between human beings and the species most similar to them morphologically, the anthropoid apes. However, no such forms can be found in the fossil record. In particular, there is no link between apes and people which would suggest descent from a common ancestor.

Wilson's 1861 president's address returns to the species question after a survey of scientific and technical activities ranging from LeVerrier's supposed discovery of the planet Vulcan, to attempts to lay a transatlantic telegraph cable, to supposed evidence for ether as a medium for light. In Wilson's comments for 1861, evidence which seemed contrary to Darwin's position is underlined. For example, the sudden proliferation of life in the Cambrian period after the apparent absence of any fossils in the pre-Cambrian clearly conflicts with Darwin's seeming commitment to the gradual development and diversification of life-forms. Wilson goes on to claim that although theories of the transmutation of species seem to to put science in conflict with religion, the evidence in favour even of Darwin's version is slight. He is especially concerned to argue against common ancestry for humans and apes. He does so by suggesting that apes and other lower animals operate by instinct while humans have few and poorer instinctual reactions and must rely, instead, on a distinctive capacity for reason. Where Darwin would claim, in *The Descent of Man*, a gradual acquisition of mental powers as a result of adaptive variations, Wilson claims a discontinuity of ability which separates special creations.

Wilson does use one result of Darwin's researches for his own purposes. He was a staunch proponent of the essential unity of the human species and of the common abilities of all normal members — a view with ethical implications.[17] He finds in Darwin's discussion of intra-specific variability a weapon against claims that there are many distinct human species with differently developed abilities.

William Dawson LeSueur (1840-1917) was educated at the University of Toronto in the 1860s, and spent his entire working life as a civil servant in the Post Office Department. His principal writings on literary criticism, on positivism, on ethics and religion, and on evolution appear between 1871 and 1895. His later writings dealt with Canadian politics and history. He was impressed by the thought of Darwin, Spencer, Comte and Mill, and so, along with Goldwin Smith and a very few others, took part in a small movement of heterodox private scholarship. These writers were among the contributors to the *Canadian Monthly and National Review* and its successor *Rose-Belford's Canadian Monthly*, during the 1870s and 1880s. In addition, LeSueur wrote for a broader international audience as a contributing editor for E.I. Youmans' *Popular Science Monthly*. This journal frequently published articles by thinkers of the stature of C.S.Peirce and Herbert Spencer (of whom Youmans was an admirer) on philosophical topics, on expositions of scientific theories for the educated public, and on early developments in the social sciences.

"Evolution and the Destiny of Man" appeared in the February 1885 number of *Popular Science Monthly* as a critical notice of the very popular *The Destiny of Man Viewed in the Light of His Origin* by John Fiske.[18] Fiske was an American thinker without an academic home [19] and a sometime associate of Chauncey Wright and C.S.Peirce. He was mightily impressed by evolutionary biology and attempted to reconcile certain religious doctrines with it. *The Destiny of Man* was occasioned by an invitation from the Concord School of Philosophy to talk on some facet of the question of immortality.

Fiske's strategy is to emphasize the emergence of human mental abilities, which abilities he takes to be non-material but a product of selective processes. These capacities, Fiske claims, have so evolved from the process by which species are generated through variation and selection. Fiske then goes a step further: not only are humans the final product of natural selection, they are the *goal* of the process of evolution, and thus are Nature's crowning glory. Humanity continues to evolve as a result of social and intellectual processes; cultural endowments allow even the weak and vicious to survive despite environmental pressures, while the division of labour allows various people to develop and exploit distinct abilities.

Although Fiske admits that we cannot know whether this evolved psychic ability — the human consciousness or soul — is immortal, he does claim that the scientific knowledge of the day counts against its being a material entity or process. He goes on to say that "He who regards Man as the consummate fruition of creative energy and the chief object of Divine care, is almost irresistibly driven to the belief that the soul's career is not completed with the present life upon the earth."[20] Although he acknowledges difficulties with the position, he still goes on the add "that the doctrine of evolution does not allow us to take the atheistic view of the position of man."[21]

LeSueur's response to Fiske is a protest against his unwarranted leaps of reasoning. Following Comte, he regards consciousness as an emergent level of reality.[22] Also following Comte, however, he distinguishes scientific intellectual endeavours from theological ones. His complaint, then, is about the injection of one style of thought, the theological, which makes "comprehensive statements" and "offers solutions to the profoundest problems," into a realm in which knowledge is advanced by a "gradual method" of step-by-step improvement of hypotheses.[23] Fiske speaks well when he confines himself to science, says LeSueur, but gets beyond evidence when he proposes a *goal* for natural selection,[24] just as he makes an unlicensed leap when he attributes "divinity" to Spencer's fundamental "unknowable" reality. LeSueur highly values truth arrived at by scientific methods, for those methods lead to knowledge. It is misleading to regard extrapolations from science as anything but speculation. There is no scientific license for Fiske's attempts to synthesize religious belief with evolutionary theory.[26] Darwinian natural selection is no goal-directed process:

> Darwin has discovered no law in nature by which good qualities (as such) are produced; he has simply discovered a law by which all kinds of qualities (differentiations) good, bad and indifferent are produced and by which the bad ones (bad, i.e., in relation to the environment) are knocked off, like so many projecting angles by the destruction of the individuals manifesting them.[27]

Early Canadian reactions to Darwin's *Origin* are marked by concern over what was taken to be insufficient evidence and a belief that since no direct evidence can be had for parts of the theory it remains a speculation on a mystery incapable of purely scientific solution. Some questions turn out to be resolvable only by revelation.

By the 1880s, however, the theory of natural selection had earned sufficient respectability that attempts were made to reconcile it with religious belief. LeSueur's objection to Fiske was that the techniques of theology were used in this reconciliation. These techniques are merely speculative and lead to no secure truth. The issues with which Fiske wished to deal are beyond knowledge because they cannot be treated by scientific methods. In this they are unlike such issues as the origin of new species as a result of the descent and variation for which both standards of demonstration and evidence exist. Revelation cannot replace science to resolve supposed mysteries. Its status is epistemologically dubious and its realm speculation about those territories beyond science's current frontiers.

There is irony to be discovered in the contrast between leSueur and the early critics of Darwin. Those early commentators, motivated in part by religious faith, objected to the methodologically speculative appearance of the Darwinian doctrine on the origin of species. By the 1880s LeSueur, the profoundly secular thinker, claims that Darwinian theory is methodologically sound and careful. However, he finds in one attempt to reconcile the acknowledged process of transmutation of species with (admittedly unorthodox) religious belief a scientifically unacceptable form of speculative leap.

Notes

1. For a useful summary of the role of both higher criticism and Darwin on *Canadian* intellectual life see Ramsay Cook, *The Regenerators* (Toronto: University of Toronto Press, 1985) p.1-25.
2. Charles Lyell, *The Principles of Geology*, 3 vols. (1830-33); William E.Buckland, *Geology and Minerology, Considered with Reference to Natural Theology* (London: Pickering, 1836) Bridgewater Treatises vol.6. The original skepticism about the antiquity of the universe dates back to scholarship of the seventeenth and eighteenth century. See Paolo Rossi, *The Dark Abyss of Time* (Chicago: University of Chicago Press, 1984).
3. An extensive debate about the efficacy of prayer occurred in *The Canadian*

Monthly and National Review during the 1870s. See Brian McKillop, *A Disciplined Intelligence* (Montreal: McGill-Queen's Press, 1979) p.157-8 and Ramsay Cook, *The Regenerators*, p.43 and following. The principal participants included William Dawson LeSueur, Agnes Maule Machar and the noteworthy expatriate George John Romanes. David Hull notes the importance of uniformity of application of natural law as one advantage claimed by Darwinians for the theory of natural selection. Lyell's success over catastrophic theories of geological change is connected with his theory's avoidance of nomological singularities. See David Hull, *Darwin and His Critics* (Cambridge, Mass.: Harvard University Press, 1973) p.63-6, 74-7. Catastrophe theories, however, are currently undergoing a new vogue in science.

4. Examples of such reviews can be found in David Hull, *Darwin and His Critics*, esp. the reviews by Thomas Wollaston, William Hopkins, Francois-Jules Pictet, Fleeming Jenkin and Louis Agassiz.

5. For a discussion of objections of this sort, see Hull, p.17-36. The inadequacy of the standard views of induction as reconstructions of how scientific verification is actually carried on, and the excessive strictness of the views is discussed there. See also McKillop, p.93-5.

6. Cf. William Hopkins' review of *The Origin*, p.228-72 in Hull and esp. p.254-65. See also comments in reviews by Pictet, p.149-50, by Henry Fawcett p.284-5 and by Fleeming Jenkin, p.342-3.

7. Jenkin's review of *The Origin* is a good example of this sort of objection. see Hull, p.303-44 and esp. the sections entitled "Variability" p.305-12 and "Efficiency of Natural Selection," p.312-20.

8. For objections of this sort, see Hull p.32. The issue is clearly put in H.G.Bronn's review of *The Origin*, p.120-5 and esp. p.122.

9. At one point they had been. See Hull, p.37-54.

10. See Hull p.32 on the problem of testing for direct special creation. See Hooker's review, p.81-5 in Hull and esp. p.84-5.

11. Peirce was one of the few to see the point. See Hull p.33.

12. See McKillop p.99-110 for a discussion of Dawson's and Wilson's responses to Darwin. See also Carl Berger, *Science, God and Nature in Victorian Canada* (Toronto: University of Toronto Press, 1982) p.39f. and Ramsay Cook, *The Regenerators* p.8-12. For an example of Dawson's substantive views of prehistoric and prehuman past, see Trevor H. Levere and Richard A. Jarrell (eds.), Curious Field-Book (Toronto: University of Toronto Press, 1974) p.148-59 and any of the many editions of Dawson's *The Origins of the Earth, And Man* and his *Archaia*.

13. Whether each species has its own proper and inviolable essence and whether there is a singular 'natural' system for classifying organisms into species was an issue of central importance in the responses to Darwin. See Hull, p.67-77. See also McKillop. For a good example of another Canadian defence of immutable species, see William Hincks' review of Thomas Huxley's *On the Origin of Species, or The Causes of the Phenomenon of Organic Nature: A Course of Lectures to Working Men* in *The Canadian Journal*, N.S. vol.8 (September, 1863) p.390-404, his "Remarks on the Principles of Classification in the Animal Kingdom in Immediate Reference to a Recent Paper by J.W.Dawson," *Canadian Journal*, N.S. vol 10 (January, 1865) p.19-30 and his "Some Thoughts on Classification in Relation to Organized Beings," *Canadian Journal*, N.S. vol.11 (January, 1866) p.31-45.

14. These are the sorts of items published in the New Series (vol.1, 1856). An earlier series, produced during the early 1850s concentrated heavily on technological topics. The New Series included, in imitation of such British publications as the *Athenaeum*, not only articles and reviews on a wide range of subjects but regular

records of weather conditions as reported by the meteorological observatory in Toronto. This Victorian passion for weather is also evident in similar reports for Montreal in the *Canadian Naturalist*. For an interesting comment on the social conditions which contributed to the development of Canadian writing and research in scientific and technological areas, see James O.Peterson, "Two Factors in the Evolution of Canadian Science and Technology," p.131-8 in Richard A.Jarrell and Norman R.Ball (eds.) *Science, Technology and Canadian History* (Waterloo: Wilfred Laurier University Press, 1978).

15. Other comments on evolution frequently appeared as articles and reviews. For example, William Hincks, professor of Natural History at the University of Toronto, contributed articles on biological classification and reviews not only of Huxley's *On the Origin of Species* but of his *Lectures on Elements of Comparative Anatomy*, (*Canadian Journal*, New Series, vol.10 (JA 1865) p.40-2.) In his writings he maintained a strong view of species as distinct, permanent natural kinds. In his opposition to the Darwinian theory of evolution he was joined by E.J.Chapman, the Toronto minerologist and expert on blowpipe analysis. See his review of Darwin, *On the Origin of species*, *Canadian Journal*, New Series, vol.5 (JL1860) p.367-87 and his review of Charles Lyell, *The Geological Evidences of the Antiquity of Man*, *Canadian Journal* New Series, vol.8 (SE1863) p.378-90.

16. See the opening of the Wilson section to follow.

17. See, for example, "The Unity of the Human Race," by D.W., *Canadian Journal*, (First Series) vol.3, no.13 (AU1855) p.302-3.

18. it had first appeared in late 1884 (Boston: Houghton, 1884, 121p.) The printing of 1890 (Boston, Houghton Mifflin and Co.) is described on the title page as the "Fifteenth Edition."

19. To see that this is not an unusual condition, note that C.S.Peirce actually held a teaching position in philosophy only for the years 1879-1884 at Johns Hopkins. See Bruce Kuklick, , *The Rise of American Philosophy* (New Haven: Yale University Press, 1977) p.105, 123. Peirce worked as a private scholar and experienced financial difficulties for much of the rest of his career. See p.123-6. Fiske was a successful writer and popularizer of Spencer's work, but a lightweight as a philosopher, at least in the opinion of Morton White. See his *Documents in the History of American Philosophy* (New York: Oxford University Press, 1972) p.212. A more extensive discussion of his role can be found in Kuklick, p.80-91. Fiske's limitations are noted there, as well, but with slightly more sympathy.

20. *The Destiny of Man as Viewed in the Light of His Origin* (1890 ed.) p.112.

21. *Ibid.*

22. Cf. his "Science and Materialism," *Canadian Monthly and National Review*, vol.11 (JA1877) p.22-8. Reprinted in A.Brian McKillop (ed.) *A Critical Spirit* (Toronto: McLelland and Stewart, 1977) p.95-105. See esp. p.100.

23. LeSueur's "Evolution and the Destiny of Man," *The Popular Science Monthly*, vol.26, no.4 (FE1885) p.456-68. p.467.

24. LeSueur, "Evolution," p.459-61.

25. LeSueur, "Evolution," p.466.

26. Fiske's response to such an objection might well be the the one he uses, elsewhere, that *synthesis* is the mark of a genuine philosophy, that it must unify and extend people's belief systems, while the Comtean demand for evidence and care in argument is mere "logic" and is marked by limited foresight. See White (ed.) p.218-225.

27. LeSueur, "Evolution," p.468.

The President's Address
Daniel Wilson

[Having surveyed scientific and technical developments for 1859, both in Canada and world wide, Wilson ends with a mention of palaentological and geological studies and their unsettling results. Then he turns to a discussion of the species question.]

In this light, I conceive, we must look upon that comprehensive question which now challenges revision in the hearing of new witnesses: *What is Species?* It is a question which forces us back to first principles, and equally affects the sciences of Palaeontology, Zoology, and Ethnology; while it has also been made to bear in no unimportant degree on the relations of Science and Theology: involving as it does the questions: — In what forms has creative power been manifested in the succession of organic life? and, Under what conditions has man been introduced into the most diverse and widely separated provinces of the animal world? It is to the comprehensive bearings of the latter indeed, that the former owes its origin; for what is the use of entertaining the question, prematurely forced upon us: Are all men of one and the same species? while authorities in science are still so much at variance as to what species really is, and writers who turn with incredulous contempt from the idea that all men are descended from Adam, can nevertheless look with complacency on their probable descent from apes! One revolutionary class of thinkers, having its representatives among the ablest men of science on this continent, incline to the belief that species is a mere logical invention of the systematiser, and that the older naturalists have converted convenient definitions and the necessary formulae of classification, into assumed realities. On the other hand, the extreme phalanx of their opponents invent a series of catastrophes, by which each geological period is closed, — the finished act, as it were, of a grand cosmic tragedy, — and all existing life is swept away, to give place to the creation of new species for the succeeding epoch of a renovated earth. This mysterious question of the origin of species is accordingly trammelled in part by that most dangerous of all hindrances to free inquiry and unbiased scientific judgment: The foregone popular

*From [sir] Daniel Wilson "The President's Address" 1860 — to the Canadian Institute [*The Canadian Journal* New Series, vol5, No.26 (MR 1860) pp. 99-127.

conclusions relative to the supposed terms in which alone it can be answered, consistently with the inspired history of creation. Hence, on the one hand, development theories and transmutation of species; but also, along with it, of the recognition of the same great general laws which now govern the natural world having been in operation throughout all the countless ages of organic being which geology reveals to us.

[Here follows a brief survey of the competing theories of species current among naturalists at the time.]

According to Mr. Darwin, the essential differences of genera are only the product of the same powers of nature through a greatly protracted epoch, which within a less prolonged period had sufficed to produce species; and under our own limited observation are seen to give rise to permanent varieties in animals and plants. From observation of phenomena occurring within our own cognizince he has arrived at the conclusion that there is in reality no essential distinction between individual differences, varieties, and species. The well-marked variety is an incipient species; and by the operation of various simple physical causes and comparatively slight organic changes, producing a tendency towards increase in one direction of variation, and arrestment, and ultimate extinction in another, the law of *natural selection*, as Darwin terms it, results, which leads to his "preservation of favoured races in the struggle for life." He thus establishes, as he conceives, a principle in nature, akin to that which man consciously sets in operation when he effects changes on domesticated animals and on plants, by altered conditions of life, and then perpetuates such as he selects by preference for his own use. The element of time — so limited in man's operations, — is for practical purposes unlimited in relation to the operation of natural causes on the development of variations in organic being in diverse directions; and as the great physical changes to which geology bears witness, supply all the means requisite for producing individual variation on a scale immensely exceeding any change observable on organic life under domestication, Mr. Darwin conceives, and produces many illustrations in confirmation of his idea, that not only the origin of species, but the wider differences which distinguish genera and all higher divisions of the organic kingdom may be accounted for by the same prolonged processes of variation and natural selection. His "Origin of Species," is no product of a rash theorist, but the result of the patient observation and laborious experiments of a highly gifted naturalist, extending over a period of upwards of twenty years, and — like the *Reliquiae Diluciancae* of Buckland, — it will be found to embody thoughts and facts of great permanent value, whatever be the final decision on its special propositions. From the high authority of the writer, his well-established character as an accurate observer, and the bold and startling nature of his views, it cannot be doubted that his work — with the promised additions to the evidence now produced — will tend to re-open the whole question, and give courage to other assailants of those views of the permanency of species, which have seemed so indispensable alike to all our preconceived ideas in natural science, and to our interpretations of revealed cosmogony. Before Mr. Darwin's "Origin of Species" appeared from the press, Sir Charles Lyell — himself no hasty or incautious doubter, — had remarked of it: "he appears to me to have succeeded by his investigations and reasonings, in throwing a flood of light on many classes of phenomena, connected with the affinities, geographical distribution, and geological succession of organic beings, for which no other hypothesis has been able, or has even attempted to account." In relation to opinions advanced on questions of such profound interest and difficulty, by a distinguished naturalist, as results of the experience and observations of many years, our attitude ought clearly to be that of candid and impartial jurors. We must examine for ourselves, not reject, the evidence thus honestly given. The experience of the past shows how frequently men have contended for their own blundering interpretations, while all the while believing themselves the champions and the martyrs of truth. All truth is of God, alike in relation to the natural and the moral law, and of the former, as truly as of the latter may we say: "if this counsel or this work be of men, it will come to nought; but if it be of God, ye cannot overthrow it; lest haply ye be found even to fight against God."

But meanwhile in another, though allied direction, truth is the gainer by this widening of the scientific horizon. In 1857 our greatest English naturalist, Prof. Owen, set forth his remarkable new system of classification of mammals, based on the form and complexity of the brain. In this novel and ingenious system he separates man, on clearly defined grounds of cerebral structure and proportions, into a distinct and crowning order of ARCHENCEPHALA; there-by supplying by anticipation, a scientific antidote to one at least of the fallacies of Professor Powell, which may be this stated: regarding the duration of time and the number of species as equally unlimited, he argues: — "While the number of species thus tends to become infinitely great, the extreme difference between man at one end and a zoophyte at the other end of the scale is constantly finite; hence the average difference between any two species tends to become infinitely small; multiplied by the number of species, it must still be equal to a finite quantity; and the product being finite, if the first factor be infinity the second must be zero."

It is scarcely necessary to observe that the tendency of species to an infinite multiplication of intermediate links, which is implied here, is a perfectly gratuitous assumption. The duration of time and the multiplication of species may be equally infinite; that it will be so we assuredly have no right to assume; but in that case the analogies which palaeontology reveals do not suggest the idea that such prolonged manifestations of the Creator's power to produce an infinite series of new forms will be exercised intermediately between those two fixed points of zoophyte and man. What if creative power should go on beyond the latter, into still higher manifestations of the divine image? Man cannot be demonstrated to be an absolute finality in organic creation. Apart, however, from any question of future creations, we look in vain among organic fossils for any such gradations of form as even to suggest a process of transmutation. Above all, in relation to man, no fossil form adds a single link to fill up the wide interval between him and the most anthropoid of inferior animals, when viewing him purely in those salient physical aspects to which the observation of the palaeontologist is limited. The Archencephale of Owen stands as the crowning masterpiece of organic creation, separated from the highest type of inferior animal organization by as well defined and broad a line of demarkation as an insular kingdom from the states, republics, and confederacies of a neighbouring continent; and if the difference between man and the inferior animals, not only in mere physical organization, but still more in all the higher attributes of animal life, be not relative but absolute, then no multiplication of intermediate links can lessen the obstacles to transmutation. One true antidote therefore to such a doctrine, and to the consequent denial of primary distinctions of species, seems to offer itself in such broad and unmistakeable lines of demarkation as Professor Owen indicates, between the cerebral structure of man and that of the most highly developed of anthropoid or other mammals.

The President's Address

Daniel Wilson

[These excerpts occur in the context of a survey of the scientific and technical advances of the year 1860]

When the views of De.Maillet, Oken, and Lamarck were reproduced in a popular form, it was not altogether without reason that the argument was affirmed to place science in conflict with religion. It seemed like an attempt, if not to dispense entirely with a supreme creative power and divine first cause, at least to reduce to the smallest conceivable minimum the controlling government of an ever-present, overruling providence; and to demonstrate a universe which having been constructed like some ingenious piece of mechanism, wound up, and set agoing, was thenceforth capable of working out its results without further oversight, until the term of its mechanical forces was exhausted, and the finger, stopping of itself on the great dial, declared that time shall be no more. The theories of spontaneous generation and the modification of organized beings by external physical agents, or by the direct operation of their own voluntary acts, have indeed found advocates among those honestly in search of guiding lights toward the hidden laws and truths of nature; but they have maintained but a feeble hold on the earnest students of science, and have for the most part been diluted into popular forms of scepticism in which all recognition of a providential government of the universe has been ignored. But the novel and highly suggestive views on the origin of species by means of natural selection, are presented to us under very different auspices. We cannot treat them with too sincere respect even while rejecting them. They are no rash and hastily formed fancies of a shallow theorist, but the earnest convictions of an eminent English naturalist of great and varied experience, set forth as deductions based on a continuous series of observations and experiments, extending over upwards of twenty years; and heralded by the favourable testimony of some of the most cautious and

*From [sir] Daniel Wilson, "The President's Address," 1861 — to the Canadian Institute. *The Canadian Journal,* New Series, Vol. 6, No.32 (MR 1861) pp. 101-120.

discriminating among his scientific contemporaries. Nevertheless, the time which has been already allowed for the critical investigation of such evidence as is advanced to sustain his comprehensive hypothesis, has only tended to discredit his transmutation theory, and add assurance to the convictions of the scientific believer in the idea of creation as the only satisfactory solution of the succession of life. Science has achieved wondrous triumphs, but life is a thing it can neither create nor account for, by mere physics. Nor can we assume even that the whole law of life can be embraced within the process of induction, as carried out by an observer so limited as man is, in relation to the sequence of time, and to the cosmical changes by which so much of the record is erased. Darwin, indeed, builds largely on hypotheses constructed to supply the gaps in the geological record; but whilst welcoming every new truth which enlarges our conception of the cosmic unity, all nature still says as plainly to us at to the Idumean patriarch: "Canst thou by searching find out God? canst thou find out the Almighty to perfection?" Assuredly it is in no spirit of sceptical presumption that Darwin has set forth his views; and I heartily accord with the claim advanced by Professor Huxley, that the arguments of an experienced and profound naturalist on pure questions of science, must be met on scientific grounds alone. But when science claims not only to disclose the nature of all living and extinct organizations, but to determine their primary origin, it is difficult even on purely scientific grounds, to avoid reasserting the truth which all nature audibly affirms, that creation owes its existence to a Creator. And at every appearance of new organic forms in the geological strata of the earth, science sacrifices no jot or tittle of its true dignity, when owning a higher law, it admits that He who, in the beginning, created the heavens and the earth, has in like manner put forth the same creative power at every successive origination of species.

The geologist in reasoning on the succession of life, has hitherto appealed to palaeontological evidence by which he traces every specific form through provinces of space uniform in their relations to the order of geological strata and therefore determinate as to the relative period of time within which they sprung into being, ran their appointed course, and were superseded by new orders of life. Yet it is not to be doubted that the record is very imperfect, and so leaves room for piecing it out with theory, hypotheses, and a comprehensive generalization. Nor need we affirm that the Lamarckian idea of an abnormal organic power of self-development; or that which assigns to external influences a modifying power on the characters of species: is wholly unsupported by observation. Neither these, nor the opinions set forth by Darwin in favour of the derivation of well determined forms of one period from others more or less diverse in earlier formations are altogether unsustained by evidence; though they can carry us but a short way in accounting for, or determining the plan of creation. They may induce us to reject the claims of many specific variations in organic form to be ranked as distinct primary species; but they leave the grand questions of the origin of species and the source of organic life, precisely where they were. We are still free to look upon the successive orders of life as the manifestations of an intelligent creative power: the intellectual conceptions of the supreme Intelligence by whom the universe subsists, wrought out, like all else in His visible creation, by material means. . . .

If the origin of species be really traceable to natural selection and the preservation of favoured races in the struggle for life, then it should be demonstrable that man is preeminently favoured in physical organization, for he has every where triumphed over all other animals. But that triumph has been the result of no such physical preeminence, but of that intellectual power bestowed on him when — as we believe on an authority to which the progress of science adds ever fresh confirmation, — God breathed into him the breath of life, and man became a living soul. . . .

[Wilson discusses the tendency of certain theorists notably Louis Agassiz, to declare, on the basis of human variability that there are a number of contemporary human species. He uses Darwin's discussion of variability in pigeons to formulate an answer.]

Looking to the tendency of such views to an ever-widening multiplicity of species, or races of men, and to the consequent diminution in a corresponding ratio, of the elements of difference between them, it is impossible, I conceive, to look the force of some of Darwin's arguments in their bearing on this momentous question. Take for example his favourite illustration, the domestic pigeon; we look in vain for the slightest trace of the transmutation of a bird of another genus into any one of the varied and widely-scattered breeds of the wild or domestic pigeon, whatever force we may recognise in the arguments by which he traces all alike back to the Columba livia. . . .

Finally he adds: "It is also a most favourable circumstance for the production of distinct breeds, that male and female pigeons can be easily mated for life." But we have only to remember that those, and all the other elements referred to, are to a far higher extent characteristic of man. Domestication and a social settled life, the permanent mating in pairs, the migration in communities, the external influences of an artificial civilization and highly diverse climatic influences for thousands of years, have all pertained to his normal condition, and may all therefore be made to yield still stronger proofs that the man of Europe, of Egypt, and of India, are alike descended of one primal stock.

Review of Darwin on the Origin of Species

J.W. Dawson

Nothing is more humbling to the scientific enquirer than to find that he has arrived in the progress of his investigations at a point beyond which inductive science fails to carry him. The physicist finds himself in this position when required to explain the nature of matter, or the cause of gravitation or cohesion, or the essence of the mysterious influences of light, heat, and electricity. The chemist is equally baffled in the presence of those mysterious atoms which are in all his processes, yet are not perceptible to his senses. The physiologist stands awe-stricken in the presence of a microscopic cell whose structure he knows, but whose origin and wonderful vital endowments he fails to comprehend. The geologist and the systematic zoologist are haunted in their dreams by those multifarious species that appear and disappear, like phantoms on the stage of geological time, yet seem so fixed and unchangeable in existing nature. True science is always humble, for it knows itself to be surrounded by mysteries — mysteries which only widen as the sphere of its knowledge extends. Yet it is the ambition of science to solve mysteries, to add one domain after another to its conquests, though certain to find new and greater difficulties beyond. Hence we find every difficult problem assailed by a constant succession of adventurers, some of them content cautiously to explore the ground and prudently to retreat where to advance is no longer safe; others gathering all their strength for a rush and a leap into an unknown and fathomless abyss. Both classes do good to science. The first show us the real nature of the difficulties to be overcome or to be abandoned as hopeless. The second we follow to the last crumbling margin of sound fact and deduction on which their feet have rested before their final plunge, and thus gain an experience that otherwise we should not have had the courage to seek.

The question of the origin of species yields in difficulty to none of the problems to which we have referred above, and Mr. Darwin's book is a noted

*First published in *The Canadian Naturalist*, Vol. 5 (1860)

instance of the second of the methods of treatment which we have indicated. We do not however value him the less on account of his boldness and rash self-sacrifice in the cause of science. We follow him with pleasure over many agreeable and instructive paths not previously explored, and we shrink back only when he leads us to the brink of a precipice, and we fail to perceive the good land which he says lies beyond, or to place confidence in the bridge, thinner than gossamer, which he has woven to bear our feet over the gulf that separates the proved ground of specific variability from the mystery of specific difference. We regard this as the most accurate and concise statement that can be made respecting the character of this book. It elaborately investigates the question of variation of species, and illustrates its laws in a very full and satisfactory manner, though giving to some of these laws an undue prominence as compared with others. It then attempts to apply the laws of variation to an entirely different series of phenomena, those of specific diversity, and finding some analogies between the characters that distinguish species and varieties, seeks on this ground to break down all specific distinction in respect to origin, and to reduce all species to mere varieties of ancient and perhaps perished prototypes.

The work thus divides itself naturally into two distinct and quite dissimilar portions: 1st. The careful induction of facts bearing on the nature and laws of variation, in which the author appears in all his strength as a patient and reliable zoologist; and 2nd. The wild and fanciful application of the results thus attained to another class of phenomena with which they have no connection except that of mere analogy. We shall endeavor to distinguish these two portions of the work, but cannot avoid treating of them together.

Variation occurs under two very different conditions. It takes place in domesticated animals and plants, and in animals and plants in a wild state. Very properly our author first examines its conditions under domestication, in which state variation is much more extensive and also more easily observed. The great variations that occur in a state of domestication are no doubt due to changed and unnatural conditions of life; but farther than this we know nothing of their precise causes. On this subject our author indulges in some preliminary speculations, and tries to rid the subject of what he terms misconceptions, some of which are, however, only facts too stubborn to be bent to his theory. For example, in speaking of the prevalent idea, that domesticated animals have been chosen by man on account, among other things, of their capacity for variation, he says: — "I do not dispute that these capacities have added largely to the value of some of our domesticated productions; but how could a savage possibly know when he first tamed an animal whether it would vary in succeeding generations, and whether it would endure other climates? Has the little variability of the ass or the guinea-fowl, or the small power of endurance of warmth of the reindeer or of cold by the common camel, prevented their domestication? I cannot doubt that if other animals and plants equal in number to our domesticated productious, and belonging to equally diverse classes and countries, were taken from a state of nature, and could be made to breed for an equal number of generations under domestication, they would vary on the average as largely as the parent species of our existing domesticated productions have varied." On reading these sentences it must occur to any reflective reader, 1st. That savages very rarely tame animals. 2d. That if savages or others attempted to tame animals indiscriminately, they would fail in many cases, and these in the very cases in which species could endure little change. 3d. Animals little variable, like the reindeer and the camel, have little geographical range, and this just because of the fixity or tenderness of their constitution. 4th. Even the capacity of breeding at all under the changed conditions of domestication, is wanting in some species. In short, there is no reason whatever to believe that species are equally variable; but, on the contrary, that they differ very much in this respect, — as naturalists have always maintained. In the same loose way he treats the doctrine of the tendency of varieties to revert to the original types of the species. This, our author admits, if established, would overthrow his whole hypothesis, and he gets rid of it by denying the evidence of reversion afforded by so many of our domestic animals and cultivated plants, and by farther affirming that such reversion, if it does occur, amounts to nothing, because produced by external causes. Certain species, by the external causes applied in domestication, are caused to vary. These causes being removed, as every one knows, they gradually lose their acquired and unnatural characteristics; but, according to Mr. Darwin, this gives no evidence of an original type, but only of the operation of other causes of change, tending in some other direction. The argument would be good if we could have species **destitute of all distinctive characters to begin with; in other words, if we could create species. But as the case stands, it is a mere *petitio principii.***

In this way our author, in the opening paragraphs of his first chapter, quietly ignores a number of facts essential to the validity of the received views of species, and so leads the unwary reader to enter on the consideration of variation with an impression already formed that varieties and species are not distinguishable. We take the liberty of entering on the inquiry in another spirit, and of beginning with the fact that we have species which have remained distinct in the whole period of human experience, and also as far back in geological time as we can trace any of them. This being premised, we may enquire what variations man has been able to effect in those species which he has domesticated, and by what processes and under what laws these changes have occurred.

[Here follows a lengthy quotation from the *Origin* in which Darwin discusses the extreme variability introduced into domestic pigeons by breeders.]

The common rock-pigeon is thus proved to highly variable in a state of domestication, so much so that naturalists not aware of all the fact, might well be excused for concluding, as some of them have done in the similar instances of the ox, the domestic fowl, and man himself, that the varieties represent several distinct species. To what then do these differences amount? (1) They are mainly in non-essential points, as colour, development of feather, etc., and they do not consequently interfere, to any important extent, with the food and habits of the animal; or if we were to represent the matter from the opposite point of view to that taken by Mr. Darwin, the constitution and instincts of the species being fixed by the law of its creation, it cannot vary beyond these. The author is clearly wrong in stating that any of them could amount to generic distinctions; that is, if genera are to be based on *structural* differences, for of these there is comparatively little, except in the one point of proportion of parts, difference in which is of specific value only, and often occurs in near varieties. (2) Many of the differences are abnormal; that is, they are of the character of monstrosities, and this separates them widely from true specific differences. (3) The varieties are perfectly fertile, which is not the case with hybrids between clearly distinct species. (4) The cross breeds revert to the characters of the rock-pigeon, showing that the specific type still remains uneradicated, or that each variety is, so to speak, a hemitropic form, which, when united with an opposite one, tends to reproduce the original form. It follows from these results, that, however likely to be mistaken for species, the varieties of the pigeon are really something essentially different from true species, and the same conclusion would hold with any animal that could be selected.

We now come to the causes of variation in a state of domestication; and here, already, in the twenty-ninth page of his volume, we find our author leaving the basis of fact and losing himself in the mazes in which he henceforth continues to wander. He attributes the varieties of domestic animals to "Man's power of accumulative selection; nature gives successive variations; man adds them up in certain directions useful to him." We object to this, as altogether a partial and imperfect statement. It is not nature that gives the variations, but external circumstances; while nature only gives a certain capacity to vary, the extent of which is the point in question. Man places animals in abnormal conditions into which their instincts and natural powers would not permit them of themselves to enter. They vary in consequence of these, sometimes suddenly, sometimes gradually, sometimes from premeditated treatment, sometimes unaccountably, sometimes in directions useful to man, sometimes the reverse. Out of all the diversities thus produced, man no doubt selects what suits him and keeps it, as far as he can, in the conditions favourable to its permanence and improvement; but such selection is a comparatively small part of the actual cause of the phenomena observed, which result really from unnatural conditions of life compelled by man.

His next step is to establish analogies between variation and specific difference, as observed in nature. Many species are doubtful; that is, naturalists are not quite decided that they may not be varieties. This is true; but such species are the exceptions, and the differences of view have arisen as much from defective observation or reasoning as from any real difficulty.

Again, in large genera the species approach each other very nearly. This is inevitable from the nature of the case, and though it may cause difficulties in distinguishing them, it proves nothing as to their not being true species. Species which range widely also are prone to vary, and this also follows from the nature of the case, great range and much variability being really cause and effect, and reacting on each other. Farther, it is stated that species belonging to large genera are more prone to vary than species belonging to small genera. This has not been established as a general principle, nor, if it should be, would it necessarily bear the interpretation put upon it. To reach the facts we must be certain that we are comparing natural genera consisting of species having true affinities of structure, and that all our generic distinctions are based on the same grades of difference. . . .

But if the reader is willing to take this for granted, Mr. Darwin will carry him a step further. He next proceeds to maintain that in nature there is a power of selection similar to that which the breeder exercises — a power of "Natural Selection" not heretofore recognised, and by virtue of which varieties are produced and developed into species. There is here a huge hiatus in the reasoning of our author. We have already shown that an excessive importance is attributed to artificial or human selection; but with all the exaggeration of its powers, it has proved insufficient to change one species into another. The pigeon, with all its varieties, is still a pigeon, and, according to our author's own conclusive argumentation, a rock-pigeon. It is not a wood-pigeon, or turtle dove, still less a partridge or a rook. But now we are asked to believe that those same natural courses which break down all the breeder's elaborate distinctions so soon as his breeds are allowed to intermix and live in a natural way, are themselves able to take up the work and do still greater marvels in the way of selection. Such a doctrine is self-contradictory, and, we believe wholly incapable of proof; but let us see how this is attempted: As might have been anticipated, natural selection being either creation or nothing, a new power is evoked as a *primum mobile*. This is the "struggle for existence," a fancied warfare in nature, in which the race is always to the swift and the battle to the strong, and in which the struggle makes the strong stronger. In a previous chapter we have been told very truly that the reason why the wealthy and skillful breeder succeeds in producing marked races is that his animals are cared for and pampered, while the savage and the poor man fail because their animals must struggle for subsistence. Nature it appears takes the opposite way, and improves her breeds by putting them through a course of toil and starvation, a struggle not for happiness or subsistence, but for bare existence. . . .

In looking for the proof of this strange doctrine, we find stated in support of it only a number of isolated and exceptional facts, many of them cases in which man interferes with the equilibrium of nature; and we have to fall back on the general statement that the struggle for existence inevitably follows from the high rate at which organic beings tend to increase but this Malthusian doctrine, though good for a single species viewed by itself, is false for the whole in the aggregate. Vegetable life and the lower forms of animal life support the higher, and these supporting forms increase far more rapidly than those that subsist on them. So much so, that vast quantities of organic food go to waste, or would do so but for the hordes of scavengers of low organization that seem specially created to gather up the fragments of nature's bounteous feast. . . .

The beautiful harmony of nature provides that the feeders shall multiple more slowly than the food, and that the food shall be kept under by the feeders. When any form does locally multiply too far, the checks appear, usually in the form of a diminished reproduction or in the more rapid removal of the infirm, the sickly and the aged. When through the slow operation of physical causes or the introduction of new species, certain forms of life can no longer find the means of subsistence, all the facts we know indicate their disappearance, not their change into forms. Nay, species verging to extinction or struggling for existence, like the red deer of Scotland, degenerate rather than improve, and must necessarily do so, so long as the laws of organic being remain what they are. In short, the struggle for existence is a myth, and its employment as a means of improvement still more mythical. . . .

The remarks that we have made on natural selection, and the struggle for existence, afford a key to the whole of Mr. Darwin's argument, which amounts to little else than a wholesale appropriation of all the effects of external conditions of existence to these supposed cause of change. We could fill pages with evidence of the entire confusion of ideas which pervades his mind on this point, but one extract must suffice, both as an indication of this confusion, and as a fair example of the argument:

[Here follows a lengthy citation from 'orgins' in which Dawson registers skepticisim about the direct effects of environment on variation and a rigorous dismissial by Dawson.]

In one respect Mr. Darwin vindicates fully his well-earned reputation as a scientific naturalist. He fairly and ably states the many objections to his view that must occur to the minds of zoologist, botanists and geologists, and manfully though unsuccessfully, attempts to cope with them. . . .

We shall only refer to the geological objection. Geology he admits shews no trace of the "finely graduated organic chain" which in his theory should connect man with the extinct kangaroo-rat like marsupials of the oolite and trias, and all our existing animals and plants with the perished creatures supposed to be their progenitors. He has but one explanation of this, the "extreme imperfection of the geological records." To illustrate this imperfection, he refers to the immense lapse of time involved in the geological record, to the small number of species known compared with this great lapse of time, to the breaks caused by the absence of fossiliferous deposits at certain periods. All these are fair abatements from the completeness of the geological series, and many of the remarks made on them are very valuable; but they do not mitigate the condemnation of the selection theory pronounced by geology. Breaks in the geological record are usually only local, and if general, might indicate actual destruction and renewal of species. Though it is true that estuary and land deposits have in most cases been preserved only in times of subsidence; this is not true of marine deposits, some of the most perfect of which mark times of elevation. Moreover, in those parts of the geological scale which are the most perfect and unbroken, there is no graduated transition of forms. Take for instance the great Silurian limestones of America, or the plant-bearing beds of the coal formation. In both we find some species perseveringly unchanged through many great deposits, and others suddenly appearing and disappearing, and this in cases where the profusion of specimens and continuity of formations preclude any supposition of much imperfection in the evidence. Nothing is more conclusive on this subject than the last of the fossiliferous deposits, next to the modern period; as, for instance, the Post-Pliocene clays and sands of Canada. These belong to a period of elevation proceeding gradually from the time of the boulder formation up to the modern era. In these deposits we have more than sixty species of invertebrate animals, all except one or two known to be now living in the Gulf of St. Lawrence. Yet in all this lapse of time not one of the species has, by natural selection or any other cause, varied more than its living relatives now do. . . .

In his closing chapters the author endeavours to shew that his theory accounts in a satisfactory manner for the typical likeness of species to each other, for the curious embryological relations of animals, and for the existence of rudimentary organs; but all these things are equally intelligible on the opposite view. If species are parts of a plan devised by an intelligent Creator, that plan must appear in their structures. If the plan embraces more general and more specialised contrivances, the latter must, in their earlier stages of growth, simulate the former. All organs, if there is a plan at all, must appear in its different parts in different degrees of relative perfection and complexity, and what we call rudimentary organs are merely the lowest of these degrees; not unless, for in many cases we know their uses, but of less relative importance than in other cases.

We have in the foregoing remarks dwelt chiefly on the points in which we believe the author to be mistaken; but we do not wish to undervalue the work. In many respects it is eminently useful. It shews, in opposition to many views maintained with much vigour on this side of the Atlantic, the great variability of species. It imposes a salutary caution on those naturalists who too readily admit geographical distribution as an evidence of specific distinctness. It illustrates by a vast fund of curious fact the obscure laws of variation and hybridity. All these pearls are not the less valuable to the judicious reader, that the author has seen fit to string them upon a thread of loose and faulty argument, and to employ them to deck the faded form of the transmutation theory of Lamarck.

[Dawson now uses a citation from The *Origin* to summarize Darwin's claims]

We may well ask what is gained by such a result, even if established. The origin of species as we now have them, it is true is mysterious, but what is gained by reducing them all to one primitive form? That would be an equal mystery, more especially if it included within itself the germs of all the varied developments of animal and plant life. By such a doctrine also we involve ourselves in a host of geological and other difficulties, and so break down the **distinction between species and varieties as to deprive our classifications of** any real value. On the contrary, if we are content to take species as direct products of a creative power, without troubling ourselves with supposed secondary causes, we may examine, free of any trammelling hypothesis, the law of their succession in time, the guards placed upon their intermixture, the limits set to their variation in each case, the remarkable arrangements for diminishing variations by the natural crossing of varieties, the laws of geographical distribution from centres of origin, and the physical causes of variation, of degeneracy, of extinction.

All these are questions to be investigated apart from any hypothesis of the common origin of different species on the one hand, or of the diverse origin of individuals apparently identical on the other; and we cannot doubt that the results will approach to the following conclusions. (1) That the origin of specific distinctness lies beyond the domain of any natural law known to us. (2) That the variations of the species are the effects of the combined influences of its natural endowments and of external circumstances. (3) That in nature specific force and causes of variation constitute antagonist powers, acting and reacting on each other, and thus producing an equilibrium which is disturbed only by the artificial contrivance of man.

Evolution and the Destiny of Man

William Dawson Le Sueur

In examining this work, small as it is, we seem to discover, as it were traces of collaboration. It has the appearance of having been written not by one Mr. Fiske, but by two Mr. Fiskes. The first is Mr. Fiske, the simple student of science and recorder of scientific facts; the second is an author who apparently can not rest content with facts as they are, but constantly strives to views them in the light of some foreign hypothesis. The second Mr. Fiske would appear to have edited the first rather than the first the second; yet the work has been done in such a way that the diverse elements can easily be distinguished and separated.

The scientific Mr. Fiske discourses thus: As the Copernican theory destroyed the notion that the earth was infinitely larger than all the heavenly bodies, and was the center of the universe, thus giving a violent shock to the theological beliefs of the period, so the Darwinian theory today has destroyed the notion, prevalent up to the present time, that man occupies a position wholly apart from the rest of the animal creation. It enables us to state that "man is not only a vertebrate, a mammal, and a primate, but [that] he belongs, as a genus, to the catarrhine family of apes"; further, that "the various genera of platyrrhine and catarrhine apes, including man, are doubtless descended from a common stock of primates, back to which we may also trace the converging pedigrees of monkeys and lemurs, until their ancestry becomes indistinguishable from that of rabbits and squirrels." There is no more reason for supposing that this conclusion will ever be overthrown than there is for supposing that the Copernican theory will be banished and the Ptolemaic restored. The facts which once furnished support to the "argument from design" have received at the hands of Mr. Darwin a very different interpretation. It is "that simple but wasteful process of survival of the fittest," which is now invoked to explain the marvels of adaptation with which Nature abounds. "The scientific Darwinian theory alleges development

*From William Dawson Le Sueur, "Evolution and the Destiny of Man" a review of
The Destiny of Man Viewed in light of his Origins by John Fiske (Boston: 1884)
First published in *Popular Science Monthly* Vol. 36, No.4, 1885.

only as the result of certain rigorously defined agencies. The chief among these agencies is natural selection." A point, however, arrived, in the development of the brute-ancestor of man, when psychical changes began to be of more use to him than physical changes; in other words, when better-developed brains began to have the advantage over better-developed muscles. From the point onward the brains of our progenitors steadily increased "through ages of ceaseless struggle," not only in size but in complexity of structure. So far, therefore, as man was concerned, "the process of zoological change had come to an end, and a process of psychological change was to take its place." A difference in kind was thus established between man and the lower animals, the result of the accumulation of differences of degree. In the same way we see a difference in kind established between a nebula and a solid sphere through the operation of a gradual process of cooling and contraction. Upon this point there should be no mistake for it is thus that all differences in kind are brought about. The result of the increasing size and complexity of the human brain, and the corresponding variety in human life, was that human beings could no longer be born in possession of full adult faculties. Infancy thus supervened as an accompaniment of increasing intellectuality. During infancy and youth the child *learns* what inheritance has not yet incorporated in its organization. Infancy, however, as a stage in individual life, is not confined to the human species. The man-like apes of Africa begin life as helpless babies, and are unable to walk, to feed themselves, or to grasp objects with precision until they are two or three months old. The difference between these and man is that the latter has a much increased cerebral surface, while the infancy of his progeny is correspondingly prolonged. Our earliest human ancestors lived, during an entire geologic aeon, "a fierce and squalid existence." Yet even during that time was there progress; cerebral surface was increasing and babyhood was lengthening. "The process of evolution is excessively slow, and its ends are achieved at the cost of enormous waste of life"; still, for innumerable ages its direction has been toward the enriching, the diversifying, and the ennobling of human existence.

Discussing "the origins of society and morality," the exponent of the Darwinian theory tells us that "the psychical development of humanity since its earlier stages has been largely due to the reaction of individuals upon one another, in those various relations which we characterize as social." Infancy created the family, and the family, by taming, in a measure, individual selfishness, founded morality. The individual once brought under the law of the family, must begin to judge of his conduct by some standard outside of himself; "hence the germs of conscience and of the idea of duty." Society has thus led to a great improvement in the quality of individual life; it has made it possible for the world to have a Shakespear, the difference between whose brain, taking creasing into account, and that of an Australian savage, "would doubtless be fifty times a greater than the difference between the Australian's brain and that of an orang-outang." Such is the measure of our intellectual progress. On the moral side humanity can boast such leaders as Howard and

Garrison. Yet the psychical development of man is not at an end. It is destined to go on, making not only intelligence greater, but sympathy stronger and more profound. It is true that the eliminating of strife "has gone on with the extreme slowness that marks all the world of evolution." Still, such a process is in operation, and upon it we build our hopes for the perfection of humanity.

So far the expounder of science. It will be observed that the statements he makes are either indisputable, or rest upon grounds of much apparent solidity. In connection with everything that he advances there is an implicit appeal to verification. "If these things are not so," he seems to say, "then what are the facts?" It will be observed, also, that we are presented with no strained conclusions, with no glosses on the text, with no doubtful or misleading metaphors, with no unwarranted suggestions. We have intelligible views, plainly and candidly expressed. The destiny of man is fairly considered in the light of his origin; but, as his origin occurred on earth, so in what precedes his "destiny" is discussed as a question of development and progress on the earth. It is modestly suggested, by no means dogmatically affirmed-the author herein agreeing with Mr. Spencer — that the influences that have raised mankind from brutehood to his present condition have not yet expended their force, but will carry him forward to further and indefinite developments of intelligence and morality.

Pass we now to consider the ideas presented, as it would almost seem, by a second Mr. Fiske, who undertakes the task of rendering innocuous or even edifying all that the first has put forward. Here we find what may perhaps best be described as a constant attempt to cut a larger garment than the cloth will allow. It is science that is supposed to supply the cloth, but, when science stints the measure, poetry and sentiments are laid under contribution. Much is done by way of suggestion, and points are so skillfully made that we need to be constantly on our guard lest we be led to mistake for knowledge what in reality is mere conjecture, or the expression of emotional longing.

But to proceed. In the preface we have a full admission that the question of a future life lies "outside the range of legitimate scientific discussion." At the same time it is maintained that we may have an "opinion" on the subject, and that our opinion on such a question "must necessarily be affected by the total mass of our opinions on the questions which lie within the scope of scientific inquiry." Here issue may be joined. If "the total mass of our opinions" on questions lying "within the scope of scientific inquiry" can guide us to an opinion on the question of a future life, then that question itself can not be said to lie "outside the range of legitimate scientific discussion." If, on the other hand, the laws and analogies which science reveals do *not* bear upon this question, then it is vain to talk of our conclusions thereon being affected by the total mass of our opinions, upon matters falling within the domain of science. In other words, there either is or is not a bridge between such questions as science commonly deals with and this question of immortality. If there is, let us walk over it and possess the farther land; if there is not , let us recognize the fact and not pretend that the laws of the physical region throw any light on questions lying beyond that region. An "opinion" on such a matter, moreover, is not worth entertaining unless we can hope for some verification of it; and we only cheat ourselves by framing "opinions" and trying to think that in some remote way they have the sanction and support of science. It might also, with some show of reason, be maintained that mere opinions on such a point are likely to do a great deal of harm, since they are apt to stand in the way of the following out of a consistent line of thought and conduct thought. A man who has merely an "opinion" is not bound by it one way or another. He may neglect the future life in the interest of the present, or the present in the alleged interest of the future, just as the inclination of the moment may lead him. The great works of the past were not wrought on the strength of an "opinion" in the present day. The work of the world in all ages has called for convictions, and it calls for them still. It is a somewhat singular thing that our author should have used the expression, "the total mass of our *opinions* on the questions which lie within the scope of scientific inquiry." The word "knowledge," I respectfully submit, was required in this place. It is our *knowledge* that can guide us to *opinions*, or, in other words, that can determine for us questions as to preponderance of evidence. An opinion that is based upon an opinion is too unsubstantial a thing to deserve any attention. the only advantage I can see in the use of the word "opinions" in the place indicated is, that it seems in a manner to help to bridge over the gap between the scientific and the non-scientific regions. The bridge, however, will not hold: it may be pretty to look at, but it has no firm anchorage.

As we have already seen, the Copernican theory destroyed the notion that man's abode, the earth, was the centre of the universe. The very foundations of theology seemed at the time to have been shaken; but today "the speculative necessity of man's occupying the largest and most central spot in the universe is no longer felt." Upon this it may be observe that what disturbed our forefathers was not the conflict between the Copernican teaching and any speculative necessity of the period, but the conflict between that teaching and the plain declarations of the Scriptures. That was the trouble. Mr. Fiske tells us that the alarm was unnecessary — that the foundations of Christian theology have not really been shaken thereby. Possibly that is the best view to take of it, seeing that the matter can not be mended.

The reason why atheism is so abhorrent to us why "we are wont to look upon it with unspeakable horror and loathing," is that "on its practical side it would remove humanity from its peculiar position in the world, and make it cast in its lot with the grass that withers and the beasts that perish." Can this statement, I ask be soberly made by a man of science speaking in the name of science? In what sense does atheism — a form of belief with the truth of falsity of which we need not at present concern ourselves — remove humanity from any peculiar position distinctly, and on scientific grounds, shown to belong to it? . . .

The "peculiar position" of humanity is what it is, and neither atheism nor any other "ism" cán make it other than it is. It is for us to discover, as far as may be, what our position is, and calmly to abide by our conclusions in the matter as long as they continue to recommend themselves to our reason. If we find that certain contrary views inspire us with "unspeakable horror and loathing" instead of with a sense of error and a desire to remove the error, we shall do well to examine ourselves as to whether we really be in the faith, whether we are not trying to atone by "horror and loathing" for indeterminateness of conviction and a deficient sense of intellectual wholeness and integrity. Such tempestuous emotions are not generally of good omen. . . .

. . . Looking at the general arrangement of the solar system and the general action of terrestrial forces, it seems but trifling to pretend that human life is in any sense an explanation of the scheme as a whole, or that man's interests have been studied in any especial manner. Such a statement may seem to border on that doctrine which, as our author tells us, justly excites "unspeakable horror and loathing"; but, with all respect, I venture to express the contrary opinion that it is a doctrine calculated to have a better moral effect than the one he labors to support. It is a doctrine which, while it tends to abate human egotism, tends also to increase our sense of responsibility. If our life is the grand culmination of creation, and if the creative power has special designs concerning us, our destinies are largely, if not wholly, taken out of our own hands. We become at once "a royal priesthood, a peculiar people." Nothing henceforth is too good for us, no "waiting upon Providence" unjustifiable. If, on the other hand, we have no guarantee that we are in any special sense the nurslings of Heaven, then it rests with us to make the best of whatever endowments we find ourselves actually possessing. We dismiss conceit from our minds and apply ourselves simply to know what is, in order that we may be able to exert the widest and most potent influence possible on our environment. . . .

A fine sentiment is uttered in the following passage: "To pursue unflinchingly the methods of science requires dautless courage and a faith that nothing can shake. Such courage and such loyalty to Nature brings its own reward." Then what is the "own reward" of such admirable conduct? It is that we are enabled to see distinctly "for the first time how the creating and perfecting of man is the goal toward which Nature's work has all the while been tending." Here I must enter a respectful protest. I can not conceive that any special conclusion whatever, however edifying or comfortable, can be correctly spoken of as the natural (for that is the force here of "own") reward of loyalty to truth. If loyalty to truth brings *its own reward*, that reward can only consist in a confirmed habit of intellectual sincerity, and whatever of other moral excellence springs from such loyalty. Surely the strict scientific stand-point which our author promised to maintain has been badly deserted, when we are told that, if we are only loyal to truth, all our conclusions will come out in the most satisfactory shape. "Be loyal to truth," I should prefer to say, "and your reward will be that you will discover the truth in larger measure than you would otherwise do, and will have the signal advantage ot being able to adapt your life to the truth instead of to fliction." That, in connection with strengthened moral character, seems to me to be the appropriate reward of loyalty to the truth, not the confirmation of any cherished theories. "The Darwinian theory," we are told "makes it (human life) seem more than ever the chief object of that creative activity which is manifested in the physical universe." But really from the scientific stand-point we are not much concerned with what things can be made to *seem*; we are concerned with what they can be proved to be. Opinion can not take the place of knowledge, nor yet of belief; and, in regard to all such questions, only knowledge and belief are of any avail. Prove to us that such and such things are so: well and good — our minds yield to evidence. persuade us that they have been supernaturally revealed: well and good also — our minds take the desired set. But give us only probable opinions, the product of a kind of pseudo-scientific casuistry, and you do nothing for us at all, except perhaps diminish in some degree our sense for truth and reality.

The word "seem," above emphasized, may be said to furnish the key-note of the whole of what may be called the apologetic element in the work before us. The first Mr. Fiske tells us what things are, and how they have come to be what they are. The second tells us what they seem like to those who wish to think that the foundations of Christian Theology have not been disturbed either by the Copernican astronomy or the Darwinian theory of the origin of species. The weakness of this kind of thing is that it may be worked in any direction and in any interest. Say what you want things to seem like, and they can easily be made to assume the desired complexion. Take an example. After animals have been devouring one another and starving one another out of existence for long ages, there appears an animal who assumes a predominance which he never afterward loses, and who goes on increasing his power and improving his position from century to century. Well, if one wishes to believe that the object toward which all this inter-mastication and inter-starvation of the myriad tribes of earth and air and sky was tending was the production of man, himself for long ages one of the most hideous of animals, there is no obstacle in the way except the complete lack of evidence in a positive sense plus the fact that the inter-mastication and inter-starvation are still going on now that man has come. If any one chooses to describe natural selection as a "simple and wasteful process," and then to say that it is "a slow and subtile" one, there is no obstacle in the way except the contrast which common sense establishes between simplicity and subtilty. . . .

There are a great many phrases and suggestions throughout the volume before us, besides those already noted, which might be quoted as showing the intention of the writer to make a kind of Darwinian philosophy *a l'usage des familles*. My space, however, is so nearly exhausted that I must pass over all but one of these. On page 117 we read that "the greatest philosopher of modern times, the master and teacher of all who shall study the process of evolution for many a day to come, holds that the conscious soul is not the product of a collocation of material particles, but is, in the deepest sense, a divine effluence." This I do not hesitate to say is a misrepresentation, involuntary no doubt, of Mr. Spencer's position. If there is any meaning in language, it makes Mr. Spencer ascribe a special divinity to mind. Mr. Spencer, however, does nothing of the kind; he holds that there is one unknowable, unconditioned being, and that this manifests itself in the two conditioned forms of mind and matter. The material particles, therefore, can claim, according to his system of thought, just as much divinity of origin as the mind or soul itself. The word "divine," moreover, is not a word to the use of which Mr. Spencer is prone, and I could not readily turn to any passage in which he employs it to express any idea of his own. He speaks in his recent articles of "an Infinite and Eternal Energy"; but of the mind, in particular, as "divine effluence," he does not speak. To say, therefore so positively that Mr. Spencer regards the mind as "in the deepest sense a divine effluence," and that in distinction to the body, and not fair, to say the least, to the distinguished philosopher to the exposition of whose views Mr. Fiske has devoted his own most serious labors.

The conclusion of the whole matter appears to be this, that there is nothing to be gained by trying to read old theology into new science. It may be, as Mr. Fiske affirms, that the foundations of Christian theology have not been shaken — no one needs to be dogmatic on the point — but, as theology is a matter of revelation and science a matter of observation it is well to keep the two as separate as possible. The method of science is a gradual method: little by little, we widen the circle of our knowledge; little by little, we improve our hypotheses. Theology makes from the first the most comprehensive statements, and offers solutions of the profoundest problems. To apply, therefore, the dicta or the general conceptions of theology to the province of science is to run much risk of injuring the work of science by the forcing of premature conclusions; admitting that theology has nothing to teach that is positively erroneous. That loyalty to truth so fittingly referred to by our author requires us to content ourselves with such conclusions as we can reach by lawful and appropriate methods. If we see a law of natural selection at work, let us try to get as clear an understanding as possible of the manner of its working; but let us be very careful how we personify it, and how we impute to our personification feelings and purposes which correspond with nothing in the facts as we know them. Nothing could be more opposed to the human idea of "work" than the process of natural selection as described by our author himself, yet he constantly speaks of the "work" of natural selection. He tells us that "in the desperate struggle for existence no peculiarity has been too insignificant for natural selection to seize and enhance"; just as if natural selection were some vigilant intelligence watching for opportunities to advance its designs. The same fact which is thus expressed in, as I think, misleadingly metaphorical language could have been expressed in honest prose by saying that "in the desperate struggle of existence no peculiarity was too insignificant to contribute to survival *or destruction*, as the case might be."

There we have he fact without any illegitimate implications; and it is thus, as it strikes me, that scientific facts should be described. Species were formed, if the theory of natural selection is sound, in very much the same way in which the others are ground off bowlders carried down by glaciers or swept away by torrents. Whatever projections happen to be in the way are knocked off; finally, the stone is reduced to a shape in which it is comparatively safe from further injury by friction. So with species. Darwin has discovered no law in nature by which good qualities (as such) are produced, he has simply discovered a law by which all kinds of qualities (differentiations), good, bad, and indifferent are produced, and by which the bad ones (bad, i.e., in relation to the environment) are knocked off, like so many projecting angles by the destruction of the individuals manifesting them.

If therefore, we believe in natural selection let us believe in it as it is, and be content to speak of it as it is. *Let us not make a god of what is, in its essence, the very negation of intelligence action.* In regard to the doctrine of immortality, there is little need for alarm, so far as the teachings of science are concerned. Science does not attack it; and if the theological grounds on which it has been received hold good, then the doctrine holds good. Let us have our own teleology if we will, only let us not mix it up with our science seeing that it can, only embarrass the growth of the latter. All will be well if we keep everything in its own place, observing proper metes and bounds.